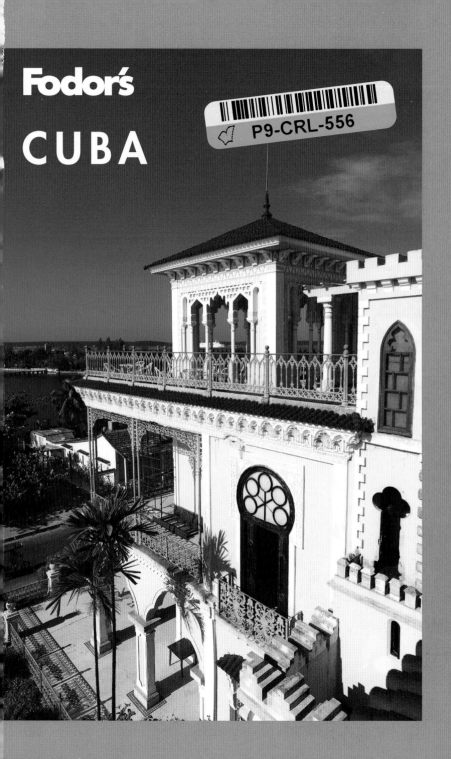

Fodor's

CUBA

P9-CRL-556

WELCOME TO CUBA

Between rolling mountains and dazzling shores, fine cigars and vintage cars, Cuba captivates visitors with its abundant tropical pleasures and cultural treasures. White-sand beaches entice sun worshippers by day, and clubs pulsing with Afro-Cuban jazz own the night. In Havana, locals debate baseball on street corners shaded by royal palms and neo-classical buildings while Studebakers whiz past. In the colonial town of Trinidad, villagers gather in plazas lit by wrought-iron lamps, and in the countryside, tobacco fields tended by *guajiros* (farmers) spread across the Viñales Valley.

TOP REASONS TO GO

★ **Architecture:** From ornate baroque palaces to grand Art Deco mansions.

★ **Beaches:** Lovely strands at Varadero and Cayo Largo and colorful corals at Playa Ancón.

★ **Music:** Afro-Cuban rumba, salsa, and mambo provide Cuba's high-energy soundtrack.

★ **Nightlife:** Sultry jazz clubs, open-air discos, and rum spice up the nights.

★ **Cigars:** Cultivated in tobacco fields in the Viñales Valley, hand-rolled in Havana.

★ **History:** You can explore Spanish castles from the 1550s and see Cadillacs from the 1950s.

12

TOP EXPERIENCES

Cuba offers terrific experiences that should be on every traveler's list. Here are Fodor's top picks for a memorable trip.

1 Trinidad

With its restored colonial mansions, manicured plazas, and neoclassical palaces, Trinidad is often called the "museum of Cuba." Centuries of architecture are on display along cobblestone streets traversed by horse-drawn carriages and lined with pastel-painted houses. *(Ch. 4)*

2 La Habana Vieja

Both crumbling and soaring, La Habana Vieja jam-packs history and culture into a lively neighborhood of vintage cars, 16th-century fortresses, and leafy courtyards. *(Ch.2)*

3 Music

Cubans move to the beat of rumba, mambo, chachachá, and more. Live music is everywhere from Havana jazz clubs to plazas in sleepy villages. *(Chs. 2, 3, 4)*

4 La Cabaña Fortress

By day this colossal fortress offers splendid views of Havana; by night a military reenactment provides thrills with a ceremonial firing of cannons over the harbor. *(Ch. 2)*

5 Festivals

Immense cultural pride makes Cuba a land of celebrations. From the fireworks competition in Remedios to the Havana Cigar Festival, there's always a party somewhere in Cuba. *(Chs. 1, 2, 4)*

6 Ernest Hemingway

Hemingway loved Cuba, and you can visit many of his favorite places such as La Floridita, a historic Havana bar (pictured), and Finca Vigía, his home for 20 years. *(Ch. 2)*

7 Partagas Cigar Factory

Cubans cigars are the ne plus ultra for many aficionados. Guided tours at Havana's best-known factory provide a fascinating glimpse into the traditional hand-rolling process. *(Ch. 2)*

8 Beach Escapes

The largest island in the Caribbean has plenty of white-sand, palm-fringed beaches, from resort-fronted Varadero to remote strands such as the lovely Playa Sirena. *(Chs. 1, 2, 4)*

9 Cienfuegos

Colonized by the French rather than the Spanish, Cienfuegos is a tidy, bayside city that shows off a different side of Cuban history with beautiful Parisian, neoclassical architecture. *(Ch. 4)*

10 Che Guevara Memorial

Presided over by a giant bronze statue of Cuba's controversial hero, this site is a fascinating place to learn about the island's recent revolutionary history. *(Ch. 4)*

11 Rum

The national drink is ubiquitous and cheap. Supermarkets and hotels sell the popular Havana Club brand, and a refreshing mojito is a good bet in any bar. *(Chs. 1, 2)*

12 Valle de Viñales

A spectacular natural landscape, worth the trip just for its towering *mogotes* (rocky outcrops), this lush agricultural region reveals a slice of everyday life in rustic Cuba. *(Ch. 3)*

CONTENTS

MAPS

ABOUT THIS GUIDE

Fodor's Ratings

Everything in this guide is worth doing—we don't cover what isn't—but exceptional sights, hotels, and restaurants are recognized with additional accolades. **Fodor's**Choice★ indicates our top recommendations. Care to nominate a new place? Visit Fodors.com/contact-us.

Trip Costs

We list prices wherever possible to help you budget well. Hotel and restaurant price categories from $ to $$$$ are noted alongside each recommendation. For hotels, we include the lowest cost of a standard double room in high season. For restaurants, we cite the average price of a main course at dinner or, if dinner isn't served, at lunch. For attractions, we always list adult admission fees; discounts are usually available for children, students, and senior citizens.

Hotels

Our local writers vet every hotel to recommend the best overnights in each price category, from budget to expensive. Unless otherwise specified, you can expect private bath, phone, and TV in your room. For expanded hotel reviews, facilities, and deals visit Fodors.com.

Top Picks		Hotels &
★ **Fodor's**Choice		**Restaurants**
	🏨	Hotel
Listings	🛏	Number of rooms
⊠ Address		
⊠ Branch address	❍	Meal plans
☎ Telephone	✕	Restaurant
🖶 Fax	✍	Reservations
⊕ Website	👔	Dress code
✎ E-mail	▭	No credit cards
✐ Admission fee	$	Price
⊙ Open/closed times		
Ⓜ Subway	**Other**	
⊹ Directions or Map coordinates	⇨	See also
	☞	Take note
	⚑	Golf facilities

Restaurants

Unless we state otherwise, restaurants are open for lunch and dinner daily. We mention dress code only when there's a specific requirement and reservations only when they're essential or not accepted. To make restaurant reservations, visit Fodors.com.

Credit Cards

The hotels and restaurants in this guide typically accept credit cards. If not, we'll say so.

EUGENE FODOR

Hungarian-born Eugene Fodor (1905–91) began his travel career as an interpreter on a French cruise ship. The experience inspired him to write *On the Continent* (1936), the first guidebook to receive annual updates and discuss a country's way of life as well as its sights. Fodor later joined the U.S. Army and worked for the OSS in World War II. After the war, he kept up his intelligence work while expanding his guidebook series. During the Cold War, many guides were written by fellow agents who understood the value of insider information. Today's guides continue Fodor's legacy by providing travelers with timely coverage, insider tips, and cultural context.

EXPERIENCE CUBA

CUBA TODAY

So near and yet so far. In spite of Cuba's proximity to the United States, its distance has been unbridgeable for Americans for half a century. However, the chill of the Cold War, which spurred U.S. economic sanctions and travel bans that have been in place since 1961, finally began to thaw on December 17, 2014, when President Obama announced an historic accord between the two nations. As U.S.-Cuba relations develop, many American travelers eager to experience what they've been missing—sizzling salsa, sugar-sand beaches, world-class cigars, and rum—are increasingly adding Cuba to their list of must-see destinations.

Vintage Appeal

The very sanctions meant to punish Fidel Castro's socialist government have only added to the island's appeal for many travelers. Five decades of U.S. trade embargo have had the effect of preserving Cuba much as it was in the 1960s. Classic tail-finned Fairlanes and chrome-laden Cadillacs that would occupy museum space anywhere else in the world are lovingly maintained and used to taxi travelers to an evening of jazz in Havana. Neglected Spanish colonial buildings surround centuries-old plazas, revealing hints of past splendor. And, in the Cuban countryside, ox-drawn plows till a landscape that's been planted in tobacco for some 400 years.

Culture Lover's Paradise

The 1999 Academy Award–nominated documentary *Buena Vista Social Club* introduced the world to the classic sound of Cuban *son*. Today's visitors to Cuba can still enjoy the sounds of this traditional music, whether in packed Havana music venues or crumbling village plazas. Live, smoking-hot salsa music is commonplace at bars and street cafés throughout the country. Grab a chair, order a drink, and enjoy the show, which invariably includes an assortment of shimmying locals, both young and old. Jazz music—once dismissed as too American in style—has been embraced, mastered, and reimagined by Cuban musicians. For just a few bucks you can experience Cuban jazz at places like La Zorra y El Cuervo, one of Havana's most famous jazz clubs.

Like their musical counterparts, Cuba's visual artists celebrate local street culture, family, and daily life. Art is everywhere—from high-end galleries in the capital city to tiny front-lawn displays. Images ranging from dancing señoritas and classic

WHAT'S NEW

Much of Cuba's appeal lies in its antiquity. Still, what's good for Cuba's citizens—chiefly, economic development and an improved standard of living—should be good for its tourists. Since 2004, Raúl Castro has introduced a number of liberal reforms, making it easier for Cubans to own private businesses like souvenir shops and *paladares* (family-run) restaurants. Foreign investment is slowly finding its way to the island, resulting in much-needed building renovations and infrastructure improvements. Ironically, it's along the cobbled streets of Old Havana that visitors are most likely to glimpse Cuba's newest developments: construction cranes gradually rising above centuries-old plazas; Spanish colonial buildings gutted, their facades left beautifully intact while the buildings' interiors cars to abstract landscapes are depicted in acrylic paintings, paper mosaics, leather, and hand-carved wooden sculptures.

Caribbean Beaches

The Caribbean's largest island offers plenty of places to soak up the sun. North and south of mainland Cuba, a long series of archipelagos provide important ecological barriers to the main island, dotting the turquoise waters with palm tree–fringed sanctuaries. Closest to Havana is Varadero, Cuba's answer to Cancun, with tourist-class, beachfront hotels sprouting up from the Hicacos Peninsula. Just above Central Cuba, a spectacular 30-mile (50-km) causeway links Cayo Santa Maria and its golden strand to the mainland, spanning sparkling swathes of aquamarine water. All-inclusive resorts at Cayo Santa Maria and other nearby beach destinations like Cayo Coco and Cayo Guillermo ensure you'll never have to leave your Caribbean paradise far behind when you head off to dinner and drinks. Along Cuba's southern shores the Canarreos Archipelago offers a sunny paradise. Farther east, the Jardines del Reina Archipelago is preserved as a national park with deep-sea fishing and spectacular coral reefs, popular with scuba divers.

Modernizing the Island

Although Cuba has been off-limits to Americans for several decades, the island nation has not been forbidden to European and Canadian visitors or to travelers from nearby Latin America. As a result, there is a decent tourism infrastructure in Cuba: comfortable, air-conditioned hotels and restaurants; plenty of English-speaking staff; even a wide array of satellite television channels (a luxury few Cuban citizens enjoy). And although some 21st-century conveniences still lag behind much of the rest of the world—namely, reliably fast Internet service and mobile phone towers—it is a refreshing sight for screen-addled eyes to see friends and family conversing and dancing rather than staring at their smartphones.

morph into new hotels, boutiques, and restaurants.

You'll witness another construction boom at Cuba's beaches, some of the Caribbean's best. Resort hotels are quickly rising from the sand. Foreign firms, primarily Spanish and Canadian, lend their brand names and manage the properties, bringing a level of service that many of the state-run lodgings still lack.

In December 2014 President Obama announced the easing of travel and spending restrictions on American visitors and Cuban ex-pats to the island, and in August 2015 the United States reopened its embassy in Havana, bringing the countries much closer to full diplomatic relations for the first time since 1961.

WHAT'S WHERE

Numbers correspond to chapters in this book.

2 **Havana.** Slightly more than 2 million people call the nation's capital, La Habana, home. Set on Cuba's north-western coast, the city overlooks the Straits of Florida, sprawling across 286 square miles (740 square km) and incorporating 15 municipalities. Habana Vieja, Vedado, and Miramar are the three districts where visitors find Cuba's famous colonial architecture, vintage cars, cigar factories, and local music clubs.

3 **Western Cuba.** This scenic region includes the three provinces of Matanzas, La Habana, and Pinar del Río, as well as the Municipio Especial (Special Municipality) of Isla de la Juventud. You'll find huge geographical diversity here: the wetlands of Ciénaga de Zapata; the premier tobacco-growing country near Pinar del Río; the mountain peaks of the central Cordillera de Guaniguanico; and the scrubby woodlands of the Península de Guanahacabibes. Bordering it all are miles of sandy beaches.

4 **Central Cuba.** Directly east of Matanzas lie the provinces of Cienfuegos, its eponymous bay-side capital, and Villa Clara. These provinces,

together with neighboring Sancti Spíritus, contain acres of lowlands planted with sugarcane and tobacco and pastureland with the dark, piney Escambray Mountains to the south. In Sancti Spíritus, Trinidad stands out for its spectacular 16th-century colonial edifices and the popular beaches of Playa Ancón. Continuing eastward, Cayo Coco and Cayo Guillermo in the province of Ciego de Avila are part of the Jardines del Rey Archipelago and rank among the best beaches in all of Cuba. Farther east is Camagüey Province, known for its quaint colonial-era capital of the same name and for the northern beach resort Santa Lucia, a scuba diver's paradise.

5 **Eastern Cuba.** The easternmost provinces of Cuba—Las Tunas, Granma, Holguín, Santiago de Cuba and Guantánamo—see fewer travelers than the other regions. Much of Cuba's musical heritage was born in Santiago de Cuba as was the Revolution that brought Fidel Castro (born in Holguín) to power. Although Guantánamo is best known for its U.S. Naval Base, the province is also blessed with fabulous beaches, the majestic Sierra Maestra, and the forests surrounding Baracoa.

Gulf of Mexico

HAVANA **2**

Artemisa Güin
San Cristóbal   Surgidero
Pinar Del Río **3**   de Batabanó

Golfo de Batab

Nueva Gerona

Cabo de San Antonio

ISLE DE LA
JUVENTUD

CUBA

1

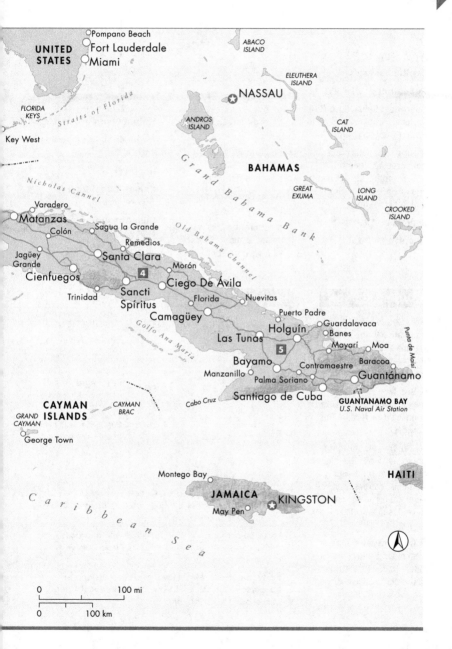

NEED TO KNOW

Havana ✪

Atlantic Ocean

CUBA

Caribbean Sea

AT A GLANCE

Capital: Havana

Population: 11,047,251

Currency: Cuban Peso (CUP) for locals; Cuban Convertible Peso (CUC$) for visitors

Money: U.S. dollars are not accepted. They can be exchanged for CUC at banks and at CADECAs at airports and in city centers.

Language: Spanish

Country Code: 53

Emergencies: 26811, 106

Electricity: 110v/60 cycles; electrical plugs have two flat prongs.

Time: Eastern standard time

Documents: Visa on arrival for up to 30 days with valid passport

Mobile Phones: GSM (900)

Major Mobile Companies: Cubacel

WEBSITES

Cuban Tourist Board: ⊕ www.gocuba.ca

CubaAbsolutely: ⊕ www.cubaabsolutely.com

GETTING AROUND

✈ **Air Travel:** José Martí International Airport in Havana is the busiest in the country, followed by Varadero and Santiago.

🚌 **Bus Travel:** Cuba's major towns and cities are connected by reliable bus services.

🚗 **Car Travel:** Car rentals are expensive and vehicles are often in short supply. Accidents can result in jail time. For most visitors, driving is not worth the risk or expense.

🚆 **Train Travel:** Cuba's rail system links all the major cities. That said, bathrooms and other facilities onboard are not well-maintained.

PLAN YOUR BUDGET

	HOTEL ROOM	MEAL	ATTRACTIONS
Low Budget	$25	$1	Casa de Don Diego Velazquez ticket, $2
Mid Budget	$50	$7	Museo Nacional de Bellas Artes—Coleccion Cubana ticket, $5
High Budget	$125	$12	Cuevas de Bellamar ticket + camera fee, $13

WAYS TO SAVE

Stay in *Casas Particulares*. Cuba's version of the B&B, *casas particulares* offer the best value in the land. Some even include breakfast in the rate.

Focus on architecture. Cuba is filled with gorgeous old architecture, and admiring structures from outside won't cost you a thing.

Enjoy free music. Most Havana restaurants and bars have free live music. In towns, bands frequently perform concerts in the central plaza.

PLAN YOUR TIME

Hassle Factor	High, due to legal restrictions by the U.S. government. Independent travelers go via a third country. Visitors with permits on organized tours can take charter flights directly from the United States.
3 days	A long weekend in Cuba is best spent soaking in the culture and history of Havana, with a day trip to the seaside resort of Varadero.
1 week	A week is enough time to get a feel for Havana, visit the lush Valle de Viñales, and spend a couple of days relaxing on the beaches of Varadero.
2 weeks	In two weeks you can explore Havana, visit the valleys and beaches of Western Cuba, stopping at the historic city of Trinidad before making your way to Santiago, Cuba's cultural capital.

WHEN TO GO

High Season: December–February and July–August are Cuba's high seasons. Tourism peaks in the winter months, when Northern Hemisphere travelers descend on the island to escape colder climates back home. July and August are popular because of school vacations.

Low Season: Cuba's risk for hurricanes is at its highest from June–November, leading to a low season that runs through June and starts up again in September, finishing at the end of November.

Value Season: March and April see fewer tourists than other months, as well as a lower risk of getting caught in a tropical storm.

BIG EVENTS

February: Expect readings, book sales, and lots of food at Havana's International Book Fair, held annually at the Caba a Fortress.

March or April: During Easter Trinidad''s Way of the Cross Procession weaves through the old city''s historic streets.

July: Santiago's annual Carnival is proof that Cubans know how to throw a good party.

September: The Anniversary of CDRs, community committees created during the Revolution to keep an eye on neighbors, is celebrated with block parties and feasts.

READ THIS

■ *Paradiso,* José Lezama Lima. A coming-of-age story set in pre-Castro Havana.

■ *Trading with the Enemy: A Yankee Travels Through Castro's Cuba,* Tom Miller. An American's travelogue of his eight-month journey through Cuba.

■ *The Cuba Reader: History, Culture, Politics,* Aviva Chomsky. A collection of media from and about Cuba.

WATCH THIS

■ *Buena Vista Social Club.* Documentary on the world-famous Cuban music club that peaked in popularity during the 1940s.

■ *Fidel.* The story of Fidel Castro's rise to power.

■ *Death of a Bureaucrat.* Comedy satirizing Cuban bureaucracy in the 1960s.

EAT THIS

■ *Ropa vieja*: Shredded meat in tomato sauce

■ *Vaca frita*: Fried beef

■ *Boliche*: Stuffed pot roast

■ *Cuban sandwich*: Ham, pork, pickles, and Swiss cheese on crusty Cuban bread

■ *Arroz con pollo*: Rice and chicken

■ *Cuban pastries*: Turnovers filled with guava and sweet cream cheese

CUBA TRAVEL FAQS

As of December 2014, legal travel to Cuba for U.S. citizens became easier for the first time in more than 50 years. However, it's not quite as easy as hopping a plane to your favorite Caribbean island. The U.S. Department of the Treasury's Office of Foreign Assets Control (OFAC) oversees the rules for Cuba visits by Americans. Here are answers to frequently asked questions for Cuba travel.

Can I go to Cuba on my own just to lie on the beach and explore the country?

Not yet. The Cuban Assets Control Regulations (CACR) lists 12 categories of activities that are approved for travel to Cuba. They include family visits, official government business, journalistic activity, professional research, educational activities, religious activities, public performances, and humanitarian projects among others. The full list is available at ⊕ *www.whitehouse.gov.*

Independent leisure visits such as staying at a beach resort are not approved activities. However, if your planned activities in Cuba meet the criteria in any of the 12 permitted categories, you can obtain a general license from OFAC by signing an affidavit stating the intent of your visit; you no longer need to apply for a specific license for each category. The Treasury Department's website provides full descriptions of what constitutes approved activities for each category. For the most part, they are common-sense definitions. Writing about Cuba on a blog won't qualify as "journalistic activity." Family visits must be with a close relative, defined as "any individual related to a person by blood, marriage, or adoption who is no more than three generations removed from that person . . . ."

> ## CUBA TRAVEL INFO
>
> As U.S.-Cuba relations develop, travel rules will continue to change. Before you plan your visit to Cuba check the U.S. Department of the Treasury website (⊕ *www. treasury.gov/ofac*) for complete, current information.

What is People-to-People Travel?

These are cultural exchange tours (which satisfy the educational category of the permitted activities) led by tour operators licensed for Cuba travel. Group sizes are usually 20 people or fewer, and itineraries are quite immersive—packed with cultural activities and lectures as well as visits to schools, artists' studios, and cooperatives.

Accommodations, food, guide services, in-country transport, and flights from Miami are included; however, the flights from Miami are on charter flights, which come at a premium. Getting to Miami is at your costTrips can range from $2,500 to $6,000 a week.

What are the flight options from the United States?

Currently, nearly all air travel from the U.S. is via charter flights from Miami. Under the new regulations, commercial airlines can operate flights to Cuba; and American, Delta, JetBlue, and United Airlines are among the first large carriers to explore options for routes (including direct flights from New York), but it may be mid-2016 or later before regular commercial service is offered.

What about flight options from other countries?

Non-U.S.-based commercial airlines fly to Cuba from many destinations. Americans who meet the OFAC travel requirements can arrange to fly commercial through a third country, such as Canada, Mexico, Panama, or the Cayman Islands—an option that can often be less expensive than taking a charter flight. Some U.S. travelers without OFAC authorization fly to Cuba this way for a leisure visit, but keep in mind that your passport will be stamped by Cuban immigration, so U.S. authorities can see that you've been to Cuba. Although very few people have been prosecuted in recent years, the penalties that are currently on the books are hefty. According to OFAC's Cuban Assets Control Regulations: "Criminal penalties for violating the sanctions range up to . . . $250,000 in individual fines."

What's the Cuban currency and can I use a credit card?

Cuba uses a dual-currency system. Cubans use the peso (CUP) to purchase everyday goods; visitors use the convertible peso (CUC), which has far greater value than the CUP. The international exchange rate is $1 CUC = $1 USD; however, there is a 10% penalty charged when exchanging U.S. dollars, and a 3% currency exchange fee. U.S. dollars are not accepted for payment, and Cuban currency is not traded internationally, so you must buy CUC in Cuba. The best places to exchange U.S. dollars for CUC are at a CADECA (a government exchange bureau) or at a Cuban BFI Bank. The main branch of CADECA is in Havana on Amargura near the Malecón, but there are also branches at airports, many resorts, and town centers throughout the island. You can often exchange at hotel front desks, but you will often receive a lower exchange rate. The Cuban government says the controversial dual system will come to an end, but the time is yet to be determined.

Longtime restrictions on U.S. credit cards in Cuba are being lifted, with Visa and MasterCard accepted as of mid-2015. American Express and Discover are coming online in the near future. With Visa and MasterCard, we recommend contacting your issuing financial institution to be sure that their specific cards are supported. Businesses are beginning to accept credit cards, but many are not set up for it, especially outside Havana, so it's always a good idea to have CUC. *(See Money Matters in Travel Smart for more information on currency and credit cards.)*

Is it true I can bring Cuban cigars and other goods to the United States?

If OFAC-approved for travel to Cuba, Americans can now bring back up to $400 worth of souvenirs, including $100 worth of cigars. However, quality Cuban cigars can sell for $25 each, so that $100 does not go far. Note that Cuban cigars sold in other countries, such as Canada, are still banned from import to the United States.

TOP TOUR OPERATORS

Independent leisure travel to Cuba does not conform to current U.S. law, so the best way for Americans to explore the country is with a licensed tour operator that provides "people-to-people" itineraries. These fully escorted, multiday excursions focus on interaction with the Cuban people. They fulfill the requirements of one of the 12 approved categories by which Americans can visit Cuba—educational travel. Jam-packed with cultural activities, itineraries may include agriculture, art, athletics, cuisine, dance, ecology, education, faith, folklore, health, history, literacy, music, politics, sociology, and theater. Some tours focus on an individual subject; others mix and match topics in a single tour. We highlight the best tour operators in alphabetical order below (*See People-to-People Tours under Tour Operators in Travel Smart for more information, as well as factors to consider when selecting such packages.*)

Access Tours. Access has two distinct specialties in its tours around the world: adventure sports and cuisine. Since the culinary aspect meshes better with the people-to-people requirements, that's the focus of its excursions to Cuba. Bring back more than memories by learning how to whip up some Cuban food and beverage recipes for your friends and family. Ropa vieja, grilled fish, and ceviche are among the signature Cuban dishes on the menu. Small group sizes—a maximum of 10—mean that everybody gets a hands-on experience in helping to prepare meals. (You don't need to do all the work; some of the meals are prepared for you as well.) Learning to make daiquiris Hemingway-style is also on the week's syllabus, as are visits to cigar and sugarcane plantations. **Destinations:** Havana, Trinidad, Valle de Viñales. **Popular packages:** Cuba Culinary Tour, 8 days, from $3,990. **What they do best:** Fun and learning with food and drink, Cuban style. ☎ *650/492–4778* ⊕ *www.accesstrips.com.*

Cultural Explorations Cuba. This operator offers an array of weeklong tours of the island with general themes. However, Cultural Explorations Cuba truly shines in its specialty tours that delve into Cuban art, churches, Judaism, cuisine, or LGBT issues. They've also entered the nascent meetings-and-incentives market in Cuba and can organize conferences and seminars for U.S.-based businesses and organizations. Standard cultural-exchange activities must be incorporated into such stays to satisfy people-to-people requirements. **Destinations:** Havana, Cayo Santa María, Cienfuegos, Playa Girón, Santa Clara, Trinidad. **Popular packages:** Journey Cuba, 7 days, from $3,599; Havana Art, 5 days, from $3,995. **What they do best:** Terrific selection of specialty tours. ☎ *561/921–2425* ⊕ *www.cultural-explorations.com.*

Drod Culinary Adventures. Second-generation Cuban-American chef Douglas Rodriguez, award-winning master of Alma de Cuba restaurant in Philadelphia, has been leading culinary-themed tours to Cuba a couple of times a year since 2014. Rodriguez takes you to markets, farms, fields, and ports and lets you participate in the selection of the best fruits and vegetables and catches of the day. Tours include stays at some of Cuba's finest hotels and meals at some of its most distinctive *paladares*—private homes licensed to open their doors to the public for dining. Standard sightseeing rounds out the tours' itineraries. **Destinations:** Havana, Camagüey, Cienfuegos, Trinidad, Varadero. **Popular packages:** Art,

Food, & Culture of Cuba, 7 days, from $4,995. **What they do best:** In-depth look at Cuban cuisine, through the guidance of a master chef. ☎ *954/693–6562* ⊕ *www. chefdouglasrodriguez.com.*

Insight Cuba. The Insight folks pioneered the people-to-people concept—they've been leading trips since 2000—and are one of the few tour operators in the world that focus strictly on Cuba. Insight really mixes it up in its itinerary offerings: a half-dozen general tours—one to two weeks in length—take in the entire island or sectors of it and give a terrific overview of the country. Alternatively, an impressive array of specialty excursions, often shorter, explore single themes such as Cuban jazz, baseball, or vintage cars. Insight can even set you up to run in the annual Havana Marathon. For a quick trip, the Weekend in Havana tour takes you on a short visit to the country's intriguing capital. Insight also customizes tours for groups, within the bounds of the people-to-people requirements, of course. **Destinations:** Havana, Baracoa, Bayamo, Camagüey, Cayo Santa María, Cienfuegos, Holguín, Las Terrazas, Pinar del Río, Remedios, Santa Clara, Santiago de Cuba, Trinidad, Valle de Viñales. **Popular packages:** Classic Cuba, 9 days, from $4,695; Undiscovered Cuba, 13 days, from $5,595. **What they do best:** Top-notch guides with experience in a country they know like the back of their hand. ☎ *800/450–2822* ⊕ *www. insightcuba.com.*

Road Scholar. Although the not-for-profit Road Scholar began life under the name Elderhostel, people of all ages participate in its highly regarded tours that focus on travel as part of lifelong learning. The company has been leading people-to-people trips to Cuba since 2011, and they come complete with the company's expert lectures and panel discussions. Road Scholar offers the standard island-wide tours, some as long as three weeks, but also in the mix are shorter tours that focus on photography, family activities, and homestays in casas particulares. New to its offerings is a study cruise that circles the island and calls at several Cuban ports. Like most such tours, the majority of Road's excursions depart from Miami, but a couple of its itineraries offer New York departures instead. **Destinations:** Havana, Camagüey, Cienfuegos, Holguín, María La Gorda, Santa Clara, Santiago de Cuba, Trinidad. **Popular packages:** The People of Cuba, 9 days, from $3,495; Cuba Today, 9 days, from $3,395. **What they do best:** Expert instructors who provide valuable background on what you're seeing. ☎ *800/454–5768* ⊕ *www. roadscholar.org.*

IF YOU LIKE

Beaches

When it comes to sugar-sand beaches and deep blue waters, many people think of the islands that surround Cuba—the Bahamas, Turks and Caicos, and Cayman Islands. But Cuba has plenty of dazzling strands that rival that of its neighbors', giving beach lovers plenty of spots to enjoy beautiful Caribbean sand and surf.

Cayo Coco and Cayo Guillermo. The white-sand beaches and turquoise sea of these two islands make them major destinations. They're also near an array of fishing and diving spots and are home to an abundance of birds.

Cayo Santa María. The 30-mile (50-km) causeway linking mainland Cuba to Cayo Santa María is spectacular in its own right, with sweeping views of turquoise water and mangroves. Several all-inclusive resorts provide worry-free lounging on the beach.

Cojímar. Ernest Hemingway loved this seaside village on the eastern outskirts of Havana. Come and admire the location that inspired *The Old Man and the Sea* and the site where the author docked his boat, *Pilar*, and enjoy a seafood lunch at La Terraza, Hemingway's favorite.

Playa Ancón. South of Trinidad, Playa Ancón offers colorful coral beds tailor-made for snorkeling and scuba diving. Above water, sugar-sand beaches and several all-inclusive hotels allow easy relaxation beneath graceful palm trees.

Varadero. East of Havana, Varadero inhabits the skinny, sandy Hicacos Peninsula, Cuba's answer to Cancún. Dozens of tourist-class hotels and restaurants will keep you well-fed and comfortable, and you'll have your fill of activities such as swimming, sunbathing, snorkeling, and shipwreck diving.

Music

Your Cuban journey will be accompanied by a veritable soundtrack of island music. There are countless genres, from classical to Latin jazz to such hybrids of European and African sounds as salsa, *timba*, conga, rumba, bolero, *son*, *danzón*, *guajira*, mambo, and *nueva* and *vieja* trova. Cover charges are cheap, except in Havana's Tropicana. The only "admission" Cuba's ubiquitous street musicians ask for is a small contribution to the cause.

Café Cantante Benny Moré, Cienfuegos. Benny Moré and his melodious tenor voice are no longer with us, but the spirit of Central Cuba's most famous singer lives on. Moré popularized the guitar and percussion *son*; those who inherited his mantle continue that tradition at this small nightspot.

Casa de la Trova, Santiago de Cuba. Santiago's is the most famous, but many cities have their requisite venue showcasing *trova*, a uniquely Cuban genre of guitar-accompanied folk music blending poetry with a little bit of protest.

Cuban National Symphony, Havana. The performers in the capital's Amadeo Roldán concert hall may be young and casually attired (white shirts and black bow ties as opposed to white tie and tails), but these professional, well-directed musicians open their hearts and truly communicate with music.

Tropicana, Havana. Sequined, feathered dancers and Cuban-style big-band music at the island's most famous cabaret evoke a bygone era when Lucy met Ricky Ricardo. It's arguably Cuba's most touristy thing to do, but the place packs 'em in night after night.

Natural Wonders

Journey beyond Cuba's cities and resorts, and you'll find vast tracts of unspoiled land on this, the largest Caribbean island.

Caleta Buena, Playa Girón. Cuba's natural attractions don't stop at the shoreline. East of Playa Girón is this exquisite limestone *cenote* (sinkhole) and coral cove. It's a beautiful site for experienced divers.

Parque Nacional Ciénaga de Zapata. The Caribbean's largest wetland makes for Cuba's premier birding site. This park in Western Cuba shelters 21 native and around 170 migratory species. Accommodations are sparse here; Varadero tour operators can fix you up with a day trip.

Parque Nacional Turquino. A short hike through the vegetation of this national park in the Sierra Maestra range brings you to Castro's camp and headquarters during the Revolution. You'll see why this remote locale made such a strategic command post.

Topes de Collantes. Just outside Trinidad loom the Sierra del Escambray, whose cool pine forests might make you think you've been transported to Minnesota from tropical Cuba. Hiking is superb here. Lack of good accommodations means the park is best visited on a day tour from Trinidad.

Valle de Viñales. Limestone hillocks (*mogotes*) punctuate the landscape in this fertile valley in Western Cuba. The panorama is, in a word, fabulous. The deep red soil is rich here, making this the island's prime tobacco-cultivating region, too.

Historic Sites

Cuba's socialist government came to power with the stated goal of building a new revolutionary society, but it didn't ignore the country's rich history, and you shouldn't either.

Basílica del Cobre, Santiago de Cuba. This may be an officially atheist country, but Cubans respect and revere their patron saint, Our Lady of Charity, to whom they attribute all manner of good fortune, present and past. Her image is housed here in a 1926 countryside basilica.

Castillo de Jagua, Cienfuegos. Set above the Bahía de Cienfuegos, this fort was built in 1745 to discourage pirates from trading with locals. It has been refurbished (even the drawbridge works), and has a historical museum, a bar, and a restaurant.

Castillo de San Carlos de la Cabaña, Havana. Every night at 9 sharp, the ceremony of the cannon draws Cubans and visitors alike to this fort. Follow this not-to-miss event with dinner at one of the restaurants in the Morro fortress area.

Mausoleo y Museo Ernesto "Che" Guevara, Santa Clara. "El Che" is entombed here at the country's most famous revolutionary sight. The hushed reverence shown by visitors demonstrates evidence of Cubans' respect for this iconic figure.

Plaza de San Juan de Dios, Camagüey. This splendid cobbled square—surrounded by 18th- and 19th-century buildings—anchors the historic district of Cuba's third largest city, Trinidad. No other Cuban city oozes history quite the way Trinidad does. The streets, with their brightly pastel-painted 19th-century buildings, are the sight here. Wander and soak up the past.

GREAT ITINERARIES

HIGHLIGHTS OF CUBA IN 8 DAYS

Cuba is not only the largest island in the Caribbean, but it may also have the most sights and attractions scattered across its diverse landscape. It could easily take more than two weeks to see the natural wonders of its mountains and forests and experience the culture and history of its towns and cities. The following itinerary takes in many of the island's best attractions across several regions, with recommended lodgings in each, offering the first-time visitor an exciting introduction to the country.

Days 1 and 2: Havana

Cuba's amazing capital is the first port of entry for most visitors, and it could keep you occupied for days. Spend your first day strolling the famous seaside walk **El Malécon**. A good starting point is Antonio Maceo Park, just east of Hotel Nacional. Continue east about 2 miles (3 km) until you reach the beautiful **Baroque Catedral de la Habana**. The next day you can take in a trio of terrific museums —the rum-themed **Museo del Ron Havana Club**, the fine arts **Museo Nacional de Bellas Artes**, and the **Museo de la Revolución**.

On either day, be sure to save some energy for the night. Visit the famous **El Floridita** (aka the cradle of the daiquiri) bar. Although touristy, it provides a classic Cuban night, with hot live music and cool daiquiris and mojitos. Or head to **Casa de la Música**, one of Havana's most popular night clubs, featuring many of Cuba's biggest modern acts.

When you're finally ready for sleep, you could stay at the historic **Hotel Nacional**, where pre-revolution anybody who was anybody stayed. For a contemporary feel,

try the **Hotel Meliá Cohiba** with its modern amenities or the intimate **Hotel Raquel**.

Days 3 and 4: Trinidad

The colonial town of Trinidad dates from 1514 and remains Cuba's best-preserved colonial architectural gem. Its streets, with their pastel-colored houses, are an attraction on their own. The **Museo de la Lucha contra Bandidos** houses a Revolution-themed museum in a former monastery, the Convento de San Francisco. Like all things Trinitario, religion rubs shoulders with Revolution here. The **Iberostar Grand Hotel Trinidad** is your best lodging choice in the city.

Days 5 and 6: Camagüey

Camagüey's labyrinth of streets reputedly confused invading pirates, and they continue to do so with visitors. Keep asking for directions; you'll get where you need to go. A pair of 18th-century churches, the **Iglesia de Nuestra Señora de la Merced** and the **Iglesia de Nuestra Señora de la Soledad** have both gone through numerous renovations and restorations through the centuries but have remained pretty faithful to their original constructions. **The Hotel Colón** evokes its 1920s heyday and is one of Cuba's snazziest city hotels.

Days 7 and 8: Santiago de Cuba

Like Havana, Santiago could keep you occupied for days. The beehive of life that is **Parque Céspedes** is best observed from the venerable **Hotel Casa Granda**, the best people-watching post in the city; it and the modern **Meliá Santiago de Cuba** are two great, affordable, places to stay. Three terrific museums sit in the center of the city: the **Museo Provincial Bacardí Moreau** documents Santiago's history; the rum-themed **Museo del Ron** acquaints you with the life and times of Cuba's best-known beverage; and the **Museo del Carnaval** portrays

artifacts from Santiago's Carnival celebration. (Try to time that last one for late afternoon when the museum stages a mini-carnival performance.) Don't forget Santiago's environs either. Cuba's Revolution began at the **Antiguo Cuartel Moncada,** military barracks outside the city. Pay your respects to revered Cuban poet José Martí at the **Cementerio Santa Ifigenia** where he is buried. Cuba's patron saint, Our Lady of Charity, is revered at the **Basílica del Cobre.** The imposing **Castillo del Morro** fortress sits out on the coast and protected Santiago from pirate invasions during colonial times. Any of the regional sites warrant a half day and can be reached by taxi. Back in the city, an evening of drink and music at the **Casa de la Trova** or drink only at the **Hotel Casa Granda** are relaxing ways to cap off a day, even if you don't stay at the latter.

VINTAGE CUBA IN 5 DAYS

Americans are often enamored with Cuba's antiquated appearance, the sense that little has changed since the early 1960s when a series of trade sanctions effectively froze the island in time. Follow this itinerary for a glance at old Cuba, beginning in Habana Vieja and ending in Remedios.

TIPS

This itinerary is, admittedly, ambitious. The entire length of the journey from Havana to Santiago de Cuba is far, about 870 km (520 miles). If you are fortunate enough to have extra days, the travel could be accomplished more leisurely. Each of the destinations on this itinerary are reached by major highways. If you travel as far as Santiago de Cuba, you may wish to break up your return journey to Havana with an overnight stop in Camagüey or Trinidad. Renting a car in Havana is expensive, but it gives you more freedom to come and go at will; however Víazul provides modern coach transportation to all these destinations. Víazul buses are very air-conditioned. Dress appropriately.

Days 1 and 2: Havana

Spend your day in Cuba's cobbled **Habana Vieja.** The **El Morro-La Cabaña Historical Military Park** stands guard over the old city on the north side of Havana Harbor, just as it has since its construction in the 16th century. Wander the ramparts of the star-shaped fortress that once kept foreign ships out of the harbor by way of a chain stretched across to the other side of the harbor. You can climb to the top of **El Morro Lighthouse** for a stunning view of all of Havana and the **Straits of Florida**, 90 miles of water that separates Cuba from Key West, Florida. Back in Old Havana, you'll want to pop into the **Cathedral of the Virgin of the Immaculate Conception**. The cathedral's Baroque exterior dates from its construction in 1748; a renovation in the early 19th century gave the interior a Classical look. Have lunch at one of Hemingway's favorite haunts, **La Bodeguita del Medio**. Quench your thirst with a mojito, just as Papa did, have a sandwich and bask in the memories of the famous people who preceded you, depicted in wall posters: Hemingway, Carmen Miranda, and Errol Flynn. Museum hop in the afternoon—vintage favorites include the **Rum Museum**, the **National Fine Arts Museum** and the **Museum of the Revolution**—and then take a taxi along **The Malecón**, the 5-mile (8-km) seawall, to your recommended accommodations, the landmark **Hotel Nacional**. The pink, twin-towered hotel was built in 1930 and has long connections to Batista, the mob's Lucky Luciano, Winston Churchill, and Marlon Brando.

On Day 2, venture out of Havana to **Cojímar**. The seaside village east of town is home to the **Fuerte de Cojímar**, a tiny fort, alongside of which is a bust of Ernest Hemingway. Here it was that Papa docked his boat, *Pilar*, chatted with fishermen, and got the inspiration for his classic *The Old Man and the Sea*. Fill up on a seafood lunch at **La Terraza**, Hemingway's favorite when he was in town, before taking off for **Finca Vigía**, Hemingway's home and office. Bull-fighting posters, the heads of game animals, and *Pilar* remain at the estate, all of it original to the time that the author lived here. Back in Havana, take a spin in a classic car, a 1956 Chevrolet Bel Air or a 1957 Ford Fairlane, en route to an evening of dinner and jazz at

Café Oriente. Cap off your evening with one last toast to Hemingway: a daiquiri at **La Floridita**, the author's favorite watering hole.

Day 3: Santa Clara

A three-hour drive from Havana, east on Autopista Nacional, takes you to the village of Santa Clara where the pivotal battle to topple the Batista regime occurred, and it's here that you'll find the **Monumento Ernesto Che Guevara**. It's impossible to miss the larger-than-life bronze statue of Che beneath which are the words, *"Hasta la victoria siempre,"* "Onward to victory, always!" attributed to the beloved Cuban revolutionary. Interred beneath the memorial are the remains of Che and a small museum dedicated to Guevara and the revolutionaries who fought alongside him. Spend time exploring Santa Clara's **Parque Vidal**, where most of the town's museums and monuments are located. The main plaza and surrounding streets are closed to traffic, and in the evenings you can experience local entertainment, watching concerts that take place in the plaza's main kiosk or on the street in front of the Casa de la Cultura. For a bargain lodging option right on Parque Vidal, you can stay overnight at the **Santa Clara Libre** hotel. On your way out of town, pass by the **Tren Blindado**, a memorial park commemorating a Batista troop train that was blown up by Che and his gang.

Day 4: Remedios

From Santa Clara continue east on Carretera a Camajuaní for about 45 minutes to Remedios, one of Cuba's oldest towns, founded in 1515. Small, but culturally rich and remarkably well preserved, Remedios is widely known for its *las Parrandas* festival in December, an all night celebration with homemade lanterns, fireworks, brass

Caribbean Sea

bands. The town's chief attraction is its **Parroquia de San Juan Batista**, a 17th-century Baroque church. Inside is a carved cedar altar with gold leaf and two rare statues of the Virgin Mary, one heavily pregnant and the other depicted as a mulatto. The exquisite ceiling is of hand-carved mahogany built to resemble the hull of a ship. The late-19th century inn **Hotel Mascotte** is the only hotel option, but there are several *casas particulares*, most of which are west of Plaza Martí.

Day 5: Caibarién to Havana

About 15 minutes east of Remedios on Circuito Nte./José Martí is Caibarién, where ox-drawn plows and horse-drawn carts are commonplace in the sugarcane fields near the town. Spanish colonial-era buildings surround the town square called the **Parque de la Libertad**, where you can dine on *cucina criollo*, authentic Cuban cooking, at a family-owned *paladare*. Listen to the local orchestra perform in the town's plaza (they play each weekend), then visit the **Reforma**, a historic sugar mill that has since been converted into a museum. Sample a cup of *guarapo* (sugarcane juice), with or without a shot of rum, then head out back to see a dozen late 19th- and early 20th-century steam locomotives, reminders

TIPS

Havana's taxis will ferry you comfortably among the city's far-flung neighborhoods. Pickpockets and gropers populate the capital's chaotic public bus system. Don't even attempt it. Outside of Havana, this itinerary confines you to a relatively small circuit in Central Cuba. The roads to the destinations listed here are decent—decent for Cuba, that is. Although renting a vehicle gives you more freedom to explore, leaving the driving to someone else is the easiest option, and Víazul, the workhorse of Cuban tourism transport, takes you to the places here in its spacious coaches. Base yourself back in Havana for the last night.

of a day when trains rumbled through here regularly to load up on sugarcane, refined sugar, and rum.

If you choose to rent a car for this itinerary, the return trip from Caibarién to Havana via the Autopista Nacional without stops should take about 4 hours.

FLAVORS OF CUBA

Food conversations in Cuba turn repeatedly to the vicissitudes of supply. The combination of food shortages and state-run restaurants has produced some remarkably undistinguished cooking over the past 50 years. If you're familiar with the Cuban-American food of South Florida, you may be surprised at the food's bland counterpart back home. Still, the sanctioning in the 1990s of privately owned restaurants called *paladares* have sparked a renaissance of authentic *cocina criollo*, traditional Cuban home cooking that does its level best to make the flavorful most of what's at hand.

Main Dishes

Pollo (chicken), *puerco* (pork) and to a lesser degree *res* (beef) and *cordero* (lamb) rank as Cuba's meat staples—too cripplingly expensive to show up often in home kitchens but filling ample space on Cuban tourist-class restaurant menus. Cuts of meat tend to be of lesser quality than most Western restaurants, frequently a bit overcooked.

Any meat may be served *estofado* (stewed). *La caldosa*, a universal favorite, combines chicken, onions, garlic, plantains, and a variety of vegetables in a rich broth left to simmer slowly. Another favorite is *cordero estofado con vegetales*, lamb stew made with sweet potato, yam, carrots and other veggies. *Ropa vieja* combines shredded beef with a *salsa criolla*. Spanish for "old clothes," *ropa vieja*, as folkloric legend has it, was named when a desperately poor man cooked old clothes to stand-in for meat to feed his children, and it was magically transformed into a delicious stew from all the love he poured into it. Other common meat dishes include *chicharrones de puerco* (pork crisps), and *masas de cerdo* (morsels of pork), often served in a *mojo criollo*.

Sauces and spices are not common in Cuba—they veer into the realm of unnecessary luxury. The most commonly found are *salsa criolla* (onion, tomato, pepper, garlic, salt, and oil), *ajiaco* (the hot red pepper *aji* combined with yuca, sweet potato, turnips and herbs) and *mojo* (garlic, tomato, and pepper).

On Cuba's eastern end, dishes are more Caribbean in style, with less of the Spanish influence found elsewhere on the island. Expect more spices and a preparation that involves cooking in coconut oil and *lechita* (coconut milk). Eastern dishes include *congrí oriental* (rice prepared with red kidney beans), *bacón* (a plantain tortilla filled with spicy pork), and *tetí* (a small, orange river fish in season between August and December).

Rice and Beans

Rice and beans, whether cooked together or served separately, are the most commonplace of sides in Cuba. They're inexpensive and have the distinct advantage of a long shelf life. Cooked slowly and often flavored with a bit of lard, they rank as savory, stick-to-your-ribs fare across the country.

Frijoles negros (black beans) and *arroz* (white or yellow rice) frequently accompany meat dishes. Variations on those themes include *moros y cristianos* (Moors and Christians), a delicious combination of black beans and white rice ubiquitous in Cuba. *Arroz congrí* is white rice with *frijoles negros dormidos* (literally "put to sleep," or cooked and allowed to stand overnight). Yellow rice takes its color not from saffron but from annatto seeds, also used to color butter.

Seafood

Traditionally, seafood isn't of primary importance in Cuban dishes; however, *pescado* (fish) staples can serve a welcome substitute for non-meat eaters at tourist-class restaurants across Cuba. Look for *corvina* (sea bass), *pargo* (red snapper), and *filet de emperador* (swordfish) with *camarones* (shrimp) and *langosta* (lobster) showing up less often.

Fruits and Vegetables

Whether it's the perishability of fresh produce or the decision to dedicate Cuba's farmland to its cash crops of sugarcane, tobacco, and coffee, you'll find little in the way of fresh vegetables or fruits. This may be just as well, as Cuba's impure water makes it inadvisable to dig into uncooked vegetables or fruits that cannot be peeled.

You will, however, see a lot of plantain, a fruit that sees 101 preparations in the Cuban kitchen. When ripe, the plantain may be cut diagonally and fried. When green, it can be sliced into *lascas* (thin wafers), fried, and salted to create *mariquitas*, or chopped into thick wedges, pounded and fried as *plátanos a puñetazos* (punched plantains). Green or mature, plantains may be boiled, mashed with a fork, dressed with olive oil and crisped pork rinds to create *fufu* or mashed and mixed with *picadillo* (ground meat) and melted cheese for a *pastel de plátano* (plantain pudding), a sort of tropical shepherd's pie.

Sweets

Not surprisingly, the denizens of the land of sugarcane love their sweets. Desserts include sweet sponge cakes called *kek* or *ke*. Specialties such as *guayaba* (guava paste) and *mermelada de mango* (mango jelly) may both be served *con queso* (with cheese). The eastern treat *cucurucho* is made of coconut, sweet orange, papaya, and honey. Cubans are big fans of ice cream. In bigger cities such as Havana and Santa Clara, the ice-cream shop Coppelia is extraordinarily popular, often identified by the long line of patrons queuing up to enter.

Rum and Cocktails

Cuba's long history of sugarcane cultivation led to its renowned *ron* (rum) industry. You'll find rum served throughout the country. Young rum, which is the least expensive version, is characterized by its colorless appearance. Artificial and caramel colorings are forbidden in Cuban rum, so the darker in tone an amber rum appears, the longer you can be assured that it has aged in oak. These are the most prized of Cuban rums, the smoothest and most caramel in flavor, and the most expensive.

If you'd like the sugar experience without the kick, have a *guarapo* (pure cane juice, thought to be an aphrodisiac) or skip the juice and get a stalk of sugar cane to chew on, a garnish often included with cocktails or Cuban coffee. Cuba also has several fine beers ranging from light lagers such as Cristal to darker varieties like Bucanero.

Fruit drinks are often served to restaurant patrons as soon as they arrive, a sort of sangria with or without alcohol. Alternates are the *mojito*, a cocktail comprised of rum, sugar, mint, soda, and lime. Cuba's classic daiquiri is made of blended light rum, lime, and ice.

KIDS AND FAMILIES

Cubans love children. There is scarcely a better way to meet locals than to travel with a youngster in tow. And Cuba is rich in activities for kids, from glorious sugar-sand beaches to energetic live street music.

Good to Know

Tourist-class hotels offer comfortable lodging for little ones, typically charging nothing extra for kids under 16 (although you may need to pay extra for a crib or roll-away cot).

Cuban restaurants often serve meals family-style, making it possible for timid eaters to try a little of this and a little of that, perhaps settling on a heaping plate of beans and rice or a second (and third?) helping of roast pork. Make sure to let your children know the importance of drinking bottled water rather than straight from the tap.

To be on the safe side, take with you any children's supplies you can't live without—diapers, medications, sunscreen, or baby food—as availability of these items can vary in Cuba.

Rental cars in Cuba do not always offer children's car seats.

Things to Do

Cuba's complicated history and its current political situation may not mean much to the kids. But there's plenty to keep youngsters occupied on this Caribbean island, beginning with a long list of outdoor recreation options.

Beaches. All beaches in Cuba are public and they're are a number of great, swimmable spots with facilities, including Playa Pilar and Playa Flamenco in the North and Playa Ancón in the South.

Santo Tomás Cavern. Set on the westernmost tip of Cuba just west of Viñales, this cave system, one of the largest in the Western Hemisphere, twists and turns underground for some 28 miles (45 km), up and over 8 levels. Explore the cavern outfitted with headlamps, clambering up and down ladders past rock formations hidden beneath fields of coffee. The 90-minute tours are led by English-speaking guides.

La Boca de Guamá. This attraction off the Autopista Nacional, near the Laguna del Tesoro, includes a crocodile farm (Criadero de Cocodrilos), an open-air Indian museum and boat rides. See the crocs' sinister smiles from the perspective of several boardwalks and raised wooden platforms before taking a boat trip to the Laguna del Tesoro, at the center of which stands a tiny island, home to a recreated Taíno Indian village. For added excitement, book a stay at one of the island cabañas of Villa Guamá, little thatched cabins that sit perched on piles above the water and are connected to one another by hanging bridges.

Cuban Baseball. In much of Latin America, soccer is king. In Cuba, baseball reigns supreme. You can catch a game at arenas across the country from October to April. In Havana, games are played by one of two home teams, the Industriales and the Metropolitanos, at the Estadio Latinoamericano, just a stone's throw from Revolution Square.

Live music. At venues across Cuba, professional orchestras and dance troupes perform music ranging from classical favorites to Spanish-inspired *son* and Afro-Cuban tumba. You're likely to stumble upon organized and impromptu concerts at centrally located city plazas as well as at Cuban restaurants and cafés.

FESTIVALS AND EVENTS

February
Go ahead, light up that stogie! At the **Havana Cigar Festival** (⊕ *www.habanos. com*) held each year in February, highlights include tobacco plantation tours in Pinar del Río, cigar-factory tours, seminars, workshops, and the release of new cigars. Proceeds from the event's closing silent auction go to the Cuban public health system.

May
Cuba takes May Day seriously. **World Workers Day** is celebrated each year beginning early on May 1 when hundreds of thousands of residents march on Havana's Plaza de la Revolución to proclaim, via chanting and banners, the virtues of the Revolution. Armed with papier-mâché replicas of the tools of their trades—cigars, taxis, musical instruments, barber's shears—the Cubans' demonstrations often turn into a street party complete with conga lines and plenty of music.

Every two years the world's premier festival for non-Western artists of all genres, the **Havana Biennale** (⊕ *www. biennialfoundation.org*) features fine visual arts, contemporary art and music from across Latin America and the Caribbean, Africa, Asia, and the Middle East. The next Biennale will be held in 2017.

July
Few Cuban festivals compete in color or exuberance with **Carnaval** in Santiago (⊕ *www.santiagodecubacity.org*). For a week in July an explosion of color, musical rhythms, and dancing fills the streets of this eastern city, Cuba's second largest. A similarly extravagant Carnaval celebration is held in late July/early August in Havana.

September
The **Benny Moré International Festival** (⊕ *www.cienfuegoscity.org*) celebrates the life and music of Cuba's biggest 1950s-era Big Band leader each September in Cienfuegos. Musicians and singers from across the island and beyond pay homage to this master of all Cuban genres, including *son*, *mamba*, and *bolero*.

October
At the **International Ballet Festival of Havana**, the finest dancers arrive from around the world each October to perform with members of the National Ballet of Cuba.

December
Although the festivities are strictly regional, little compares with the unique *parrandas* in Cuba's Villa Clara Province. Held between Christmas and New Year's Day in Remedios, Caibarién, and a dozen other Villa Clara villages, the Mardi Gras-style parties involve much song, elaborate costuming, floats and plenty of rum. But the centerpiece of the fun involves massive fireworks competitions between villages.

The **International Festival of Latin American Film** (Festival Internacional de Cine Latinoamericano ⊕ *www.habanafilmfestival. com*) has become one of the Western Hemisphere's finest film festivals. Held annually at venues across Havana the first week in December, the event focuses on new cinema and the rising stars of Latin-film directing.

In mid-December world-renowned musicians attend Havana's prestigious **International Jazz Festival** (⊕ *http://jazzcuba.com*). Although venues around town stage concerts, the biggest and best are always held at the Teatro Mella with Cuban jazz legend and pianist Chucho Valdés starring in the opening event.

HAVANA

Updated by
Esme Fox

In this historic seaport, long known as the Key to the New World, classic American cars clatter along streets lined with Spanish architecture and pulsating with African and Caribbean rhythms. Old Havana's Baroque facades, massive-columned palaces, and lush patios whisper tales of Cuba's colonial past. Everywhere, Spanish, African, Caribbean, and American flavors boil in a dynamic and sensual brew.

"If I get lost, look for me in Cuba..." wrote Spanish poet Federico García Lorca. If you visit Havana, you'll soon understand why. The city is a mixture of opulence and decay, old world and new, socialism and capitalism, Europe, Africa, and America.

Once-elegant buildings crumble behind Corinthian columns, while an increasing number are undergoing renovations and restorations that previsage what will be a new, and hopefully glorious, unique historic city. Meanwhile, rickety 1950s Chevrolets and Oldsmobiles crisscross the capital, acting as economical community taxis while tiny motorized *coco-taxis* and bicycle-powered *ciclo-taxis* roll by. Many things here are in disrepair; yet all this seems only to add to Havana's rough allure. Graham Greene and Ernest Hemingway drank deeply of it and were inspired; Ava Gardner and Winston Churchill—to name a few—were similarly enchanted.

Havana, like the rest of Cuba, is on the brink of change, and being the capital, it's leading the charge. You'll see still the classic cars and crumbling colonial mansions the city is famous for, but clear signs of renovation and gentrification are all around. Already, Habana Vieja's main plazas and their surroundings are well on the way to being restored to their former glory, and those who still want a glimpse of the Cuba we know had better be quick.

As well as its impressive architecture decaying or restored, Havana offers an intoxicating mix of rhythms, rum, revolution and history. Its museums are fascinating and varied, covering everything from money and tobacco to African and Asian cultures, rum, ballet and even playing cards. Whatever your interests—old forts and castles, contemporary theater, decorative arts, cars, or beaches—the city has something that will please everyone.

In the last couple of years, relaxation of certain laws has meant that a wave of new accommodations options have opened up to tourists, such as private apartments or rented houses, not to mention new and inventive bars, restaurants, and *paladares* popping up on the scene. Today, the city has an air of excitement about it, and although it still has a long way to go, its citizens are looking forward to the future and where it will take them.

TOP ATTRACTIONS

TOP ATTRACTIONS

Colonial architecture. Havana is home to some of the most spectacular colonial architecture to be found anywhere in the world. Many buildings may be crumbling and dishevelled, but this gives them a stoic, tenacious appearance.

The Malecón. Havana's atmospheric esplanade is the place to be when the sun sets, watching the streaking colors over the Bahía de la Habana. Families, couples, and friends all come to enjoy the show, making this one of the best spots for people-watching in the city.

Vintage cars. One of the most iconic symbols of Cuba is the classic car, the majority of which can be found in Havana. A drive down the Malecón in an open-top rose-colored Cadillac is a quintessential Havana experience.

Music. Music is the soul of Cuba and in Havana you'll find it everywhere—pulsating through streets, floating out of restaurants and bars, performed in hotels, and of course beating in the clubs.

Habana Vieja. Old town is packed with enough colonial treasures, magnificent buildings, and cultural museums to make it the must-see neighborhood in Havana.

ORIENTATION AND PLANNING

GETTING ORIENTED

In the middle of Havana Province and edged by the Straits of Florida to the north, the city of Havana is officially divided into 15 municipalities, which themselves often contain various neighborhoods. For the purposes of touring the city, it's best to divide the city into six main areas.

Moving from east to west (and, roughly, from old to new) you'll find Habana Vieja, with its many historical charms; Centro Habana, with the scenic Paseo de Martí (Prado), the Capitolio, and the 7-km (4-mile) seaside Malecón; Vedado, which is reminiscent of both Manhattan and Miami; and Miramar, with its grand mansions. Across Havana Harbor are the fortresses—El Morro and La Cabaña—and the Cristo de la Habana statue, as well as the municipality known as Regla and other sights in Eastern Havana.

Habana Vieja. The highlight of any trip to Havana will be a stroll through Habana Vieja with its colonial palaces, Baroque churches and historic plazas. Parts of this district have been meticulously restored, while others remain in crumbling disrepair.

Centro Habana. This is where *habaneros* go about their lives. Children play baseball, and from the dusty urban streets you can witness gleeful singing, dancing, and the regular commotion of life in a setting of urban sprawl.

Vedado. Vedado is a vast area that hosts a great mix of historical landmarks, hotels, restaurants, and nightlife. Taxi rides to attractions such as the Museo de Artes Decorativos or UNEAC can be combined with strolls through leafy streets filled with stately mansions.

Miramar. Miramar is an upscale neighborhood where you'll find few, but interesting attractions. The vast neighborhood has a series of oceanfront resorts and hosts the Miramar Trade Center.

Eastern Havana. The small towns to the east of the city have become somewhat of an extension of Havana itself, but still manage to retain their own charm. They're best visited to discover more about Cuba's Santería religion or to follow the Hemingway trail.

Playas del Este. This 9 km (5 ½ miles) string of white-sand beaches—popular with tourists and locals—lies about a half-hour drive from Havana and makes for an idyllic escape from the hustle and bustle of the city.

PLANNING

WHEN TO GO

November through May is high season, and temperatures are more moderate than at other times of the year. February is Cuba's coolest month, with temperatures in the 24°C to 26°C (75°F to 79°F) range. Don't rule out a visit during May through October; although this is hurricane season and the weather is hot and humid, there are fewer tourists and generally lower rates.

PLANNING YOUR TIME

You could very easily spend five days in Havana and still not get to see everything it has to offer. If you have a week in the area, we suggest four of five days in the city, combined with a two or three-day beach break in the Playas del Este, about 11 miles (18 km) east of the city. The best way to explore the city is to begin your time in Habana Vieja (the historic old town) and the fortresses across the bay, then slowly work your way west through Centro Habana and Vedado, leaving half a day at the end to visit the farthest and most modern area of Miramar with its magnificent mansions. If you have a couple of extra days, head east to the other side of the Havana Port to visit the small towns of Regla and Guanabaco, famous for their connections to the Santería religion. You may also wish to explore farther south to visit Finca Vigía, the former home of Ernest Hemingway, as well as Parque Lenin.

GETTING HERE AND AROUND

BUS TRAVEL

Havana's famous *camello* buses, with their camel-like humps, are no more. Instead you'll find a more modern fleet of Chinese-made buses ambling their way around the city and its outskirts. The bus is definitely the cheapest (less than CUC$1 per journey), but you may find that deciphering all the routes can be a little complicated. For bus travel to other parts of the island, contact either the bus company Víazul or Transtur, both of which operate comfortable air-conditioned fleets of modern buses.

Contacts Víazul. ⊠ *Calle 26 y Av. Zoológico, Nuevo Vedado* ☏ *7883–6092* ⊕ *www.viazul.com.*

CAR TRAVEL

Driving in Havana and its environs isn't as daunting as you might think; there are relatively few cars on the roads, and most drivers aren't overly aggressive. Remain alert and flexible and watch out for bicycles, ciclo-taxis, and coco-taxis—not to mention pedestrians looking for *botellas* (rides). Road surfaces are uneven, so if you drive, keep your eyes glued to the pavement. Cubans beep their horns often, though rarely in a belligerent way; this is a courteous way to let other drivers know you're coming through.

Parking isn't generally a problem in Havana as there are still relatively few automobiles circulating. Even around Plaza de las Armas or Plaza de San Francisco de Asís it's usually possible to find a parking spot. You will, however, encounter freelance parking attendants who will keep an eye on your car for a dollar up front, a bargain automobile-security system.

TAXI TRAVEL

Taxis are generally inexpensive by European or North American standards, providing you're ready to bargain, but hardly any of them have the official meters. You can grab them from in front of hotels, hail them on the streets, or call them. Official taxis are often Hyundais, Mercedes, or Russian-made Ladas. Ciclo-taxis (bicycle rickshaws) are breezy and slow, offer a scenic ride, and cost about the same as auto taxis. Coco-taxis (motor scooter–powered conveyances) are another option. Always negotiate the price before you get in any type of cab. The fares vary in price, but from Vedado to La Habana Vieja you should be paying about CUC\$6; from Miramar it would be about CUC\$10.

If you want to pay a fraction of that price, take an American-made 1950s vehicle at Parque Central. In these community taxis, or *carros* as they're called, expect to pay half a convertible peso to Vedado, but note that you will share your ride in what can be a really tight fit. The community taxis follow set paths, mostly along Calle 23 (La Rampa) in Vedado, and don't expect to veer from the set road.

All taxis were recently regrouped to operate under the government's Cubataxi brand.

Contacts Cubataxi. ☎ *7855–5555.*

RESTAURANTS

Shortages of raw materials and a bureaucratized approach to food preparation in state-owned restaurants have produced many a mediocre meal, but with the privateer restaurants leading the way, Cuban cuisine is coming back. For the best cooking in Havana, seek out the *paladares* (privately owned establishments; the name, which literally means "palates," was cribbed from a popular Brazilian soap opera in which the heroine makes her fortune with a roadside restaurant named "El Paladar de Raquel"). Call ahead to reserve a table if you go to a paladar, and never believe a taxi driver who swears to you that the place is closed; he gets a commission for taking you to the place he is flacking for.

HOTELS

If you're interested in exploring colonial Havana, the most convenient and aesthetically pleasing place to stay is La Habana Vieja. More than a dozen hotels, all part of the Habaguanex chain connected with the city's restoration operation, offer lodging in Old Havana. A stay in one of these places means that your lodging expenses help finance the refurbishment of this neighborhood. Hotels in Centro Habana at the periphery of the old city are close to La Habana Vieja, as well as the paladares and attractions of Centro Habana, Vedado, and Miramar. One of the most unique of these is Hotel Los Frailes, where staff are dressed as Franciscan friars.

Many lodgings are concentrated in the Vedado district, where the otherwise dusty but architecturally splendid Hotel Nacional or the mammoth Hotel Habana Libre reign supreme. The central Hotel Saratoga—across from Havana's famous Capitolio—is a high-class boutique hotel that sets the standard in Cuba for its superior design, general comfort, and service levels. The Meliá Cohiba and the NH Capri probably have the best services and infrastructure, along with the Meliá Habana; the Château Miramar is a nice smaller option for families. Many of the top hotels, including the Meliá Cohiba, Meliá Habana, Hotel Nacional, Tryp Habana Libre, NH Parque Central, and Santa Isabel have executive floors with separate check-in facilities and business centers with Internet, email, fax, and phone services.

A popular alternative to the main hotels is staying in a *casa particular* (a private home that rents guest rooms). The opportunity to help individual Cubans directly, as well as the chance to live more like a Cuban, makes this an attractive alternative. Specific private accommodations are difficult to recommend (people go in and out of business rapidly as a result of ferocious taxation), but there are many excellent options, some located in stunning old colonial homes or even stately mansions. The houses are well-kept and often have better facilities than many of the top hotels. Usually rooms come with air conditioners, fans, private bathrooms, refrigerators, and safes, all in good working order. You'll find casas particulares all over Havana, so you still have the freedom to choose which area of the city you want to stay in. Prices vary from around CUC$25–CUC$40 per night and breakfast usually costs an extra CUC$5 per person, invariably consisting of huge platters of fresh fruit, bread, eggs (any way you want), juice, and coffee. While it's difficult to reserve ahead directly with the casa owner, you can book via third-party websites. This is highly recommended, as the best ones fill up quickly. A reliable site is Casa Havana Particular (⊕ *www. casahavanaparticular*), a member of the Cuba Casa Particular Association, where you can read descriptions and see photos of each casa before you book. All the houses on the site have been reviewed by the association's travel team, ensuring quality throughout. Payment is made directly to the casa owner upon departure.

WHAT IT COSTS IN CUBAN CONVERTIBLE PESOS			
	$	$$	$$$	$$$$
Restaurants	under CUC$12	CUC$12–CUC$20	CUC$21–CUC$30	over CUC$30
Hotels	under CUC$75	CUC$75–CUC$150	CUC$151–CUC$200	over CUC$200

Restaurant prices are the average cost of a main course at dinner or, if dinner is not served, at lunch. Hotel prices are the lowest cost of a standard double room in high season.

TOURS

Cubatur, one of Cuba's state-run agencies, has very professional staff that can help you make arrangements for anything from a guided tour to a table at the Tropicana. The agency, or other similar service agencies, can be found in any of the main hotels where you will be staying. Havanatur and Cubanacán also have offices in many of Havana's top hotels and can arrange cultural and ecological tours as well as excursions to beaches. The staff does it all—from car rentals to plane tickets. Paradiso is a small company that offers cultural tours and guided excursions of all kinds.

Habana Tour Bus, operated by the Transtur bus company, is a modern double decker hop-on-hop-off type bus, like those you find in many of the world's top tourist cities. It offers three different routes and stops at all the major sites. Tickets cost CUC$5 per person and are valid all day long. A good starting point is the Parque Central, in front of the Hotel Inglaterra.

Cubanacán. This large company also owns and runs many of Cuba's hotels and is a great source for organizing accommodations, domestic travel, tours around the country, and excursions. They can also book tickets for some of Havana's top cabaret shows. ✉ *Calle 41 No. 2213, e/Calles 22 y 24, Miramar* ☎ *7204–9605* ⊕ *www.viajescubanacan.cu.*

Cubatur. A big travel and tourism agency, Cubatur can organize everything you need for your trip to or around Cuba. In Havana, they offer two main guided city tours, one concentrating on colonial Havana and the other on the more modern side of the city; there's also an additional one in an old classic car. Other tours include day-trip excursions to Viñales and Cayo Largo and an overnight trip to Santa Clara and Trinidad. ✉ *Calle 23 esq. de L, Vedado* ☎ *7833–3569* ⊕ *www.cubatur.cu.*

Havanatur. A variety of services are offered from car rentals to accommodations booking, themed tours around the entire island or tickets to the Tropicana. In Havana they offer one main city tour, which visits most of the major sights in the historic center. They also offer a separate Hemingway tour, as well as one to see the nighttime cannon ceremony at the Fortress of San Carlos Cabaña. In addition to this, a number of guided day trips are offered to Viñales, Varadero, and Cayo Largo. Their offices are located in many of the major city hotels including the Hotel Tryp Habana Libre, the Iberostar Parque Central, and the Meliá Habana. ✉ *Calle 23 y M, 23 y P, Vedado* ☎ *7201–9874* ⊕ *www.havanatur.cu.*

Infotur. The official National Tourist Office has branches all over the country, as well as a few places in Havana. This is a one-stop-shop tourism agency, where you can book lodging, transport, excursions, tours, and tickets for entertainment venues. It's best to speak to them directly for a full list of what they offer. The offices in Havana Vieja are better located, but the main office in Miramar is on Calle 28, e/3ra y 5ta Avenidas. ⊠ *Calle Obispo 524, e/Calles Bernaza y Villegas, La Habana Vieja* ☎ *7866–6333* ⊕ *www.infotur.cu.*

Paradiso Turismo Cultural. This small company specializes in cultural tours and excursions of all kinds, including five main Havana tours, each with its own focus—aromas and flavors, rhythm and color, folklore and Santaria religion, Hemingway, or family. They also offer a variety of courses and workshops such as photography, painting, music, and dancing. Those who want to experience nightlife or live-music scenes, but would rather go with a group, should book with Paradiso, too. ⊠ *Ave. 5ta 8202, e/Calles 82 y 84, Miramar* ☎ *7214–0701* ⊕ *www.paradiso.cu.*

EXPLORING

To see La Habana Vieja and its many colonial palaces and Baroque churches at their best, plan to tour on foot. Although you could spend days here, you can easily see the highlights of Old Havana in two days. Make the fortresses across the bay a side trip from La Habana Vieja, and save the sights farther east, as well as the Playas del Este, for another day. Centro Habana also has many historic sights, and it is here that you will truly see the sprawling everyday life of Cubans. The Capitolio, Chinatown, and Parque Central are must-sees for tourists, but a stroll in the southern reaches of Centro Habana and its dusty streets are an eye-opener. A tour of Centro Habana can begin and end at the Hotel Inglaterra and Parque Central. El Malecón, from La Punta all the way to La Chorrera fortress at the mouth of Río Almendares (Almendares River), is an important part of Havana life and a good hour's hike.

Vedado stretches from Calzada de Infanta to the Río Almendares and is difficult to explore on foot. Taxi rides to objectives such as the Museo de Artes Decorativos or UNEAC can be combined with strolls through leafy streets filled with stately mansions. Miramar, which stretches southwest across the Río Almendares, was the residential area for wealthy Habaneros and foreigners before the Revolution. A tour of its wide, tree-lined avenues is best made by car.

The streets in La Habana Vieja and Centro Habana have been, in European fashion, given such poetic names as Amargura (Bitterness), Esperanza (Hope), or Ánimas (Souls). Note that some streets have pre- and postrevolutionary names; both are often cited on maps. Throughout the city, addresses are also frequently cited as street names with numbers and/or locations, as in: "Calle Concordia, e/Calle Gervasio y Calle Escobar" or "Calle de los Oficios 53, esquina de Obrapía." It's helpful to know the following terms and abbreviations: "e/" (*entre*) is "between"; *esquina de* (abbreviated "esq. de") is "corner of"; and *y* is "and."

CLOSE UP
Havana's Place in History

For almost 250 years the maritime hub of Havana was little more than a staging area for Spanish convoys loaded with New World treasures and bound for Europe. Cuba's campaign for independence began along with its 19th-century prosperity, and Havana was often in the eye of the storm. During the Ten Years War (1868–78), Cuba's first attempt to break free of Spain, the city was a haven for conservatives loyal to the mother country. Havana would later become a hotbed of liberalism and the nerve center for phase two of the independence movement—sparked by the eloquent revolutionary José Martí—which led to the Second War of Independence (1892). In 1898, Havana harbor was the last port of call for the *Maine*, a major U.S. military vessel, which was blown up (depending on whose history books you read) by accident, by Americans, or by pro-annexationist Cubans. This event led to the Spanish-American War, the end of Spanish sovereignty, and the beginning of heavy U.S. involvement in Cuban affairs.

Though the 1950s Revolution against dictator Fulgencio Batista began on the eastern end of the island, Fidel Castro's most charismatic moment was his triumphal entry into Havana on January 1, 1959. Castro's regime improved the quality of life for most Cubans, especially in the areas of education and medicine. But the collapse of the Soviet Union combined with the long-standing U.S. blockade has caused severe shortages of goods. A steady flow of visitors from Canada and Europe have helped to improve matters. Havana today is a work in progress, rough and real, caught in its own history and struggling toward an uncertain future.

LA HABANA VIEJA

La Habana Vieja is a thick concentration of colonial architecture and humanity—a vibrant wedge of restoration work and tumultuous street life all set to music. Dubbed "Key to the New World" for its strategic position at the confluence of the Atlantic, the Caribbean, and the Gulf of Mexico, Havana was the staging point for the riches shipped back to Spain, and the tremendous wealth of this era is reflected in the plazas and mansions sprinkled throughout the old city. This opulent colonial patrimony also bears witness to the social inequities that led to the Revolution, which, in turn, resulted in the unusual conditions that make present-day Old Havana a unique blend of colonial splendor and contemporary squalor.

Development of Havana began on the eastern edge nearest the harbor and moved west. Unlike the standard models for Spain's imperial capitals, the city has no main square. Plaza de Armas, as the seat of colonial rule, comes closest to this role historically, though its position on the edge of the bay (and the city) deprives the square of the required centrality. Plaza Vieja (originally called Plaza Nueva) was created as a space for markets and festivities instead of for the military and the government. Plaza de San Francisco was Havana's third square, followed by the Plaza de la Catedral, originally known as La Ciénaga (the swamp) for its marshy terrain. La Habana Vieja's fifth square was the Plaza del Santo Cristo.

More than half surrounded by the Bahía de la Habana (Havana Bay), Calle Águila, the only street that begins and ends at the sea (running from the Ensenada de Atares to the Malecón), is officially the western limit of La Habana Vieja, although the true border is Calle de Bélgica (more often known by its old name as Egido), which becomes Monserrate at its center and Avenida de las Misiones at its northern extreme.

La Habana Vieja is composed of a dozen north–south streets intersected by 20 east–west arteries, forming more than 100 surprisingly symmetrical (for 16th-century urban planning) blocks. Innumerable mansions and palaces, nearly two-dozen cultural centers and museums, six churches, and five convents are crowded into this 1½-square-miles municipality. Calle Brasil (Teniente Rey) roughly divides La Habana Vieja into a southern sector including Plaza Vieja and Plaza del Santo Cristo, and a northern sector that includes Plaza de Armas, Plaza de San Francisco, and Plaza de la Catedral.

GETTING HERE AND AROUND

The old, historic part of the city is best explored on foot, as the streets are narrow and many of the streets around the five main plazas are pedestrianized. If your feet are getting tired though, flag down a bicycle taxi, which can easily navigate around the many road works in the area. Just remember to agree to the price in advance.

TOP ATTRACTIONS

Camera Obscura. On the northwestern corner of Plaza Vieja, located on the top floor of the early 20th-century Villa Gómez, you'll find the city's fascinating Camera Obscura, gifted to Cuba by Spain's Council of Cadiz. Housed in a darkened room, with a small hole in the ceiling, visitors can watch the real-life scenes on and around Plaza Vieja being played out in a large dish right in front of them. The camera is the only one of its kind in Latin America and the Caribbean and one of only 74 in the world today. ⊠ *Calle Mercaderes, esq. de San Ignacio, Plaza Vieja, La Habana Vieja* ☎ *7866–4461* ⊡ *CUC$2* ☉ *Daily 9–5:30.*

Casa de la Obrapía. This house is named for the *obra pía* (pious work) with orphans that was carried out here in colonial times. Its elaborately wrought Baroque doorway is thought to have been carved in Cádiz around 1686. The architecture of the interior patio is based on North African *fondouks* (inns) and, later, of Spanish *corralas* (patios). There's much to see here: arches of different sizes and shapes, vases decorated with paintings by Spanish painter Ignacio Zuloaga, as well as a collection of old sewing machines and needlecraft paraphernalia. ■ TIP➜ The Alejo Carpentier artifacts (including the car he used in Paris) are still there, but locked up in a special room that you must get permission ahead of time to see. ⊠ *Calle Obrapía 158, La Habana Vieja* ☎ *7861–3097* ⊡ *Free* ☉ *Tues.–Sat. 9:30–5, Sun. 9:30–12:30.*

Casa Natal de José Martí. On January 28, 1853, Cuba's *padre de la patria* (father of the nation), José Martí, was born of Spanish parents in this humble house. When a child he prophetically announced, "Five generations of slaves must be followed by a generation of martyrs." At

HAVANA GREAT ITINERARIES

IF YOU HAVE 3 DAYS

In La Habana Vieja, do a whirlwind tour of Plaza Vieja, Plaza de la Catedral, and Plaza de Armas, with a stop at the famous La Bodeguita del Medio (or, for better scenery and fewer tourists, Restaurante Paris, in front of the cathedral) for a mojito. Take a taxi through the harbor tunnel to the fortresses. Have dinner at La Divina Pastora before (or after) the 9 pm cannon blast at the Castillo de San Carlos de la Cabana. On day two, explore Centro Habana; visit the Capitolio, the Casa del Habano Part-agás, and the Parque Central before having a daiquirí at El Floridita. In the afternoon, walk the length of Calle Obispo from El Floridita to Plaza de Armas; stroll the Paseo del Prado or El Malecón. On day three, visit the Necrópolis Cristóbal Colón before touring Vedado's impressive town houses and the mansions of Miramar. Dine at El Aljibe, then head for the Tropicana cabaret and its kitsch reviews or, for something more local and less touristy, the local acts at Casa de la Música.

IF YOU HAVE 5 DAYS

On the first day, explore the many sights in La Habana Vieja's southern half, starting at the Casa Natal de José Martí and ending at the Plaza Vieja. On day two, take in the Plaza de la Catedral and the Plaza de Armas before wandering along Calle de los Oficios, with its many art galleries. In the early evening, taxi through the harbor tunnel to the fortresses. Visit the Museo del Che and the Museo de la Cabaña in the Castillo de San Carlos de la Cabaña, have dinner at La Divina Pastora before or after the 9 pm cannon blast at La Cabaña.

age 15 he wrote a newspaper piece judged treasonous by the Spanish governors, and after time in a Havana prison followed by exile to the Isla de la Juventud, he was exiled to Spain, where he later studied law. Martí then spent 14 years in the United States, working as a newspaper reporter. Three volumes of poetry and several books of essays established him as the most brilliant Latin American writer and political analyst of his day.

Martí's words stirred both moral and financial support for Cuban independence. In mid-April 1895, as part of a revolutionary plan that was months in the making, Martí joined General Máximo Gómez on Santo Domingo (Dominican Republic). The two set out for Eastern Cuba, where General Antonio Maceo awaited them. A month later, on May 19, 1895, Martí became one of the first casualties of the Second War of Independence, when he charged, mounted on a white steed, into a Spanish ambush during a battle at Dos Ríos. His lyrics in "Guantanamera," are premonitory: *"Que no me entierran en lo oscuro / a morir como un traidor / yo soy bueno y como bueno / moriré de cara al sol."* ("May they not bury me in darkness / to die like a traitor / I am good, and as a good man / I will die facing the sun.") The memorabilia in this museum range from locks of the young Martí's hair to the shackle he wore around his ankle as a prisoner to letters, books, and poetry. Look for the martyr's spurs and ammunition belt, a rare 1893 photograph of Martí with Máximo Gómez in New York, and another of the Manhattan office on Front Street where he worked on the Cuban independent newspaper *Patria*. ⊠ *Calle Leonor Pérez (Paula) 314, La Habana Vieja* ☎ *7861–3778* ☞ *CUC$1.50* ⊙ *Tues.–Sat. 9:30–5, Sun. 9:30–1.*

FAMILY **Castillo de la Real Fuerza.** Constructed in 1558 by order of Spanish king Felipe II three years after an earlier fortress was destroyed by the French pirate Jacques de Sores, this classic, moat-enclosed fortress was the residence of the local military commanders until 1762. The tower, added in 1632, is topped by the famous *Giraldilla* (weather vane), a nod to the one atop the Giralda minaret in Seville, the city whose Casa de Contratación (House of Trade) oversaw financial and shipping operations between Spain and its territories in the Americas. Havana's favorite symbol—it's even on the Havana Club rum label—the Giraldilla honors Doña Inés de Bobadilla, Cuba's lone woman governor, who replaced her husband, Hernando de Soto, when he left to conquer Florida (and search for the Fountain of Youth) in 1539. De Soto and his expedition went on to explore much of North America and were among the first white men to cross the Mississippi River. He died in 1542, but Doña Inés spent years scanning the horizon, awaiting his return. The current Giraldilla is a copy of an earlier bronze one toppled by a hurricane and now on display in the Museo de la Ciudad de La Habana. Today the museum houses an exhibition on Cuban navigation, dating from 1577 to today. On display are miniatures of the galleons that once passed through the island with gold coins, treasures, and documentation of maritime life over the centuries. ⊠ *Plaza de Armas, e/Calle O'Reilly y Av. del Puerto (Calle Desamparado/San Pedro), La Habana Vieja* ☎ *7864–4488* ☞ *CUC$3* ⊙ *Tues.–Sun. 9:30–5.*

Fodor's Choice **Catedral de la Habana.** Cuba's Cervantes Prize–winning novelist, Alejo
★ Carpentier, may have borrowed from St. Augustine when he described the city's cathedral as "music made into stone," but the words—like the bells in the structure they describe—ring true and clear. Work on the church was begun by the Jesuits in 1748, who weren't around to see it finished in 1777 (King Carlos III of Spain expelled them from Cuba in 1767). The facade is simultaneously intimate and imposing, and one of the two towers is visibly larger, creating an asymmetry that seems totally natural. The two bells in the taller, thicker tower are said to have been cast with gold and silver mixed into the bronze, giving them their sweet tone. In *Our Man in Havana*, Graham Greene describes the statue of Columbus that once stood in the square as looking "as though it had been formed through the centuries underwater, like a coral reef, by the action of insects." This is, in fact, exactly the case: coral, cut and hauled from the edge of the sea by slaves, was used to build many of Havana's churches. Look carefully and you'll see fossils of marine flora and fauna in the stone of the cathedral. ⊠ *Plaza de la Catedral, La Habana Vieja* ☎ *7861–7771* ☞ *Free* ⊙ *Weekdays 10–4:30, Sat. 10–2, Sun. 9–12:30; Mass weekdays 6 pm, Sat. 3 pm, Sun. 10:30 am.*

El Templete. This Neoclassical, faux-Doric temple was built in 1828 on the site of the city's first Mass and its first *cabildo* (city council) meeting. The cabildo took place under a massive *ceiba* (kapok) tree, which was felled by a 19th-century hurricane. The present tree—planted in the little patio in front of El Templete in 1959, the year of the Revolution—is honored each November 19, the day celebrating Havana's founding. It's said during a special ceremony, if you walk three times around the tree and toss a coin toward it, you'll be granted a wish—provided, of course, that you keep your wish secret. El Templete is also the site of a triptych by French painter Jean-Baptiste Vermay portraying the first Mass, the first cabildo, and the municipal personalities who participated in the building's opening ceremonies. It's also home to the ashes of the painter and his wife, who—along with 8,000 other habaneros—were victims of the 1833 cholera epidemic. ⌧ *Plaza de Armas, La Habana Vieja* ⌫ *CUC$1.50* ☉ *Tues.–Sun. 9:30–5.*

Iglesia Santo Cristo del Buen Viaje. Although originally founded in 1640 as the Ermita de Nuestra Señora del Buen Viaje, the present church was built in 1755. The advocation to the *buen viaje* (good voyage) was a result of its popularity among seafarers in need of a patron and a place to pray for protection. The Baroque facade is notable for the simplicity of its twin hexagonal towers and the deep flaring arch in its entryway. Traditionally the final stop on the Vía Crucis (Way of the Cross) held during Lent, the church and its plaza have an intimate and informal charm. This is the plaza where Graham Greene's character Wormold (the vacuum-cleaner salesman/secret agent) is "swallowed up among the pimps and lottery sellers of the Havana noon" in *Our Man in Havana.* ■TIP➜ **Don't miss the view from the corner of Amargura: you can see straight down Villegas to the dome of the old Palacio Presidencial (Presidential Palace).** ⌧ *Plaza del Cristo, La Habana Vieja* ☎ *7863–1767* ⌫ *Free* ☉ *During Masses (daily at 10 and 5).*

Iglesia y Convento Menor de San Francisco de Asís. The Latin inscription over the main door of this church and convent dedicated to St. Francis reads: "non est in toto sanctior orbe locus" ("there is no holier place on earth"). As it's now a museum and concert hall, it may no longer be earth's holiest place, but it certainly is one of the loveliest. Built in the 16th century, in 1730 it was restored in a baroque style, resulting in a richly adorned facade with fluted conch-like tympanums over the doors and windows. Just inside the door you'll see tombs beneath a glass floor panel. Churches were used as cemeteries until Bishop Espada founded what is now the Necrópolis Cristóbal Colón in 1868, a detail all Cubans seem to know and cherish. Note also the 19th-century grandfather clock made by Tiffany. The rooms to the right of the nave house archaeological finds and art exhibits. Precisely 117 steps lead to the top of the 141-meter (463-feet) tower, the tallest in Havana. ⌧ *Plaza de San Francisco, La Habana Vieja* ☎ *7861–3312* ⌫ *CUC$2 (includes entrance to museum inside)* ☉ *Mon., Tues., Thurs., and Fri 9–4:30, Wed. and Sat. 9–6, Sun. 9–2.*

Fodor's Choice
★
Museo del Ron Havana Club. Housed in an elegant 18th-century mansion, this is one of Havana's best museums. A stop here provides a look at the history of Cuba's sugar industry, as well as the insides of a rum distillery—including a model *central* (sugar mill) with miniature steam engines—and the craftsmen (such as the coopers, or barrel makers) who were a part of it. Your ticket includes a guided tour, rum tastings, and the opportunity to take photos. The Havana Club shop is a good

place to stock up on a few bottles, while the attached bar is great for an after-tour mojito. ⊠ *Calle San Pedro 262, esq. de Calle Sol y Av. del Puerto (Calle Desamparado/San Pedro), La Habana Vieja* ☎ *7861– 8051* ⊕ *www.havana-club.com* ☑ *CUC$7* ⊙ *Museum: Mon.–Thurs. 9–5:30, Fri.–Sun. 9–4.30; Havana Club Bar: Mon.–Sun. 9–9.*

NEED A BREAK?

Cafe O'Reilly. This newly opened café, housed in a beautiful old colonial building, complete with original tiles, is quickly becoming one of Havana's best coffeehouses. The rich coffee aromas waft halfway down the street, and inside the sound of bubbling percolators is complemented by cloth coffee bags, old coffee trade maps, and photos of coffee farmers covering the walls. As well as coffee anyway you want, the café also serves snacks such as sandwiches, ice creams, and salads. ■ TIP→ This is a great place to buy some freshly roasted Cuban coffee beans to take back home with you. ⊠ *Calle O'Reilly 203, La Habana Vieja.*

Museo del Tabaco. This small museum, housed above a tobacco and cigar shop, provides insight into Cuba's tobacco culture, as well as the history of tobacco within the country. There's a good exhibit on the growing of the tobacco plant and also collections of vintage lighters and old cigar advertisements. Entry is free, but a guided tour is recommended to get the most out of your visit (it requires a small donation). ⊠ *Calle Mercaderes 120, La Habana Vieja* ☎ *7861–8166* ☑ *Free; fee for guided tour* ⊙ *Tues.–Sat. 9:30–4:30, Sun. 9:30–1.*

Museo Numismático. This museum contains a collection of various coins and banknotes from around the world, as well as those from Cuba. Highlights include a collection of 1,000 gold coins dating between 1860 and 1928. There's also the entire chronology of Cuban banknotes from the 19th century to the present day on display. ⊠ *Calle Obispo 305, e/ Calles Aguiar y Habana, La Habana Vieja* ☎ *7861–5811* ☑ *CUC$1.50* ⊙ *Tues.–Sat. 9:30–5, Sun. 9:30–1.*

Palacio de los Capitanes Generales. At the western end of the Plaza de Armas is the former residence of the men who governed Cuba. A succession of some five-dozen Spanish captain-generals (also called governors) lived here until 1898, and the U.S. governor called it home prior to the Revolution. The wooden "paving" on the plaza in front of it was installed on the orders of a 17th-century captain-general, who wanted to muffle the clatter of horses and carriages so he could enjoy his naps undisturbed. Today the palace is the **Museo de la Ciudad de la Habana,** with such unique treasures as a throne room built for the king of Spain (but never used); the original Giraldilla weather vane that once topped the tower of the Castillo de la Real Fuerza; and a cannon made of leather. Groups of *pioneros* often gather in the gallery here for art-history classes, and you can buy art books in the on-site shop. Inside it to the right is a plaque dated 1557; it commemorates the death of Doña Maria de Cepeda y Nieto, who was felled by a stray shot while praying in what was then Parroquia Mayor, Havana's main parish church. The tomb in the pit to the left holds the remains of several graves discovered in the church cemetery. ⊠ *Plaza de Armas, Calle Tacón, e/Calle Obispo* *y Calle O'Reilly, La Habana Vieja* ☎ *7869–7358* 🖳 *CUC$5 to see lower floor and to be guided around upper floor* ☉ *Tues.–Sun. 9:30–5.*

Planetarium. Built in 2010 to commemorate the 400th anniversary of Galileo's astronomical discoveries, the modern planetarium doesn't seem to fit in with the rest of Plaza Vieja's colonial grandeur; nonetheless, it makes for an interesting visit. Inside there's a scale model of the solar system, as well as a range of interactive games and a large viewing theater, which currently only has audio descriptions available in Spanish. ■TIP➔ **Reservations must be made in advance.** ✉ *Plaza Vieja, Calle Mercaderes, La Habana Vieja* ☎ *7864–9544* 🖳 *CUC$10* ☉ *Wed.–Sat. with showings at 10, 11, 12:30, and 3:30.*

Plaza de Armas. So-called for its use as a drill field by colonial troops, this plaza was the city's administrative center and command post almost from the beginning. The statue in the center is of Manuel de Céspedes, hero of the Ten Years War, Cuba's first struggle for independence from Spain. Today, this is the city's most literary square; an army of erudite secondhand booksellers encircles it during the day.

Nearby is the Palacio de los Capitanes Generales, across from which are El Templete and the Castillo de la Real Fuerza. Note that there are often concerts in the plaza on Sunday evenings—events not to be missed.

On the northwestern corner of Plaza de Armas is the **Palacio del Segundo Cabo**, which at the time of writing was undergoing renovation. When complete, it will become the Center for Interpretation of the Cultural Relations between Cuba and Europe. Opposite this, on the other side of the plaza, you'll find the **Museo Nacionale de Historia Natural de Cuba** (Cuba's Natural History Museum), which is home to a rich collection of Cuban flora and fauna, as well as various mineral samples and fossils. ✉ *Calle Obispo, La Habana Vieja* 🖳 *CUC$3* ☉ *Tues. 1:30–5, Wed.–Sun. 10–5:30.*

Plaza de la Catedral. The square that surrounds and is named for the Catedral de la Habana is one of La Habana Vieja's most beautiful spots. In addition to the cathedral, you'll find several elegant mansions that once housed the city's aristocrats.

The **Casa de los Marqueses de Aguas Claras** (1751–75), in the square's northwestern corner, was built by Antonio Ponce de León, the first Marquis of Aguas Claras and a descendent of the discoverer of Florida, Juan de Ponce de León. Today the building contains the Restaurant Paris, a stylish eatery whose tables fill a verdant interior courtyard as well as the upper floors. On the square's western edge is the 19th-century **Casa de Baños** (Bath House), which was built on the spot where an *aljibe* (cistern) was constructed in 1587. It served as the main municipal water supply and as a public bathing house. The narrow cul-de-sac next to the Casa de Baños is the Callejón del Chorro (Alley of the Water Fountain), named for an aqueduct that ended here in Havana's early days.

Wander along the square's eastern edge for a look at the early 18th-century **Casa de Lombillo,** which today houses a number of changing art exhibitions. ✉ *San Ignacio and Empedrado, La Habana Vieja.*

Museo de Arte Colonial. Directly across the square from the cathedral, the museum's rich collection of colonial objects ranges from violins to chamber pots. It's in the Casa de Luis Chacón—also known as Casa del Conde de Bayona after the son-in-law of the original owner—which dates from the 17th century and which saw its first restoration in 1720. ⊠ *Calle San Ignacio 61, La Habana Vieja* ☎ *7862–6440* ⊠ *CUC$5* ⊙ *Tues.–Sun. 9:30–5.*

NEED A BREAK?

Dulcería Bianchini. Down the small side street of Callejón del Chorro, just off the Plaza de Catedral, you'll find the cute Bianchini café and bakery. With its funky red walls, glass chandeliers, and mismatched shabby-chic furniture, it's the perfect stop to refuel with a coffee and a sweet treat. Very different from Havana's usual fare of sponge cakes laden with layers of multicolor cream, owner Katia Bianchini has taken inspiration from her Swiss and Italian ancestors to create a range of homemade cookies, cakes, and muffins. The chocolate soufflé is a must-try. Another branch of the café is at Calle Sol 12. ⊠ *Plaza de Catedral, Calle San Ignacio 68, Callejón del Chorro, La Habana Vieja* ⊕ *www.dulceria-bianchini.com.*

Plaza Vieja. What is now called the Old Square was originally Plaza Nueva (New Square), built as a popular alternative to Plaza de Armas, the military and government nerve center. Later called Plaza del Mercado (Market Square) as Havana's commercial hub, Plaza Vieja was the site of executions, processions, bullfights, and fiestas—all witnessed by Havana's wealthiest citizens, who looked on from their balconies. The original Carrara marble fountain surrounded by four dolphins was demolished in the 1930s when President Gerardo Machado (1871–1939) built an underground parking lot here. Today the square's surrounding structures vary wildly in condition, though all of them are noteworthy. Don't miss the splendid view west down Calle Brasil (Teniente Rey) to the Capitolio.

The impressive mansion on the square's southwestern corner is the **Casa de los Condes de Jaruco** (1733–37), the former seat of the Fondo Cubano de Bienes Culturales (BFC; Cuba's version of the National Endowment for the Arts). Its lush main patio is surrounded by massive, yet delicate, pillars. Look for the ceramic tiles along the main stairway and the second-floor stained glass windows. Today the building houses members of the Génesis Galerías de Arte and an upstairs restaurant. On the second floor La Casona Galería de Arte displays the works of contemporary Cuban and international artists, while on street-level Diago Galería de Arte shows the works of native Cuban painters. To your left as you exit is the interesting 1762 Elias Durnford painting *A View of the Market Place in the City of the Havana* [sic].

On the square's southeastern corner, the **Palacio Viena Hotel** (also known as the Palacio Cueto) is a 1906 Art Nouveau gem that was occupied by several-dozen families after the Revolution. The intense floral relief sculpture and stained-glass windows are still intact, if a little sooty, on all five stories. This building has perennially been under renovation, and it's anybody's guess when the grand structure will once again take its place in the square.

On the square's western edge is the 1752 **Casa de Juan Rico de Mata** (*Calle Mercaderes 307*), now housing the Fototeca de Cuba, a contemporary photography gallery that has rotating temporary exhibitions of Cuban and international photographers. Also along the western edge, heading north, you'll see the planetarium, housed in an old cinema, and the Camera Obscura, located in the 20th-century Villa Gómez. The **Casa de las Hermanas Cárdenas** (*Calle San Ignacio 352*), on the square's eastern side, was once used by Havana's first philharmonic society. It's now home to the Centro de Desarrollo de Artes Visuales (Center for the Development of Visual Arts), which hosts temporary exhibits.

In the 18th-century **Casa del Conde San Estéban de Cañongo** (*Calle San Ignacio 356*), you'll find the Artesanías para Turismo workshop. Strangely, a permanent exhibition here presents Wallonia, French Belgium, and its industry and agriculture, as well as its most noteworthy comics like Tintin. Apparently the exhibition was granted after Belgian interests put up the money to restore the building. There would probably be much more exciting ways to use this prime property than a pedantic exhibit that ultimately gives little to the creative life of the community.

While wandering along San Ignacio, notice the faded "vapores cuba–españa" ("steamboats cuba–spain") sign on the wall inside the entryway of **No. 358**. The 18th-century **Casa del Conde de Lombillo** (*Calle San Ignacio 364*; not to be confused with the Conde de Lombillo house in the Plaza de la Catedral) has lovely original murals in amber hues with faded blue and green floral motifs decorating its facade. Today it houses the charming Café Bohemia, which has upstairs suites for rent. The restoration of the 17th-century **Colegio del Santo Angel** (*Calle Brasil/Teniente Rey 56, esquina de Calle San Ignacio*) almost a decade ago. It was originally the house of Susana Benitez de Parejo, a wealthy young widow who departed for Spain in the mid-19th century; it was later used as an orphanage for boys under 12 years of age and then as a music conservatory until it collapsed in 1993, leaving only the facade standing. Now housing an excellent restaurant and 11 luxury apartments, this is one of the finest triumphs of the restoration work in Plaza Vieja. ⊠ *Calle San Ignacio and Muralla, La Habana Vieja.*

WORTH NOTING

Casa de Africa. This museum showcases a collection of art and various cultural artifacts from all over Africa. There's also a room dedicated to the *orishas* (Yoruban deities) upstairs. Look out for the interesting collection of African instruments upstairs. Live Afro-Cuban music is played here from 3 to 5 pm on the first Saturday and second Tuesday of every month. ⊠ *Calle Obrapia 157, e/Calles Mercaderes y San Ignacio, La Habana Vieja* ☎ 7861–5798 ⊠ *Free* ☉ *Tues.–Sat. 9:30–5, Sun. 9:30–1.*

Casa de Asia. Housing an array of cultural treasures from all over Asia, this two-floor museum is well worth a look. It showcases a collection of exquisite Japanese kimonos, intricately carved Chinese cabinets,

La Habana Vieja and Centro Habana

Bahía de la Habana

CENTRO

0   1,000 ft
0   500 m

Cantonese porcelain from the 18th and 19th centuries, as well as various stone statues, ancient swords, and instruments. ⊠ *Calle Mercaderes 111, La Habana Vieja* ☜ *Free* ⊙ *Tues.–Sat. 9:30–5:30, Sun. 9:30–1.*

Casa Simón Bolívar. Housed in an elegant colonial mansion, this museum is dedicated to the life of Simón Bolívar, a Venezuelan military leader who was instrumental in the revolutions against the Spanish Empire. He was credited with helping to liberate Bolivia and was also president of Gran Colombia, as well as dictator of Peru. The museum houses a range of paintings, photos, and documents pertaining to Bolívar, as well as a selection of his medals. There's also a section of the museum dedicated to Venezuela, showcasing indigenous art and ceramics, and an exhibition about the life of former president Hugo Chávez. ⊠ *Calle Mercaderes 160, La Habana Vieja* ☎ *7861–3938* ☜ *Free* ⊙ *Tues.–Sat. 9:30–5, Sun. 9:30–1.*

Centro Wifredo Lam. Dedicated to and named for the great Cuban Surrealist painter Wifredo Lam, who was known as the Cuban Picasso, this gallery and museum is just behind the Catedral de la Habana in the elegant, 18th-century Casa del Obispo Peñalver. The center hosts temporary shows with works by contemporary Cuban and South American artists. Lam, born in 1902, studied in Spain and fought with the republic against Franco. He later fled to France, where he was influenced by Pablo Picasso, Georges Braque, and the poet André Breton, among others. He returned to Cuba to support the Revolution, and later returned to Paris, where he died in 1982. His best works hang in the Cuban collection of Havana's Museo de Bellas Artes. ⊠ *Calle San Ignacio 22, esq. de Calle Empedrado, La Habana Vieja* ☎ *7864–6282* ⊕ *www.wlam.cult.cu* ☜ *Free* ⊙ *Mon.–Sat. 10–5.*

Iglesia del Espíritu Santo. Havana's oldest church (circa 1638) was built by Afro-Cubans who were brought to the island as slaves but who later bought their freedom, a common phenomenon in Cuba. Fittingly, today it's the only church in the city authorized to grant political asylum. Its interior has several notable paintings; notice especially the representation of a seated, post-Crucifixion Christ on the right wall. The crypt under the left of the altar contains catacombs. The three-story belfry to the left of the church is one of La Habana Vieja's tallest towers. ⊠ *Calle Acosta 161, esq. de Calle de Cuba, La Habana Vieja* ☎ *7862–3410* ☜ *Free* ⊙ *Weekdays 8:30–4.*

Museo Armería 9 de Abril. This old gun shop, and now gun museum, contains the vast personal arms collection of Fidel Castro, as well as other weapons used during the Revolution. There is also a small permanent exhibition detailing the events of April 9, 1958, when Castro and his people attempted a general strike. ⊠ *Calle Mercaderes 157, e/ Calles Lamparilla y Obrapia, La Habana Vieja* ☎ *7861–8080* ☜ *Free* ⊙ *Tues.–Sun. 9:30–5, Sun. 9:30–2:30.*

Museo de la Farmcia Habanera. This still functioning Art Nouveau pharmacy may sometimes be short on drugs, but it is certainly long on design. Founded by a Catalan apothecary in 1874, it was built in the elaborate Modernist style universally favored by 19th-century pharmacies. The carved wooden racks and shelves backed by murals painted on glass are especially ornate, and the ceramic apothecary jars, though probably empty, are colorfully painted. Also known as La Reunión (note the inscription on the wall behind the counter), this pharmacy was a famous meeting place, a sort of informal neighborhood clubhouse. ⊠ *Calle Brasil (Teniente Rey) 251, esq. de Calle Compostela, La Habana Vieja* ☎ *7866–7554* 🖘 *Free* ◷ *Daily 9–5.*

Museo Naipes. Housed in Plaza Vieja's oldest building, this unusual museum is completely dedicated to playing cards. It's home to a collection of more than 2,000 cards from all over the world, with some dating back to the 18th century. ⊠ *Plaza Vieja, Calle Muralla 101, La Habana Vieja* ☎ *7860–1534* 🖘 *Free* ◷ *Tues.–Sat. 9:30–5, Sun. 9:30–1.*

CENTRO HABANA

The Centro neighborhood has a little something for everyone. This is where many habaneros go about their everyday lives … working, living, shopping, and eating. History buffs will appreciate the eclectic mixture of monuments and monumental architecture from the 17th through the 20th centuries. Art lovers will enjoy its Museo Nacional de Bellas Artes, and connoisseurs of all things Cuban will appreciate its offerings of cigars, rum, and Revolution at the Museo del Ron, the Fábrica de Tabacos Partagás cigar factory, and the Museo de la Revolución.

The area consists of a large commercial zone filled with hotels, bars, theaters, and museums, and behind them, a sprawling area of residential streets and hole-in-the-wall cafés. It's very busy and noisy, with lots of traffic, so going for a pleasant stroll isn't ideal, although the area still makes for an interesting insight into Cuban life. The best areas to explore are the Barrio Chino (Havana's Chinatown); the elegant Paseo del Prado, which takes you down to the Malecón; and the bustling pedestrianized Boulevard San Rafael, behind the Hotel Inglaterra.

GETTING HERE AND AROUND

The main part of Centro Havana is easily walkable from Habana Vieja, but unless you're visiting Parque de la Fraternidad and the nearby museums such as the Museo Nacional de Bellas Artes and the Museo de la Revolución, the easiest way to get around is by taxi.

TOP ATTRACTIONS

Capitolio. Modeled after Washington, D.C.'s domed Capitol building, Havana's Capitolio was built in 1929 and is rich in iconography. The statue to the left of the entrance stairway represents Work (considered a masculine ethic); that on the right is of Virtue (a perceived feminine attribute). Some 30 bas-reliefs on the main door depict events in Cuba's history. The giant main hall is called the Salon de los Pasos Perdidos (Hall of the Lost Steps), allegedly for the fading reverberations of footsteps. It's dominated by the gigantic bronze statue of Minerva (once known as La República). Set into the floor at her feet is a diamond (presently a replica) from which all distances on the island are measured. The former Senate Chamber is at the end of the right-hand corridor; the one-time Chamber of Representatives is on the far left. The on-site restaurant, El Salón de los Escudos, serves a reasonable lunch; the Café Mirador offers lighter fare. The building has been undergoing renovation for about the last four years and it is not yet known when it will be complete. The outside is still worth a look though, even though it's covered in scaffolding. ⊠ *Paseo de Martí (Prado), Centro Habana.*

Edificio Bacardí. Built in 1930, the former Bacardí rum headquarters (the family elected not to brave the Revolution and now makes rum in Puerto Rico) is an Art Deco outburst best admired from the roof of the Hotel Plaza across the street. Its terra-cotta facade is covered with nymphs, sylphs, salamanders, and undines; its bell tower is capped with a brass, winged bat you'll recognize from the Bacardí rum label (or from the coat of arms of the House of Aragón, a clue to the family's Catalonian heritage). Visitors can't go inside, but it's worth a look at the outside nonetheless. ⊠ *Calle San Juan de Dios 202, esq. de Av. de la Bélgica (Monserrate), Centro Habana.*

Estudiantes de Medicina. A fragment of Havana's early ramparts commemorates the spot where eight medical students were unjustly executed for independence activism by the Spanish governors in 1871. At night the monument is beautifully illuminated, the work of the electrical engineer Félix de la Noval. You'll see amber light representing rifle fire; it can't, however, extinguish the white light (against the wall), which symbolizes the ideals of independence. ⊠ *Paseo de Martí (Prado) y Av. del Puerto (Calle Desamparado/San Pedro), Centro Habana.*

Fábrica de Tabacos Partagás. Tobacco is a fundamental part of Cuban life, and a look inside a cigar factory makes for an interesting trip—despite the high entry fee and the pricey cigars. Now in its new location on Calle San Carlos, instead of the old iconic orange and white building behind the Capitolio, the Fábrica de Tabacos is a good place to learn about the cigar-making process. ■ TIP➜ **Guided tours of the factory are only available on weekday mornings and must be booked in advance, which can be done at any of the major hotels in the city.** Although interesting and informative, the tours are fairly rushed and only last 15 to 20 minutes. Many of the rooms are also closed to visitors. Those who wish to purchase cigars at the end of the tour can do so around the corner at the H. Upmann Empresa de Tabaco Torcido store. ⊠ *Calle San Carlos 816, Centro Habana* ☎ *7878–5166* 🎫 *CUC$10* 🕓 *Factory visits weekdays 9–1.*

FAMILY **Memorial Granma.** A glass enclosure behind the Museo de la Revolución shelters the *Granma*, the yacht that transported Castro and 81 guerrillas back to Cuba from exile in Mexico in 1956. Bought from an American, the 38-foot craft designed to carry 25 (presumably unarmed) passengers nearly foundered during the week-long crossing. It eventually ran aground at Oriente Province in Eastern Cuba, but it was two days behind schedule. The saga gets worse: Castro's forces were ambushed and only 16 survived, including Fidel, Che, Raúl Castro, and Camilo Cienfuegos. The park around the yacht is filled with military curios: tanks, jeeps, the delivery truck used in the 1957 assault on the Palacio Presidencial, and an airplane turbine, allegedly from a U-2 spy plane downed during the 1962 Cuban Missile Crisis. ⊠ *Calle Colón, e/Av. de la Bélgica (Misiones/Edigio/Monserrate) y Calle Agramonte (Zulueta),*

Centro Habana ☎ 7862–4091 ✉ CUC$8 for combined ticket to memorial and Museo de la Revolución ☉ Daily 10–5.

Monumento Máximo Gómez. This bronze equestrian monument honors the great military leader of Cuba's 19th-century wars of independence. It was erected in 1935 in modern Havana's most pivotal location—in an important traffic circle and at the entrance to the tunnel leading to the fortresses across the harbor. The Dominican-born General Gómez led the *mambises* (a term used by the Spanish for Cuban rebels) in the Ten Years War, refused to surrender when an unsatisfactory treaty was signed in 1878, left the island, and returned with José Martí almost 20 years later to continue the fight in the 1895 Second War of Independence. Martí died in the opening battle; fellow general Antonio Maceo fell in December of 1895, but Gómez survived. ⊠ *Av. del Puerto (Calle Desamparado/San Pedro), e/Calle Agramonte (Zulueta) y Av. de las Misiones (Bélgica/Edigio/Monserrate), Centro Habana.*

Fodor's Choice
★

Museo Nacional de Bellas Artes—Colección Cubano. Havana's fine-arts museum occupies two separate buildings, each of which deserves careful exploration. The original location on Calle Trocadero, finished in 1954, occupies the site of what was once a market. Designed by Alfonso Rodríguez Pichardo, the building, a compact prism with a large central courtyard, seems to breathe light. It now contains a varied and exciting Cuban collection. The third floor has 16th- to 19th-century colonial religious paintings, portraits, landscapes, and street scenes. Rooms 3 and 4 follow the 1927–38 beginning and consolidation of Cuban modern art. On the second floor, in rooms 5–8, are works by artists from the 1950s to 1990s. The power, color density, and intensity of Cuban painting is extraordinary, as is the rush through 500 years of history—from Armando Menocal's chained Columbus embarking for Spain in 1493 to Servando Cabrera Moreno's *Guernica*-like depiction of the 1961 Bay of Pigs invasion and beyond to more contemporary pieces. Paintings to look for include the sensual *El Rapto de las Mulatas* by Carlos Enríquez, *Gitana Tropical* (sometimes known as the "Cuban Mona Lisa") by Victor Manuel Garcia, *Maternidad* by Wifredo Lam, *Recibido en Mal Estado* by Zaida del Río, and *Mundo Sonádo* by Tonel (Antonio Eligio Fernandez). ⊠ *Calle Trocadero, e/Av. de la Bélgica (Misiones/Egido/Monserrate) y Calle Agramonte (Zulueta), Centro Habana ☎ 7863–9484 ⊕ www.bellasartes.cult.cu ✉ CUC$5; CUC$8 for combined ticket with Colección de Arte Universal ☉ Tues.–Sat. 9–5, Sun. 10–2.*

Museo Nacional de Bellas Artes—Colección de Arte Universal. The collection is housed in the splendid Centro Asturiano finished in 1928 (in answer to the Centro Gallego across the Parque Central), a building designed by Spanish architect Manuel del Busto, as dazzling as the collection it contains. Its sweeping stairway was inspired by the Paris Opera House, and its immense stained glass window alludes to the discovery of America. The collection ranges from Roman, Greek, and Egyptian ceramics and statuary to European art from the Italian, German, Flemish, Dutch, Spanish, French, and British schools. In addition there are rooms devoted to the art of the United States, as well as displays of Asian, Mexican, Antillean, and South American works.

Works by Joseph Turner, Sir Joshua Reynolds, Francisco José de Goya, Bartolomé Estaban Murillo, Zurbarán, Brueghel, Canaletto, Peter Paul Rubens, Velázquez, Sorolla, and Zuloaga, among others, are displayed here. ⊠ *Calle Obispo, e/Av. de la Bélgica (Misiones/Egido/Monserrate) y Calle Agramonte (Zulueta), Centro Habana* ☎ *7863–9484* ⊕ *www. bellasartes.cult.cu* ⊠ *CUC$5; CUC$8 for combined ticket to Colección Cubano* ☉ *Tues.–Sat. 9–5, Sun. 10–2.*

Fodor's Choice **Museo de la Revolución.** Batista's Palacio Presidencial, unsuccessfully
★ attacked by students on March 13, 1957, was converted into the Museum of the Revolution after Castro's 1959 victory. The Russian tank outside was used by Cuban forces to repel the Bay of Pigs invasion. The marble staircase and the magnificent upstairs ceiling mural tell one story, while galleries with displays of items from colonial times to the present tell another; the contrast is effective. Photographs of tortured revolutionaries, maps tracing the progress of the war, the bloodstained uniforms of rebels who fell in the 1953 Santiago de Cuba Moncada Barracks attack, and photos of Fidel and Che complete a comprehensive tour of the Revolution's history. ■TIP➜ **Don't miss Cretin's Corner for a look at some familiar faces.** ⊠ *Calle Refugio 1, Centro Habana* ☎ *7862–4098* ⊠ *CUC$8 for combined ticket to museum and Memorial Granma* ☉ *Daily 9–5.*

Parque Central. Across from the Hotel de Inglaterra and the Gran Teatro de la Habana, this park has always been a hub of Havana social activity. Centered on a statue of (who else?) José Martí and shaded by royal palms and almond trees, this is *the* place for heated debates on Cuba's national passion—baseball. The Hotel Plaza is on the park's northern end. On its southern end, notice the opulent 1885 Centro Asturiano, now the home of the Museo de Bellas Artes and its Arte Universal collection. ■TIP➜ **This is one of the best places to hire a classic open-top American car and driver for a tour around the city or a sunset drive down the Malecón.** ⊠ *Calle Refugio 1, Centro Habana.*

WORTH NOTING

Asociación Cultural Yoruba de Cuba. The Asociación Cultural Yoruba provides a close look at African culture. The bigger-than-life *orishas* (Yoruban deities) on display are all identified and explained in English, French, and Spanish. It is also a place where people still come to pray and give offerings to the various *orishas*. Depending on the day, you may even get to witness a Santería ceremony or ritual here, which the public are welcome to attend. The association is near the Parque de la Fraternidad Americana, a shady space around a sacred ceiba tree planted in 1928 with soil from each of the free countries of the Americas. ⊠ *Paseo de Martí (Prado) 615, e/Calle Montes y Calle Dragones, Centro Habana* ☎ *7863–7415* ⊠ *CUC$5* ☉ *Daily 9–5.*

**OFF THE
BEATEN
PATH**
Callejón de Hamel. This neighborhood project, directed by and featuring the painting (note the vivid street murals) and sculpture of Salvador Gonzalez Escalona, is an ongoing Afro-Cuban educational and artistic event. All the quirky sculptures you see here have been made out of recycled materials—look for the story of Saint-Exupéry's *Little Prince,*which has been painted into an array of bathtubs at the far end of

the street. Afro-Cuban music groups Rumbo Morena and Eroso Obba perform here every Sunday from noon to 3 pm, enthusiastically watched by locals and tourists alike. ⊠ *Off Calle San Lázaro, e/Calle Ánimas and Calle Soledad, Centro Habana* ☎ *7878–1661* ⛾ *Free.*

Iglesia del Santo Angel Custodio. This prim little white church is a required visit for literature buffs hot on the trail of scenes from the novel by Cirilo Villaverde (1812–94), *Cecilia Valdés (o la Loma del Angel).* The novel's bloody denouement takes place on the steps here during a marriage scene straight out of Racine. A plaque on a wall across from the church door lauds Villaverde's portrait of 19th-century Cuban life. Villaverde, in fact, made literary history with the stark social realism with which he portrayed the inhuman treatment of slaves in his novel. (One scene, for example, depicts plantation owners complaining bitterly about their foreman whipping slaves so early in the morning that the screaming and the crack of the lash disturbs their morning slumber.) The neo-Gothic church is, indeed, on La Loma del Angel (The Hillside of the Angel). With its pure, vertical lines, it's markedly different from La Habana Vieja's hulking Baroque structures. Originally erected in 1690 and rebuilt in 1866, Santo Angel del Custodio was the site of the baptisms of both José Martí and Félix Varela, the priest, patriot, and educator credited with having "first taught Cubans to think." Martí, Varela, and Villaverde were all key contributors to the cause of Cuban independence. ⊠ *Calle Compostela 1, esq. de Calle Cuarteles, Centro Habana* ☎ *7861–0469* ⛾ *Free* ⊙ *Tues.–Sat. 10–6:45, Mass at 5 pm; Sun. 8–11:30, Mass at 9 am.*

Palacio de Aldama. Just past the Parque de la Fraternidad Americana's southwest corner is this Italianate mansion built in 1840 by the Spanish merchant Domingo de Aldama. His son, Miguel de Aldama, worked for Cuban autonomy from Spain until his palace was sacked by the Spanish authorities in 1869. Don Miguel fled to the United States, where he continued his work as an activist for Cuban independence until his death in 1888. The building isn't open to visitors, but the massive columns and monumental size of the place are striking proof of the economic power of the 19th-century Cuban sugar barons, dubbed the *zacarocracia* by Cuban journalists and historians. ⊠ *Av. Simón Bolívar (Reina) 1, Centro Habana.*

VEDADO

Vedado is a good area from which to wander west along the waterfront Malecón to the fortress-restaurant Santa Dorotea de Luna de la Chorrera, at the mouth of the Río Almendares. From here you can either tour the forest—the Parque de Almendares on the west side of the river—or continue southwest on a drive through the Miramar district, with its beautiful mansions, famous hotels, good restaurants, and legendary nightclubs. Vedado is also a good jumping-off point for the Necrópolis Cristóbal Colón, Havana's showcase cemetery crammed with heroes, legends, and elaborate memorials. The monolithic Plaza de la Revolución, farther south, is another short taxi hop from Vedado.

In colonial days this area was placed off-limits—that is, *vedado* ("vetoed," or forbidden)—to provide protection from the pirates that attacked Havana from the west. Trespassers, whether friend or foe, faced a stiff penalty: loss of an arm or a leg. The forest has long been replaced by fast-moving traffic, skyscrapers, and wide streets, but the name remains. Although a walk through this neighborhood involves long distances and won't be as pleasant as one through La Habana Vieja, don't avoid it entirely—there are plenty of leafy-green side streets and noteworthy sights.

GETTING HERE AND AROUND

The best ways of getting to and around Vedado is by regular taxi or coco taxi, as attractions here are fairly spread out. You won't see many bicycle taxis around here either. It's worth getting out and exploring a few of the streets on foot though to discover the incredible architecture here, and, of course, El Malecón should be strolled.

TOP ATTRACTIONS

FAMILY
Fodor's Choice
★

El Malecón. Havana's famous Malecón, sheltered by a sea wall, runs west for 7 km (4 miles) from La Punta (where it's also known as Avenida Antonio Maceo) and the harbor's entrance to the Santa Dorotea de Luna de la Chorrera fortress, near the mouth of the Río Almendares. Although it was designed in 1857 by a Cuban engineer, it wasn't built until 1902, thanks, in part, to the American capital that flowed to the island after the Spanish-American War. Once an opulent promenade flanked by brightly painted houses, the Malecón today is dark and dilapidated, the houses crumbling, and the wide limestone walkway broken and eroded. Yet it still has its charms. As it faces north, it offers spectacular views of both sunrise and sunset—perhaps accounting for the belief that there's not a single habanero who hasn't professed love eternal here at one time or another. Crashing waves and the rainbows created from their spray and the sun adds to the Malecón's magic.

As you walk, look for rectangles carved into the stone. These were once (and are still used as) sea baths, which fill at high tide and allowed people to splash about, safe from both currents and sharks. Just west of the Hotel Nacional you'll come to **Monumento al Maine**, honoring the 260 American sailors killed in the 1898 explosion of that U.S. warship, which was visiting Havana in a display of American might. The event lead to what the United States calls the Spanish-American War (for Cubans this was the final stage of their War of Independence, which began in 1868) followed by a period of heavy U.S. involvement in Cuban affairs. A plaque dedicated by the Castro government here reads: "To the victims of the *Maine*, who were sacrificed by imperialist voracity in its eagerness to seize the island of Cuba." ⊠ *Havana.*

Museo de Artes Decorativos. The house containing this museum was built in 1927 and owned by José Gómez Mena, one of Cuba's wealthiest aristocrats. The collection is a staggering display of treasure and taste: antique furniture; Aubusson rugs; a Louis XVI *secrétaire*; Ming vases; paintings by Tocqué, Nattier, and Largillière. Don't miss the impressive *comedor* (dining room) with its vast array of silverware or the main *salón* , dripping with chandeliers. ⊠ *Calle 17, No. 502, e/Calle D y Calle E, Vedado* ☎ *7830–9848* 🖃 *CUC$5* 🕐 *Tues.–Sat. 9:30–5.*

Museo de la Danza. This interesting and well laid-out museum explores Cuba's relationship with dance, specifically ballet. It focuses mainly on the history of ballet from the 18th century onward, but also has smaller exhibits looking at contemporary dance, as well as Spanish flamenco. Look out for the ballet shoes signed by Margot Fonteyn. The last two rooms focus on Cuba's national ballet, as well as its director, choreographer, and prima ballerina Alicia Alonso, who is now in her nineties. ⊠ *Línea 365, Vedado* ☎ *7831–2198* ⊕ *www.balletcuba.cult. cu* 🖃 *CUC$2* 🕐 *Tues.–Sat. 10–5.*

Museo Memorial José Martí. The highlight of the Plaza de la Revolución is the memorial at its center. It consists of a massive granite sculpture of the national hero—in a seated, contemplative pose—on a 30-meter (98-foot) base and a 139-meter (456-foot) tower constructed of marble from La Isla de la Juventud (where Castro was imprisoned for his attack on the Moncada Barracks). The museum contains first editions of Martí's works, drawings, maps, and other memorabilia. Also on display are the original plans for both the monument and the square. You can also climb to the top observation deck for some views of the city. ⊠ *Plaza de la Revolución, Vedado* ☎ *7882–0906* 🖃 *CUC$1 for exterior of statue, CUC$3 for museum, CUC$3 for tower observation deck, CUC$5 for combined ticket* 🕐 *Mon.–Sun. 9:30–4:30.*

Necrópolis Cristóbal Colón. The Christopher Columbus Cemetery sprawls behind a huge ceremonial arch and is a repository for a great deal more than just the deceased. Founded in 1868 by Bishop Espada, it's a veritable pantheon of monuments commemorating poets, novelists, musicians, soldiers, statesmen, and rank-and-file citizens. Cuban novelist Cirilo Villaverde and Cervantes-laureate Alejo Carpentier are here, as are the martyrs of the *Granma* yacht landing, the students killed in the 1957 assault on the Palacio Presidencial, and Buena Vista Social Club member Ibrahim Ferrer Planas. This is also a place full of extraordinary legends, some of them macabre. You can learn all about them on a guided tour (highly recommended; you can arrange for one in English for a small fee at the hut just inside the grounds to the right). Be sure to ask about the story of La Milagrosa (The Miraculous). ⊠ *Calle Zapata y Calle 12, Vedado* ☎ *7834–6528* 🖃 *CUC$5* 🕐 *Mon.–Sun. 8–6.*

FAMILY **Parque Coppelia.** Named for the 1870 ballet by the French composer Léo Délibes, this Vedado park and its ice-cream emporium are Havana institutions. The *Star Wars*–type flying saucer in the middle of the square was the Revolution's answer to the many ice-cream parlors that, prior to 1959, were highly discriminatory. This state-owned establishment serves more than 25,000 customers daily. While many Cubans prefer waiting in the long lines and paying with the more accessible "national" pesos, tourists or those willing to fork out convertible pesos have that option. The parlor once offered a legendary number of flavors, but after the Special Period (the national emergency declared upon the collapse of the Soviet Union, after which Cuba suffered severe shortages of everything from fuel to food) supplies became scarce, and a flavor a day became the rule. While at first glance the fearfully long lineups don't make the place very attractive—especially if a few scoops of ice cream provide the light at the end of the tunnel. But ice cream is only an alibi here. Cubans tend to chatter, mix, and mingle while waiting. Forget Facebook; this is a real-life social-networking venue. ☒ *Vedado.*

Fodor'sChoice
★
Plaza de la Revolución. This plaza in upper Vedado may seem grandiose and soulless, but it has several monuments with a lot of heart. Since the Revolutionary victory of 1959, it has been the official parade ground for events ranging from the annual May Day celebration to the 1998 visit of Pope John Paul II. A political, administrative, and cultural hub, the square is surrounded by army, police, Communist Party, and other ministries. In better days Castro's whereabouts, which were always a mystery, included visits to these government centers, though he was just as likely to be coaching the national baseball team, resting in one of his many secret Havana residences, or off fishing on the Península de Zapata. It's hard to miss the giant etching of Che Guevara on the **Ministerio del Interior** (Ministry of the Interior) at the plaza's north-western edge. It bears the words "hasta la victoria siempre" ("always onward to victory"). On the square's western edge, across Avenida Carlos Manual de Céspedes, is the **Teatro Nacional**, Cuba's most important theater. Other highlights of the Plaza de la Revolución include the **Museo Memorial José Martí** at its center, the **Museo Postal Cubano** around the corner from the Ministerio de Comunicaciones (Communications Ministry), and along Plaza de la Revolución's northern edge is the **Biblioteca Nacional José Martí**, Cuba's largest library. ☒ *Avenida Carlos Manuel de Cespedes, Vedado.*

Biblioteca Nacional José Martí. Along Plaza de la Revolución's northern edge is the National Library, which, with 2 million volumes, is Cuba's largest. You must call in advance to book tours of the building. ☒ *Plaza de la Revolución, Vedado* ☎ *7811–9442* ⊘ *Mon. 8:15–1:30, Tues.–Fri. 8:15–6:15, Sat. 8:15–4:30.*

WORTH NOTING

Museo Napoleónico. Housed in the graceful mansion of former Cuban politician Orestes Ferrera, this museum is dedicated in part to the French military leader Napoleon Bonaparte (who never set foot in Cuba), and in part to the architecture and style of the house itself, which was built in 1926, around the same time as the Capitolio. The museum's collection, which has been amassed by Ferrera, as well as sugar magnate Julio Lobo includes one of Napoleon's famous hats, his toothbrush, a lock of his hair, his medals, pistols and swords. Don't forget to look up at the beautiful original frescoes on the walls or miss Ferrera's stunning wooden library on the third floor. You can also walk out onto the beautifully tiled balconies for one of the best views over Havana. ☒ *Calle San Miguel 1159, esq. de Ronda, Vedado* ☎ *7879–1460* 🎫 *CUC$3, CUC$5 with a guide* ⊘ *Tues.–Sat. 9:30–5, Sun. 9:30–12:30.*

Museo Postal Cubano (*Postal Museum*). Just east of the etching of Che Guevara and around the corner from Ministerio de Comunicaciones (Communications Ministry), you'll find this museum dedicated to the Cuban postal service. As well as documenting the history of the country's postal service, it also displays hundreds of stamps from all over the world, old Roman and Greek tablets dating as far back as the year 2300 BC, letters, and old seals. Keep a look out for Cuba's postal rocket, a unique experiment which was carried out in 1939. ⊠ *Plaza de la Revolución, Vedado* ☎ *7882–8255* 🎫 *Free* ☉ *Mon.–Thurs. 8–5:30, Fri. 8–4:30.*

Union Nacional de Escritores y Artistas de Cuba (*UNEAC*). Occupying what was once the Casa Juan Gelats, one of Vedado's finest early 20th-century mansions, the National Union of Writers and Artists is the site of cinematic events, lectures, and prose and poetry readings, as well as musical performances. On Wednesday evenings (5–8 pm) you can see trova or Afro-Cuban performances, while Saturday (9 pm) is the night of boleros. Have a seat at the bar with a Cuba Libre, and you are likely to end up chatting with some of the creative types that appear here. Writers, filmmakers, artists gather here, as their union offices are in the building. The building across Calle H from this one is an important UNEAC annex. ⊠ *Calle 17 y Calle H, Vedado* ☎ *7832–4551* 🎫 *Lectures and readings free, musical performances usually cost around CUC$5* ☉ *Daily 9–9.*

MIRAMAR

At the beginning of the 20th century, Cuban magnates and American businessmen built their houses in Miramar, which begins west of the tunnel under the Río Almendares and ends at the Río Jaimanitas. One of the best ways to get to know the area is to go for a stroll down 5th Avenue, where most of these impressive mansions, stately homes, and embassies are located. Aside from this, the area doesn't have as many sights as the rest of the city. However, there are some interesting spots that deserve a look, in particular the Fundación de la Naturaleza y El Hombre. But keep in mind that these sights are pretty spread out, so unless you're eager for some long-distance hiking, it's best to tour this part of town by car, or hire a taxi for the afternoon. Public transport here is scarce, as indicated by the mobs of school children *pidiendo botellas* (hitchhiking; literally "asking for bottles," as in favors or baby bottles).

GETTING HERE AND AROUND

Distances in Miramar are vast and there's hardly any public transport, so you're best hiring a taxi from the center. The journey from the historic center will be about 20 to 30 minutes, depending on where you want to go. Taxis are also pretty hard to find in Miramar so you may want to ask your taxi to wait or come back for you.

TOP ATTRACTIONS

FAMILY **Acuario Nacional.** At the national aquarium, you can learn about many of Cuba's 900 species of fish. Dolphin shows are very popular, and there are also sea lion shows. At the time of writing, the aquarium was open, but undergoing refurbishment. ⊠ *Calle 60 y Av. 1, Miramar* ☎ *7203–6401* 🎫 *CUC$1 adults, CUC$7 kids* ☉ *Tues.–Sun. 10–6; dolphin shows at 11, 3, and 5; sea lion shows are at noon and 4.*

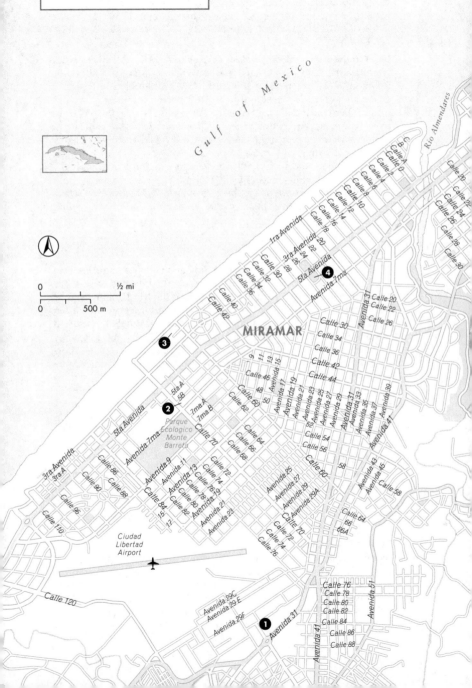

Vedado and Miramar

Gulf of Mexico

Río Almendares

Calle 0
Calle 2
Calle 4
Calle 6
Calle 8
Calle 10
Calle 12
Calle 14
Calle 16
Calle 18
Calle 20
Calle 22
Calle 24
Calle 26
Calle 28
Calle 30

1ra Avenida
3ra Avenida
5ta Avenida
Avenida 7ma

Calle 30
Calle 32
Calle 34
Calle 36
Calle 40
Calle 42

MIRAMAR

Calle 31
Calle 20
Calle 29
Calle 26

Calle 30
Calle 34
Calle 36
Calle 42
Calle 44

9 11 13 15
Calle 46
48 50
Avenida 17
Avenida 19
Avenida 21
Avenida 23
Avenida 25
Avenida 27
Avenida 29
Avenida 31
Avenida 33
Avenida 35
Avenida 37
Avenida 39
Avenida 41
Avenida 43
Avenida 45

5ta A
5B
7ma A
7ma B

Parque
Ecológico
Monte
Barreta

5ta Avenida

Calle 60
Calle 62
Calle 64
Calle 66
Calle 68

Avenida 7ma

Calle 70

3ra Avenida
3ra A

Calle 86
Calle 90
Calle 88
Calle 96

Avenida 9
Avenida 11
Avenida 13
Calle 84
15
17

Calle 72
Calle 74
Calle 76
Calle 78
Calle 80
Calle 82
Avenida 19
Avenida 21
Avenida 23

Calle 54
Calle 56
52

58

Calle 60

Avenida 25
Avenida 27
Avenida 29
Avenida 29A

Calle 64
66
66A

Calle 70
Calle 72
Calle 74
Calle 76

Calle 58
Calle 59

Calle 110

*Ciudad
Libertad
Airport*

Calle 120

Avenida 29C
Avenida 29 E
Avenida 29F

Avenida 31

Avenida 41
Avenida 51

Calle 76
Calle 78
Calle 80
Calle 82
Calle 84
Calle 86
Calle 88

① ② ③ ④

0   ½ mi
0   500 m

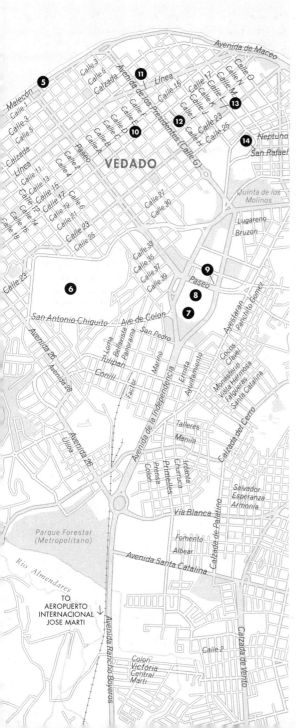

Fundación de la Naturaleza y El Hombre. This small, but fascinating museum focuses on the 17,422 km (10,825 miles) canoe journey lead by archaeologist and diplomat Antonio Nuñez Jimenez down the Amazon River from 1987 to 1988. The exhibits document the journey from Ecuador back to his native Cuba, as well as showcasing various pre-Colombian artifacts brought back with him. Also on display is the actual canoe in which Jimenez traveled. ✉ *Av. B5 6611, e/Calles 66 y 70, Miramar* 📞 *7209–2885* 🌐 *www.fanj.org* 💳 *CUC$2* ☉ *Weekdays 8:30–2:30.*

WORTH NOTING

Museo de la Alfabetización. Located in a former military airfield, which has now been turned into a giant school complex called Ciudad Libertad, this museum is dedicated to the literacy crusade of 1961. During this time students and teachers took to the countryside to teach illiterate peasants to read and write. ✉ *Av. 29E y Calle 76, Marianao, Marianao* 📞 *7267–9526* 💳 *CUC$3* ☉ *Weekdays 8–noon and 1–4:30, Sat. 8–noon.*

Parque Emiliano Zapata. This park is dedicated to the Mexican revolutionary agrarian reformist Emiliano Zapata (1889–1919). The Iglesia de Santa Rita, next to the park, is notable for its tower and for the sculpture of Santa Rita (by Rita Longa, whose work adorns the entrance to the Museo Nacional de Bellas Artes–Colección Cubana) just inside to the left. With sensuous lips, smooth features, and graceful curves, the work was branded as too erotic to display by the early 20th-century chaplain, and the sculpture was hidden away until the mid-1990s. ✉ *Ave. 5, e/Calle 24 y Calle 26, Miramar.*

HABANA DEL ESTE

Havana's eastern reaches have several interesting sights. The Regla neighborhood has strong Afro-Cuban traditions, and nearby Guanabacoa is known for its excellent museum dedicated to Santería, an Afro-Cuban religion.

Hemingway fans must make the trip to the small fishing village of Cojímar—home to Gregorio Fuentes, Hemingway's friend and boatman—and Finca Vigía, Hemingway's home in San Francisco de Paula.

GETTING HERE AND AROUND

You can visit Regla and Guanabacoa as an extension of a tour of the fortresses or on a separate side trip. Transportation to and around them can be a combination of ferries or launches, taxis, trains, and walks. To see the Hemingway highlights drive along the Carretera Central 13 km (8 miles) southeast of Havana to San Francisco de Paula, and spend a few hours looking through Hemingway's house, preserved exactly as it was the day he left it, never to return. Afterward, drive up to Cojímar on the Circunvalación (Ring Road) for lunch at one of Papa's favorite haunts, La Terraza, overlooking the mouth of the River Cojímar.

TOP ATTRACTIONS

FAMILY **Castillo de San Carlos de la Cabaña** (*La Cabaña*). In 1762 Lord Albemarle took El Morro for the English after a 44-day siege. A year later, Carlos III recovered Cuba in exchange for Florida and promptly ordered the construction of what was then the largest fort in the Americas. Sprawling across the hill east of El Morro, the fortress was named for the Spanish king and for the typical Cuban cabanas or *bohíos* (cabins) that once occupied the site. With the capacity to house 1,000 troops, this immense bastion was said to be so big that Carlos was given a telescope with which to admire it from Madrid.

The infamous **Foso de los Laureles** (Graveyard of the Laurels) was the execution wall where hundreds died during the wars of independence. The 9 pm *ceremonia del cañonazo* (ceremony of the cannon shot) is a must-see event filled with nostalgia and mystery. First, a lamplighter lights the gas lanterns. Then, a crier (a recruit with a voice so good he's been signed on permanently even though his military service ended years ago) begins an eery plainsong chant that reverberates throughout the fortress and, when the wind is right, across the bay to La Punta: *"Silencio; ha llegado la noche / Las luces están encendidas / Nuestro cañon se llama Capitolino / A las nueve sonará"* ("Silence; night has fallen / The lanterns are lit / Our cannon is named Capitolino / At nine it will sound"). Finally, a detail of some half-dozen soldiers dressed in scarlet 18th-century uniforms marches in and loads and fires the cannon, which makes a deafening noise (cover your ears).

La Cabaña's two museums are of moderate interest. The **Museo de la Cabaña** documents Cuba's military history, and the **Museo del Che** is dedicated to the life of Ernesto "Che" Guevara, who ranks alongside José Martí as one of Cuba's national martyrs. ✉ *Carretera de la Cabaña, Habana del Este* ☎ *7862–4092* 💲 *CUC$6 for entrance to fort, CUC$8 for nighttime cannon ceremony* ⏲ *Daily 10–10.*

FAMILY **Castillo de San Salvador de la Punta** (*La Punta*). On a point (hence, the name) directly across from El Morro, La Punta took 11 years to build (1589–1600), under the supervision of the same Italian military engineer—Juan Bautista Antonelli—responsible for its sister fortress. The two forts are so close, it's said that voice communication is possible in calm weather. In the early 17th century, a heavy chain was stretched between them, sealing the port at night and during attacks. Today the fortress has an even more romantic role in the city's unfolding drama: it's a favorite spot for lovers. At the time of writing, it was closed to the public due to ongoing renovations, but walking around the outside still makes for an impressive view. ✉ *Paseo de Martí (Prado) y Av. del Puerto (Calle Desamparado/San Pedro), Habana del Este.*

FAMILY **Castillo de los Tres Reyes del Morro** (*El Morro*). Begun in 1589, Havana's landmark fort is named for the Reyes Magos—the Magi or Three Kings of Bethlehem, who are the patrons of its chapel—and for the fact that it occupies a *morro* (promontory) at the harbor entrance. It and its sister fort across the way, La Punta, made Havana the safest port in the Americas at a time when both pirates and imperialists helped themselves to whatever could be had. Built into cliffs, El Morro was furnished with a battery of 12 cannons christened La Batería de los Doce Apóstoles (The Battery of the Twelve Apostles) facing the sea and another dozen, called Las Pastoras (The Shepherdesses), nearer the ramparts. The active lighthouse flashes its beam over Havana every 15 seconds. Inside the castle, across a moat and drawbridge, are stables, the chapel, dungeons, and a wine cellar. You'll also find the fortified vaults, which contain the **Museo del Morro,** with displays on the fortress itself; the **Museo de la Navegación,** with navigation and seafaring artifacts; and the **Museo de Piratas,** with exhibits and bits of folklore on pirates. The armory displays weapons from around the world. ⊠ *Carretera de la Cabaña, Habana del Este* ☎ *7863–7941* 🖭 *CUC$6 for the fort, CUC$2 extra for lighthouse* ⊙ *Daily 8–7, lighthouse 10–noon and 2–7.*

Cojímar. The fishing village Hemingway described in *The Old Man and the Sea* is modeled after this sleepy maritime hamlet where the author's wooden sportfishing craft, *El Pilar,* was berthed. El Torreón, the small fortress built here after the English used Cojímar as a landing point in their 1762 attack on Havana, is the site of a Hemingway bust made of brass boat propellers donated by Cojímar fishermen.

Wander around town; Gregorio Fuentes—Hemingway's skipper and pal from 1935 to 1960—once lived at Calle Pezuela 209. Gregorio provided Hemingway with a great deal of inspiration. The writer, having based the novel on the then thirtysomething Gregorio, was at a loss for a title until Gregorio shrugged and commented that, as far as he could tell, it was just about *"un viejo y el mar"* ("an old man and the sea"). ⊠ *Cojímar.*

NEED A BREAK?

La Terraza. Cojímar would merit a visit even without its literary significance as home of **La Terraza** . From the opening *curaçao*—a frozen daiquirí made with a blue bitter-orange liqueur—and *majuas* (tiny deep-fried fish) through the *ranchito de mariscos* (fish, lobster, and shrimp stewed in tomato, onion, and peppers), everything is very good here. The graceful mahogany bar dangerously dignifies the act of drinking, and the Hemingway memorabilia aren't overdone. ⊠ *Calle Real y Candelaria, Cojímar* ☎ *7763–9486.*

El Cristo de La Habana. Sometimes referred to as El Cristo de Casa Blanca for the eastern Havana municipality above which it stands, the 18-meter (59-foot) Carrara-marble colossus by Cuban sculptress Jilma Madera is said to be the largest open-air sculpture ever created by a woman. It was unveiled in 1958, a year before the Revolution and a year after the student assault on Fulgencio Batista's Palacio Presidencial. It's said that Batista's wife, praying for her husband to escape the shootout alive, vowed to erect a statue of Christ like that in Rio de Janeiro if her prayers were answered. Batista survived, and the statue was built while he tortured and murdered political opponents—especially students— with renewed brutality. For this reason, there's a certain official coldness toward the site. Certainly the sculpture itself is less interesting than the views (from its base) of the harbor and La Habana Vieja and the ambience of the park—a popular local picnic spot—that surrounds it. ⊠ *Carretera de Casa Blanca, Habana del Este* 🖭 *Free* ⊙ *Daily 10–10.*

FAMILY
Fodor's Choice
★
Finca Vigía. Even those convinced that they've outgrown their thirst for Hemingway will feel a flutter of youthful romanticism on a visit to Finca Vigía (Lookout Farm), the American Nobel Prize–winner's home from 1939 to 1961. The excellent guides will show you his weight charts—faithfully kept on the bathroom wall and never varying much from 242.5 pounds—a first edition of Kenneth Tynan's *Bull Fever* by the toilet; the lizard preserved in formaldehyde and honored for having "died well" in a battle with one of Hemingway's five-dozen cats; the pool where Ava Gardner swam naked; Hemingway's favorite chair (ask about what happened to people who dared sit in it); his sleek powerboat, *El Pilar*; and much, much more. ⊠ *San Francisco de Paula* ✢ *Follow Careterra Central for 14 km (9 miles) outside Havana* ☎ *7891–0809* ⊕ *www.hemingwaycuba.com/* 🎫 *CUC$3* ⊗ *Mon.–Sat. 10–4, Sun. 9–1.*

Guanabacoa. Once a small sugar and tobacco center, Guanabacoa is inhabited primarily by the descendents of slaves who worked the fields here. Though the town, which is full of colonial treasures, is now part of sprawling Havana, its old Afro-Cuban traditions and religions have been kept alive. ⊠ *Guanabacoa.*

Museo Histórico Municipal de Guanabacoa. Installed in a handsome, if somewhat rundown, colonial mansion, this museum exhibits a comprehensive history of Guanabacoa, with emphasis on its ethnic and religious traditions. For a deeper understanding of Santería as well as of the Palo Monte and Abakua sects that have been so important in Afro-Cuban sociology and history, this is an important visit. ⊠ *Calle Martí 108, Guanabacoa* ☎ *797–9117* 🎫 *CUC$2, CUC$3 with a guide* ⊗ *Mon.–Sat. 9:30–5:30, Sun. 9–1.*

WORTH NOTING

FAMILY
Parque Lenin. This vast amusement park was popular with Cubans before the 1992 collapse of the Soviet Union. The penury of the Special Period, however, has caused the carousels and other fairground attractions to be shut down. Developed on what was once a farming estate 20 km (12 miles) southwest of Havana, the 745-hectare (1,841-acre) park contains rolling meadows, small lakes, and woodlands. Look for the Monumento Lenin, a mammoth granite sculpture of the Russian Revolutionary. The Monumento a Celia Sánchez has photographs and portraits of Cuba's unofficial First Lady. The park's offerings also include art galleries, ceramics workshops, and a movie theater, although keep in mind that much of it is rundown. Horseback riding, boating, and swimming are options here as well. You can have a good meal in Las Ruinas and stay overnight in the comfortable motel. ⊠ *Carretera de la Presa, Habana del Este* ☎ *7647–1100* 🎫 *CUC$3* ⊗ *Sept.–June, Wed.–Sun. 9–5:30; July and Aug., Tues–Sun. 9–5:30.*

Regla. Probably named for a West African Yoruba deity, this seafarers' and fishermen's enclave retains a rough vitality. Originally a camp for black slaves—especially of the Ibibio, Bantu, and Yoruba tribes—Regla's Afro-Cuban roots are strong.

The waterfront **Iglesia de Nuestra Señora de Regla**, the first stop as you leave the ferry, was built in 1810. It's famous as the home of La Virgen de Regla (The Black Virgin of Regla), a black Madonna who cradles a white infant. Identified with Yemayá, the Yoruban orisha of the sea, the Virgin is the patron saint of motherhood and of sailors. On September 8 both Catholic and Santería celebrations honor her. There's a procession through the streets to the wailing of dirge music. The faithful also fill the church—dressed in their finest and wearing something blue, the color of the sea and of Yemayá—waiting their turn to touch the virgin or their favorite icons and crucifixes in side chapels. At the water's edge, women standing ankle-deep in the harbor's oily waters sing or pray to Yemayá, sometimes tossing in a coin or launching offerings of flowers, oranges, or melons. A branch of the Museo Municipal de Regla, just to the right of the church, has a display of Afro-Cuban orishas. There's also a shrine to Yemayá in the entryway of a private house, two doors up at No. 15. ⊠ *Habana del Este.*

Museo Municipal de Regla. This museum offers insight into Regla's history. During the Revolution, this area was a rebel stronghold known as *La Sierra Chiquita* (The Little Sierra; as opposed to the Sierra Maestra where Fidel and his forces operated). Close to but outside and largely separate from Havana, Regla was a convenient place for clandestine activity. Photographs of the Regla heroes and heroines (such as Lidia Doce) who were tortured and murdered by the Batista regime line the walls. Also on display is a copy of the first edition of Eduardo Facciolo's *La Voz del Pueblo Cubana*, dated June 13, 1852, as well as a room dedicated to the *orishas* (deities of the Santaría religion). The museum can also organize guided tours of Regla for CUC$5 per person. ⊠ *Calle Martí 158, Habana del Este* ☎ *7797–6989* ⊠ *CUC$2; CUC$3 with a guide* ⏱ *Mon.–Sat. 9–5, Sun. 9–noon.*

BEACHES

The Playas del Este (Eastern Beaches) are just 20 to 30 minutes from Havana on the same coast road, La Vía Blanca, that takes you to Varadero. Full of sun worshippers and local flavor, these sands have an atmosphere like that of a daytime disco by the sea. Although a morning of basking in the sun is conceivable, it's really more of a full-day operation.

There are a number of ways to get to the Playas del Este. The first is by private taxi from your hotel, which is a good idea if you're taking all your luggage with you. If you're just going for the day, take the hop-on, hop-off tour bus, which leaves from opposite the Hotel Inglaterra and will take you as far as Santa María del Mar. It costs CUC$5 per person. Alternatively, take a shared mini-bus taxi, which leaves from near the Estación Central de Ferrocarriles (Central Train Station) and will only cost you a couple of CUCs each. It will also take you all the way to Guanabo and is handy for those staying in casas particulares there. Carros can be taken along the highway to get from one beach to another and horse-drawn carriage taxis can be used to get around the town of Guanabo.

Bacuranao. Lying 18 km (11 miles) east of Havana, this tranquil crescent of sand surrounding a quiet lagoon is the first you'll come to along the Playas del Este. This is about as natural as they come, with a scattering of palm trees for shade and a few locals who will offer to catch some fresh fish and cook it for you or scale a tree to get you a coconut. Coral reefs and an 18th-century Spanish galleon lie far off shore, meaning that you'll occasionally see scuba-diving excursions here, too. Look for the Villa Bacuranao, hidden by rocks and trees, at one end of the beach, a quiet two-star resort with a swimming pool, restaurant, and inexpensive basic rooms to rent. **Amenities:** food and drink. **Best for:** solitude; swimming. ⊠ *Via Blanca, Bacuranao, Playas del Este, Playa Tarará.*

Mi Cayito. In between Santa María and Boca Ciega, you'll find a lively sweep of white sand, proudly flying the rainbow flag. This is Playas del Este gay beach, full of buffed beach bodies, sun beds, and a party-like atmosphere. Most hotels in the surrounding area are also gay-friendly. **Amenities:** food and drink; water sports. **Best for:** partiers. ⊠ *Mi Cayito, Av. Aventura, Playas del Este, Playa Santa María del Mar.*

Playa Boca Ciega. Just beyond the Laguna Itabo and the mouth of the Río Boca Ciega you'll find a small, but lively stretch of sand, mostly used by those staying at the nearby Hotel Blau Arenal. There's always something going on here such as salsa lessons or limbo competitions. **Amenities:** food and drink. **Best for:** partiers. ⊠ *Calle 1ra, Guanabo, Playa Santa María del Mar.*

Playa de Santa María. Locals will tell you that this is the best and prettiest beach of the Playas del Este, and it's certainly the liveliest, too, popular with both tourists and visiting habaneros. Here you'll find the Hotel Club Tropicoco and the Hotel Atlantico, behind the dunes. Think beachside restaurants, sun beds, massage tents, live Cuban music, water sports, and individual food vendors, selling everything from tamales to pizza and boxes of rice and beans. **Amenities:** water sports; food and drink. **Best for:** partiers; swimming. ⊠ *Av. Aventura, Santa María del Mar, Playa Santa María del Mar.*

Playa El Mégano. Just 2 km (1 mile) east of Playa Tarará is a wide stretch of white sand, which marks the very beginning of the popular Playa de Santa María. Here you can rent sun beds or pedalos and enjoy the facilities of a simple beachside café. There's also on-sand dining, catered by the hotels located behind the dunes. It's busier than Bacuranao and Playa Tarará, but still quiet enough to find your own stretch of sand. **Amenities:** water sports; food and drink. **Best for:** walking. ⊠ *Via de la Mar, Playa Megano, Playa Santa María del Mar.*

Playa Guanabo. If you head farther east from Playa Boca Ciega, you'll come to the bustling town of Guanabo and its pretty golden-sand beach with calm clear waters. With its many bars, restaurants, shops, and horse and carriage–style taxis, Guanabo is a popular weekend getaway spot for local habaneros. This is also where you'll find the greatest concentration of *casas particulares*, which can often have better facilities than many of the area hotels. The beach has a relaxed vibe during the day, with inexpensive sail and pedal boats for rent, but it gets busier in the evenings with impromptu rum and dance parties. **Amenities:** food and drink; water sports. **Best for:** sunset; swimming. ⊠ *Calle 3ra, Guanabo, Playa Santa María del Mar.*

Playa Jibacoa. Santa Cruz del Norte, 10 km (6 miles) east of Playa Guanabo, is an industrial town that's home to Cuba's greatest distillery, the Ronería Santa Cruz, where the ubiquitous Havana Club rum is made. Don't let the offshore oil rigs or the less than pristine waters here deter you from continuing. Just 3 km (2 miles) east of Santa Cruz is the best and least spoiled of all of the beaches near Havana. Nestled between headlands at the mouth of the Río Jibacoa, its white sands are backed by cliffs that overlook crystal clear, aquamarine waters. Divers will appreciate the coral reefs here, while terrestrial types can follow hiking trails from the beach into the backcountry. The Breezes Hotel here is one of the finest beach hotels in Cuba. **Amenities:** food and drink; water sports. **Best for:** snorkeling; walking. ⊠ *Via Blanca, Playa Jibacoa, Santa Cruz del Norte.*

Playa Tarará. Two km (1 mile) east of Bacuranao is a small stretch of white sand that's only accessible via a modern private residential area; tourists are welcome for a small fee. It's home to the 50-berth Marina Tarará/Club Naútica, site of the Old Man and the Sea Fishing Tournament every July. Here you can arrange boat rentals, yacht cruises, fishing trips, and diving or snorkeling excursions. There are also accommodations and a good restaurant at the Hotel Villa Armonía Tarará. **Amenities:** food and drink; water sports. **Best for:** snorkeling. ⊠ *Via Blanca, Tarará, Playa Tarará.*

WHERE TO EAT

Shortages of raw materials and a bureaucratized approach to food preparation in state-owned restaurants have produced many a mediocre meal, but with the privateer restaurants leading the way, Cuban cuisine is coming back. For the best cooking in Havana, seek out the *paladares* (privately owned establishments; the name, which literally means "palates," was cribbed from a popular Brazilian soap opera in which the heroine makes her fortune with a roadside restaurant named "El Paladar de Raquel").

Although Havana may not offer a head-spinning number of irresistible gastronomical options, things are improving. Your best bet is to avoid many of the state-owned restaurants and stick with the top paladares as much as possible, where the food is usually fresh and authentic. In recent years, laws on private enterprises in Cuba have relaxed, meaning that new and innovative paladares are springing up all time, offering a range of flavors for all budgets and tastes. Today you won't just find the traditional-style paladares, with their cozy and clandestine atmospheres, but also those that are modern, funky and chic. The Vedado, Miramar, and Playa districts are prime paladar habitats, as the Habaguanex chain dominates most of La Habana Vieja. Centro Habana has the most famous of all, La Guarida. Call ahead to reserve a table if you go to a paladar, and be wary of taxi drivers who swear to you that the place is closed; they often get a commission for taking you to the place they are flacking for.

State-owned establishments, with a few exceptions (such as El Aljibe), are mediocre at best. However, they're often in settings you may find hard to resist, despite the overpriced and uninteresting fare. Some hotel restaurants (not the cafeterias or buffets) are noteworthy, especially the Chez Mérito in the Hotel Presidente and the Aguiar in the Hotel Nacional. Two caveats: beware of elegant but empty establishments, and opt for simple criollo fare over sophisticated or "international" creations unless you are in the top hotels.

HABANA VIEJA

Home to atmospheric plazas, quaint cobbled streets, and majestic colonial mansions, Habana Vieja is filled with many restaurants and cafés, varying in price and quality. The majority of the eateries here are state-owned and are often located within the area's historic hotels, however more paladares have opened up in the last few years, meaning more variety and quality. You'll hardly ever need to reserve a table in this area, unless it's in one of the more popular paladares, which generally offer better customer service too.

$$ ✕**Bodegón Onda.** In a quiet corner next to the Hotel El Comendador, this restaurant offers an array of tapas, which includes various seafood offerings. On top of that, it also offers grilled fare such as vegetables, chicken, pork, and fish. Tapas servings vary from CUC$1 to CUC$3, a great deal in any destination. Seafood tapas menus can be had for CUC$12 for two persons. Service is rather slow, but friendly. ⑤ *Average main: CUC$12* ⊠ *Calle Obrapía 55, La Habana Vieja* ☎ *7864–6021.*

SPANISH

$ ✕**Cafe de los Artistas.** Located down the trendy Callejón de Peluquerros, lined with new paladares, bars, and art galleries, this eatery offers some of the tastiest and most innovative cuisine in Havana Vieja. Think Cuban-style fajitas or wild rice with peanuts and curry. Vegetarians will be delighted with the choices, which include a savory eggplant cake, topped with a tomato salsa and melted cheese. The decor here matches the excellent food, with bare brick walls, original tiles, stained glass windows, and old black-and-white photos lining the walls. ⑤ *Average main: CUC$7* ⊠ *Calle Aguiar 22 e/Ave. de las Misiones y Pena Pobre, (Callejon de los Peluquerros), La Habana Vieja* ☎ *7866–2418* ⊟ *No credit cards.*

INTERNATIONAL

$$ ✕**Café del Oriente.** One of the most sophisticated-looking eateries in Havana Vieja, this upscale restaurant sits on the atmospheric Plaza de San Francisco. Try for the upstairs corner table, which overlooks the plaza and has a view of the Sierra Maestra boat terminal, the Iglesia y Convento Menor de San Francisco de Asís, and the Lonja del Comercio (Commerce Exchange) across the way. The food is overpriced and only fair, but the suave decor does offer a nice ambience. Tempting dishes here, prepared by head chef Ernesto Rosario, include seafood à la crème or prawns sautéed with rosemary. ⑤ *Average main: CUC$20* ⊠ *Calle de los Oficios 112, La Habana Vieja* ☎ *7860–6686.*

CAJUN

Cuban Cuisine

Carne de cerdo or *puerco* (pork) and *pollo* (chicken) dishes are common, with *res* (beef), *pargo* (snapper), *cherna* (grouper), *camarones* (shrimp), and *langosta* (lobster) close behind. In the paladares, which can't legally serve beef and lobster, look for *conejo* (rabbit), *cordero* (lamb), and *cangrejo* (crab). Bananas, plantains, and *viandas* (tubers) such as potatoes, yams, and yuca (also known as cassava or manioc) are staples.

Standard *criollo* (creole) dishes include *frijoles negros con arroz* (black beans with rice); pollo *asado en salsa criolla* (grilled in a sauce of tomato, onion, and *ají*—a hot, red pepper); *pierna de puerco asado en su jugo* (roast leg of pork in its own gravy); *aporreado de res*, *aporreado de tasajo*, or *ropa vieja* (different names for shredded beef in salsa criollo); *enchilado de* langosta (stewed in peppers, tomato, onions, and garlic); langosta *a la mariposa* (grilled and served with lemon); *frituras de malanga* (crisp, fried wedges of a tuber that tastes like a tangy potato); and *yuca con mojo* (cassava in salsa criolla).

There are seemingly endless ways to prepare plantains in Cuba, among them *chicharrones de plátano* (finely sliced and salted plantain chips, also known as *mariquitas*); *tostones* (fried chunks of green plantain); and *plátanos a puñetazos* (literally, "punched plantains"; banana or plantain half cooked, taken out, placed under a cloth and hammered flat with a fist before being placed back in the pan to finish browning). Keep your eyes peeled for typical criollo desserts such as *casco de guayaba* (guava paste) or *mermelada de mango* (mango marmalade), both served *con queso* (with cheese).

Wine is increasingly available as proper storage at stable temperatures improves. Vintage Riojas and Ribera de Duero wines show up from time to time, though the price of good wine (CUC$20–CUC$25) compared to a 1-convertible peso bottle of local beer is a factor difficult not to keep in mind. Torres wines from Catalonia's Penedès region and from Chile are also frequently available. Mojitos (light rum, sugar, mint, lemon juice, and club soda) and daiquirís (blended light rum, lime, sugar, and crushed ice) are Cuba's most famous rum drinks. The two most popular and widely available Cuban beers include the standard light lager, Cristal and the darker Bucanero.

$$
INTERNATIONAL

✕ **El Figaro.** Another popular addition to Callejón de Peluquerros (Barbers' Alley), El Figaro's tagline is *comida sin pelos* (food without hairs). The menu, which was set up by the grandson of Cuba's celebrity chef Gilberto Smith Duquesne, is full of gourmet, stylized Cuban dishes, as well as international favorites such as ceviche or gazpacho. Try the signature dish of lobster cooked in coffee, cream, white wine, and cognac. ■TIP→ **Come later in the evening to watch old movies projected onto the outside wall (like a drive-in movie theater), while sampling one of their 15 varieties of mojitos.** $ *Average main: CUC$15* ⊠ *Calle Aguiar 18 el Av. de las Misiones, La Habana Vieja* ☎ *7861–0544* ▭ *No credit cards.*

$$
SPANISH

✕ **El Mesón de la Flota.** Opened on the site of a warehouse that was frequented by Spanish sailors in colonial times, this little hideaway serves

2

such creditable Spanish specialties as *tortilla de patata* (potato omelet) and *gambas al ajillo* (shrimp sautéed with garlic). The flamenco performances (nightly at 9) provide a bracing shot of atmosphere, although the Café Taberna just a couple hundred meters on tends to attract the crowds these days. $\boxed{\$}$ *Average main: CUC$15* ✉ *Calle Mercaderes 257, e/Calle Amargura y Calle Brasil (Teniente Rey), La Habana Vieja* ☎ *7863–3838* ⊟ *No credit cards.*

$ ✗ **Jardín del Oriente.** Those on a budget should try this lovely little place
CUBAN located in the gardens of Café del Oriente, which is just around the corner. A favorite with locals on their lunch break, tables are set among the tropical plants and trickling fountains, and it's always packed. Typical Cuban fare is served, as well as an array of filled baguettes. Portions are big and you won't pay more than CUC$5 for any of the main meals. $\boxed{\$}$ *Average main: CUC$5* ✉ *Calle Amargura 12, e/Oficios y Mercaderes, La Habana Vieja* ☎ *7860–6686* ⊟ *No credit cards.*

$$ ✗ **La Paella.** In the Hostal Valencia, this restaurant specializes in paella,
SPANISH just as its name suggests, and has won high praise for its Valencian dishes. House suggestions include grilled Caribbean seafood, Yoruba lobster with béchamel sauce, and buttered shrimp. In keeping with the cuisine, the large, airy dining room has a terra-cotta floor, a rustic feel, and is dressed in traditional Spanish furnishings. A signed image of a notable bullfighter, another of the running of the bulls, and even a memento to former president Fidel Castro Ruz dating from 1989 adorn the walls here. $\boxed{\$}$ *Average main: CUC$14* ✉ *Calle de los Oficios 53, esq. de Calle Obrapía, La Habana Vieja* ☎ *7867–1037.*

$$ ✗ **Mama Inés.** Ask anyone in Havana Vieja which places they recom-
CREOLE mend to eat and they'll almost always mention Mama Inés. Owned by chef Erasmo, who has cooked for everyone and anyone including presidents and diplomats, this intimate colonial-style paladar serves classic Creole dishes using the freshest ingredients. Erasmo himself is very humble and friendly, and always comes out of the kitchen to check on diners. Dishes are a little overpriced for what they are, but you are being cooked for by a famous chef. $\boxed{\$}$ *Average main: CUC$16* ✉ *Calle Obrapia 60, e/Oficios y Baratillo, La Habana Vieja* ☎ *7862–2669* ⊟ *No credit cards.*

$ ✗ **Nao Bar Paladar.** Located in a quiet alley near the waterfront, this cozy
CUBAN and intimate paladar serves up tasty Cuban dishes with an emphasis on seafood. Seated under old wooden beams and surrounded by colorful antique lamps, you can sit back and enjoy the rhythms of the house band Legendario Havana. Try the Cuban tamales or malanga fritters with honey to start, followed by the giant mermaid lobster or fresh catch of the day. Like most places in Havana, you won't find many vegetarian options on the menu, but the staff here will be happy to cook up something special for you if you ask (and it won't just be an omelet or rice and beans). $\boxed{\$}$ *Average main: CUC$10* ✉ *Calle Obispo 1 e/San Pedro y Baratillo, La Habana Vieja* ☎ *7867–3463* ⊟ *No credit cards.*

$ ✗ **Restaurante Europa.** From its beginnings as the 19th-century Europa
CAJUN Café, the onetime famous colonial-style café and candy shop has reopened as a restaurant serving Cuban and international cuisine. As is typical here, a band plays live Cuban music, greeting visitors walking

Where to Eat and Stay in La Habana Vieja and Centro Habana

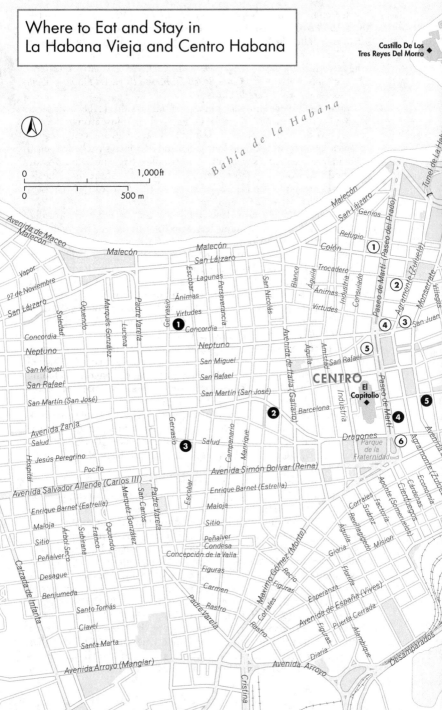

Castillo De Los Tres Reyes Del Morro ◆

Bahía de la Habana

0 — 1,000ft
0 — 500 m

CENTRO

El Capitolio ◆

Restaurants ▼

Hotels ▼

down Obispo towards the port. Dishes are uninspiring, but if you just want a cheap and simple lunch, this place is good. Plates include basic grilled chicken fillets, traditional Cuban hashed beef, and simple sandwiches cooked by chef Ernesto. There's an extensive cocktail list and an impressively stocked bar. As is often the case in Cuba, the restaurant even sells tobacco products. ⑤ *Average main: CUC$5* ✉ *Calle Obispo 112, adjacent to Aguiar, La Habana Vieja* ☎ *7866–4484* ⬛ *No credit cards.*

$$ ✕ **Restaurante Paris.** Formerly named El Patio, Restaurante Paris is still
CAJUN a romantic and atmospheric option for a meal. It might be hard to pick a spot here: tables are either out on the Plaza de la Catedral or in the patio of the colonial house in which the restaurant is located. The criollo menu is complete, and although the food and service fall short of the spectacular settings, the quality of the ingredients is good. Most notable are the array of seafood dishes, such as lobster in salsa criollo or grilled fish. ⑤ *Average main: CUC$12* ✉ *Plaza de la Catedral 54, La Habana Vieja* ☎ *7867–1035* ⬛ *No credit cards.*

$ ✕ **Taberna El Molino.** Located at the rear of the quiet and elegant Hotel
CUBAN Marqués de Prado Ameno, the decor here is simple and understated and dishes range from alluring fare like grilled seafood, langoustines, or filet mignon to the simple, homey stuffed chicken and vegetables that Cubans seem to favor. The best options are its two signature dishes—cider chicken or honey pork. Desserts are uninspiring, including such standbys as cheesecake, chocolate cake, and ice cream, but try the strong but tasty Café Cubano to top off your meal. ⑤ *Average main: CUC$10* ✉ *Hotel Marqués de Prado Ameno, Calle O'Reilly 253, e/ Cuba y Aguiar, La Habana Vieja* ☎ *7862–4127.*

$$ ✕ **Vuelta Abajo.** An elegant, intimate spot in the Hostal Conde de Vil-
CAJUN lanueva, this restaurant specializes in dishes from Vuelta Abajo, Cuba's best tobacco-growing region. Try the pollo *yumurino* (in a criollo sauce) or the colonial-trapiche fish fillet, which is garnished with a piece of sugarcane dressed in a ginger sauce. ⑤ *Average main: CUC$15* ✉ *Hotel Conde de Villanueva, Calle Mercaderes 202, La Habana Vieja* ☎ *7862–9293* ⊕ *www.habaguanexhotels.com.*

CENTRO HABANA

Centro has the fewest dining options, but there are a few decent budget places located around the city's Chinatown. Although mostly devoid of Chinese people, the Barrio Chino has a few Chinese restaurants in among its colorful street signs and dragon-adorned archways. These places are also very popular with locals, whom you're unlikely to find in many of the Habana Vieja restaurants. Besides this, it's also home to the city's most famous paladar La Guardia, which was even the setting for the movie, *Fresa y Chocolate* (*Strawberry and Chocolate*). Make sure you book ahead for this one. You can also get a decent meal at one of the big hotels, although it's not far to walk into Habana Vieja for a wider variety of options.

$ ✕ **Hanoi.** Also known as Casa de la Parra (House of the Grape Arbor),
CUBAN this simple, yet elegant restaurant only specializes in typical criollo

and Cuban food, despite the name. Sit inside under old wooden beams or outside on the patio under shady grape vines while dining on the classic menu that includes such dishes as *morros y cristianos* (rice and beans), *boniato cocido* (boiled yam), various grilled meats, and fish and vegetable fried rice. Although the price is right, make sure to check your bill before paying as sometimes they overcharge. $ *Average main: CUC$5 ⊠ Calle Brasil (Teniente Rey) y Calle Bernaza, Centro Habana ☎ 7867–1029 ▭ No credit cards.*

$
CHINESE CUBAN

✕**La Flor de Loto.** While both its decor, neighborhood, and context may be Chinese, this restaurant has very little to do with the Orient. (Frankly, rare is the Asiatic face at any Havana Chinese eatery.) Very popular with locals, there's always a queue halfway out the door. The restaurant's menu includes a wide variety of food that is popular with Cubans. The grilled chicken criollo-style is grand and not dry at all, while the shrimp in a cream sauce is delicious. Prepare yourself for king-size portions. Daily offerings and the chef's selections are stapled to the menu daily. $ *Average main: CUC$5 ⊠ Salud 313, e/Gerrasio and Escobar, Barrio Chine de Cuba (in front of Callejon Cerrada del Paseo), Centro Habana ☎ 7860–8501 ▭ No credit cards.*

$$$$
LATIN AMERICAN
Fodor's Choice
★

✕**La Guarida.** Still Havana's most famous paladar, La Guardia has reached almost legendary status. Enrique Nuñez and his wife, Odeysis, have transformed their early 20th-century town house into a fine paladar. It's so photogenic that scenes in *Fresa y Chocolate (Strawberry and Chocolate)* were filmed here. The three-floor climb up the squalid but picturesque stairway generates an appetite-enhancing adrenaline. The daily special is never what Enrique and Odeysis need to get rid of but rather what they hope will make you happiest. Look for *cherna compuesta a lo caimanero* (with coconut and spices) or *conejo al aceite de oliva con caponata* (cooked in olive oil with a sauce of eggplant, peppers, and onion). On Sunday the restaurant is open only for brunch from noon to 4. $ *Average main: CUC$40 ⊠ Calle Concordia 418, e/ Calle Gervasio y Calle Escobar, Centro Habana ☎ 7886–9047 ⊕ www. laguarida.com ▭ No credit cards ⌖ Reservations essential.*

$
CAJUN

✕**Los Nardos.** Situated right across from the Capitolio, it might be easy to miss Los Nardos if it wasn't for the long queues. Popular among locals, hefty portions of red snapper, rabbit or chicken and lamb stew are served up daily. There's virtually no exterior signage, and the restaurant is decorated with locally crafted wooden lamps, tables, and chairs, giving the dining room an eclectic decor and a romantic ambience. Make sure that you are on the first floor—and not the upper floor, which is another less stellar eatery. $ *Average main: CUC$8 ⊠ Paseo del Prado 563, e/ Dragones y Teniente Rey, Centro Habana ☎ 7863–2985 ▭ No credit cards.*

$
CHINESE

✕**Tien-Tan.** Its name means "heaven's temple" in Mandarin, and this temple to Chinese cuisine has enough worshippers that you'll be lucky to find a spot inside. No matter, though, as there are tables outside as well—all the better for watching passersby on Chinatown's wildest street. Prices vary wildly depending on what you order, and while the food is cooked by Chinese chef Xio Luo, it could be a little fresher. Certain dishes (such as the crispy duck) must be ordered in advance.

$ *Average main: CUC$10* ⊠ *Calle Cuchillo 17, e/Calle Zanja y Calle San Nicolas, Centro Habana* ☎ *7861–5478* ▭ *No credit cards.*

VEDADO

In Vedado you'll find some of the city's best paladares hidden away in top-floor penthouses, graceful colonial mansions, and old factories. Reservations are always recommended, as these places fill up fast. Although, if there's just one or two of you and you're willing to wait for a table, you'll usually get a spot. Many of the top hotels in the area also have particularly good restaurants. Those on a budget should do as the Cubans do and try out one of Vedado's numerous pizza stands (there's one every couple of blocks).

$$$$
EUROPEAN

✕ **Aguiar.** For decades, the elegant dining room in the Hotel Nacional has been one of the city's premier establishments. Despite the table-side shrimp-and-rum flambé performances, which are always entertaining, the atmosphere is generally subdued—even when the place is full. The wine list is excellent, though pricey. $ *Average main: CUC$35* ⊠ *Hotel Nacional, Calle O y Calle 21, Vedado* ☎ *7836–3564* ⊕ *www. hotelnacionaldecuba.com* ⚭ *Reservations essential.*

$$
ECLECTIC

✕ **Café Laurent.** This chic paladar, situated in the penthouse of a Vedado apartment block, could very well be located in Paris or Barcelona with its funky decor and gourmet cuisine. Choose to dine inside the bright dining room, plastered in newsprint, or outside on the breezy terrace, which offers dreamy views of Havana. With a heavy emphasis on seafood with a Creole twist, the menu also offers meat and vegetarian options, all beautifully presented—think red snapper with clams, lobster and shrimp brochettes, tuna carpaccio, or slow-roasted lamb. $ *Average main: CUC$14* ⊠ *Penthouse, Calle M 257, e/19 y 20, Vedado* ☎ *7831–2090* ⊕ *www.cafelaurent.ueuo.com* ⚭ *Reservations essential* ▭ *No credit cards.*

$$
CUBAN
Fodor's Choice
★

✕ **Decamerón.** Ring the bell of this cozy paladar to be let into a series of intimate rooms packed with an eclectic array of antique clocks, vintage musical instruments, paintings, lamps, and vases. For something typically Cuban with a gourmet twist, go for the *ropa vieja* (shredded beef in Creole sauce) with crunchy sweet potatoes. If you're looking for something a little more international, try the sirloin steak with blue cheese sauce or one of the excellent pasta dishes. Of the house specialties, the flaky tuna and vegetable tartlet starter or the lemon pie for dessert are particularly good. $ *Average main: CUC$13* ⊠ *Linea 753, e/ Paseo y Calle 2, Vedado* ☎ *7832–2444* ⚭ *Reservations essential* ▭ *No credit cards.*

$$
INTERNATIONAL
Fodor's Choice
★

✕ **El Cocinero.** Housed in an old renovated oil mill, this place is easy to find, as the paladar's name is branded in giant letters across the towering brick chimney. Located at the edge of Vedado, it might be a bit of a trek to get here, but it's definitely worth it for one of Havana's trendiest eateries. Step inside to the clanging of an old ship's bell (indicating a new customer has arrived) and climb the winding staircase into the mill itself. Stop on middle level for the industrial-chic restaurant, where tasty Cuban and international favorites are served, or head on up to the atmospheric terrace to enjoy gourmet snacks and cocktails. There's everything here, from lobster tail, fish croquettes, and octopus cooked in garlic to ribs, lamb curry, and goat-cheese club sandwich. $ *Average main: CUC$16* ⊠ *Calle 26, e/Calles 11 y 13, Vedado* ☎ *7832–2355* ⚓ *Reservations essential* ⊟ *No credit cards.*

$$
FRENCH FUSION

✕ **Le Chansonnier.** Once a private French restaurant, Le Chansonnier has now emerged into one of Havana's hottest paladares under the direction of Hector Higueras. In its modern chic interior, dine on fusion specialities such as seafood gazpacho, aubergine au gratin, roast chicken with mushroom cream, and their signature duck terrine. Make a visit the bathrooms to see the amazing artwork created by Damián Alquiles. $ *Average main: CUC$17* ⊠ *Calle J, No. 257, e/Calles 15 y Línea, Vedado* ☎ *7832–1576* ⊕ *www.lechansonnierhabana.com* ⚓ *Reservations essential* ⊟ *No credit cards.*

MIRAMAR

Surrounded by stately mansions, embassies, and international hotels, it's not surprising that Miramar is home to some of the best state-owned restaurants and paladares. You'll generally pay more here than in other areas, but that's to be expected, considering the location. Everything is very spread out, so that even if you're staying here, you'll almost certainly need to call a taxi. Remember, if you're coming from other areas in the city, you'll need to budget about CUC$10 each way for a taxi to get here. A few of the better paladares can be found along the water's edge, offering excellent sea views and an excellent choice for a romantic evening out.

$$
SEAFOOD

✕ **Don Cangrejo.** Located near the seafront in the open air, this is one of Havana's best seafood restaurants. Shrimp, crab, lobster, grouper, snapper: every type of seafood available in the Antilles seems to find its way through this bustling kitchen. At night, the restaurant turns into one of Miramar's most popular nightclubs, with a host of live bands and DJs. $ *Average main: CUC$17* ⊠ *Av. 1, e/Calle 16 y Calle 18, Miramar* ☎ *7204–3837.*

$$
CAJUN

✕ **El Aljibe.** One of the better state-owned restaurants, El Aljibe offers a pretty open-air setting and live music while you dine. The criollo fare here is reasonably priced and served gracefully, and the place is always filled to the brim with clued-in diners (including such celebrities as Omar Linares, Cuba's finest former baseball player), as well as bus loads of tourists. The roast chicken in bitter-orange sauce, served with black beans and rice is famous, and it's worth coming here just to try it. $ *Average main: CUC$13* ⊠ *Av. 7, e/Calle 24 y Calle 26, Miramar* ☎ *7204–1584* ⊟ *No credit cards.*

$$
ECLECTIC

✕ **La Fontana.** Set in a scenic garden, around small ponds and fountains, this is one of Miramar's best paladares, which also functions as a bar and lounge with good cocktails and some great live bands. Specializing in a variety of grilled meats, which are cooked on an outdoor charcoal grill, this place will definitely satisfy the carnivores among you. Other excellent dishes include shrimp teriyaki and fish fillet with clams in a green herb sauce. Vegetarians meanwhile will be happy with the starters of eggplant or fried chickpeas and mains of grilled vegetable

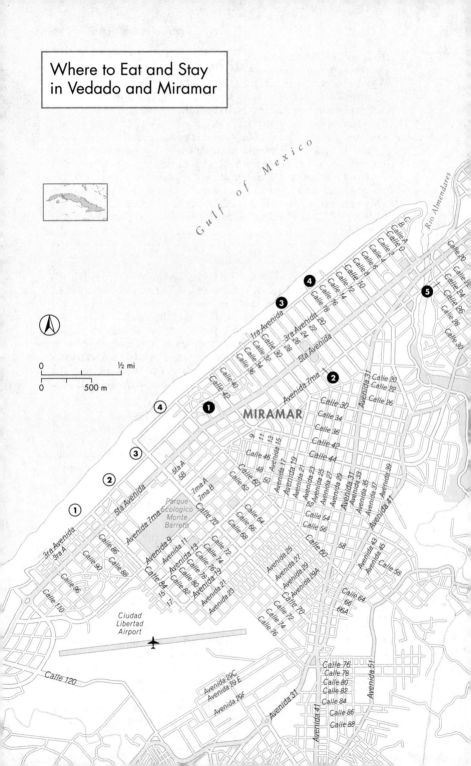

Where to Eat and Stay in Vedado and Miramar

Gulf of Mexico

Río Almendares

MIRAMAR

Parque Ecológico Monte Barreto

Ciudad Libertad Airport

½ mi

500 m

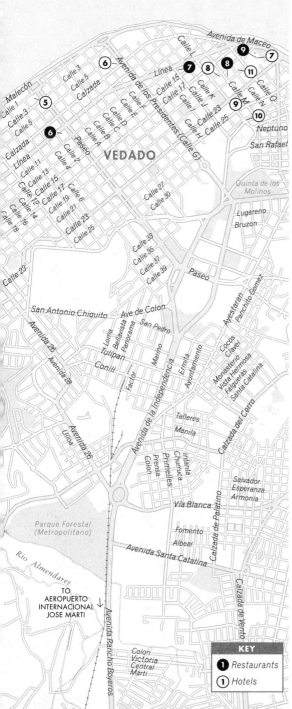

platters, risottos, and pastas. Sometimes there is an extra cover charge for the music. $ *Average main: CUC$19* ⊠ *Av. 3, No. 305, esq. de Calle 46, Miramar* ☎ *7202–8337* ⊕ *www.lafontanahavana.info* ▭ *No credit cards.*

$ ✕**Vistamar.** Overlooking the Straits of Florida, this cozy little paladar is
CAJUN set in an attractive Miramar home, and provides alfresco dining with, as its name suggests, fine views—well, at sunset anyway (at night, it's blacker than Hades out there). The dishes are good quality and specialties include octopus and lobster tails. The lemon pie also comes highly recommended. Spectacular views, good food, and live Cuban tunes— what more could you ask for? $ *Average main: CUC$10* ⊠ *Av. 1, No. 2206, e/Calle 22 y Calle 24, Miramar* ☎ *7203–8328* ▭ *No credit cards* ⌕ *Reservations essential.*

HABANA DEL ESTE AND PLAYAS DEL ESTE

Dining options in Habana del Este are scarce and you will mostly be relying on basic local cafés or hole-in-the-wall pizza joints. La Divina Pastora is one exception, located across the water, next to Havana's impressive fortresses. If you're staying in Playas del Este and don't fancy eating at your hotel all the time, the town of Guanabo has a couple of good options.

$$ ✕**La Divina Pastora.** Although prices are on the high side, the romantic
CUBAN location makes them worth it. Standing at the foot of El Morro, this restaurant offers splendid views over Havana and is a good spot for dinner after the *cañonazo*at La Cabaña. Your best bet is lobster; kept alive in an on-site tank, it's guaranteed to be fresh. $ *Average main: CUC$12* ⊠ *Parque Historico Militar Morro–Cabaña, Habana del Este* ☎ *7937–807* ▭ *No credit cards.*

$ ✕**Paladar el Piccolo.** This place is a little far out of town, but hitch a
ITALIAN ride on one of Guanabo's quaint horse and carts, and for a couple of CUC's, you'll be there in no time. Set in a rustic dining room with a large outdoor patio and open kitchen, this lively paladar serves some of the best pizzas you will find in the whole of Cuba. Watch as your pizza is cooked in a traditional wood-fired oven in front of you. $ *Average main: CUC$9* ⊠ *Ave. 5 y Calle 502, Guanabo, Habana del Este* ☎ *796–4300* ▭ *No credit cards.*

$ ✕**Paladar Maeda.** In a small residential area on top of a hill in Guanabo,
CUBAN this charming paladar is the best in town. What's more is that it actually
Fodor's Choice does feel like you're dining in someone's home, unlike some of Havana's
★ more modern paladares. Here you'll dine on modern Cuban classics and an excellent array of fresh seafood dishes, in a pretty garden, filled with flowers, grape vines, and trickling fountains. Try the grilled fish with salsa verde. There are no vegetarian choices on the menu, but if you ask, they'll make you up a giant *parilla de verduras* (grilled platter of mixed vegetables), straight from the barbecue. If you like it, you can even opt to stay here, as they also have a couple of rooms for rent upstairs. $ *Average main: CUC$10* ⊠ *Calle Quebec 115, e/Calles 476 y 478, Bellomonte, Guanabo, Playa Santa María del Mar* ☎ *7796–2615* ▭ *No credit cards.*

WHERE TO STAY

Let your interests dictate where you stay. If you love history and architecture, pick a hotel in La Habana Vieja or Centro. Just be aware that while hotels in Habana Vieja are charming and colorful, they do not offer all the amenities that you might find in large international chain hotels. Wi-Fi service is generally not available, but almost all hotels offer some kind of paid public Internet option. The Habaguanex chain hotels are based on unique and interesting concepts. For example, Hotel Los Frailes is in an old mansion and is designed as a sort of cloister, complete with monks in friars' robes. Conde de Villanueva is designed specifically for cigar lovers, and Hotel Ambos Mundos plays up its association with the American writer Ernest Hemingway. Most of these hotels are recommendable.

If you like to party until the wee hours, Vedado offers a Manhattan atmosphere with plenty of nightlife. If you seek peaceful sea breezes, consider staying in Miramar. If you can't decide, head for the Hotel Saratoga, with its rooftop pool, historic setting, unparalleled service in Cuba—and a stone's throw from the historic sites of La Habana Vieja. The closest resort areas to Havana are the Playas del Este, the best of which is Memories Jibacoa; stay here if you want to be in relative proximity to the capital (about 30 minutes east by car) but want more of a resort experience directly on the beach.

Hotel reviews have been shortened. For full information, visit Fodors. com.

LA HABANA VIEJA

Hotels here ooze old-world charm and colonial grandeur, and while many of them are slightly run-down and could do with an upgrade, the airy patios, marble columns, and colorful facades more than make up for it. Located within walking distance to many of the city's major sights, you won't have to venture far or spend your time riding around in taxis. The old buildings, narrow streets, and constant street repairs and renovations mean that it can be slightly noisier here than other areas, but you can't beat it for charisma and photographic appeal.

$$
HOTEL
⬚ **El Mesón de la Flota.** Named for a *mesón* (tavern) frequented by Spanish sailors in colonial times, this hotel in the heart of the Old City has five rooms with every modern amenity and spotless bathrooms. **Pros:** the hotel and facility staff are amenable; just steps from Plaza Vieja; very big rooms. **Cons:** the downstairs bar may well be too much noise for some guests of this bustling area; rooms do not have the grand colonial style of some of the other hotels. Ⓢ *Rooms from: CUC$140* ✉ *Calle Mercaderes 257, e/Calle Amargura y Calle Brasil (Teniente Rey), La Habana Vieja* ☎ *7863-3838* ⊕ *www.habaguanexhotels.com* 🛏 *5 rooms* ⏐⊙⏐ *Breakfast.*

$$
B&B/INN
⬚ **Hostal Valencia.** Although the bougainvillea-draped central patio is more reminiscent of Seville and Andalusia, the theme at this restored 18th-century mansion is really Valencia. **Pros:** creative room design. **Cons:** the showers tend to be on the weak and lukewarm side; hotel doors

close at midnight, making it impossible to experience Havana's night-life. $ *Rooms from: CUC$140* ✉ *Calle de los Oficios 53, esq. de Calle Obrapía, La Habana Vieja* ☎ *7867–1037* ⊕ *www.habaguanexhotels. com/en/hotels/hostalvalencia.asp* ⤴ *14 rooms* ⊠*| Breakfast.*

$$$ ⊞ **Hotel Ambos Mundos.** Hemingway stayed here in 1928 on his first trip
HOTEL to Havana; he went on to make it his hideaway before moving to Finca Vigía in 1939. **Pros:** the hotel's vibrant piano bar is reminiscent of Rick's American Café from the classic film Casablanca.; great views from the restaurant. **Cons:** rooms are decidedly dated; general maintenance is poor. $ *Rooms from: CUC$173* ✉ *Calle Obispo 153, La Habana Vieja* ☎ *7860–9530* ⊕ *www.hotelambosmundos-cuba.com/* ⤴ *52 rooms, 3 suites* ⊠*| Breakfast.*

$$$ ⊞ **Hotel Conde de Villanueva.** In a 19th-century house that once belonged
B&B/INN to a Spanish financier, this is a far cry from your typical cookie-cutter-style hotel. **Pros:** a unique thematic hotel where old-style elegance is prized over the contemporary; central Habana Vieja location is ideal. **Cons:** certainly not for those with an aversion to secondhand smoke. $ *Rooms from: CUC$173* ✉ *Calle Mercaderes 202, La Habana Vieja* ☎ *7862–9293* ⊕ *www.habaguanexhotels.com* ⤴ *9 rooms* ⊠*| Breakfast.*

$$$ ⊞ **Hotel del Tejadillo.** Just a block from the harbor, a few steps from the
B&B/INN cathedral, and very near Plaza de la Catedral, this hotel is made up of three houses from the 18th, 19th, and 20th centuries. **Pros:** great location near the Cathedral; beautiful room decor with wrought-iron and chunky wood furniture. **Cons:** some rooms have no windows; the breakfasts could be better. $ *Rooms from: CUC$173* ✉ *Calle Tejadillo 12, La Habana Vieja* ☎ *7863–7283* ⊕ *hoteltejadillocuba.com* ⤴ *26 rooms, 6 suites* ⊠*| Breakfast.*

$$$ ⊞ **Hotel El Comendador.** Before becoming the home of Don Pedro
B&B/INN Regalado Pedroso y Zayas in 1801, this building—one of the earli-est in the original town of San Cristóbal de La Habana—served as a *cabildo*, a jailhouse, a butcher shop, and then a fish market. **Pros:** it has the feel of an airy apartment in Paris; overlooks Havana's harbor; rooms are tastefully restored. **Cons:** interior patio could do with a touch-up and a lick of paint; if you need anything you always have to go to the Hotel Valencia reception around the corner. $ *Rooms from: CUC$173* ✉ *Calle Obrapía 55, La Habana Vieja* ☎ *7867–1037* ⊕ *www.habaguanexhotels.com* ⤴ *14 rooms* ⊠*| Breakfast.*

$$$ ⊞ **Hotel Florida.** Today a light, elegant reception area leads onto a colo-
HOTEL nial archway that gives the hotel an old-world atmosphere, making it one of the top choices in Habana Vieja. **Pros:** the colonial-style patio is one of the best in Habana Vieja; live piano music every night. **Cons:** the busy street front can be noisy; not all the guest rooms are up to par. $ *Rooms from: CUC$173* ✉ *Calle Obispo, esq. de Via Cuba, La Habana Vieja* ☎ *7862–4127* ⊕ *www.hotelfloridahavana.com* ⤴ *21 rooms, 4 suites* ⊠*| Breakfast.*

$$$ ⊞ **Hotel Marqués de Prado Ameno.** This 18th-century town house is a
HOTEL more private and tranquil property than others in the area—the inner courtyard's hanging tropical plants make it feel like a real private hide-away from the busy, crowded surrounding streets. **Pros:** an intimate environment in a unique architectural space; great on-site restaurant.

2

Cons: some of the rooms have no windows; rooms on the small side. ⑤ *Rooms from: CUC$173* ✉ *Calle O'Reilly 253, e/Cuba and Aguiar, La Habana Vieja* ☎ *7862–4127* ⊕ *www.habaguanexhotels.com* ⇨ *16 rooms* ⦿*Breakfast.*

$$$
HOTEL

Hotel Raquel. Majestic and regal best describes the hotel's elegant Baroque facade and impressive lobby, with its soaring marble columns and domed stained glass roof. **Pros:** lovely roof terrace with amazing city views; romantic option. **Cons:** some rooms have no windows; it can get a bit noisy early in the mornings; Internet isn't reliable. ⑤ *Rooms from: CUC$168* ✉ *Calle Amargura 103, esq. de San Ignacio, La Habana Vieja* ☎ *7860–8280* ⊕ *www.hotelraquel-cuba.com* ⇨ *25 rooms* ⦿*Breakfast.*

$$$
B&B/INN

Hotel San Miguel. Carrara-marble floors, intricate plaster carvings, and rich woodwork make this one of Habaguanex's best La Habana Vieja restoration projects; the discreet reception area is an architectural jewel. **Pros:** the terrace offers some of the best views of the harbor; a very private spot perfect for reading and relaxing; architectural details are breathtaking. **Cons:** the bathrooms are a bit on the small size; only decent views from the terrace. ⑤ *Rooms from: CUC$173* ✉ *Calle de Cuba 2, esq. de Peña de Pobre, La Habana Vieja* ☎ *7862–7656* ⊕ *www.habaguanexhotels.com* ⇨ *10 rooms* ⦿*Breakfast.*

$$$$
HOTEL

Hotel Santa Isabel. This 17th-century building is so stately that the Counts of Santovenia made it their home until 1867, when it became one of Habana Vieja's most elegant hotels; today, it's one of the neighborhood's most modern lodging options. **Pros:** rarely is a soul seen in the vast lobby, ensuring plenty of privacy; rooms have spectacular views of the harbor or Plaza de Armas. **Cons:** customer service can be on the poor side; the hotel tends to overbook and send people elsewhere upon arrival. ⑤ *Rooms from: CUC$272* ✉ *Plaza de Armas, Calle Baratillo 9, La Habana Vieja* ☎ *7860–8201* ⊕ *www.habaguanexhotels.com* ⇨ *17 rooms, 10 suites* ⦿*Breakfast.*

$$$
HOTEL

Palacio O'Farrill. Adjacent to Havana Bay and Cathedral Square, this hotel was once the house of Don Ricardo O'Farrill, descendant of an Irish man who made his fortune in the sugar trade. **Pros:** the changing architectural styles as you climb up through the hotel; central location. **Cons:** low water pressure and lukewarm temperatures in the showers; the breakfasts could do with an upgrade. ⑤ *Rooms from: CUC$173* ✉ *Calle Cuba 102, esq. de Calle Chacón, La Habana Vieja* ☎ *7860–5080* ⊕ *www.habaguanexhotels.com* ⇨ *38 rooms* ⦿*Breakfast.*

$$
RENTAL

Suite Havana. Until recently the only accommodations options available in Cuba were hotels and casas particulares; now, however, laws have been relaxed and Cubans are allowed to rent out whole apartments or houses. **Pros:** some of the best-quality accommodations you'll find in Havana; daily cleaning service and breakfast; central location. **Cons:** the street below can get a bit noisy. ⑤ *Rooms from: CUC$117* ✉ *Calle Lamparilla, 62 altos, e/Mercaderes y San Ignacio, La Habana Vieja* ☎ *7582–96524* ⊕ *www.suitehavana.com* ⇨ *2 rooms* ⦿*Breakfast* ▭ *No credit cards.*

CENTRO HABANA

Bustling Centro's hotels are a little more modern than those in Habana Vieja, but still iconic in their way, giving off a time-warped 1950s vibe. This is where local Cubans go about their everyday life giving you more of an insight into the Havana of today and its citizens. Most accommodations options here are situated around the lively Parque Central, where you can watch animated baseball debates, rent an old classic car, or go for a romantic horse-and-carriage ride around the city. You're also located within walking distance to the city's best museums and the atmospheric Paseo del Prado where you can walk down to the Malecón and the sea.

$
HOTEL

Hotel Caribbean. Although it's no Shangri-la, this budget option is ideally located on the border of La Habana Vieja and Centro. **Pros:** great location; rooms have a/c and private baths. **Cons:** the decor is very basic and not grand like some of the others; it's quite rundown. $ *Rooms from: CUC$40* ⊠ *Paseo de Martí (Prado) 164, Centro Habana* 🕾 *7860–8210* ⊕ *www.islazul.cu* ☜ *40 rooms* ❑ *Breakfast.*

$$
HOTEL
Fodor's Choice
★

Hotel Inglaterra. Inaugurated in 1875, this is Cuba's oldest hotel and there's much to admire here—photographs of old Havana, intricate Andalusian tiles, the shield of Spain's Catholic kings behind the bar. **Pros:** you can't beat the location of this hotel at the foot of La Habana Vieja; the patio has live music daily. **Cons:** room design and amenities are below standard, especially considering that this is a historic property. $ *Rooms from: CUC$129* ⊠ *Paseo del Prado 416, Centro Habana* 🕾 *7608–593* ⊕ *www.hotelinglaterra-cuba.com* ☜ *83 rooms* ❑ *Breakfast.*

$$
HOTEL

Hotel Plaza. There's something charming about the entrance way of the Plaza, despite its cavernous, tourist-packed hallways. **Pros:** historic Art Nouveau–style lobby; great roof terrace; plenty of drinking and dining options. **Cons:** rooms are a bit shabby and most have seen better days; some visitors have reported dirty rooms. $ *Rooms from: CUC$82* ⊠ *Calle Agramonte (Zulueta) 267, Centro Habana* 🕾 *7860–8583* ⊕ *www.hotelplazacuba.com* ☜ *188 rooms* ❑ *Breakfast.*

$$$$
HOTEL
Fodor's Choice
★

Hotel Saratoga. Located right across from the Capitolio and overlooking the Parque de la Fraternidad, this is easily the best international-class business hotel in Cuba. **Pros:** great amenities and services; Havana's most notable international-class business hotel; rooftop pool with Capitolio views. **Cons:** pool can get crowded. $ *Rooms from: CUC$240* ⊠ *Paseo de Prado 603, Centro Habana* 🕾 *7868–1000* ⊕ *www.hotel-saratoga.com* ☜ *96 rooms* ❑ *Breakfast.*

$$$$
HOTEL
Fodor's Choice
★

Iberostar Parque Central. This vast hotel, which is right on the park for which it's named, offers many modern creature comforts as well as a convenient location. **Pros:** it has a good business center with Internet; on-site cigar bar; great location on Parque Central. **Cons:** the busy neighborhood is loud and bustling. $ *Rooms from: CUC$261* ⊠ *Calle Neptuno, e/Paseo de Martí (Prado) y Calle Agramonte (Zulueta), Centro Habana* 🕾 *7860–6627* ⊕ *www.iberostar.com* ☜ *427 rooms* ❑ *Breakfast.*

$$
HOTEL

Mercure Hotel Sevilla. The setting for several episodes in Graham Greene's *Our Man in Havana*, this hotel is technically in Centro Habana but right on the edge of La Habana Vieja. **Pros:** superb view at the rooftop restaurant. **Cons:** food here is lamentable; the hotel's past is more glorious than its present. $ *Rooms from: CUC$143* ⊠ *Calle Trocadero 55, Centro Habana* ☎ *7860–8560* ⊕ *www.mercure.com* ⇲ *178 rooms* ⦿ *Breakfast.*

2

VEDADO

Leafy Vedado can provide a quiet respite from the hustle and bustle of Centro and Habana Vieja, where you can stroll along wide boulevards and pass magnificent crumbling mansions, without being hassled. Accommodations standards here are slightly higher than you'll find elsewhere in the city and well-known international chains own many of the hotels. Distances are farther and you'll have to take taxis to reach many of the city's most important sights and museums, however, you're also closer to some of the city's best restaurants and live-music venues.

$ ⛭ **Hotel Colina.** Set on and named for the famous hill occupied by the
HOTEL   Universidad de la Habana, the Colina has a down-at-the-heel 1950s-era charm and a drop or two of student (read: revolutionary) chic that seems to attract a predominately French clientele. **Pros:** good location; good value. **Cons:** hotel is somewhat hard to find. $ *Rooms from: CUC$55* ⊠ *Calle L, e/27 and Jovellar, Vedado* ☎ *7836–4071* ⊕ *www.islazul.cu* ⇲ *87 rooms* ⦿ *Breakfast.*

$$$$ ⛭ **Hotel Meliá Cohiba.** This mammoth glass-and-steel hotel looms over
HOTEL   the western end of the Malecón and has very little to do with the Havana of Baroque churches and colonial palaces, but it also rates among Cuba's best. **Pros:** the vast lobby is an impressive sight; Internet center. **Cons:** the hotel is a tad far from the city's core and major sights. $ *Rooms from: CUC$250* ⊠ *Calle Paseo, e/Calle 1 y Calle 3, Vedado* ☎ *7833–3636* ⊕ *www.melia-cohiba.com* ⇲ *342 rooms, 120 suites* ⦿ *Breakfast.*

$$$ ⛭ **Hotel Nacional.** Officially the Hotel Nacional de Cuba, this elegant
HOTEL   establishment recalls another era, as it's filled with memorabilia of such famous (and infamous) guests as Winston Churchill, Ava Gardner, Frank Sinatra, and Meyer Lansky—the Nacional still buzzes. **Pros:** more than a hotel, this property speaks to Cuba's history, and its past is symbolic; great bar; views from the clifftop garden are fantastic. **Cons:** has maintenance issues and is more run-down than it should be; thin walls between rooms. $ *Rooms from: CUC$175* ⊠ *Calle O y Calle 21, Vedado* ☎ *7836–3564* ⊕ *www.hotelnacionaldecuba.com* ⇲ *426 rooms, 16 suites* ⦿ *Breakfast.*

$$ ⛭ **Hotel ROC Presidente.** If the shady lobby bar and a refreshing bever-
HOTEL   age don't soothe your weary traveler's soul, then head immediately to your comfortable room overlooking the pool and the Straits of Florida beyond. **Pros:** close to government offices and on the edge of the Malecón; great restaurant; breakfast can't be beat. **Cons:** this property deserves higher standards of maintenance. $ *Rooms from: CUC$117* ⊠ *Av. de los Presidentes y Calzada (Av. 7), Vedado* ☎ *7838–1801* ⊕ *www.roc-hotels.com* ⇲ *158 rooms, 2 suites* ⦿ *Breakfast.*

$$ 🏨 **Hotel Victoria.** A few blocks from the Malecón, this Gran Caribe hotel
HOTEL may be modest, but it has much to recommend it. **Pros:** one of the few
smaller hotels in the area; free dance lessons are offered on Friday and
Saturday. **Cons:** the furniture has seen better days. $ *Rooms from:
CUC$91 ✉ Calle 19, No. 101, esq. de Calle M, Vedado ☎ 7833–3510
⊕ www.hotelvictoriacuba.com ✇ 31 rooms* ⦿ *Breakfast.*

$$ 🏨 **NH Capri La Habana.** Originally built in 1957, the hotel was once a
HOTEL famous hangout for mobsters and gangsters, but after a long period
of closure, it has undergone a complete renovation and re-opened in
2014 under the management of the Spanish NH hotel chain. **Pros:** it's
one of the few hotels that has reliable Internet; it's 100% non-smoking,
which makes a refreshing change from most Havana hotels. **Cons:** it's
a little far from most of the major Habana Vieja sights. $ *Rooms from:
CUC$140 ✉ Calle 21, e/Calles N y O, Vedado ☎ 7833–97200 ⊕ www.
nh-hotels.com ✇ 220 rooms* ⦿ *Breakfast.*

$$$ 🏨 **Tryp Habana Libre.** This high-rise monster is, at least, easy to find,
HOTEL even if it's not nice to look at, but rooms are functional and modern;
some offer astounding sea views, especially on the upper floors. **Pros:**
the hotel is squarely in central Vedado and on the main thoroughfare
leading into central Havana; large outdoor pool; great bars and restau-
rants. **Cons:** some visitors have reported dirty rooms. $ *Rooms from:
CUC$171 ✉ Calle 23 (La Rampa) y Calle L, Vedado ☎ 7834–6100
⊕ www.melia.com ✇ 572 rooms* ⦿ *Breakfast.*

MIRAMAR

With its wide avenues and glamorous homes, Miramar is Havana's
most modern neighborhood. Full of embassies, consulates, and houses
belonging to wealthy diplomats, you won't find any crumbling colonial
columns here. What you will find is newer hotels, with modern facilities
sea views, and large swimming pools, and excellent restaurants, pal-
adares, and nightlife spots. The down side? There are very few sights
in Miramar, and you can expect about a 20- to 30-minute taxi ride to
reach the major ones.

$ 🏨 **Château Miramar.** If you're looking for a smaller Miramar hotel,
HOTEL this is one of the most viable options. **Pros:** the only Miramar hotel
with charm and personality; close to the water. **Cons:** far from central
Havana; no shuttle. $ *Rooms from: CUC$47 ✉ Av. 1, e/Calle 60 y 70,
Miramar ☎ 7204–1952 ⊕ www.hotelescubanacan.com ✇ 41 rooms,
9 suites* ⦿ *Breakfast.*

$ 🏨 **Hotel Comodoro.** Although popular with package tours, the Como-
HOTEL doro isn't as impersonal as you might expect from a hotel that rou-
tinely houses hundreds of guests. **Pros:** located in a green, isolated,
and secluded part of Havana; four on-site restaurants. **Cons:** has some
maintenance issues and property could do with a makeover; far away
from major sights. $ *Rooms from: CUC$59 ✉ Av. 3 y Calle 84, Mira-
mar ☎ 7204–5551 ⊕ www.hotelescubanacan.com ✇ 251 rooms, 158
bungalows, 18 cabanas* ⦿ *Breakfast.*

$$$$ 🏨 **Hotel Meliá Habana.** Located in a distant corner of Havana, this is
HOTEL one of the city's stellar, modern properties frequented by business and

leisure travelers. **Pros:** offers a shuttle service to and from Old Havana several times daily; largest urban hotel swimming pool in Cuba. **Cons:** the bathroom fixtures are not as stellar as the property itself. $\boxed{\$}$ *Rooms from: CUC$211* $\boxtimes$ *Av. 3, e/Calles 76 and 80, Miramar* $\textcircled{\small{☎}}$ *7204–8500* $\oplus$ *www.melia-habana.com* $\rightleftharpoons$ *397 rooms* $\lvert \odot \rvert$ *Breakfast.*

$\$\$

HOTEL **H10 Habana Panorama.** A vast complex overlooking the Caribbean Sea, the hotel is close to the National Aquarium and is a few hundred meters from the Miramar Trade Center. **Pros:** this hotel offers a free shuttle service to Habana Vieja; has three on-site restaurants and two pools. **Cons:** like many hotels the lobby can get very smoky; the area by the water is very rocky and full of rubbish. $\boxed{\$}$ *Rooms from: CUC$110* $\boxtimes$ *Av. 3ra y Calle 70, Miramar* $\textcircled{\small{☎}}$ *7204–0100* $\oplus$ *www.h10hotels.com* $\rightleftharpoons$ *317 rooms* $\lvert \odot \rvert$ *Breakfast.*

PLAYAS DEL ESTE

If you want to get away from the city for a few days, without a long distance bus journey, the Playas del Este are an ideal option with all-inclusive resort-style hotels right on the beach front. Unfortunately, you might not get the highest quality in rooms or food, but you can't beat the location. Those who want to stay in casas particulares should head to Guanbo, where the largest concentration can be found.

$\$\$

HOTEL **Gran Caribe Club Hotel Atlántico.** It won't take your breath away, but this modern, all-inclusive hotel has acceptably furnished and equipped bungalows. **Pros:** best rooms have great Atlantic views; close to Havana. **Cons:** facilities are a bit outdated; the buffet is poor. $\boxed{\$}$ *Rooms from: CUC$110* $\boxtimes$ *Av. Las Terrazas, Playa Santa María del Mar* $\textcircled{\small{☎}}$ *7797–1085* $\oplus$ *www.gran-caribe.com* $\rightleftharpoons$ *92 bungalows* $\lvert \odot \rvert$ *All-inclusive.*

$\$\$

HOTEL **Hotel Memories Jibacoa.** This adults-only resort, now owned by the Memories hotel group, is one of Cuba's best. **Pros:** best beach resort close to Havana; beach is clean. **Cons:** beachfront is small and lacks privacy. $\boxed{\$}$ *Rooms from: CUC$148* $\boxtimes$ *Playa Arroyo Bermejo, Via Blanca, Santa Cruz del Norte* $\textcircled{\small{☎}}$ *4729–5122* $\oplus$ *www.memoriesresorts.com* $\rightleftharpoons$ *250 rooms* $\lvert \odot \rvert$ *All-inclusive.*

NIGHTLIFE AND PERFORMING ARTS

Music is a Cuban passion rivaled only by baseball and the Revolution itself. *Everyone* here knows who El Médico de la Salsa (The Salsa Doctor) is and what type of music he plays. Los Van Van, Beny Moré, and Compay Segundo are all celebrities on the order of Frank Sinatra, the Beatles, or Elvis. Caribbean, Spanish, African, and American rhythms have been combined to create more than three-dozen musical styles, which are themselves evolving into still more varieties. To experience the music of Cuba is to learn about it, and Havana offers plenty of opportunities for both. The city also has splashy cabaret revues as well as jazz haunts and cafés that offer quieter entertainment.

Dance performances—from traditional ballet to traditional Afro-Cuban—are also options. If your Spanish is good, you'll appreciate the active film, theater, and literary scenes. You don't need any Spanish to enjoy the art exhibited in Havana's many galleries. Attire at theaters and other venues ranges from cocktail dresses and jackets and ties to blue jeans and shorts. Tickets are nearly always available (check with your hotel concierge) at box offices and are very inexpensive by European or North American standards.

Cartelera, a Spanish-English weekly published by the Instituto Cubano del Libro and usually available free at major hotels, lists concerts, plays, and other artistic events. *Opciones* is another bilingual weekly publication with cultural listings. The *Programación Cultural,* published monthly in Spanish by the Oficina del Historiador de la Ciudad (Office of the City Historian), has what is probably the most complete schedule of events. Ask for a copy at Museo de la Ciudad in the Plaza de Armas.

NIGHTLIFE

HABANA VIEJA
BARS AND CAFÉS
Café Paris. This 24-hour standby usually offers entertainment by one of the city's excellent trios. No matter how many times you have heard "Guantanamera," these performers always give it new meaning. If you can't find much else going on in Havana Vieja at night, you can guarantee something will be happening here. This place has become so popular, in fact, that it's hard to find a seat either inside or out. ⊠ *Calle San Ignacio 22, esq. de Calle Obispo, La Habana Vieja* ☎ 7862–0466.

Café Taberna. Named after its one-time owner Juan Bautista Taberna, this was Havana's first café when it opened at the very same spot in 1772. The rhythms of in-house band Conjunto Roberto Faz and their guests are some of the best you'll hear in Havana Vieja. The tall ceilings, retro atmosphere, and impressive wooden cocktail bar give this resto-bar a notable place among Havana Vieja establishments. ■TIP→**Tickets for a dinner and performance must be booked in advance.** ⊠ *Calle Brasil/ Teniente Rey, esq. de Calle Mercaderes, La Habana Vieja* ☎ 7861–1637.

Dos Hermanos. Located next to the Museo del Ron, you'll step back in time when you walk through the door, and get the feel for life along the wharf. This, too, was once a Hemingway haunt, and it was also frequented at one time or another by Marlon Brando and Federico García Lorca. ⊠ *Av. del Puerto/Calle Desamparado/San Pedro y Calle Sol, La Habana Vieja* ☎ 7861–7845.

Fodor'sChoice
★ **El Floridita.** This time warp of a restaurant was known to have been a hangout of Ernest Hemingway and prides itself as being the "cradle of the daiquiri." In 1953, *Esquire* even dubbed the bar one of the seven most famous in the world. It's always jam-packed with tourists dancing away to a hot Cuban band any time of day or night. The atmosphere is dark and austere, with oversize waiters dressed in undersize red-and-white formal wear plying away daiquiris or other cocktails. A life-size sculpture of Hemingway overlooks the bar eternally. ⊠ *Calle Obispo 557, La Habana Vieja* ☎ 7867–1299 ⊕ *www.floridita-cuba.com.*

Factoría Cerveza Plaza Vieja. Situated right on the atmospheric Plaza Vieja, this place is always full (day or night), and there's usually some excellent live music. As the name suggests, this spot specializes in beer, which it brews itself. Choose from light, dark, black beer or malt served in large pint-size glasses or beer tubes, so that you can serve yourself right from your table. If you get a little peckish, check out the pizzas and salads, or meat from the outdoor grill. ✉ *Calle San Ignacio, esq. de Muralla, Plaza Vieja, La Habana Vieja* ☎ *7866–4453.*

La Bodeguita del Medio. Havana's best-known bar is a great place to hoist one for Hemingway. It's always packed with tourists looking expectantly toward the door as if Papa himself were about to swagger in and belly up to the bar. According to the man himself, this is *the*place to order a mojito, as seen by the author's quote written on the wall "My mojito in La Bodeguita, My daiquiri in El Floridita." In reality the mojitos are no better here than anywhere else, but it's the atmosphere that counts. There's also an upstairs restaurant serving up typical criollo fare. Walls here are pasted with visitors' notes and pictures of the many notables that have passed through over the years, including Nat King Cole and Harry Belafonte. ✉ *Calle Empedrado 207, La Habana Vieja* ☎ *7862–4498.*

La Lluvia de Oro. This is one of your best bets for late-night entertainment in Havana Vieja, even though these days it's mostly full of tourists. It's also always full of life and is a good starting point for a night on the town. Impromptu salsa dancing often breaks out here later on in the evening, too. ✉ *Calle Obispo 316, esq. de Calle Aguiar, La Habana Vieja* ☎ *7862–9870.*

Monserrate. This place hops all evening long, usually to the tune of a hot trio. Just across the road from here you'll see the Castillo del Farnés, where Fidel Castro used to hang out during his student days. It's not particularly notable for food or drinks, but is worth a look for historical reference. ✉ *Av. de la Bélgica/Misiones/Edigio/Monserrate, esq. de Calle Obrapía, La Habana Vieja* ☎ *7860–9751.*

Fodor's Choice
★

O'Reilly 304. For somewhere that's set firmly in the modern day (and to see what Havana's future is all about), head to O'Reilly 304, a funky gin and tapas bar set up by owner José Carlos. Downstairs is packed with locals and tourists, eyeing up the elaborate cocktails mixed by bartender Wilson Hernandez (among the best you'll see or taste anywhere in the world), while upstairs, surrounded by bare-brick walls, patrons enjoy innovative tapas dishes such as *ceviche*, *croquetas*, or tacos (between CUC\$3 and CUC\$6 per dish). ✉ *Calle O'Reilly 304, La Habana Vieja* ☎ *7612–425.*

Sloppy Joe's. In 1917, a Spaniard named José Abeal y Otero, who had worked in both Cuba and the United States for many years as a bartender, decided to open up his own business in an old Havana warehouse. Known for its messy service and lack of hygiene, it was dubbed Sloppy Joe's. As the years went on, and the establishment improved its appearance, and it became a haven for American businesspeople, eventually reaching legendary status and attracting celebrities such as Ava Gardner, Frank Sinatra, boxer Joe Louis, and yes, Hemingway, too. It was also here that Joe invented the sloppy joe—a sandwich filled with *ropa vieja* (shredded beef in Creole sauce). After the revolution, in 1960, the bar closed down and remained closed until 2013, when it was restored to its former glory. Today it's one of Havana Vieja's classiest establishments, and although cocktails are a little pricer than other venues, it makes a great stop for one or two. ⊠ *Calle Zuleta 252, e/Animas y Virtudes, Centro Habana* ☎ *7866–7157.*

VEDADO

BARS

Café Cantante "Mi Habana". On the upper edge of Vedado near the Plaza de la Revolución, this lively disco-bar often has musical performances and dance or comedy shows. It's very popular with locals and is a great place to experience nightlife away from the touristy Havana Vieja venues. ⊠ *Calle Paseo y Calle 39, Vedado* ☎ *7879–0710.*

Café Madrigal Bar. Housed upstairs in a stunning peach-color mansion in leafy Vedado, this quirky bohemian cocktail bar is something very different from the usual Havana venues. Its bare brick walls are filled with unusual artwork, old vintage cameras and rolls of film, and its dimly lighted tables make it both cozy and romantic. Sit at the back on the old comfy sofa or out on the atmospheric balcony with dazzling city views. Popular with both locals and visitors, it's open Tuesday–Sunday 6 pm–2 am. ⊠ *Calle 17, No. 809, e/Calles 2 y 4, Vedado* ☎ *7831–2433.*

El Gato Tuerto. Just steps from the Hotel Nacional, this dark and smoky bar offers live boleros-style music downstairs and a less than average restaurant upstairs. It can be a great option once the tunes get going later on into the night. ⊠ *Calle O, e/Calle 17 y Calle 19, Vedado* ☎ *7838–2696.*

Fabrica de Arte Cubano. Located in the same old oil factory as the restaurant El Cocinero, this place has quickly become one of Havana's hippest night spots. Open Thursday—Sunday from 8 pm to 4 am, an array of performances are scheduled from jazz and contemporary dance to theater, DJs, and exhibitions. There's also a wine-and-tapas bar and various intimate spaces to chill out. ⊠ *Calle 26, e/Calles 11 y 13, Vedado* ⊕ *www.fabricadeartecubano.com* ☜ *CUC$2.*

Piano Bar La Torre. This classy lounge offers giddy views and fabulous music from Wednesday to Sunday 9 pm–midnight. There's also a restaurant downstairs, which is open for lunch and dinner. ⊠ *Calle 17, e/ Calle M y Calle N, Vedado* ☎ *7838–3098.*

LIVE MUSIC

Cabaret Parisién. The ever-popular and always hopping Hotel Nacional, offers up another winning performance with its wild cabaret show. The lively show is followed by equally wild dancing by the audience. ■ TIP→ **If you don't want to fork out for the Tropicana, then this is the place to come.** The cover charge is CUC$35; CUC$50 gets you both dinner and the performance. ⊠ *Hotel Nacional, Calle O y Calle 21, Vedado* ☎ *7836–3663.*

Casa de la Música. Havana's best known and most popular night club and live-music venue is not to be missed. The club has two locations, one in Centro and one in Miramar; the Miramar location is a bit classier and more laid-back. They both attract big-name Cuban acts such as Los Van Van, however, they also perform reggaeton, boy-band Latin pop, and even electronica. Try to find out ahead of time who will be playing, so you're not disappointed. Entry prices vary from CUC$5 to CUC$25 depending on the band. ⊠ *Av. de Italia (Galiano), e/Concordia y Neptuno, Centro Habana* ☎ *7204–0447.*

Jazz Café. Situated in a shopping complex across the road from the Meliá Cohiba hotel is Havana's *other* jazz place, and a good one it is. The many jam sessions and the introduction of new jazz groups mean there's lots of improvisation and hot young musicians, as well as big-name acts. It acts like a jazz-cum-supper club, where tickets include dinner and a cover charge for the music. ⊠ *Galerías de Paseo, Calle Paseo y Calle 1, Vedado* ☎ *7862–6401* ⌨ *CUC$10.*

Jazz Club La Zorra y el Cuervo. Don't be alarmed. You must enter through an old English red phone box, before you descend into the city's premier jazz venue. Unlike most of Havana's music venues, the sounds make you snap your fingers and shake your head instead of everything else. Shows are held nightly, and the great-value CUC$10 cover includes two cocktails. ⊠ *Calle 23/La Rampa, e/Calle N y Calle O, Vedado* ☎ *7833–2402.*

MIRAMAR
BARS AND CLUBS
Casa de la Música Miramar. The Miramar branch of the famous Casa de la Música, also has excellent live bands. ⊠ *Av. 35, esq. de Calle 20, Playa* ☎ *7204–0447* ⌨ *CUC$5–CUC$25.*

LIVE MUSIC
Habana Café. In the downstairs lobby of the Hotel Meliá Cohiba, this nightclub and cabaret offers a show with a torrid mix of live music and red-hot dance performances. When the main performance is over, patrons and professional dancers both join in the fray. It also offers an à la carte menu from 9 pm to 2:30 am. ⊠ *Hotel Meliá Cohiba, Calle Paseo, e/Calle 1 y Calle 3, Vedado* ☎ *7833–3636.*

La Cecilia. This dinner and show spectacle has a feather-clad chorus, who dance to incandescent salsa. The place goes disco between and after performances and also hosts a lot of good bands. It's mainly frequented by tour groups. ⊠ *Av. 5, e/Calle 110 y Calle 112, Miramar* ☎ *7204–1562.*

Tropicana. Havana's most famous floor show, under the direction of Tomas Morales, is in a district just south of Miramar. Reserve a table (this place fills up fast), which comes with a bucket of ice for your half bottle of Havana Club, and you're set for the night. More than 200 gorgeous dancers picked from Cuba's many dance troupes are guaranteed to get your attention. The cover of CUC$75–CUC$95 per person(depending on seating) is astronomical for Cuba, but the lush, outdoor venue is unforgettable. The performance includes an array of vignettes, with the dancers adorned in sometimes wild, elaborate costumes including fruity-color feathers and headgear, and passionate music and dance reminiscent of the old world on the island. Shows are held daily at 9:30 pm, and when they finish, the place becomes a disco. ⊠ *Calle 72, e/Calle 43 y Calle 45, Marianao* ☎ *7267–1717* ⊕ *www. cabaret-tropicana.com* ⌨ *CUC$75–CUC$95.*

PERFORMING ARTS

DANCE, MUSIC, AND THEATER

Live Cuban music and dance performances are regularly held in the city's many cultural centers. Some of these centers also host more traditional music and dance shows as well as literary events, plays, and art exhibits. At UNEAC, for example, you can find everything from lectures to performances of Santería rituals. The Palacio del Segundo Cabo in the Plaza de Armas is another literary and artistic hub.

If your Spanish is good, try to take in a play. These are held not only in theaters and cultural centers but also in such surprising venues as the Museo de la Ciudad in the Palacio de los Capitanes Generales, the Casa Natal de José Martí, and the Museo de Arte Colonial.

Havana teems with dancers. Drop by the Escuela Provincial de Ballet (Provincial Ballet School) at Calle L and Calle 19 and have a look at the 220 little swans-in-training. Each year 45 of 800 nine-year-old applicants begin working here. After five years, some 15 of them (and those chosen from the six other provincial schools) make it to the new Escuela Nacional de Ballet (National Ballet School) at Calle Prado y Calle Trocadero, under the supervision of the Ballet Nacional de Cuba's director and prima ballerina, Alicia Alonso. Other large dance troupes include Christi Dominguez's Compañia de Ballet de la Televisión Cubana (Ballet Company of the Cuban Television Network), the Compañia de Dansa Contemporánea de Cuba (Cuban Contemporary Dance Company), and the Ballet Nacional Folklórico (National Folklore Ballet). Reinaldo Suarez's Danz-Art and Regla Salvent's Compañia de Dansa del Cuerpo Armónico are among the city's many small ensembles, along with Marianela Bovan's Danza Abierta and Rosario Cárdenas's Danza Combinatoria.

CULTURAL CENTERS

Casa de la Amistad. Housed in a stunning pink mansion in leafy Vedado, this is the place to come to hear excellent groups performing Afro-Cuban and other traditional music. It's open on Saturday night only and the cover charge depends on the band playing. ⊠ *Calle Paseo 406, esq. de Calle 17, Vedado* ☎ *7830–3114.*

Casa de la Comedia. has a full and ever-changing roster of events, including comedy shows, which take place on weekends at 7 pm. ⊠ *Calle Justiz 18, esq. de Calle Baratillo, La Habana Vieja* ☎ *7863–9282* ☑ *CUC$2.*

Casa de la Trova. This is a good place to hear traditional Cuban music and has a great authentic vibe. The best time to come is on Friday starting at 6 pm. ⊠ *Calle San Lázaro 661, e/Calle Gervasio y Calle Padre Varela/Belascoaín, Centro* ☎ *7879–3373.*

Dos Gardenias. This large complex, which also contains a variety of restaurants, always offers some type of musical event. The Video Bar is open from 10 pm and offers music and comedy nights for an entry fee of CUC$5, while the Salon Boleros opens nightly at 10 pm for boleros-style music. ⊠ *Av. 7 y Calle 26, Mindanao* ☎ *7204–2353.*

THEATERS

Teatro Amadeo Roldán. Home of the Sinfónica Nacional (National Symphony), which is currently directed by Enrique Perez Mesa, the performances here are much better than the ages and outfits of the musicians (who look for all the world like a high school band) would suggest. Listen to them deal with Handel's *Water Music* or Prokofiev's 7th, especially the allegro movements. ⊠ *Calzada, e/Calle D y Calle E, Vedado* ☎ *7832–4521.*

Teatro Julio Antonio Mella. Home of the Danza Contemporánea de Cuba, this is the standard venue for contemporary theater, as well as for dance. ⊠ *Calle Línea/Calle 7, No. 657, esq. de Calle A, Vedado* ☎ *7833–5651.*

Teatro Nacional. Cuba's most important theater is used for classical music and ballet performances, as well as for contemporary theater and dance productions. ⊠ *Plaza de la Revolución, Calle Paseo y Calle 39, Vedado* ☎ *7878–0711.*

Teatro Trianon. This theater stages plays by contemporary playwrights. ⊠ *Calle Línea e/Calle Paseo y Calle A, Vedado* ☎ *7830–9648.*

SHOPPING

Until recent times, shopping lists in Cuba were short: *puros habanos* (cigars) and rum. In recent years the availability of an increasing number of products on the market has changed the landscape. While prices are prohibitive to most locals, even cellular phones are now available to Cubans. The result of a slow-but-sure openness has also resulted in more shopping opportunities for tourists.

Look for *muñequitas,* little dolls representing orishas. Handmade goods—from wood and leather items to terra-cotta pieces—cinema posters and other graphics, musical instruments, and photographs from the Revolutionary period also make interesting buys. The light-cotton men's shirt known as the *guayabera* is Cuba's national garment, worn by everyone from taxi drivers to El Comandante himself. Practical (side pockets) and elegant (embroidered), the guayabera is worn loose (not tucked in) for coolness, and is considered flattering to middle-age figures.

The state agencies ARTEX and Fondo de Bienes Culturales have shops throughout Havana that sell postcards, books, CDs, cassettes, rum, cigars, and crafts. *La Habana: Touristic and Commercial Guide,* a booklet published by Infotur, lists the locations of the city's many Tiendas Panamericanas, which sell toiletries and other basic items.

Bargaining is expected, but unlike shopkeepers in other countries where this is true, Cubans ask very low prices to begin with and don't move far. It generally feels better to pay the extra dollar or two. At this juncture, it means a lot more in Cuban hands than in yours.

HABANA VIEJA

CLOTHING

Quitrín. Set up some 30 years ago by the Federation of Cuban Women, this successful shop now has a number of outlets throughout Cuba. It sells off-the-rack guayaberas, as well as linen and cotton dresses and pants. ⊠ *Calle Obispo 161, esq. de San Ignacio, La Habana Vieja* ☎ *7862–0810.*

GIFTS AND SOUVENIRS

Habana 1791 Aromas Coloniales. More like a working museum than a shop, this unique fragrance store sells a range of scents created from natural products all found in Cuba. Peruse the rows of old bottles and then head back into the gorgeous fountain-filled patio to view the working laboratory, where the perfumes are still created. ⊠ *Calle Mercaderes 156, La Habana Vieja* ⊗ *Mon.–Sat. 10–7, Sun. 11–2.*

Longina Música. Located on the pedestrianized Calle Obispo, this shop sells an excellent selection of music and Cuban musical instruments. ⊠ *Calle Obispo 360, e/Habana y Compostela, La Habana Vieja* ☎ *7862–8371.*

Palacio de la Artesanía. For tobacco, rum, Cuban music, and all manner of crafts, don't miss this unique shopping mall, housed in the 18th-century colonial Palacio de Pedroso. ⊠ *Calle de Cuba 64, e/Calle Cuarteles y Peña Pobre, La Habana Vieja* ⊗ *Daily 10–7.*

Piscolabis. A unique gift and souvenir shop located in between Plaza de Armas and Plaza Catedral, Piscolabis sells an eclectic range of jewelry, glasswork, wood carvings, and metalwork. It also serves great coffees, so that you can sit down and relax in between browsing. ⊠ *Calle San Ignacio 75, La Habana Vieja* ☎ *7284–0355.*

Fodor's Choice ★ **Taller Experimental de Grafica.** In the small alleyway just off Plaza Catedral, this vast workshop, which started in 1962, is one of the best places to buy unique artwork in Havana. Watch the printmakers and artists at work and then head into the shop to choose your very own piece. ⊠ *Callejón del Chorro 62, La Habana Vieja* ☎ *7862–0979* ⊗ *Weekdays 9–4.*

MARKETS

Fodor's Choice ★ **Almacenes de San José.** Havana's biggest and best craft market is in an old shipping warehouse, next to the water in Havana Vieja. It's a rabbit-warren-like maze filled with all manner of handicrafts, from carvings and jewelry to paintings, leather work, and touristy Che merchandise. There are also toilets and a few food and drink stalls. ⊠ *Av. Desampardos y San Ignacio, La Habana Vieja* ⊗ *Mon.–Sat. 10–6.*

SPECIALTY SHOPS

Casa del Habano Hotel Conde de Villanueva. Located on the first floor of the Hotel Conde de Villanueva, this classic old cigar shop is the place to stock up, selling a full array of Habanos' offerings. With its cozy velvet chairs and old-fashioned bar, it's also the perfect place to escape the heat and bustle of the street and hideaway for a quiet smoke and a coffee. ⊠ *Calle Mercaderes 202, e/Calle Lamparilla y Amargura, La Habana Vieja* ☎ *7862–9293* ⊕ *www.habaguanex.com.*

HABANA CENTRO

SPECIALTY SHOPS

La Casa del Habano Partagás. Although the cigar factory itself has moved to another location, there's still a good cigar shop on the premises. Its knowledgeable staff sell a wide selection of cigars and tobacco, and there's also a small bar inside where you can enjoy a coffee or a mojito with your smoke. ⊠ *Calle Industria 520, e/Calle Dragones y Barcelona, Centro Habana* ☎ *7866–8060.*

VEDADO

MARKETS

Ferria 23 y M. This excellent and eclectic handicraft market is very near the Hotel Nacional and is open weekdays 9–5, selling anything from souvenirs, paintings, and clothes to locally produced jewelry. ⊠ *Av. 23 y M, Vedado.*

MIRAMAR

SPECIALTY SHOPS

Casa de la Música. This small store is attached to the Miramar Casa de la Música nightclub and sells CDs and musical instruments. ⊠ *Calle 20, No. 3309, esq. de Av. 35, Miramar* ☎ *7204–0447.*

Casa del Habano, La Quinta. The many locations of the ubiquitous tobacco emporium make shopping for tobacco convenient. ⊠ *Av. 5, No. 1407, e/Calles 14 y 16, Miramar* ☎ *7209–4040.*

La Maison. The evening fashion shows (10 pm) here will knock your eyes out—more for the human display than for the textiles—and the luxury clothing is on sale duty-free. They also have a good selection of guayaberas. Entry to the fashion shows costs CUC$10. ⊠ *Calle 16, No. 701, esq. de Av. 7, Miramar* ☎ *7204–1541* ⊕ *www.netssa.com/lamaison.htm.*

SPORTS AND THE OUTDOORS

BASEBALL

Cuba, a recognized baseball powerhouse, has teams capable of beating Major League U.S. clubs, as the Cuban National Team's 12–5 victory over the Baltimore Orioles (in Baltimore) amply demonstrated in May 1999. To watch Cubans play baseball is to see poetry and passion in motion.

Estadio Latinoamericano. Top league teams play from November through May in the 55,000-seat Estadio Latinoamericano . Find out from your hotel's concierge when the games are scheduled or visit the website. Tickets are cheap. ⊠ *Calle Zequeira 312, Cerro, Vedado* ☎ *7870–6576* ⊕ *www.baseballdecuba.com.*

FISHING

Marina Hemingway. About 20 minutes southwest of Havana the marina's home to the Ernest Hemingway International Marlin Tournament each May and June. Here you can arrange fishing, yachting, diving, and snorkeling trips—regardless of your level of skill or your budget. Scuba diving costs from CUC$30 per dive (there are discounts if you book multiple dives), and snorkeling excursions go for CUC$35. A two-hour, deep-sea fishing outing in the Gulf Stream will cost CUC$40 and CUC$15 for every additional hour, and a fish-trolling excursion will cost CUC$120 for four hours. Yacht rentals range from CUC$250 to CUC$300 a day to CUC$2,000 to CUC$3,000 a week. ⊠ *Calle 248 y Av. 5, Santa Fé* ☎ *7204–6653* ⊕ *www.hemingwayyachtclub.org.*

Marina Tarará/Club Naútica. July sees the Old Man and the Sea Fishing Tournament, and the staff at this marina can fill you in on this competition. They also charter boats and run diving, snorkeling, and deep-sea fishing excursions in the Gulf Stream. ⊠ *Calle 5, e/Calle 2 y Calle Cobre, Playas del Este, Playa Tarará* ☎ *796–0242.*

GOLF

Club de Golf Habana. The club is a 15-minute (and roughly CUC$20) taxi ride south of downtown Havana. Though a little rough, the course offers a good walk in the sun, and the swimming pool and "Hole 19" bar are both good places to relax after a round. Clubs and caddies are available at an extra cost, if you require them. If you'd like to play, call ahead to be sure there's not a tournament on. ⊠ *Carretera de Vento, Km 8, Habana del Este* ☎ *7845–4578* ▣ *CUC$20 for 9 holes* ⅄ *9 holes, par 35.*

WESTERN CUBA

Updated
by Dorothy
MacKinnon

From the westernmost, pristine strands of María la Gorda to Varadero's internationally popular white-sand beaches; from the castaway islands of the southern Archipiélago de los Canarreos to the vertebral Cordillera de Guaniguanico— Western Cuba holds a wide range of geographical treasures. Both the Valle de Viñales with its distinctive *mogotes* (limestone hillocks) and the bird-filled wetlands of the Península de Zapata are quintessential Cuban destinations.

Western Cuba's provinces of Matanzas, Artemisa, and Pinar del Río, along with the Municipio Especial (Special Municipality) Isla de la Juventud, offer attractions that range from the traditional tobacco plantations of Viñales to the cosmopolitan beaches of Varadero to the wilds and wetlands on the Península de Zapata. In addition, pristine beaches and nonpareil diving opportunities can be found off—among other spots—Cayo Levisa, the Península de Guanahacabibes, Cayo Largo, and the Zapata Peninsula.

Traveling west from Havana, there's little in the way of distraction until you reach Las Terrazas nature reserve in tiny Artemisa Province. Next up is Pinar del Río, Cuba's prime tobacco-growing country. The dramatically scenic Valle de Viñales (Viñales Valley) is famous for its curious *mogotes* (hillocks), freestanding limestone formations from the Jurassic era, sheltering huge caves surrounded by *hoyos* (holes), valleys, or depressions filled with rich red soil ideal for the cultivation of tobacco. Far to the west, the Península de Guanahacabibes is a UNESCO-classified nature preserve on the Straits of Yucatán and a prime diving and snorkeling site.

To the east of Havana, you pass through the country's newest province of Mayabeque—notable only for its workaday sugar refineries, offshore oil wells, and rum factories—on the way to Matanzas Province. The capital city, Matanzas, once dubbed "the Athens of Cuba" for its artistic and literary lights, is now enjoying a slow, but steady renaissance after decades of neglect. To the east of the city is Cuba's premier beach resort—Varadero, a glittering, sandy paradise studded with all-inclusive, resort hotels. On the slender Península de Hicacos, Varadero has yacht marinas, a golf course, discotheques and cabarets, and miles of silver sands. The once-prosperous town of Cárdenas, southeast of Varadero, is worth visiting to gain some insight into Cuba's recent political history and to witness some of its former architectural glories.

On the far south shore of the province, the Península de Zapata is an ornithologist's and diver's paradise, with wildlife-rich wetlands, sandy beaches, coral reefs and limestone sinkholes filled with brightly colored fish. Playa Girón, at the mouth of Baía de Cochones (Bay of Pigs), attracts divers, too, as well as Cold War history buffs.

TOP REASONS TO GO

Beaches. Dazzling, white-sand beaches in Varadero, Pinar del Río, the Zapata Peninsula and in the Archipiélago de Canarreos vary from virtual outdoor discotheques to vast strands all but devoid of human life.

Scuba Diving and Snorkeling. Cuba is becoming one of the Caribbean's great diving and snorkeling destinations, with coral reefs, underwater caves, and sunken shipwrecks to explore, as well as aquatic life that includes 900 species—from rays and barracudas to triggerfish.

A Plethora of Resorts. The contemporary resorts of Varadero and Cayo Largo are hermetically sealed vacation paradises, catering variously to party-loving singles, active families, comfortable retirees, and affluent hedonists lapping up luxury. Water sports, golf, spas, dance, and Spanish classes are just some of the activities to choose from.

Iconic Scenery. The massive Cordillera de Guaniguanico mountain range encompasses some of the most scenic landscapes in Cuba: the dramatic Soroa waterfall, the evergreen Terrazas nature preserve, and the enchanting Valle de Viñales.

Working Plantations. Tobacco and coffee plantations have vied for supremacy for centuries in Pinar del Río province, traditionally one of Cuba's most backward regions. Visiting these economically crucial plantations gives you an insight into Cuba's history and culture, as well as some tasting opportunities.

Almost 100 km (62 miles) south of the mainland lies the Isla de la Juventud, the largest island in the Archipiélago de los Canarreos. Apart from some pre-Columbian cave paintings and a few beaches and dive sites, the hard-to-reach island is not a major tourist destination. With its history as a penal colony, the island's major interest is political, specifically the Presidio Modelo (Model Jail), where a young Fidel Castro spent 18 months and penned his famous "La Historia me absolverá" ("History will absolve me") speech. The main tourist activity lies offshore, to the east of the main island, on Cayo Largo, with its own airport and a string of all-inclusive beach resorts.

ORIENTATION AND PLANNING

GETTING ORIENTED

Caves, beaches, underwater reefs and wrecks, flora and fauna—from hummingbirds to whale sharks—all abound in Western Cuba. Pinar del Río's *vegas* (tobacco fields), the mogotes of Viñales, the Robinson Crusoe-esque simplicity of Cayo Levisa's virgin beaches, the faded glory of the city of Matanzas, and Varadero's long string of all-inclusive hotels are all worlds unto themselves. The swampy Península de Zapata, with its crabs, crocodiles, and endemic birds, and the dive sites near María la Gorda, Playa Girón, and the Isla de la Juventud offer quieter pleasures.

Pinar del Río Province. A short distance west of Havana, this province attracts nature lovers for its pine-forested mountains, nature preserves, and plantations. Settled in the 18th century, the province was built on a mixture of tobacco, sugar, and coffee plantations.

Archipielago de los Canarreos. Isla de la Juventud caters less to tourism and isn't easy to visit. Nearby Cayo Largo does have direct flights from Havana, giving access to a few upmarket resorts and dive sites on a par with Varadero and the northern Cayos.

Matanzas Province. Cross the impressive, arched Bacunayagua Bridge, the highest in Cuba, and you are at the western boundary of the province that is home to Cuba's best-known resort town, Varadero. Of the 4 million visitors to Cuba annually, 1 million head for Varadero. Matanzas, the faded, but once-elegant, capital, is known as the city of bridges—28 in total—while Cárdenas, a little to the east, is famous for its horse-drawn carriages, which are still the main mode of public transport.

PLANNING

WHEN TO GO

La Seca is the February–to–April dry period in Cuba's western and central zones; with temperatures down to 25°C–27°C (77°F–81°F) and rains scarce, this is a good time to go. Peak vacation times in spots such as Cayo Largo and Varadero fall during Christmas and Easter breaks, when package-tour groups fly in from all over the world. If people-watching and partying are what you're looking for, this is the time to come. If not, visit in November, early December, or early May. Reserve early for Easter and Christmas.

PLANNING YOUR TIME

Apart from the popular Varadero beach hotels where every detail from airport pickup to daily activities is organized for you, exploring the remoter areas of Western Cuba requires an adventurous spirit and a laid-back attitude. Pinar del Río Province is best explored from a base in the town of Viñales, which has reliable, comfortable bus service from Havana, lots of lodging options, and a wide choice of restaurants. The best way to independently explore the countryside around the town is by bicycle or on a guided walking tour. Allow two to three days here to absorb the bucolic beauty of the landscape. Most tourists see the Zapata Peninsula on a whirlwind, guided bus tour. To really get the most out of the peninsula's national park, you should base yourself in Playa Girón or Playa Larga and hire a naturalist guide. Try for a stay of two days here to get an early-morning start on a bird-watching or wildlife walk.

The easiest option is to book a week's stay at an all-inclusive Varadero hotel and take daily, guided tours to diving and snorkeling sites on the Zapata Peninsula, and city tours of Matanzas and Cárdenas. A more interesting option is to relax at the beach for a week, then add a night or two in Matanzas, staying at the exquisitely restored Hotel E Velasco, taking in a concert at the Teatro Sauto, or attending a ball game at the Palacio de los Cocodrilos.

GETTING HERE AND AROUND

AIR TRAVEL

Some international charter flights go directly to Varadero and Cayo Largo, mostly from Canada and Europe. From Havana, there are short-hop flights to Cayo Largo, Varadero, Isla de la Juventud, and Pinar del Río.

Pinar del Río's airport, Aeropuerto Álvaro Barba, is 2 km (1 mile) north of town. The airport serving Varadero—Aeropuerto Juan Gualberto Gómez—is 16 km (10 miles) west of the peninsula.

BUS TRAVEL

Bus service to Western Cuba from other parts of the mainland is the cheapest way to travel. Buses between the Varadero station and Havana's Terminal Ómnibus are quick and frequent. Most tourists choose air-conditioned Víazul buses for comfort and reliable service.

■ TIP→ Be sure to allow plenty of time between connections because even these buses do not always stay on schedule.

Bus Information Varadero Station. ⊠ Autopista Sur y Calle 36 ☎ 4529–1473 station on hwy., 4566–3396 at Varadero airport. **Viazul Bus.** ⊕ www.viazul.com.

CAR TRAVEL

The Autopista Nacional, a multilane, central artery designated A-1, connects all points in Western Cuba. For speed and safety, this is undoubtedly the best route to take, although the Carretera Central (Central Highway)—a standard two-lane highway that traverses the Cuban mainland from one end to the other—is more scenic, winding through little towns and villages. The road to take between Havana, Matanzas, and Varadero is the Vía Blanca, a four-lane freeway in even better condition than the A-1. The Carretera 3-1-16 (also known as Carretera de la Ciénaga de Zapata) connects the Autopista Nacional A-1 at Australia with Playa Girón.

Provincial roads in Western Cuba are usually in fair to good condition, though even the Autopista Nacional, the island's greatest freeway, has occasional heaves and holes and should never be driven at high speeds. Stray animals, horse-drawn carts, hitchhikers, and (on the Península de Zapata) migratory crabs are the worst driving hazards. There are no toll roads.

Gasoline availability is generally good with stations distributed around Matanzas, Havana, and Pinar del Río Provinces. The only ones *not* to pass without filling up are at the town of Isabel Rubio in western Pinar del Río Province and at Australia, the turnoff for the Península de Zapata.

Outside Varadero and Nueva Gerona, car rentals are difficult to arrange. They're available in the town of Pinar del Río and Playa Girón.

Car Rental Contacts **Transtur.** ☎ 4561–4410 in Varadero, 8277–1454 in Pinar del Río ⊕ www.transtur.cu.

TAXI TRAVEL

A taxi between Havana and Matanzas takes about an hour and costs CUC$120, or whatever you can negotiate. Try to negotiate the fare to CUC$75; it's only 100 km (62 miles). Taxis around Western Cuba are generally available between major points, though rates can be high.

Most drivers will ask for about one convertible peso per kilometer for travel within a city or town or small area. In Pinar del Río, tourist taxis can be arranged at the Hotel Pinar del Río. In the town of Varadero, taxis wait outside the Hotel Cuatro Palmas; the fare from one end of the peninsula to the other shouldn't exceed CUC$10. In Matanzas, taxis are available at the Plaza de la Vigía.

In Nueva Gerona, taxis gather at the corner of Calles 32 and 39, while horse-drawn buggies wait at the ferry terminal; the fare for a buggy to a hotel should be about CUC$2. In Cárdenas, which has almost no cars, a horse-drawn carriage is the way to go.

TRAIN TRAVEL

Trains run three or four times a week, between Havana and Pinar del Río. Book well ahead, because trains are often booked solid, especially around peak holiday times. There is train service between Havana and Matanzas on the slow, electric Hershey train. It's more of an excursion than a reliable way to get to Matanzas.

RESTAURANTS

Dining in the provincial capitals and towns is spotty; some places are acceptable while others seem fortunate to be able to provide nourishment at all. Pinar del Río for example, has no notable restaurants. Varadero has several good Italian, Chinese, criollo, and international options; buffets in hotels tend to be mediocre but the more luxurious resorts offer more sophisticated fare in their à la carte restaurants. You have to go off the beaten path to find such local specialties as crocodile tail (said to be an aphrodisiac) in the Zapata Peninsula, roast pork on the Isla de la Juventud, and lobster at María la Gorda.

Reservations aren't necessary, except in Varadero—especially at the upscale restaurants. Tipping is important to Cubans; an extra CUC here or there is much appreciated.

HOTELS

There are luxurious hotels in Varadero and Cayo Largo, a couple of charming hotels around Viñales, adequate accommodations at María la Gorda, and one ecologically sensitive hotel in the reserve around Soroa. Lodging on the Península de Zapata ranges from simple farms *bohíos* (thatch-roof cabins) to a few basic beach hotels around Playa Girón. In towns and cities outside Havana, rooms are available in *casas particulares* (private houses), though quarters may be cramped and basic. In Viñales, almost every third house in town is now a casa particular.

Hotel reviews have been shortened. For full information, visit Fodors. com.

WHAT IT COSTS IN CUBAN CONVERTIBLE PESOS			
$	**$$**	**$$$**	**$$$$**
Restaurants under CUC$12	CUC$12–CUC$20	CUC$21–CUC$30	over CUC$30
Hotels under CUC$75	CUC$75–CUC$150	CUC$151–CUC$200	over CUC$200

Restaurant prices are the average cost of a main course at dinner, or, if dinner is not served, at lunch. Hotel prices are the lowest cost of a standard double room in high season.

TOURS

Most hotels have a tour desk offering local tours, operated by the countrywide, state-owned tour companies. (⇨ *See Travel Smart*).

NEXUS Tours. With more than 20 years of experience organizing tours for Canadian visitors, this reliable company understands North American expectations and can arrange everything from transfers to hotels to sightseeing bus or adventure tours to nights out on the town throughout Western Cuba and beyond. Their attention to detail and professionalism outshine the Cuban government tour operators. They also have excellent bilingual guides, who are well versed in local history. The head office is in Varadero, conveniently close to all the popular hotels. There are also NEXUS tour desks in some Varadero hotels. ✉ *Varadero* ☎ *4566–2970* ⊕ *www.nexustours.com.*

Paradiso. With the slogan "Get to know Cuba through its culture," this government-run agency has offices in Western Cuba in Viñales, Pinar del Río, and Varadero. Their new website features news of cultural events in Cuba, describes their culture-based tours, and lists all the contact information for their offices throughout Cuba. ✉ *Calle 26 No. 106, e/ Calle 1 y Calle 3, Matanzas* ☎ *4561–2506* ⊕ *www.paradiso.cu.*

VISITOR INFORMATION

Infotur has offices in the town of Pinar del Río, Varadero, and Boca de Guamá in the Zapata Peninsula. Look for Cubanatur offices in the main hotels of the major towns and cities in Western Cuba, all of which also serve as de facto tourist-information offices.

PINAR DEL RÍO PROVINCE

Settled during the early 18th century (relatively late in the Spanish colonial era), this province was dubbed La Cenicienta, or Cinderella, for its reputation as a newcomer and for its poverty and good-heartedness. Depending on which view of the Cuban mainland's shape you prefer, the province forms either the head of the crocodile or the tail of the shark. Once the home of the Guanahatabey aboriginal people, the region was taken over by the Ciboney in their flight from the Taíno civilization that dominated until the arrival of the Spanish.

Tobacco, sugar, and coffee plantations have been rival influences in what has remained one of Cuba's lesser developed regions. Famous as the producer of the world's finest tobacco leaves, the area spawned the

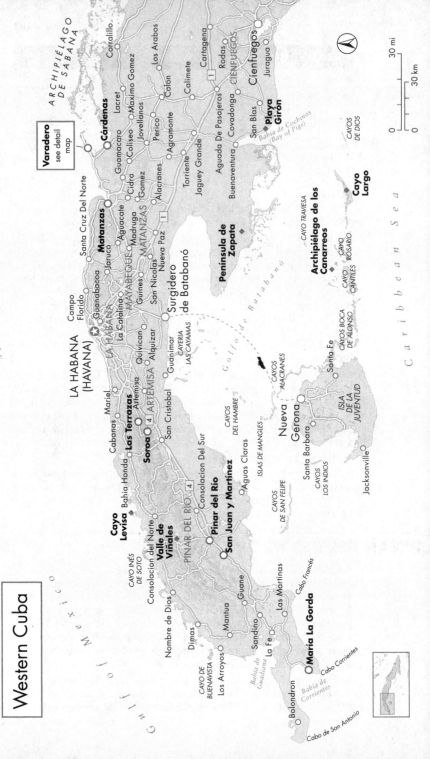

stereotype of the typical *pinareño* (native of Pinar del Río): a straw-hatted, oxen-driving *guajiro* (peasant) with a drooping mustache and a home-rolled cigar clenched between his teeth. On the positive side, pinareños are also reputed to be noble and simple citizens with an extraordinary capacity for hard work and generosity. Be prepared to be invited into homes for anything from sweet black coffee to black beans and rice.

The province's spine is the Cordillera de Guaniguanico, a 160-km (99-mile) -long mountain range. The Valle de Viñales is Pinar del Río's most scenic tobacco country, with a patchwork of fields interwoven among the odd limestone outcroppings, reminiscent of Chinese landscape paintings. The best tobacco, however, is grown in Vuelta Abajo, literally, "turn down"—so called, according to one theory, for its location southwest of the provincial capital. The pine-forested mountain retreats around Las Terrazas and Soroa draw day visitors from nearby Havana. At the westernmost part of the province, the beaches, coral reefs, and dive sites at María la Gorda attract visitors, along with the reptile life and bird migration corridor in the Guanahacabibes Peninsula UNESCO biosphere reserve.

GETTING HERE AND AROUND
The best way to get to the on-island destinations in this region is by Víazul buses, which are comfortable, air-conditioned, and cost-effective. It is about CUC$6 from Havana to Las Terrazas and CUC$12 to Viñales.

SOROA AND LAS TERRAZAS

75 km (47 miles) southwest of Havana.

Known for its exquisite orchid and botanical garden and its 22.5-meter (75-feet) waterfall, El Salto, Soroa has been dubbed "El Arco de Cuba" for the rainbow that sometimes hovers over the falls. The area is a good place to take a walk in the woods or a tour of the agricultural community of Las Terrazas, 17 km (11 miles) east of Soroa and part of a biosphere reserve established by UNESCO in 1985. You can have lunch in the community or spend a night at the ecological retreat Hotel Moka. The area is named for the terraces that were originally carved into the forested slopes by French coffee planters who came from Haiti at the end of the 18th century. The *terrazas* are now tiers of workers' and artisans' living quarters, along with craft shops and restaurants.

GETTING HERE AND AROUND
Coming from Havana, you will reach Las Terrazas and the Hotel Moka first, just over the border in Artemisa Province. After leaving the Autopista Nacional at the well-marked turnoff at Km 51, pass through the toll gate 4 km (2½ miles) north and continue into the park (CUC$7 entrance fee). Soroa can be reached via the mountain road through the reserve or from the autopista turnoff at Km 80.

EXPLORING
Fodor's Choice
★

Jardín Botanico Orquideario Soroa. Covering 35,000 square meters, this hillside botanical garden is a wild tangle of flowering vines, fragrant gingers, waist-high begonias and epiphyte-laden trees growing out of rocks. The centerpiece is a tidy greenhouse filled with blooming orchids. Back in the 1940s, a wealthy Havana lawyer and orchid fancier hired a Japanese gardener to design this glorious garden in his daughter's memory. Stone pathways bordered by plant-covered rocky outcroppings wind uphill to a lookout. The footing is a little precarious and the garden is quite wild, but beautiful. Birds abound, so be sure to bring along binoculars. The garden is also a study center for budding botanists and there is an expert guide on hand. ⊠ *Carretera de Soroa, Km 7, Soroa* ⊹ *Next door to Hotel Villa Soroa* ☎ *4852–3871* 🖂 *Entrance fee CUC$3, additional CUC$1 to bring camera or CUC$2 to bring in a video camera* ☉ *Daily 8:30–4:30.*

WHERE TO EAT

$ ✕ **Eco-Restaurante El Romero.** A rarity in carnivorous Cuba, this is a vegetarian restaurant with an innovative take on local organic and wild ingredients. You enter under a green arbor smothered by blue flowers and descend a few steps to an intimate, two-tier restaurant with a valley view. On the menu: tempura vegetables, creative salads, a bean pancake accompanied by a stuffed tomato, or the house specialty: "*boliche*," mashed yuca and sweet potato balls filled with vegetables in a cream sauce. There's also a vegetable paella. Portions come in three sizes for different-size appetites: small, medium, and large, and are priced accordingly, making it easy to sample and share. ⑤ *Average main: CUC$10* ⊠ *Main road, below Hotel La Moka, Las Terrazas* ☎ *4857–8555* ⊟ *No credit cards.*

VEGETARIAN

$ ✕ **Restaurante El Salto.** This riverside terrace restaurant overlooks the footbridge that leads to the famous waterfall. The idyllic setting and river view make up for an uninspiring menu of simple Cuban fare featuring chicken and the house specialty, *Soroa Tentación,* a stew of shredded beef with tomatoes, onion, and garlic. The house drink, the daiquiri *cascada,* is made of various colors of alcohol, in honor of the rainbow that often appears over the falls. The entrance fee to climb the 250-meter path to the waterfall is CUC$3. Unfortunately, the waterfall is usually dry by April, before the rainy season begins. ⑤ *Average main: CUC$7* ⊠ *Carretera de Soroa, Km 8, Soroa* ⊹ *Just south of Hotel Villa Soroa* ☎ *4582–2122* ⊟ *No credit cards.*

CUBAN

WHERE TO STAY

$$ ⛺ **Hotel Moka.** On the highest forested part of Las Terrazas Biosphere Reserve, this "ecologically" designed hotel makes its point with a huge carob tree growing in the lobby, its branches escaping through skylights. **Pros:** good restaurant; verdant terraces; bathtubs. **Cons:** wine list at restaurant is pricey; extra charge for Wi-Fi. ⑤ *Rooms from: CUC$120* ⊠ *Km 51 , Autopista a Pinar del Río, Communida Las Terrazas, Las Terrazas* ☎ *4857–8600* ⊕ *www.hotelmoka-lasterrazas.com* ⊟ *No credit cards* 🛏 *42 rooms* ⦿ *Breakfast.*

HOTEL
FAMILY

SPORTS AND THE OUTDOORS

Exploring the Sierra del Rosario can provide a day or two of exercise and fresh air. Guides are available for nature hikes (expect to pay about CUC$3 per hour per person, three people maximum). From Las Terrazas, the trails called La Delicias and La Serafina are the two most beautiful, each about 4 km (2½ miles) or two hours long. El Salto, the waterfall, is accessed from Soroa via a concrete stairway leading down from the well-marked Bar Edén. The so-called Baños Romanos (Roman Baths) are below the falls.

BIRD-WATCHING AND HIKING

Villa Soroa. To arrange guided hikes and bird-watching in Soroa, contact the Villa Soroa. There are morning and afternoon birding hikes (8–10:30 am and 3–5:30 pm; CUC$10 per person, both CUC$25). Hikes, including an easy one-hour hike to view the "Wonders of Soroa" or a longer, three-hour "Nature and History" mild hike, cost CUC$10 per person. ⊠ *Villa Soroa, Carretera de Soroa, Km 8, Soroa* ☎ *4852–3556* ⊕ *www.hotelescubanacan.com.*

SHOPPING

On Moka Alley in Las Terrazas you can browse in some no-frills but interesting artisan shops.

Café de María. This homey café has a tiny terrace with a view over the valley. Try the chocolate-vanilla espresso, liberally dusted with dark cocoa and accompanied by a cookie (CUC$1). You can take home a hand-sewn cloth bag of this dark-roasted coffee for CUC$4. ⊠ *Moka Alley, Las Terrazas.*

El Cusco Bazaar. This shop is full of hand-made textiles and wood and fabric creations, from rag dolls to decorative boxes to children's clothes. ⊠ *Moka Alley, Las Terrazas.*

El Ilang. You can sniff colognes made from local flowers and herbs and buy hand-decorated vials of your favorites (CUC$5–CUC$6). Ilang is made from flowers of the ilang-ilang tree, the same basis for Chanel No. 5 perfume. ⊠ *Moka Alley, Las Terrazas* ✛ *On next level down from Eco-Restaurante El Romero.*

VALLE DE VIÑALES

212 km (131 miles) southwest of Havana, 137 km (82 miles) west of Soroa, 26 km (16 miles) north of Pinar del Río.

Fodor'sChoice
★
The valley is justly ranked among Cuba's most beautiful landscapes, an expanse of lush green studded with the famous *mogotes*—freestanding, flat-topped, sheer-sided rock formations. Don't fail to stop at the Hotel Los Jazmines *mirador* for a breathtaking view over the valley; immense *mogotes* tower over deep green *vegas* that stretch into the distance and are backed by the Sierra de los Órganos (so-called for the peaks' resemblance to the pipes of an organ). The *mogotes* are the remains of the limestone *meseta,* or plateau, that rose from the sea some 160 million years ago to form the Cordillera de Guanabanico. Subsequent erosion left a karstic terrain replete with sinks, ravines, underground streams, and *hoyos*—rich depressions of red soil ideal for cultivating tobacco. The hidden canyons and natural tunnels leading into them provided shelter for pre-Columbian peoples and later for communities of *cimarrones* (runaway slaves).

The valley's flora includes many unique treasures: the underbrush, ferns, and rare cork palms on the *mogotes*; the silk-cotton tree, *Ceiba pentandra*; the royal palm; the caiman oak; and the mariposa, Cuba's national flower. Fauna includes the world's smallest hummingbird, the *zunzuncito* (Bee Hummingbird), as well as various endemic snails.

The town of Viñales itself is a national monument and, officially, both the town and surrounding area are a UNESCO World Heritage Site. Calle Salvador Cisneros, the wide main street, is flanked by stately tile-roofed houses, shaded by uniform rows of colonnaded arcades, all painted different colors. Since *paladares* (restaurants in private homes) were recently made legal, there is a string of more than 14 new bars and restaurants on this main street. Many other houses on the street are now *casas particulares*, private homes that rent rooms. The de rigueur José Martí monument sits in the large main square, bordered by the church and the elegant arches of the Cultural Center. Tree-shaded benches allow for some respite from the heat of the day. Throughout the town, the new prosperity is palpable in freshly painted and renovated houses.

GETTING HERE AND AROUND

Taxis are pricey because fuel is very expensive, and although vintage cars look great from the outside, many of them have no seat belts or air-conditioning. Your best bet for getting around Valle de Viñales is to book day tours with your hotel tour desk, or rent a bicycle.

TOURS

Infoturs lead tours in the town of Pinar del Río. Paradiso leads tours in the town of Viñales.

Infotur. For local tourist information, visit this official Cuban tourist office in the middle of town, in a grand, old hotel painted rose with red awnings. ⊠ *Hotel Vueltabajo, Calle Martí 103, esq. de Rafael Morales, Pinar del Río* 📠 *4872–8616.*

Paradiso Tours. This official government tourist office organizes guided walks in and around town, and dance lessons in the Cultural Center. ⊠ *Calle Salvador Cisneros 65* 📠 *4879–6258* ⊕ *www.paradiso.cu.*

EXPLORING

TOP ATTRACTIONS

Cueva del Indio. This spectacular and massive cave is named for the aboriginal Guanahatabey. Dripping with limestone formations, it's spooky enough to thrill even grown-ups. Visitors enter the cave through a narrow opening and follow a well-beaten, dimly lighted stone trail for 255 meters (842 feet), narrowing and widening until you reach a high-ceilinged grotto and an underground river. You board a boat here for a short cruise (300 meters [990 feet]) past illuminated stalagmites. The guide points a laser at shapes and if you really use your imagination you can just make out a champagne bottle, a skull, a crocodile, a sea horse, and even the *Niña, Pinta,* and *Santa María.* The boat takes you out of the cave through a narrow, vine-draped opening in the rock. Souvenir vendors await as you disembark. Don't miss the chance to have your photo taken atop Tomás, a huge, but placid, water buffalo. His handler will even lend you his straw hat so you can really look the part of a guajiro; a tip is expected. ■TIP→ **This is a popular spot on the tour-bus circuit, so try to come early or late in the day for a chance to have**

the cave more to yourself. ⊠ *On road to San Vicente ✛ 6 km (4 miles) north of Viñales* ☎ *4879–6280* 🖃 *CUC$5* ⊘ *Daily 9–5.*

WORTH NOTING

El Palenque/Cueva de José Miguel. The dimly lighted, rough 140-meter (462-foot) tunnel piercing this mogote opens onto an eerily quiet open space ringed by high limestone rocks. There's a rather shabby replica of a Cimarron campsite with life-size figures of escaped slaves. But if you arrive before a tour group, it's quite peaceful here. The thatch-roof, outdoor bohío-style restaurant in this clearing has a huge brick oven to roast chicken and pork; a main course and dessert costs less than CUC$6. At the entrance to the cave, sheltered by the rock over-hang is El Palanque de los Cimarrones, a popular disco/bar/restaurant that stays open late and all night on Saturday. ⊠ *Km 32 on Hwy. 241, toward San Vicente ✛ 4 km (2.5 miles) north of Viñales* ☎ *4879–6290* 🖃 *CUC$3* ⊘ *Cave: daily 9–6; restaurant: daily 9–4; disco/bar: nightly 9 pm–3:30 am.*

Jardín Botanico de las Hermanas Caridad y Carmen Miranda. This slightly oddball, 100-year-old garden surrounds a farmhouse on the northern edge of town. It was started by a man, whose daughters both lived here into their nineties and created an idiosyncratic world for themselves. Billows of bougainvillea blossoms, flowering shrubs, and fruit trees are populated by dolls and toys, mostly threadbare now and even a little macabre in places. It's not terribly tidy but it is interesting, with chickens clucking around and gardeners at work. After a stroll through the shady garden, you can sit on wicker chairs and sample some fruits. The house is full of antique furniture and photos, which a grand-neice of the sisters will happily show you. ⊠ *Northern end of Calle Salvador Cisneros* ☎ *4879–6274* 🖃 *Donations accepted* ⊘ *Daily 8–7.*

Mural de la Prehistoria. Across the massive rock face of Mogote Dos Hermanas, Diego Rivera disciple Leovigildo González (or the 25 farm-ers he directed) painted this immense—200 x 300 meters (660 x 990 feet)—luridly colored mural of prehistoric men and creatures, between 1959 and 1962. Commissioned by Fidel Castro, the painting is sup-posed to depict the evolutionary process in the Sierra de los Órganos. ■**TIP**➔ No need to pay the entrance fee; you can see it just as well from the road. ⊠ *Valle de Viñales ✛ 5 km (3 miles) west of Viñales* 🖃 *CUC$1* ⊘ *Daily 9–5.*

Museo Municipal Adela Azcuy. In a rather shabby building, this small, eclectic collection displays odd objects and photographs that focus on local history, including antique farm tools. You'll see some stirrups, weapons, weights, locks and keys, and branding irons from Spanish colonial times, as well as personal objects that belonged to the museum's namesake, a top-ranked woman warrior who fought for Cuba's inde-pendence in the 19th century. A bronze bust of Captain Adela Azcuy herself stands on the street in front of this house, where she spent much of her life. The museum organizes two- to three-hour guided walking tours in the town of Viñales, CUC$8 per person. Make reservations for the tour the day before at the museum. ⊠ *Calle Salvador Cisneros,* *across from Casa de Don Tomás, Viñales* ☎ *4879–3395* ✉ *CUC$3* ⊙ *Tues.–Sat. 8–5, Sun. 8–noon.*

WHERE TO EAT

$ ✕ **Casa de Don Tomás.** Despite the bevy of new eateries along the main
CUBAN street, this is still the classiest place in town, set in the most charming
of Viñales's oldest houses. The white clapboard house, circa 1889, has
neat, blue trim and shutters, and guests enter along a garden path under
an arbor of vines. Both the excellent traditional food and the charming
service make this place memorable. Diners can choose a table on the
front veranda, in the garden terrace, or in the interior dining rooms
decorated with sepia vintage photos. The *delicias de Don Tomás*, a rice
casserole with ham, pork, chicken, lobster, and sausage, is a favorite, as
is the *tasajo a lo guajiro* (shredded beef in a criollo sauce). The signature
cocktail here is the Trapiche, a refreshing blend of pineapple juice, rum,
and honey with a sugarcane swizzle stick. ⑤ *Average main: CUC$10*
✉ *Calle Salvador Cisneros 141* ☎ *4879–6300.*

WHERE TO STAY

$$ ⌂ **Horizontes La Ermita.** Sunrises and sunsets viewed from this elegant
B&B/INN hotel's hilltop setting are unequaled. **Pros:** views are wonderful; close to
FAMILY town. **Cons:** only a dozen rooms actually have great views; bathrooms
are small and have showers only. ⑤ *Rooms from: CUC$90* ✉ *Carret-
era La Ermita, Km 1.5, on west side of town* ☎ *4879–6071* ⊕ *www.
hotelescubanacan.com* ⇝ *62 rooms* ⑩ *Breakfast.*

$$ ⌂ **Hotel Los Jazmines.** Western Cuba's grande dame of hotels is painted
HOTEL rosy pink and is highlighted by arcs of stained glass windows over
FAMILY shuttered French doors that open onto balconies with spectacular, panoramic views of the valley and its limestone *mogotes* (steep-sided hills).
Pros: the best rooms have great views and are in the old part of the
hotel, near the pool; the pool itself is an Olympic-size expanse on the
edge of a terrace. **Cons:** most rooms are on the small side; pool needs
some paint and repairs; no elevators in main building. ⑤ *Rooms from:
CUC$90* ✉ *Carretera de Viñales, Km 23* ✛ *5 km (3 miles) from Viñales*
☎ *4879–6205* ⊕ *www.hotelescubanacan.com* ⇝ *70 rooms* ⑩ *Some
meals* ☞ *Rate includes breakfast and dinner for 2.*

CAYO LEVISA

110 km (68 miles) west of Havana, 52 km (32 miles) north of Viñales.

The Archipiélago de los Colorados runs west along Cuba's northern
coast, beginning at Cayo Paraíso, a famous haunt of Hemingway who
moored his fishing boat *Pilar* here. A plaque erected near the wooden
dock at Cayo Paraíso on the 90th anniversary of his birth immortalizes
Hemingway's love for this pristine spot, which, in fact, he named (old
navigational charts identify it as Cayo Megano).

Cayo Levisa is the next key to the west. Easily visible 5 km (3 miles)
offshore, it has 4 km (2 miles) of white-sand beaches along its northern
edge and offers excellent diving and snorkeling. Lobsters and black
coral are the main aquatic attractions.

3

GETTING HERE AND AROUND

Since the *cayo* is only 140 km (87 miles) from Key West, anyone embarking here needs to show a passport. The boat leaves at 9 am and 5 pm from the Coast Guard station at Palma Rubia, and leaves Cayo Levisa at 10 am and 6 pm for the run in to Palma Rubia. Boat fare is CUC$10 per passenger one way, CUC$19 round-trip, with a cocktail included. To get to the boat landing, turn north off the northern-coast circuit just after the town of Las Cadenas.

WHERE TO STAY

$$

B&B/INN

☶ **Hotel Cayo Levisa.** This quiet, castaway-island resort is devoted to diving and snorkeling. **Pros:** an isolated, idyllic, romantic spot; excellent diving and snorkeling. **Cons:** insects abound, depending on the season, so bring insect repellent; simple rooms, nothing fancy. ⑤ *Rooms from: CUC$91* ✉ *Cayo Levisa* ☎ *4875–6506* ⊕ *www.hotelescubanacan.com* ⤴ *33 bungalows* �‖ *All meals.*

PINAR DEL RÍO

178 km (110 miles) southwest of Havana, 26 km (16 miles) south of Viñales.

Named for the stands of pine trees that once shaded the banks of the Río Guamá, Pinar del Río has been Cuba's tobacco city since its first land grants were allocated in 1544. Viñales and Vuelta Abajo were the island's great tobacco plantations, and Pinar del Río prospered as the tobacco market town and manufacturing center, even after the rest of the island turned almost exclusively to the cultivation and export of sugarcane.

Today the city (population 137,000) is a bustling but dilapidated provincial capital with major hospitals and government offices. The streets are filled with horse-drawn surreys and pedal taxis, the main modes of public transport, and lined with crumbling building facades and crooked utility poles supporting tangles of cables. Like the fading revolutionary murals on abandoned building walls, the city suffers from severe neglect. It's a sobering sampling of life in Cuba, away from the major tourist sites. A small cigar factory, along with a distillery that produces *guayabita* (a brandy-like liqueur made from sugarcane and guava) offer up-close looks at surviving small-scale industries. The highlight, though, is a visit to a museum that itself is a relic of a fantastical architectural past.

GETTING HERE AND AROUND

Hire a taxi from your hotel, or book a day-long bus tour. If you drive a rental car, park it as soon as you can, and hire pedal cabs to get you around town.

TOURS

Infotur. Visit this official tourist office for local information and a chance to step inside the vintage Vueltabajo Hotel, the grandest building in town, painted rose with red awnings. ✉ *Hotel Vueltabajo, Calle Martí 103, esq. de Rafael Morales* ☎ *4872–8616* ⊕ *www.infotur.cu.*

EXPLORING

TOP ATTRACTIONS

Fodor's Choice ★ **Museo Ciencias Naturales.** Installed in a fantastical Moorish palace, dripping with carved stone griffins, this museum is even more fascinating for its outlandish architecture and quaint, old-fashioned displays than for its hodgepodge, natural history collection. Built by a wealthy doctor in 1909, this private residence was known as the Guasch Palace. After the Revolution, the doctor's son "gifted" the building to the state and it was officially renamed after a self-taught, 19th-century Cuban scientist named Tranquilino Sandalio de Noda. The exhibits include dusty dioramas of desiccated stuffed specimens, from antelope to zebra, plus an array of mounted animal heads on the walls. There's a room dedicated to butterfly and moth collections, and a shell collection is displayed in showcases held up by carved seahorses. The delightful surprise here is the interior garden where, amid Art Nouveau painted floor tiles, intricately carved wooden doors and tropical plants, a giant concrete model of a demonically grinning tyrannosaurus Rex reigns. ■ TIP➜ **Pay the extra to bring in your camera; there are photo ops everywhere you look.** Across the street from the museum there are two side-by-side, brightly colored restaurants competing for lunch business. ✉ *Palacio Guasch, Calle Marté Este 202* ✛ *West edge of town, on road to Havana* ☎ *4877–9483* ✑ *CUC$1, CUC$2 for camera* ☉ *Mon.–Sat. 9–5, Sun. 9–1.*

WORTH NOTING

Fábrica de Bebidas Guayabita. On a narrow side street south of the city center, this small distillery occupies a former rum factory. Just about every process is done by hand, from pouring the tiny guayabita berries into huge, wooden fermenting barrels, to bottle washing, to tapping corks into the bottles, to affixing the old-fashioned labels. Visitors can taste the finished product in the shop. The dry version, which ferments for three months, is a fiery blast of brandy; the sweet version is more like a plum *eau de vie.* A bottle costs around CUC$6. It's noisy, messy and often crowded with tour groups, but it's a glimpse of how a truly authentic Cuban product is still being produced. ■ TIP➜ **It's not easy to find, so hire a pedal cab.** ✉ *Casa Garay, Calle Isabel Rubio 189* ✛ *1 block west, then 1 block south of cathedral San Rosendo* ✑ *CUC$3* ☉ *Daily 8:30–5.*

Fábrica de Tabacos Francisco Donatien. This traditional cigar factory, in a stately, colonnaded building that was the city jail until 1961, offers a more intimate visit than some of the major Havana cigar factories. You can watch a Montecristo in the making, as a guide explains the process. In a long, high-ceilinged hall, mostly young men—sporting trendy, shaved hair-dos—sit at old-fashioned, wooden tables, carefully destemming aged tobacco leaves, which look like thin strips of leather, then slowly rolling layers of different tobacco. The rolls are placed in plastic molds, pressed, then tested with an air compressor for the right consistency. You might hear the *lector* (reader) entertain the cigar rollers by reading newspaper articles from *Granma* or novels, but it's more likely you'll hear popular music from a radio. You purchase your ticket in the air-conditioned Casa del Habano across the street, where you can also buy cigars and souvenir humedors. ⚠ **No cameras are allowed in**

the cigar factory. ✉ *Calle Antonio Maceo 157* ☎ *4877–3069* 💲 *CUC$5* 🕐 *Weekdays 9–noon, 1–4.*

NIGHTLIFE

Rumayor. Just outside town, this Afro-Cuban restaurant and nightclub puts on a cabaret show on an outdoor stage with 20 high-energy, sexy dancers (male and female) plus singers on Thursday, Saturday, and Sunday nights. The bar opens at 9 and the hour-long show (CUC$5) starts at 11. You can dine first at the adjoining airy, all-wood and bamboo, *bohío*-style restaurant that's decorated with huge African masks. Also open for lunch, the restaurant is famed for its *pollo ahumado* (smoked chicken). The bar and cabaret are the city's top nightspots. ✉ *Carretera Viñales, Km 2, northeast corner of town* ✛ *Turn off highway leading to Viñales, and follow a tree-shaded broad avenue 50 meters (164 feet)* ☎ *4876–3051.*

SAN JUAN Y MARTÍNEZ

23 km (14 miles) southwest of Pinar del Río, 209 km (130 miles) southwest of Havana.

The finest-quality tobacco leaves come from Vuelta Abajo—the region southwest of Pinar del Río city—thanks to a combination of abundant rainfall throughout the year (except during the growing season). And although the countryside here is relatively drab, it's the mecca that *puro* (cigar purists) must visit. Some 80,000 acres of tobacco are planted annually in the province, and the best of it is found around San Luis and San Juan y Martínez.

The main street in San Juan y Martínez is lined with pastel-color, columned houses, typical of the province. Other than a café or two and the odd *paladar,* this sleepy tobacco town has little to offer. A visit to a tobacco farm is the main reason for lingering in Vuelta Abajo. Drop in at any plantation and the farmers will show you the crops, techniques, and drying barns, and possibly invite you for lunch.

GETTING HERE AND AROUND

To get to this out-of-the-way community, you will need to hire a taxi or rent a car.

MARÍA LA GORDA

123 km (74 miles) southwest of San Juan y Martínez, 150 km (93 miles) southwest of Pinar del Río, 328 km (203 miles) southwest of Havana.

Three hours west of Pinar del Río, over a bumpy road, you reach this world-renowned pristine beach and dive site, on the Bahía de Corrientes. It's named for a voluptuous young woman who was allegedly captured by pirates, then repatriated. Sadder, perhaps, but more business-savvy, she proceeded to set up a brothel. What makes the trip today worthwhile are the idyllic, virgin beaches and jewel-clear water, ideal for diving and snorkeling. Along the road, there's also the chance to encounter boar, deer, crocodiles, wildcats—though you're more likely to see Cuba's ubiquitous land-crab population headed for the seashore to lay eggs.

The flat, scrub-forested Península de Guanahacabibes was the final refuge for Cuba's Ciboney aboriginals fleeing first the Taíno and then the Spanish conquerors of the late 15th and 16th centuries. Today, the most sought-after inhabitants on the 90-km-long (56-mile-long), 30-km-wide (19-mile-wide) peninsula are the 190 resident and migratory species of birds, including 11 endemic species. Listed as an IBA (Important Bird and Biodiversity Area) by BirdLife International, the peninsula is a bird-watcher's mecca, especially in spring and fall, when multitudes of birds following the Mississippi Flyway pass over.

GETTING HERE AND AROUND
Because there is no public bus service to Maria la Gorda, you will need to arrange a transfer through your hotel, or rent a car.

EXPLORING
Parque Nacional Península de Guanahacabibes. At the end of the road from Pinar del Río, the village of La Bajada lies at a junction: the road to the left heads to Playa María la Gorda (14 km [9 miles] south), the one to the right takes you into the park, a UNESCO Biosphere Reserve. The drive out to Cuba's western tip at Cabo de San Antonio, 54 km (33 miles) over a rough dirt track, is a long haul to undertake, unless you're eager to explore the wilderness. If you go, bring food and drink; a cooler and a few sandwiches are advised. Your best transportation bet is to take a bus from Pinar del Río (about CUC$39) or book a tour with Gaviota, one of the state-owned tour companies, which also operates the hotel in María La Gorda. ⊠ *Bahía de Corrientes* ☎ *4875–0366.*

WHERE TO STAY
$

B&B/INN

▦ **CIB María la Gorda.** You can't get more off-the-beaten path than at this simple, beachfront hotel; it's the best option in this snorkeler's paradise, with a top-notch diving center that attracts an international clientele. **Pros:** a no-frills but romantic setting that offers some of the best dives in the hemisphere. **Cons:** difficult to reach. ⑤ *Rooms from: CUC$50* ⊠ *Bahía de Corrientes* ✛ *143 km (88 miles) southwest of Pinar del Río* ☎ *4877–8131* ⊕ *www.gaviota-grupo.com* ⇨ *55 rooms* ⑩ *Breakfast.*

SPORTS AND THE OUTDOORS
SCUBA DIVING AND SNORKELING
Centro Internacional de Buceo María la Gorda (*María La Gorda International Dive Center*). Run by the Villa María la Gorda hotel, the Centro Internacional de Buceo María la Gorda has three, 41-foot equipped dive boats and eight dive masters, with programs ranging from initiation dives (CUC$44) to 20-dive packages (CUC$384). The proximity of the prime diving areas just 200 meters (656 feet) out, the sunlit, underwater caves, the variety of fish, and the abundance of black coral 15 meters (50 feet) down all conspire to make this an extraordinary place to dive. Try to come outside of high season, when the dive boats may be filled to 15-diver capacity. ⊠ *Bahía de Corrientes* ☎ *4877–8077* ⊕ *www.villamarialagorda.com.*

ARCHIPIÉLAGO DE LOS CANARREOS

Of Cuba's 4,000 islands, most of them specks, the largest is the Isla de la Juventud (Isle of Youth), the main island in the Archipiélago de Canarreos. South of Havana, in the Golfo de Batabanó, it was previously called La Isla de los Piños (Isle of Pines) for the native pine forest that once covered it. The roughly circular, 50-km-diameter (31-mile-diameter) island was originally a colony for exiles and later the site of a prison (Fidel Castro was jailed here for 18 months). After the Revolution, Castro's Third World experiment in communist universities and field work, known as the Youth Brigades, was based here—hence the island's name change.

Isla de la Juventud is a special municipality (as opposed to a full-fledged province) and has little to offer tourists outside of some diving sites, a group of caves with pre-Colombian paintings, and its political history. Nueva Gerona, the only important town, is where some 60,000 of the island's 100,000 residents live.

GETTING HERE AND AROUND

There are two daily flights from Havana to Rafael Cabrera Mustelier Airport on Isla de la Juventud, on Aerocaribbean Airlines, a Cuban airline. Try to reserve well in advance as internal flights are very often booked days or weeks before flight days.

Taking a ferry to the island is possible but daunting. The ferry ride takes about three hours, on noisy catamarans that hold about 200 passengers, and you must arrive at the ferry terminal, at each end, at least two hours before departure. The catamaran leaves from the town of Surgido de Batabanó, a bus ride from Havana, once a day, (about CUC$13) for the crossing; and returns to the mainland at 9 am (CUC$11). You must buy tickets for the bus and ferry in advance in Havana at the Agencia Viajero. You can buy return ferry tickets only on the island itself, at the Naviera Cubana Caribeña ferry terminal in Nueva Gerona. On Fridays and Sundays there is one extra departure.

CAYO LARGO

177 km (110 miles) southeast of Havana, 120 km (74 miles) east of the Isla de la Juventud.

If a carefree, quiet beach vacation is what you're looking for, secluded Cayo Largo, encircled by a coral reef, is ideal. Add in 20 km (13 miles) of pristine, white-sand beach bordering an endless turquoise Caribbean sea and all-inclusive hotels that cater to your every need, and you have Varadero without the crowds and without the frenzy. Though contact with Cuban life and culture is limited, you'll meet lots of Italians and Canadians, who enjoy direct flights to this popular getaway island. In fact, four of the hotels are exclusively Italian. Although the island is more expensive than the mainland, it has the added attractions of a couple of designated, clothing-optional (CO) beaches, a gay-friendly vibe, and a first-class marina that caters to every activity in, on, and under the water. The only caveats are the seas here can be rough and mosquitoes do accompany sunsets, so come prepared. The major hotels are grouped fairly closely together along the south coast, but there are still miles of undeveloped beachfront and close-in keys to explore, on foot and by boat.

Tourists arrive at Vilo Acuña International Airport, Cayo Largo's small airport, on international fights from Canada or Europe, or on a 45-minute Cuban domestic flight from Havana or Varadero. Cayo Largo is about 180 km (112 miles) southeast of Havana. All of the island's hotels are within easy taxi/bus transfer distance from the airport.

BEACHES

Playa Sirena. This superb 3-km (2-mile) white-sand strand is the only beach on the island with picture-perfect palm trees. All the hotels arrange ferry and bus shuttles to this sliver of a peninsula off Cayo Largo's western tip. The marina here, shared by all the hotels, has a restaurant and a bar and a full range of water sports, including diving, snorkeling, and boat rentals from kayaks to pedal boats to Hobie Cats. If the beach gets too crowded, you can arrange a boat to take you to nearby, deserted keys such as Cayo Rico and Cayo Iguana. For a taste of the best of Cayo Largo, without renouncing the cultural experience of Cuba, there are day-trip packages from Havana and Varadero that include a 40-minute flight, half a day and lunch on Playa Sirena, snorkeling the offshore reef, and a visit to Cayo Iguana. **Amenities:** food and drink; toilets; water sports. **Best for:** snorkeling; walking. ⊠ *Cayo Largo.*

WHERE TO EAT

$ ✕ **Taberna del Pirata.** Lobster is the specialty at this breezy terrace res-
SEAFOOD   taurant near the Cayo Largo Marina. Along with *criollo* recipes featuring fresh fish, there's standard chicken-to-pizza fare. It's more than the beach shack it may seem at first sight, with a good wine list and unobtrusive live music from a local trio. $ *Average main: CUC$8* ⊠ *Cayo Largo Marina* ☎ *4524–48212* ▭ *No credit cards.*

WHERE TO STAY

$$$$ ⛱ **Sol Cayo Largo.** At the quieter, far-western end of Playa Lindarena, this
RESORT   is the most sophisticated, luxurious hotel on Cayo Largo. **Pros:** attractive pool and gardens; elegant, sophisticated decor. **Cons:** some rooms are not very close to the beach. $ *Rooms from: CUC$250* ⊠ *Playa Lindarena* ☎ *4524–8260* ⊕ *www.meliacuba.com* ⟳ *244 standard rooms, 44 superior sea view, 8 junior suites* ⏉ *All-inclusive.*

MATANZAS PROVINCE

Formerly Cuba's sugarcane-producing heartland, Matanzas Province now plays host to more than one-quarter of all visitors to Cuba, thanks to the concentration of all-inclusive resorts in nearby Varadero. The city of Matanzas, with its immense deep-water harbor, was a sugar- and slave-trading port of great importance during colonial times. Once deemed the Athens of Cuba for its cultural vigor, and the Cuban Venice for its two rivers and 28 bridges, Matanzas is slowly reviving, thanks to the infusion of tourism dollars earned by locals who live in the city; it's more than worth a visit. Varadero has more than four-dozen major hotels along the slender Península de Hicacos, between the Atlantic Ocean and the Bahía de Cárdenas, and more behemoth hotel complexes are under construction. East of the tourist hub, the city of Cárdenas has a character and charm all its own, if somewhat dilapidated. The Península de Zapata, beginning with the vast national park and ending at the Bahía de Cochinos (Bay of Pigs) and the fascinating Museo Playa Girón, offers an increasingly popular combination of flora, fauna, and history.

GETTING HERE AND AROUND

The best way to get to and from Matanzas Province is by Víazul buses, which are comfortable, air-conditioned, and relatively inexpensive. To drive here, take the wide and quick Vía Blanca (White Way), which runs 100 km (62 miles) east from Havana and then another 40 km (25 miles) on to Varadero. With views of the coast and the Valle de Yumurí, the Vía Blanca is one of Cuba's finest highways. The so-called Hershey train—a four-hour run from the Casablanca district across Havana harbor—is the other classic way to visit Matanzas. Including lunch, a quick tour of central Matanzas could take two to four hours, plenty of time to get the feel of this once-opulent 19th-century town. Flights are scheduled regularly from Havana to the province's most popular tourism destination of Varadero.

MATANZAS

100 km (62 miles) east of Havana.

Matanzas, which means "killings," takes its unfortunate name from the slaughter in 1510 of survivors of a Spanish shipwreck by an indigenous tribe. Ironically, the city was also Cuba's early livestock abattoir and exporter of meat to Spain. Despite its rather gruesome name, the city today has an optimistic energy about it, with tidy streets lined with elegant pastel-hued facades of Neoclassical buildings, many under restoration. The architecture, museums, and restored churches make the city well worth investigating. The San Juan and Yumurí rivers cut through the city center and empty into the vast Bahía de Matanzas, still an important sugar port. Breezes off the bay cool and freshen the city streets and there are panoramic views from high above the city. During the day, the city is fairly quiet, but comes to life at night when the residents—many of whom work in the nearby Varadero hotels—come home. Head for the Parque de la Libertad where most of the action is in town.

EXPLORING

TOP ATTRACTIONS

Monserrate Heights Mirador. For a spectacular view of the city and the bay, hire a taxi to take you up to Monserrate Heights, a pleasant park that's also the site of La Ermita de Monserrate, a handsome, colonial-Spanish style church. Built in 1875, the church is a shrine to the patron saint of Catalonians who emigrated to Cuba. The view in the opposite direction is of the Yumuri River valley. If you manage to make the long, uphill climb here, there is a snack bar in the park where you can refresh yourself. ⊠ *Ermita de Monserrate, top of Calle 312 ✛ Reparto Los Mangos.*

Fodor's Choice   **Museo Farmacéutico Triolet.** The city's main, not-to-be-missed sight is this
★   perfectly preserved, 19th-century natural-medicine pharmacy. Estab-
lished in 1882 by Ernesto Triolet and his son-in-law, Juan Fermín de
Figueroa, this gorgeous emporium looks out onto the Parque de Libertad through large stained glass windows. The pharmacy closed its
doors in 1964, and has been preserved exactly as it was on that day,
down to the huge, ornate cash register; the log book with handwrit-
ten recipes for each prescription; the rolls of brown paper to wrap the
glass bottles that were individually filled and labeled; and the ceiling-
high, handsome wood-and-glass cases holding hundreds of decorative
porcelain jars. Guided tours take you to the distillery behind the shop,
where the pharmacists manufactured their world-famous trademark
syrups and tonics. Medicine bottles, embossed with the pharmacy's
name, were made in Philadelphia and shipped to Cuba. Don't miss
the bronze crocodile used to compress and calibrate the corks that,
before the screw-top, sealed vials. The tour continues upstairs in the
lavish living quarters of the owners—natural medicine was obviously
a profitable business. An art gallery on the mezzanine floor showcases
stained glass works—including small glass bird mobiles for sale—made
by a studio that occupies the top floor. ⊠ *Calle Milanés (Ca. 83), esq.
de Calle Santa Teresa (Ca. 290)* ✣ *Southwest corner of Parque de la
Libertad* ☎ *4524–3179* 🖼 *CUC$3* 𝄞 *Mon.–Sat. 10–6, Sun. 8–noon.*

Parque de la Libertad. This attractive, leafy square is the heart of the
city. A bronze statue of 19th-century liberal revolutionary leader José
Martí presides over the plaza, accompanied by a startling sculpture of a
screaming, bare-breasted woman representing Cuba breaking free from
her chains. Around the square are beautifully restored Neoclassical
buildings, including the Museo Farmacéutico Triolet, the restored Sala
de Conciertos José White, and the magnificently refurbished Velasco
Hotel, next door to the handsome Velasco Theater. Nearby bookshops
and cafés are bustling, and there's almost always some music or street
theater going on in the square. ⊠ *Bordered by Calles 79, 83 (Calle del
Medio), 290, and 288.*

WORTH NOTING

Catedral de San Carlos. Recently restored on the outside, this massive,
Neoclassical church with two ornate towers is famous for its interior
frescoes. In front of the church, there is a huge ceiba tree with a heavy,
metal bell hanging from one of the branches, commemorating the bells
that were rung to call in slaves from the sugar plantations. On the
ground below lies a large, antique metal gear from a sugar mill. ⊠ *Calle
del Medio between Milanés y Calle 282* ☎ *4524–8342* 𝄞 *Weekdays 8–
noon and 2:30–5, Sun. 9–noon.*

Hershey Railway. Once the property of the Hershey chocolate barons,
Cuba's first electric railway was built in 1917 to haul sugarcane and
workers to the sugar refinery. Now the quaint electric engine slowly
pulls three passenger cars with wooden benches to a picturesque station
in Matanzas, making many stops along the way. The ride usually takes
about three to four hours to travel 95 km (60 miles). It's an interesting
trip, but you can't be on a tight schedule, because the train isn't always
on time and sometimes doesn't even get from Havana to Matanzas

on the same day. The best train to take is the 12:21 pm train from the Casablanca station in Havana, or the 12:09 from Matanzas, but always check the most current schedule first. You buy the tickets on the train. ⊠ *Calle 67/San Blas y Calle 155/San Alejandro ✛ 2 blocks from ferry terminal, in Reparto Versalles neighborhood* ☎ *4524–7254* ⌨ *CUC$3* ☉ *3 departures daily; call for exact schedule.*

Iglesia de San Pedro Apóstol. This architecturally eclectic church was built in 1870 by architect Daniel Delaglio, who also designed the city's emblematic Teatro Sauto. The church's Neoclassical symmetry is broken by a jumble of towers, turrets, domes, and cupolas. The bright yellow interior has rich, fluted columns behind the main altar. ⊠ *Calle 57 y Calle 270 ✛ Near Hershey train station in Reparto Versalles.*

Museo Provincial Matanzas. This distinctive, slate-blue building with two tiers of graceful arcades recalls the city's mid-19th-century heyday. It was built in 1838 for the wealthy del Junco family and since 1980 has housed a collection of artifacts, photographs, memorabilia and tools—some of them gruesome—chronicling the sugar and slave industries, on which the city's wealth was built. For an extra CUC$5 you can take photos. ⊠ *Calle 272 y Calle 83 ✛ Facing Plaza de la Vigía and Sauto Theater* ☎ *4524–3195* ⌨ *CUC$2* ☉ *Tues.–Sat. 9–noon and 1–4:40, Sun. 9–noon* ⌨ *CUC$5 extra to take photos.*

Plaza de la Vigía. A little overwhelmed by passing traffic, this landmark square is the cultural hub of Matanzas, with the Matanzas Provincial Museum on one corner and the magnificent, neoclassical Sauto Theater (currently closed for restoration) taking up a whole side. In the middle of the square is the marble statue of an anonymous independence fighter known as *El Soldado Desconocido* (The Unknown Soldier). A couple of cafés face the theater and there's a modern art gallery (free) to browse. ⊠ *Calle 272 y Calle 83 ✛ At entrance to city, off main road heading to Varadero.*

Puente Concordia. This once-elegant, arched bridge over the Yumurí Estuary used to set a Parisian, Seine-like scene. Built in 1878, with two imposing carved columns at each end, it connected the barrio of Versalles, named for resident wealthy French coffee planters, and the city. Although it's currently in sad shape, it's still one of the most striking pieces of Matanzas architecture. The Cuban government used to give replicas of the columns as official gifts to visiting dignitaries. ⊠ *Calle 272, as it crosses Yumurí River.*

Teatro Sauto. On the Plaza de la Vigia, the massive, white Teatro Sauto is one of Cuba's finest and best-preserved Neoclassical structures. Also known as the Teatro Antillano, or Theater of the Antilles, it was built in 1863 at the peak of the city's prosperity. The theater is currently undergoing a major restoration and is closed indefinitely, but you can't miss seeing this landmark building. ⊠ *Plaza de la Vigia* ☎ *4524–2721.*

WHERE TO EAT

$ ✕ **Café Vigía.** This lively café, with a large, covered terrace overlooking
CUBAN the plaza, is the perfect place to grab a table and a cool drink and enjoy the view of the Sauto Theater. Inside, the scene is vintage 19th century, with wood floors, Corinthian columns supporting the high ceiling, a

long, polished-wood bar, and vintage photographs on the walls. Stained glass transoms top the arched windows, while a cool breeze wafts in from the bay, and there are ceiling fans to keep the air moving. Open daily from breakfast to late at night, the menu is inexpensive snack fare, including pizza, large beakers of beer to share and, of course, every coffee concoction. There's a modern art gallery next door, and a little farther along, an interesting book shop that sells artistic, handmade books using old photos, hand-written text, and drawings. The café is a good bathroom stop after visiting the nearby Provincial Museum. ⑤ *Average main: CUC$6* ⊠ *Plaza del Vigía, Calle Magdalena, esq. de Calle Medio* ✛ *Across from Sauto Theater, at entrance to Matanzas* ☎ *4525–3076* ▤ *No credit cards.*

WHERE TO STAY

$
HOTEL
Fodor's Choice
★

🖃 **Hotel E Velasco.** Brilliantly restored, this elegant hotel built in 1902 is a gem, set on the pleasant Parque de la Libertad. **Pros:** exquisite decor; great location. **Cons:** smallish standard rooms. ⑤ *Rooms from: CUC$58* ⊠ *Parque de la Libertad, Calle Contreras, e/Santa Teresa and Ayuntamiento* ☎ *4525–3880* ⊕ *www.hotelescubanacan.com* ⤴ *13 rooms, 4 suites* ⑩ *Breakfast.*

NIGHTLIFE AND PERFORMING ARTS

Danzón. Matanzas is the birthplace, officially in 1879, of *danzón*, Cuba's national dance. It's a fusion of European contradance (*habanera* in Spain) and Afro-Cuban rhythms. The city holds an annual Danzón Festival every November, with a dance competition that attracts competitors from all over Cuba. For information about *danzón* and other cultural events, check the city's website. ⊠ *Matanzas* ⊕ *www.atenas. cult.cu.*

Sala de Conciertos José White. This exquisite, Neoclassical concert hall is named after a 19th-century violinist/composer who was exiled for his nationalist leanings. It was the first place that *danzón*, Cuba's national dance, was performed. The building has been under restoration for two years and should open by January 2016, as a venue for concerts and cultural events. ⊠ *Plaza de la Libertad* ✛ *Next door to Hotel E Velasco* ☎ *4526–0153.*

SPORTS AND THE OUTDOORS

BASEBALL

FAMILY **Victoria a Girón.** Matanzas is a fanatical baseball town, with a top first-division team called Los Cocodrilos. You will see images of the grinning, green crocodile mascot everywhere. Games are held from October to March in the 30,000-seat stadium Victoria a Girón, also known as El Palacio de los Cocodrilos. A ticket to the game costs a foreigner about CUC$3. The street the stadium is on is named after Cuba's most famous baseball player, Martín Dihigo, a pitcher and second baseman who played for the Cuban Stars in the Negro Leagues in the United States from 1923 to 1936. He also played in the Mexican and Cuban Leagues and was elected to the American Baseball Hall of Fame in 1977. He was revered in Cuba and served as Cuba's Minister of Sports for 12 years. A little farther past Victoria a Girón sits Palmar de Junco. Built in 1874, this stadium was the site of Cuba's first baseball game and is now a national monument, as well as home to the provincial sports academy. ⊠ *Av. Martín Dihigo s/n* ☎ *4524–8813 stadium, 4525–3551 Infotur tourist office* 🖅 *CUC$3.*

VARADERO

140 km (87 miles) east of Havana.

Depending on your travel tastes, Varadero could be a tropical, carefree paradise or mass tourist inferno. It's Cuba's most popular tourist destination, for two good reasons: Playa Azul, a spectacular, stretch of white-sand beach; and the all-inclusive resorts that rival those of similar resort areas anywhere in the world (and remove all the logistical stresses of traveling independently in Cuba). Varadero is also a good base for catamaran cruises, sport fishing, and excursions to Matanzas, Cárdenas, and the Península de Zapata. Although most of the hotels are managed by foreign companies, they all offer basically the same tours operated by Cuban-owned tour operators,

This narrow peninsula—really an elongated island separated from the mainland by the Laguna Paso Malo—is just over 20 km (12 miles) long and is edged by seemingly endless, white-sand beaches and clear waters in mesmerizing blues, greens, and aquamarines. You can almost walk the beach from one end to the other, but there are a few rocky sections. At an average width of 700 meters (770 yards), Varadero extends northeast to Punta Hicacos, Cuba's northernmost point. Laid out in three longitudinal avenues intersected by 69 cross streets, Varadero town is easy to navigate. It's a warren of more than 50 hotels, plus restaurants, shops, and nightclubs.

Originally inhabited by the Taíno, Varadero was settled by the Spanish in the late 16th century. In the late 19th century, families from Cárdenas began to build summer houses here. In 1883 the first town council established a plan for building baths and recreational facilities. The Varadero Hotel opened in 1915, and in 1926 the du Pont de Nemours family—the powerful American industrialists whose early fortune was made in gunpowder—bought most of the peninsula and built a large estate complete with a golf course. Other wealthy *norteamericanos* followed, including Al Capone.

By the 1950s, numerous hotels were under construction; they followed the example of the Hotel Internacional, a quintessential den of iniquity complete with a casino, mobsters, and abundant available women. After 1959, the Revolution declared the elitist enclave public property, and rank-and-file Cubans were allowed on the beach. Varadero then became a favorite Russian resort, where Eastern European tourists frolicked in the sun and guzzled mojitos right under Uncle Sam's nose. Today it's favored by Europeans and Canadians, attracted by reasonable prices for all-inclusive beach holidays ranging from affordable, midrange family hotels to pricey, superluxurious spa resorts. More hotel complexes are currently under construction, filling the few available sites left.

GETTING HERE AND AROUND

The best way to get oriented and find your way around Varadero is to board one of the double-decker buses that ply the peninsula daily from 8 am to 8 pm. The all-day, hop-on-and-off fare is CUC$5; both the red bus (Transtur) and the white Gaviota bus accept the same ticket.

TOURS

Infotur. The official government tourist office has information on local tours here, in the center of town and also out on the peninsula, in the Centro Comercial Hicacos. ⊠ *In Hotel Aguazul, Calle 13, esq. de 1ra Av.* ☎ *4566–2966, 4566–7044 in Centro Comercial Hicacos* ⊕ *www.infotur.cu.*

NEXUS Tours and Paradiso Tours also provide excellent service for Varadero. ⇨ *See Tours at the beginning of this chapter.*

EXPLORING

TOP ATTRACTIONS

Delfinario Varadero. For a pleasant break from the beach, you can watch a troupe of acrobatic dolphins show off their tricks in a 35-minute show (CUC$20) and take photos (an extra CUC$5). If you want to dive in and swim with the dolphins, it costs an extra CUC$60. You can also have your photo taken with a dolphin in the background (CUC$5). ⊠ *Delfinario* ✣ *Opposite Marina Chapelin, south of Hotel Blau Varadero* ☎ *4566–8031* 🎫 *CUC$20* ☉ *Daily 9–5, performances at 11 and 3:30.*

WORTH NOTING

Cueva de Ambrosio. Discovered in the 1960s, this cave contains aboriginal drawings of concentric circles and other pre-Columbian symbols, thought to be more than 3,000 years old. To get to the cave entrance, you must follow a shady path 300 meters (990 feet). ⊠ *Autopista Sur, near Royalton Hicacos Hotel* 🎫 *CUC$3* ☉ *Mon.–Sat. 9–4:30.*

Museo Municipal. Housed in one of Varadero's prettiest early 20th-century summer houses, built entirely of wood and painted sky blue with white trim, this collection chronicles Varadero's early days as a resort. Of special interest are photographs of Che and Fidel "taking" the Hotel Internacional after the Revolution. ⊠ *Calle 57, esq. de Av. Playa* ☎ *4561–3189* 🎫 *CUC$1* ☉ *Tues.–Sun. 10–7.*

Parque Josone. Once the estate of a wealthy sugar-mill owner, since 1940 this public park, open daily, has been a tranquil spot with extensive gardens and a small lake with swans and flamingos. Rowboats are available for rent (less than CUC$2), and there's a small public pool, and open-air concerts some nights. ⊠ *Av. 1 y Calle 56* ☎ *4566–2740* 🎫 *Free* ☉ *Daily 9 am–midnight.*

BEACHES

Fodor's Choice
★
Playa Varadero (*Playa Azul*). Visitors know it as Varadero, but locals call this 20-km (12 ½-mile) stretch of white-sand Caribbean beach Playa Azul, for the intense azure skies mirrored in the blue water. This spectacular beach along the north shore of the Hicacos Peninsula, is on a narrow finger of land that juts out into the Florida Straits. It segues into shallow, warm Caribbean waters, ideal for swimming and paddling. You can walk for miles along the beach, past the variously color-coded

cabanas and lounge chairs of the 50 or so hotels that have access to the beach. There are, however, a few rocky areas where the sand disappears, so don't set off on a long beach walk without sandals or beach shoes. Although the hotel properties and lounges are for guests only, there is no rule against walking along the shore and taking a dip in the sea whenever you need to cool off. Most hotels supply kayaks or small boats, but divers and snorkelers will have to take excursions to other waters. Sunsets and sunrises are spectacular all along the beach. You can even have the beach to yourself when other hotel guests have departed for the dinner and evening shows. **Amenities:** food, drinks, lounge chairs and sun shades, toilets and showers, provided by hotels all along the beach, for guests only. **Best for:** swimming, sunning, walking, jogging, sunsets. ⊠ *Avenida Playa ✛ Playa Varadero stretches along the north shore of the Hicacos Peninsula, 140 km (88 miles) east of Havana, at the eastern end of the Via Blanca Highway.*

WHERE TO EAT

$$
STEAKHOUSE

✕ **Barbacoa Steak House.** Close to a cluster of hotels, this popular steak house is in an attractive colonial-style villa, with a covered, arched terrace. Specialties include Chateaubriand, grilled beef, or strip loin. The restaurant also serves a variety of seafood plates, including grilled lobster with garlic and butter and mahimahi fillets. It's an excellent, well-priced option for those who have exhausted their culinary choices in one of the many nearby all-inclusive resorts or are just interested in more private dining. Decor is classical, tasteful, and almost elegant. ⑤ *Average main: CUC$16* ⊠ *Calle 64, esq. de 1ra Av.* ☎ *4566–7795.*

$$
SPANISH

✕ **El Mesón del Quijote.** The most romantic Varadero restaurant sits atop a small hill, beside what appears to be an antique round stone tower. It's actually part of the aqueduct system the duPonts built to supply their estate. A metal sculpture of Don Quijote, mounted atop his spindly horse, points a lance in the direction of the tower. Cuban and international specialties are on offer inside the candlelit restaurant—count on paella and *fabada marinera* (seafood bean stew)—with innovative touches from the creative chefs. The menu also includes the usual filet mignon, lobster, fish, and shrimp. The restaurant makes an interesting night out for visitors tiring of their all-inclusive packages. ⑤ *Average main: CUC$14* ⊠ *Carretera de las Américas, Reparto La Torre* ☎ *4566–7796.*

$
CUBAN

✕ **La Bodeguita del Medio.** First-rate Cuban cooking and excellent *mojitos* are served in this Varadero replica of Havana's Bodeguita del Medio—the famous Hemingway haunt—graffiti included. The food is carefully prepared, the prices are more than reasonable, and the musical trio is one of the reasons diners linger late into the evening. Diners can add their own poems, names, and graffiti to the restaurant's walls. ⑤ *Average main: CUC$10* ⊠ *Av. de la Playa y Calle 40* ☎ *4566–7784.*

WHERE TO STAY

$$$
RESORT
FAMILY

▦ **Barceló Solymar Arenas Blancas Resort.** If an active beach vacation is what you're looking for, this centrally located, really big, all-inclusive resort combines two properties that share a plethora of pools, restaurants, and activities. **Pros:** lots of restaurant and pool choices; close enough to town to walk; affordable. **Cons:** the young, party-hardy

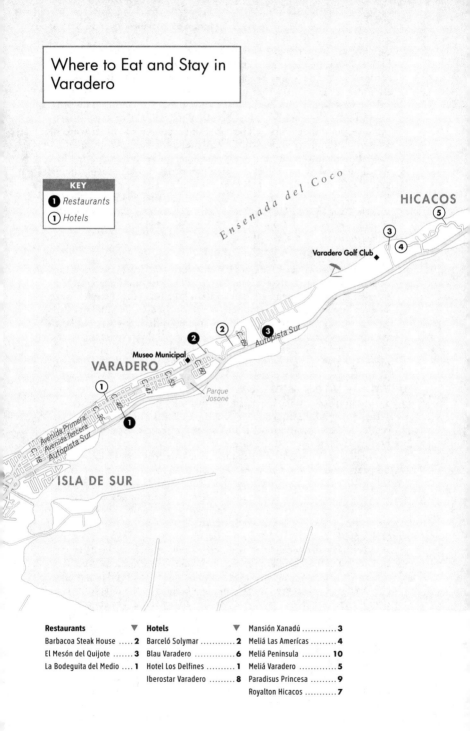

Where to Eat and Stay in Varadero

KEY

① Restaurants

① Hotels

Ensenada del Coco

HICACOS

VARADERO

ISLA DE SUR

Museo Municipal

Parque Josone

Varadero Golf Club

Autopista Sur

Avenida Primera
Avenida Tercera
Autopista Sur

Nicholas Cannel

⑨ ⑧ ⑦ ⑥

Autopista Sur

PENINSULA DE HICACOS

CAYO
LIBERTAD

⑩

Marina

VARADERITO

Bahía de Cárdenas

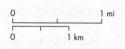

0   1 mi

0   1 km

crowds can keep you up well into the night; must love a bustling atmosphere. ⑤ *Rooms from: CUC$200* ✉ *Carretera Las Americas Km 3* ✛ *200 meters (656 feet) from Varadero town center* ☏ *4561–4499* ⊕ *www.barcelo.com* ⟳ *525 rooms in Solymar, 358 rooms in Arenas Blancas* ⏐◯⏐ *All-inclusive.*

$$$$ ⊞ **Blau Varadero Hotel.** This towering, sloping structure has the bold-
RESORT   est architecture in Varadero and an excellent reputation as a family-
FAMILY   oriented resort. **Pros:** very much family-oriented with a great menu of activities; 24-hour snack bar at the beach. **Cons:** waits for elevators can be tedious, especially with small children; half the rooms face the road and the bay; bit of a walk from rooms to the beach. ⑤ *Rooms from: CUC$278* ✉ *Carretera de Las Morlas, Km 14.5* ☏ *4566–7545* ⊕ *www.blau-hotels-cuba.com* ⟳ *383 rooms, 12 suites* ⏐◯⏐ *All-inclusive.*

$$ ⊞ **Hotel Los Delfines.** One of the best values in Varadero, this cheerfully
RESORT   retro property is right in the center of town, though it nevertheless has a great beachfront. **Pros:** the price is right without giving up all resort features; the vibe is retro Cuban; right in town, so close to restaurants, shops. **Cons:** the property is located in a town setting, so it's less private than some of the outlying resorts. ⑤ *Rooms from: CUC$100* ✉ *Av. 1ra, e/Calle 38 y Calle 39* ☏ *4566–7720* ⊕ *www.islazul.cu* ⟳ *103 rooms* ⏐◯⏐ *All-inclusive.*

$$$$ ⊞ **Iberostar Varadero.** This top-of-the-line, rather grandiose resort has
RESORT   an impressive pool with dramatically eclectic design elements, includ-
Fodor's Choice   ing domed temples on islets, connected by Venetian bridges. **Pros:** the
★   property feels less resort-like and more hotel-like; spectacular stretch of beach. **Cons:** far from the city and alternative dining or entertainment options. ⑤ *Rooms from: CUC$400* ✉ *Carretera Las Morlas Autopista, Km 17.5* ☏ *4566–9999* ⊕ *www.iberostar.com* ⟳ *324 rooms, 62 suites* ⏐◯⏐ *All-inclusive.*

$$$ ⊞ **Mansión Xanadú.** Built by the duPont family, this grand, three-story
B&B/INN   1920s mansion is Varadero's only true boutique hotel; with only a half-dozen rooms, it often sells out. **Pros:** the ocean views are unparalleled; the experience of 1920s-style luxury is unique. **Cons:** the charm of living in such a beautiful hotel is mitigated by the steady flow of tourists flocking into the property daily; rooms in need of repair and renovation. ⑤ *Rooms from: CUC$168* ✉ *Av. de las Américas, Km 8.5* ☏ *4566–8482* ⊕ *www.varaderogolfclub.com* ⚶ *Varadero Golf Club* ⟳ *6 rooms* ⏐◯⏐ *Some meals.*

$$$$ ⊞ **Meliá Las Américas.** Strictly a resort for grown-ups, Las Americas over-
RESORT   looks the Varadero golf course with its small lakes on one side, and a postcard-perfect beach on the other. **Pros:** has some of the best amenities of Varadero properties; relatively calm atmosphere; decidedly golf-focused because of its proximity to the course. **Cons:** atmosphere is a little staid but not stuffy; exterior of hotel needs refurbishing. ⑤ *Rooms from: CUC$490* ✉ *Playa de las Américas, Autopista del Sur, Km 7* ☏ *4566–7600* ⊕ *www.meliacuba.com* ⚶ *Discounted rates at Varadero Golf Club* ⟳ *236 rooms, 14 suites, 90 bungalows* ⏐◯⏐ *All-inclusive.*

$$$$ ⊞ **Meliá Peninsula Varadero.** This upscale, family-focused resort has a
RESORT   village-like feel, with avenues of palm trees leading to white-clapboard,
FAMILY   Key West-style buildings. **Pros:** in the top tier of hotels with an excellent

set of amenities and facilities; excellent hotel for kids of all ages. **Cons:** you can't walk into town, isolated location means that you are basically resort-bound; within easy reach of new Gaviota Marina and Las Morlas shopping and dining. $ *Rooms from: CUC$315* ⊠ *Parque Natural Punta Hicacos, Autopista del Sur* ☎ *4566–8800* ⊕ *www.melia.com* ⟿ *581 rooms, 15 suites* ¡○¡ *All-inclusive.*

$$$
RESORT

⌂ **Meliá Varadero.** Varadero's first luxury hotel remains in the top tier of area resorts with six wings that fan out like flower petals from a lush circular atrium; the quality of the rooms and five à la carte restaurants don't disappoint. **Pros:** offers a host of colorful activities and is always full of life; close to downtown Varadero and golf course. **Cons:** exterior is dated and showing signs of age; sometimes longish elevator waits. $ *Rooms from: CUC$200* ⊠ *Playa de las Américas, Carretera de las Morlas* ☎ *4566–7013* ⊕ *www.melia.com* ⟿ *490 rooms: 331 classic, 68 classic with sea view, 21 premium ocean; 33 Level Two, 6 suites, 1 grand suite* ¡○¡ *All-inclusive.*

$$$$
RESORT
Fodor's Choice
★

⌂ **Paradisus Princesa del Mar Resort & Spa.** One of the best of Varadero's all-inclusives, this resort stands out as an all-suites, adults-only luxury property with five lagoon pools swirling around lush gardens and handsome, three-story buildings with Spanish-colonial architectural flourishes. **Pros:** spacious suites; endless pools; beautiful gardens. **Cons:** as far away as you can be from town and night spots. $ *Rooms from: CUC$300* ⊠ *Carretera Las Morlas, Km 19.5* ☎ *4566–7200* ⊕ *www.meliacuba.com* ⟿ *388 rooms, 242 suites* ¡○¡ *All-inclusive.*

$$$$
RESORT
Fodor's Choice
★

⌂ **Royalton Hicacos Resort & Spa.** Varadero's reigning luxury resort for adults creates an aura of castaway-island seclusion, amid swaying Royal palms, tropical gardens and an unequaled beachfront that's dotted with thatch-roofed shelters. **Pros:** top-notch design elements and comfort; unparalleled, personalized service; blends castaway-island seclusion with urbane sophistication. **Cons:** the center of Varadero is a long way off. $ *Rooms from: CUC$300* ⊠ *Autopista, Km 15* ☎ *4566–8844* ⊕ *www.royaltonresorts.com* ⟿ *404 rooms* ¡○¡ *All-inclusive.*

NIGHTLIFE

Most of the all-inclusive hotels offer nightly shows, from floor-show extravaganzas with dancers, to Michael Jackson tributes, to water-ballet spectaculars that combine choreographed acrobatics, gymnastics, and dance moves. Small combos travel from lobbies to bars and poolsides to supply dance music. But if you want to break out of the programmed entertainment, there are a few Varadero clubs to consider.

The Beatles Bar. The Beatles live again, every night at this restaurant/club, bordering Parque Josone. There's a live, cover band providing rock-and-roll and Beatles tunes pretty much all night long. Bring a camera and pose with the life-size bronze statues of the Fab Four here. There's also dancing indoors and outdoors on a large patio terrace. ⊠ *Av. 1ra y Calle 59* ✛ *Northern edge of Parque Josone* ☎ *4566–7329.*

La Comparsita. The best thing about this open-air nightspot is the chance to dance under the stars, among locals and tourists, to a mix of Cuban bands and international hits. Just check the weather report before you head out. The cover charge includes beer and Cuba libres (rum and coke). ⊠ *Calle 60 and Calle 3* ☎*4566–7751* ⎗*CUC$7.*

La Cueva del Pirata. If you're in a swashbuckling mood, check out the pirate-themed floor show in this natural cave, followed by a very loud disco that doesn't stop till 3 am, Monday through Saturday. The dance floor is usually packed with a young crowd. Cover charge is CUC$10. ⊠ *Autopista del Sur, Km 12* ☎*4566–7751* ⎗*CUC$10* ☉ *Closed Sun.*

Mambo Club. Reminiscent of the heyday of '50s Latin nightclubs, this nostalgic venue still has the dramatic two-level stage for dancers to descend. The entire place is, in fact, a throwback to the '50s and if you're lucky to be here on a crowded night, the mambo rhythms emanating from the orchestra will have everyone up dancing. If you don't know how, there's an instructor on hand. Drinks are included in the entrance fee. ⊠ *Carretera de las Morlas, Km 14* ☎*4566–8565* ⎗*CUC$10.*

SHOPPING

Not surprisingly, Varadero is well supplied with souvenir shops and arts-and-crafts goods. Along the main street in town, there are outdoor markets set up every couple of blocks where you can search for something different among the standard souvenirs that are also sold at almost every hotel gift shop. A new, upscale shopping center is being built at the far end of the peninsula, the Centro Comercial Las Morlas, part of the huge, Gaviota Marina complex. It should be fully operational by 2016 and offer a wider selection of upscale souvenir shops and art galleries.

AREAS AND MALLS

Centro Comercial Caimán. While wandering through Varadero's street markets, look for this cluster of shops. ⊠ *Av. 1, e/Calle 61 y Calle 62* ✢ *A few blocks north of Parque Josone.*

BOOKS

Librería Hanoi. Like all book stores in Cuba, the stock here is strong in the usual sociopolitical tracts approved by the regime, but this shop also has a good collection of paperbacks in English. ⊠ *Av. 1 y Calle 44* ☎*4566–8917.*

SPORTS AND THE OUTDOORS

All the hotels offer virtually the same outdoor activities and sports tours. The most popular tour on the water is a catamaran cruise with snorkeling, sunning and picnicking on a tiny island, and a visit to a dolphin center (around CUC$100). Dive shops also organize tours by bus to dive and snorkeling spots on the Zapata Peninsula (⇨ *see Peninsula de Zapata*). Arrangements for water sports can be made through hotel tour desks.

FISHING

Marlin Náutica y Marinas at Marina Chapelin. Fishing charters, which last five to seven hours, set off at 8:30 am daily, from this marina halfway along the peninsula. Fishing is strictly catch and release, four fishers to a boat, for about CUC$320. ⊠ *Autopista del Sur, Km 13* ☎*4566–8440, 4566–7550.*

GOLF

Varadero Golf Club. The scenic 18-hole Varadero Golf Club, built in 1936 by the duPont family, was Cuba's first golf course, complete with lakes and a bay view. If you book online, the greens fee is CUC$132, which includes your cart and bag. Clubs are included, as well, if you didn't bring your own. A caddie will set you back another supplement. Many hotels have special discounts for guests, notably the Meliá Las Americas, which overlooks the course. ☒ *Av. de las Américas* ☎ *4566–8481* ⊕ *www.varaderogolfclub.com* ✎ *CUC$132.*

SCUBA DIVING

Gaviota Marina Dive Center. At the far end of the peninsula in the Gaviota Marina, this relatively new dive center has well-maintained gear and access to 32 dive sites, including a coral reef with tunnels, underwater caves, and some ship wrecks in its own underwater marine park. The center also organizes snorkeling trips. ☒ *Autopista sur, Km 21* ✛ *Far end of peninsula, in Gaviota Marina* ☎ *4566–7755* ✎ *CUC$50.*

SKYDIVING

SkyDive Varadero. Just west of the bridge into Varadero, this skydiving outfit offers skydiving training and tandem jumps with a professional instructor. If you really want to learn, there's a two-week course for CUC$3,000. But if you already have parachute training, a jump will cost you CUC$30 (CUC$25 extra for gear). Bring your license and logbook. ☒ *Vía Blanca* ☎ *45666–2828* ⊕ *www.skydivingvaradero.com.*

CÁRDENAS

10 km (6 miles) east of Varadero.

This once-elegant town, modeled after Charleston, SC, was founded in 1828 as a sugar-exporting port with a neat grid of streets lined with Neoclassical facades. The streets remain but, apart from some restored churches and public buildings, the state of dilapidation is sobering. Ironically, this is where many hotel workers from the glitzy Varadero hotels live. Anyone who wants to experience "the real Cuba" can take a town tour in a traditional horse-drawn *caleta* (cart) for less than CUC$10. The city's historical fame rests on being the first town in Cuba to raise the national flag in 1850. A mercenary force of Kentuckians and Mississippians led by a Venezuelan named Narciso López briefly captured Cárdenas from the Spanish, hoping to provoke a national uprising that failed to materialize. More recently, Cárdenas became famous as the original home of Elián González, the boy who became enmeshed in a tug-of-war in 2000 between his Cuban father and his anti-Castro relatives in Miami, after his mother died during a furtive boat escape to the United States from Cuba.

A gigantic stone crab, commemorating the city's history as a crab fishery, marks the town line as you approach from Varadero; sculptures of a bicycle and a fittingly broken-down *caleta* mark the other end of town. With barely a car in the streets, there's a dramatic simplicity and some charm to what lies in between. The main attraction here is the fascinating Museo Oscar María de Rojas and an excellent new restaurant.

EXPLORING
TOP ATTRACTIONS

Fodor's Choice
★

Museo Oscar María de Rojas. This beautifully restored museum, housed in an elegant, colonnaded 1918 building, is worth a visit for its wide-ranging exhibits on everything from archeology to ethnology to numismatics to colonial weaponry. Perhaps most interesting is the re-creation of the original exhibition space, as it would have been presented 100 years ago, in a high-ceilinged hall with an upper, wooden gallery. Lots of natural light illuminates the quirky, Victorian-era potpourri of natural-history exhibits, from bugs, butterflies, *polymitas* (snails with multicolored shells), to preserved fleas in nuptial dress, viewed under a magnifying glass. Antique buttons and buckles, pen nibs, death masks, a Masonic lodge throne in the shape of a peacock—you never know what oddity you will come across. On the historical side, there are the usual photographs of Cárdenas heroes of the wars of independence and the Revolution and a gruesome reminder of the risks rebels took, in the form of the garotte used to strangle victims to death. The museum has a beautiful, bright inner courtyard displaying some lovely, early 19th-century furniture, as well as an ornate horse-drawn hearse. ⌧ *Calle Calzada 4 y Calle 13* ✢ *Facing Parque Estrada Palma* ☎ *4552–4126* 📧 *CUC$5* ☺ *Mon.–Sat. 9–6, Sun. 9–1.*

WORTH NOTING

Museo a la Batalla de Ideas. Inspired by the diplomatic battle to repatriate Elián González, the five-year-old rescued off the coast of Florida in 1999, this museum, in a restored, neoclassical-style firehouse, is an ideological examination of the opposing Battle of Ideas between Cuba and the United States. Inaugurated in 2001 by Fidel Castro himself, the concept is a perfect example of how any threat to Cuba's sovereignty quickly becomes a rallying cry for unity in Cuba and grist for the propaganda mill. Other exhibits focus on the history of Cuba's battle to achieve and maintain its national sovereignty, displaying such wide-ranging "artifacts" as two English cannonballs fired in 1756, and the cross given to Elián by Reverend John Brown Campbell. ■TIP➜ **If you can read Spanish, the museum provides an excellent insight into the official Cuban mind-set.** There's a great view of the town and the harbor from the roof terrace. ⌧ *Av. José Martí 523* ✢ *E/Calle 11 y Calle 12, near Oscar María Rojas Museum* ☎ *4552–1056* 📧 *CUC$2, CUC$5 extra for camera* ☺ *Tues.–Sat. 9–noon, 1–5, Sun. 9–1.*

Parque Colón. You can sightsee in one of the horse-drawn carriages (less than CUC$10) that wait for hire in the plaza facing the town's central park, which also has the oldest statue of Columbus in the New World (erected in 1858). Overlooking the statue, the mid-19th-century **Catedral de la Inmaculada Concepción** is oddly framed by two conical towers and is in desperate need of repair. However, the Neoclassical cathedral is known for its stained glass windows, best admired from inside. To enter, walk around the church to the back door at No. 359. Don't miss the tiny chapel in the conical tower at the northeast corner. ⌧ *Av. de Cespedes, e/Calle 8 y Calle 9.*

WHERE TO EAT

$ ✕**Restaurante Don Qko.** Pronounced "Cuco," this excellent Cuban res-
CUBAN taurant is hidden off a dusty side street in a surprise oasis of tropical
Fodor's Choice plants and shrubs. Tables are arranged around a curvaceous pool and
★ in a chic dining room that's decorated in black and white. As refreshing and attractive as the decor and setting are, the main event here is
the innovative Cuban cuisine, creatively building on traditional dishes.
A delectable starter of "*tostones*" takes typical fried, mashed plantains
and raises it to a whole new level, forming plantain tarts filled with
minced pork and melted cheese, and served with a sweet and sour sauce.
A main course of *Asado con sabor y tradicion* is pork, slow-roasted,
then simmered in red wine and garlic. For dessert, try the light, fluffy
cloud of coconut flan, with caramelized fresh coconut. The separate bar
is straight out of the 1960s, with swivel stools and yellow and black
leather banquettes. The iced daiquiri is perfection. Service is polished
and friendly and the owner, Alexe, is an enthusiastic, obliging host. A
daily lunch special here, including appetizer, main course of chicken or
meat, plus sides and a drink will set you back only CUC$6.25. ⑤ *Aver-
age main: CUC$7* ⊠ *Av. Céspedes, main street through town, esq. de
Calle 21* ☎ *4552–4572* ⊘ *Closed Tues.* ▭ *No credit cards.*

PENÍNSULA DE ZAPATA

*100 km (62 miles) southwest of Cárdenas, 190 km (118 miles) south-
east of Havana.*

Home to the country's—and the Caribbean's—largest wetland, the
Península de Zapata is world-renowned for superb bird-watching and
fly-fishing. Its pristine coastline also provides excellent dive and snorkeling sites. The peninsula backs onto the Bahía de los Cochinos (Bay of
Pigs), named for the *cochinos cimarrones* (free-range or runaway pigs)
that Spanish colonists lost or deliberately stocked in the Zapata swamps
during the 16th century. In more recent history, the Bay of Pigs became
famous as the site of the failed 1961 invasion attempted by Cuban exiles
with the backing and training of the U.S. CIA.

The peninsula remains a fairly remote, undeveloped area, with very
limited and basic lodging options. But for divers and birders, it's a must.
For curious travelers with limited time, the Varadero hotels organize
day trips to the best diving and snorkeling sites, as well as visits to the
popular crocodile-breeding center.

GETTING HERE AND AROUND

Take one of the day bus tours offered by your hotel or hire a taxi with
a guide. You can also rent a car and explore on your own.

TOURS

Infotur. On the dock where boats depart for the Laguna Tesoro, you
can pick up maps and brochures of the area and talk with a tourism
official. ⊠ *La Boca de Guamá, boat dock, Playa Girón* ✛ *At entrance
to Criadero de Cocodrilos.*

EXPLORING
TOP ATTRACTIONS

FAMILY **Criadero de Cocodrilos.** From the safety of wooden walkways, you can observe some 3,000 crocodiles in various stages of development at this breeding center-cum-tourist attraction. The original enterprise was the idea of Celia Sánchez, one of Fidel Castro's close companions and advisers, who was determined to restore the failing crocodile and caiman populations in the Cienaga Swamp. Today, buses crowd the parking lot bringing tour groups for the guided tour, which takes about 45 minutes. Along the way you can stroke a baby crocodile and have your photo taken cradling a three-year-old croc. The guides fill you in on such crocodilian factoids as: these naturally aggressive creatures can jump 1 meter (3 feet) high and run as fast as a horse for 80 meters (264 feet), reaching speeds of up to 60 kph (37 mph). So stay on the walkway! After visiting with the crocodiles, if you're not too sensitive, you can lunch on crocodile steaks at two on-site restaurants, La Boca and El Ranchón. The Ranchón is smaller and cheaper, and has live music to accompany your reptilian repast (CUC$10). The entrance fee to the breeding center includes a soft drink or glass of juice. Boat tours to the Laguna de Tesoro model village leave from a dock here. ⊠ *Complejo Turistica La Boca, Km 19 on road south of Australia, Playa Girón* 🕾 *4591–5662* 🖼 *CUC$5* 🕙 *Daily 9:30–5* 🖙 *Kids under 2 years, free.*

Fodor's Choice **Parque Nacional Ciénaga de Zapata.** Bird-watchers from all over the world
★ flock to this national park in hopes of feasting their eyes on some 190 bird species, including 21 endemic species. Even if you're not a passionate birder, you can still enjoy watching a mass of wading birds—flamingos, wood storks, sandhill cranes—feeding here. The park forms about half of a UNESCO Biosphere Reserve that also includes the Las Salinas Wildlife Sanctuary. The combined reserve covers 4,520 sq km (1,641 sq miles) encompassing mangroves, cactus, dry woods, savannahs, salt pans and forest, providing habitat for reptiles, mammals, and all those birds. It's a mecca for fly-fishermen and hikers, as well. Bird-watching platforms on the way out to Las Salinas offer a chance to see some of the endemic species, such as the eponymous Zapata Rail and Zapata Wren, along with the red, white, and blue *tocororo*—Cuba's national bird and the *zunzuncito* (Bee Hummingbird), the smallest bird in the world. The main access to the park is via Playa Larga at the head of the Bahía de los Cochinos. Check in at the park office in Playa Largo a day before you plan to visit the vast park, to plan which area you want to explore, pay your entrance fee (CUC$10), and make arrangements for hiring a guide (CUC$10). ⊠ *Playa Larga ✛ Km 15, Carretera 316, south of Australia* 🕾 *4598–7249 park office* 🖼 *CUC$10 entry fee, CUC$10 guide fee* 🕙 *Park, daily sunrise–sunset; park office, daily 9–5.*

WORTH NOTING

Finca Fiesta Campesina. At this casual farm-cum-zoo visitors can see two of Cuba's distinctive animals: the *manjuarí,* a primitive water creature with an alligator-like head and a fish body, and the *jutía,* a large-eared, muskrat-like tree rat, once prized for *guajiro* stews. Scattered around the farm yard there are deer, peacocks, rabbits, ducks, and guinea fowl. At the *guarapa* bar, you can buy a glass of fresh-pressed cane juice, with or without rum (CUC$2). The musical entertainment is provided by a caged Cuban Bullfinch, a small black bird, so prized for its song that Cubans organize bird-song competitions. There's no entrance fee to the farm but there are souvenir kiosks scattered around, and an open-air restaurant ($) mostly set up for tour-group buffets. ⊠ *1 km south of village of Australia* ✢ *Turn off Autopista Nacional at Km 142 and travel south through village of Australia* ☎ *4591–2045 for restaurant* ⊙ *Daily 8–5.*

La Cueva de los Peces (*Cave of the Fish*). South of Playa Larga, on the east side of the Bay of Pigs, lies this natural aquarium in a 61-meter-deep (201-foot-deep) *cenote* (a flooded sinkhole filled with multicolor fish that swim in from the bay via a subterranean passage). Diving through the banks of fish and the lush subaquatic vegetation is superb. There is no entrance fee—you walk along a short, shaded trail to the pool and dive in. There's a makeshift, on-site dive shop with tanks, as well as snorkeling gear to rent. If you plan on doing a lot of snorkeling and care about hygiene, bring along your own mask. You can also snorkel from the beach, across the road from the entrance to the cenote. La Casa del Pescador *(see Where to Eat, below)* is next to the cenote. ⊠ *Carretera e/Playa Larga y Playa Girón at Km 18* ☎ *5341–7297 dive shop* ⊙ *Dive center: daily 8–5.*

La Laguna del Tesoro (*Treasure Lagoon*). According to legend, Taíno aboriginals dumped gold and other loot in this lake to hide it from the Spanish. No treasure has ever been found, although Taíno relics have been recovered from the lake and are now displayed in the **Museo Guamá.** The museum is part of an impressive replica of a Taíno village on an island, complete with 32 life-size figures of Taínos going about their daily business, created by Cuban sculptor Rita Longa. The lake is stocked with largemouth bass for visiting fishermen who stay in the cabins dotted around the lake. Access to the museum is by boat, leaving from the Criadero de Cocodrilos dock. The outboard motorboats, some with sunshades, travel 4 km (2½ miles) along a canal into the lagoon. The boat trip takes about 30 minutes and costs CUC$12, including entrance to the museum. The first boat leaves at 9 am and the last one at 4 pm. ✢ *5 km (2½ miles) east of Boca de Guamá via Canal de la Laguna* ⊙ *Daily 9:30–5:30*

WHERE TO EAT

$$ ✕ **La Casa del Pescador.** Tucked alongside the shaded trail that leads to La CUBAN Cueva de los Peces, this small but decent open-air restaurant offers seafood, lobster (when available), fish or crocodile options, complete with soup, salad, and sides. $ *Average main: CUC$12* ⊠ *Cueva de los Peces, Playa Girón* ✢ *On trail to fish pool* ☞ *Daily noon–4* ▭ *No credit cards.*

WHERE TO STAY

$ ▦ **Batey de Don Pedro.** Ten *bohíos* , simple, traditional cabins with thatch B&B/INN roofs, ceiling fans and private bathrooms are scattered around a field with a few shade trees. **Pros:** a unique lodging experience; inexpensive; decent restaurant. **Cons:** very basic; hot water in only 5 cabins; mosquitoes could be a problem at night because there are no mosquito nets. $ *Rooms from: CUC$24* ⊠ *Off Autopista Nacional at Km 142,*

Australia ⚓ 1 km (½ mile) south of Finca Fiesta Campesina ☎ *4591–2825* 🛏 *10 cabins, 2 rooms* 🍽 *Breakfast* 💳 *Credit cards accepted when phone works; extra meals are cash only.*

$ 🏨 **Horizontes Villa Guamá.** Once a Castro bass-fishing refuge (*Bohío 33 B&B/INN* was El Comandante's), this odd hideaway is perched on 12 little islands in the Laguna del Tesoro. **Pros:** excellent value for the money; adventurous locale. **Cons:** cold water only; vicious mosquitoes; upkeep leaves much to be desired. 🟢 *Rooms from: CUC$62* ✉ *Laguna del Tesoro* ☎ *4595–9100* 🛏 *44 cabins* 🍽 *Some meals* 💳 *Breakfast and dinner are included in room rate.*

$ 🏨 **Villa Playa Larga.** Bay breezes help cool these basic, crinkle-top roofed *HOTEL* bungalows that dot the lawn of this large property, which borders a good, sandy beach. **Pros:** good beach; as close as you can get to Peninsula de Ciénaga National Park. **Cons:** no nightlife here but the stars above you; bare-bones furnishings and food. 🟢 *Rooms from: CUC$64* ✉ *Playa Larga, facing the beach* ☎ *4598–7212* 🌐 *www.hotelescubanacan.com* 🛏 *60 rooms, including 8 triple occupancy* 🍽 *Breakfast.*

SPORTS AND THE OUTDOORS
BIRD-WATCHING
Ciénaga de Zapata National Park Birding. To get the most out of birding in Parque Nacional Ciénaga de Zapata, check in at the park office to choose which area of the park to explore. Park guide/biologist Frank Medina can help you choose your spots, and serve as your guide. Or spend a full morning on foot with independent, bilingual guide Orestes Martínez Garcias, aka "El Chino." For CUC$25 per person, he can help you spot some of the 190 or so bird species here, including 21 Cuban endemics and 17 globally threatened species. ✉ *Gran Parque Natural Montemar, Playa Girón* ⚓ *Peninsula de Zapata* ☎ *5398–7142 cell phone for Orestes Martínez, 5262–8196 national park office* 📧 *chino. zapata@gmail.com.*

DIVING
International Dive Center. There are at least 12 dive and snorkeling sites along the east side of the Bay of Pigs and beyond Cayo Largo. All of them are supplied by this dive center, which is based in Hotel Playa Girón. You can also rent gear and tanks directly at Cueva de Peces and Punta Perdix. Diving is all done from the shore, so no boats are needed. ✉ *Hotel Playa Girón, Playa Girón* ☎ *4110–7206 Hotel Playa Girón* 💰 *CUC$25 per dive; CUC$5 for snorkeling gear.*

FISHING
Cienaga National Park Fishing. Fly-fishermen have two options: bass fishing in the Laguna del Tesoro, based in the Villa Guamá; or fly-fishing along the Río Hatiguanico or in the Salinas de Brito, both in the Cienaga National Park, for tarpon, bonefish, shad and snook, all strictly catch-and-release. For eight hours of fishing in the park, CUC$240 covers boat, guide, fishing permit, and refreshments; each extra person is charged CUC$69. Book at the national park office in Playa Largo. ✉ *Cienaga National Park office, Playa Girón* ⚓ *Playa Largo* ☎ *4598–7249 park office* 📧 *usopublico@eficz.co.cu.*

PLAYA GIRÓN

125 km (78 miles) south of Varadero.

A popular destination for diving and snorkeling, this beach town is famously known as the site of the Bay of Pigs invasion. On April 17, 1961, much of the ill-fated invasion took place here. More than 1,100 men of the 1,300 Cuban exiles who made up the landing force were captured, with more than 110 killed. (Five minutes in close contact with the mosquitoes of the Zapata swamp will explain a lot about this fracas.) In December 1962, most of the prisoners were returned to the United States in exchange for Cuban prisoners in the United States and a ransom of $53 million in supplies. Even today, "*La Victoria*" is one of Cuba's great rallying points and sources of pride.

About 2,000 people live in sleepy Playa Girón village in the middle of which stands a billboard that reads: *Playa Girón—la primera derrota del imperialismo norteamericano en américa latina* (Playa Girón—the first defeat of U.S. imperialism in Latin America). Along the road between La Boca de Guamá and Playa Girón, you'll also see concrete slabs commemorating Cuban defenders who fell in the invasion, as well as a huge billboard noting the spot the invaders managed to reach before retreating. The beach itself is quite windswept, protected from rough seas by an unsightly, concrete sea wall, which is crumbling, so it's not the ideal tropical beach scene.

GETTING HERE AND AROUND

Book a guided bus tour or hire a taxi to get you here. This is one area where a rental car is really the best way to explore. There's no problem finding parking places here.

EXPLORING

Caleta Buena. Just east of Playa Girón, the sea has formed a series of natural pools by entering through underwater caves, creating the largest flooded cavern in Cuba. The bottom of sponge and coral is a polychromatic marvel, as are the many tropical fish. Experienced, well-equipped divers can follow a 25-meter (83-foot) tunnel through the limestone leading out to the sea. The on-site dive shop charges CUC$25 for a dive, including gear; and CUC$5 to rent snorkeling gear. There's no need for boats as the dive area is close. Night dives can also be arranged. The on-site restaurant is open until 5 and specializes in shrimp and lobster. There's a CUC$15 charge that includes lunch and drinks, and access to the natural pool. In spring, be prepared for roads covered with dead land crabs and their attendant vultures. ⊠ *Playa Girón* ✛ *9 km (6 miles) east of Playa Girón* ☎ *4559–5589* 🖂 *CUC$15; snorkel equipment rental CUC$5; diving equipment rental CUC$25* ☉ *Daily 10–5.*

Museo Playa Girón. Propaganda aside, this museum celebrating "the first rout of Yankee imperialism in Latin America" is a sobering testament to the harsh social conditions that provoked the Revolution, especially in this historically poorest part of Cuba, where there were no schools or hospitals pre-Revolution. The main focus is on the counterrevolutionary events after 1959 leading up to the Bay of Pigs invasion, and the story of the invasion itself. Particularly affecting are the photos of fallen

Cuban soldiers, accompanied by such personal effects as photos of their families or an old-fashioned fob watch. There's also a 15-minute film to watch. For military buffs, a restored British Hawker Sea Fury plane, used by the Cuban Air Force, stands guard at the museum entrance. For an extra CUC$2, you can hire a guide to elaborate on the exhibits. ⊠ *Playa Girón* ⊹ *At entrance to Villa Playa Girón hotel* ☎ *4598–4122* 🎫 *CUC$2* ⊙ *Daily 9–5.*

BEACHES

Playa Girón. This windswept stretch of beige sand extends along the length of the Hotel Playa Girón property. Pretty beach umbrellas and lounges for hotel guests dot the beach. Access is through the hotel. Despite the pleasant, colorful umbrellas, the view from the beach is marred by a huge, crumbling concrete sea wall, a barrier against rough Caribbean seas. On the positive side, the wall keeps the inner beach calm for swimming. If you can look beyond the unsightly concrete, sunsets here are beautiful and cooled by strong breezes. Diving and snorkeling sites are a short drive from the beach. **Amenities:** food and toilets in Hotel Playa Girón. **Best for:** swimming; sunsets. ⊠ *7206 Hotel Playa Girón* ⊹ *Playa Girón is 50 km (32 miles) south of the small town of Australia, at the bottom of the west side of the Bay of Pigs, facing the Caribbean Sea.*

WHERE TO EAT

$$
CUBAN
✕ **Punta Perdíz.** This open-air restaurant—built within the prow of a boat—is the flagship of the Complejó Punta Perdíz, with beachfront, thatch-roof shelters and beach chairs and a dive shop. The restaurant has fine views over the water from its upper deck but, sadly, the buffet menu is uninspiring. The CUC$15 buffet price is only worth it if you plan on spending the day here, imbibing the included bar drinks, and enjoying the beach lounges under thatch-roof shelters facing the sea. The snorkeling is excellent; dives cost CUC$25 a tank. The only place to change clothes is in the inadequate, cramped restaurant bathroom, so bring a large towel along with you. There are outdoor, cold-water showers and basins to rinse off salt water and snorkeling and diving gear. 🛒 *Average main: CUC$15* ⊠ *Carretera Playa Larga–Playa Girón, Km 52* 🚫 *No credit cards* ⊂ *Beach: daily 10–5; restaurant: daily 10:30–4:30.*

WHERE TO STAY

$
HOTEL
🏨 **Villa Playa Girón.** This formerly dismal hotel has had a recent makeover with many improvements, including air-conditioning in all the rooms and spruced up interiors. **Pros:** close to museum and dive sites; decent organized tours; kids under 12 stay free. **Cons:** basic rooms; unsightly sea wall spoils view. 🛒 *Rooms from: CUC$60* ⊠ *Playa Girón* ☎ *4598–7206* ⊕ *www.hotelescubacan.com* ↪ *120 rooms* 🍽 *All-inclusive.*

SPORTS AND THE OUTDOORS

DIVING

Punta Perdiz Diving Center. Two, close-in, shore-dive sites cover a colorful coral reef and a series of caverns and overhangs to explore. If the weather is calm and there's no current, the snorkeling is good here, too. Dives and gear rental (CUC$25) are supplied by the on-site dive shop. ⊠ *Punta Perdiz* ⊹ *About 8 km (6 miles) east of Playa Girón* ⊂ *Dive shop: daily 8–4.*

4

CENTRAL CUBA

Updated by
Jeffrey Van
Fleet

Cuba's geographic heart beats with the rhythms of Afro-Cuban music, of turquoise waves crashing on white-sand beaches, and of life unfolding in splendid colonial cities. Its coral reefs are awash in color, its mangrove swamps attract flamingos by the thousands, and its lush mountain valleys are filled with birdsong of all types.

Inviting beaches border Central Cuba to the north and south. In between are varied landscapes—from mountains to mangroves—dotted with historic cities. Unlike that of many Caribbean islands, Cuba's early history centered on life in cities, and scattered across this region are three of the nation's seven original "villas"—Trinidad, Sancti Spíritus, and Camagüey—as well as the colonial town of Remedios. In each, time-worn churches and mansions line cobbled streets and tidy parks; in the verdant countryside beyond, old farmhouses overlook sugar plantations, royal palms tower over pastures populated by the people's cattle, and children in red-and-white uniforms play outside one-room schoolhouses.

Central Cuba's northern and southern coasts have many beautiful stretches of sand. The beach count leaps dramatically when you include the hundreds of *cayos* (keys) that flank the shores. More and more visitors are discovering the northern cayos, collectively called the Jardines del Rey (Gardens of the King). In the south, the less accessible archipelago known as the Jardines de la Reina (Gardens of the Queen) is visited only by diving excursions.

ORIENTATION AND PLANNING

GETTING ORIENTED

The region is easy to reach and explore, thanks to the central, mostly flat highway that traverses the island from Havana to Eastern Cuba. The road becomes only slightly hilly east of Santa Clara, where it passes near the northern extreme of the Sierra de Escambray, the verdant mountain range that dominates the southern corner of Villa Clara and about half of Cienfuegos and Sancti Spíritus provinces. Various roads wind into the mountains from Trinidad and Cienfuegos. One connects the two cities via Topes de Collantes; another, more direct route runs along the coast. The more easterly provincial capitals of Ciego de Ávila and Camagüey are surrounded by flat ranch land, with roads running north and northeast to the coast.

Villa Clara, Cienfuegos, and Sancti Spíritus Provinces. These provinces are the home to historic cities, a half-dozen beaches, and natural attractions that range from highland forests to coral reefs.

TOP REASONS TO GO

Beaches. Each central province has a bit of shoreline, and many of the beaches here are lovely: turquoise shallows and powdered ivory sands shaded by coconut palms. Central Cuba's best beaches are on its northern keys—Villa Clara's tranquil Cayo Las Brujas, and Ciego de Ávila's more developed Cayo Coco and Cayo Guillermo.

Colonial Architecture. Several cities have histories that date from the arrival of the Spanish. Trinidad, the best-preserved of these communities, has block upon block of cobblestone streets lined with 18th- and 19th-century structures.

Scuba Diving and Snorkeling. Diving possibilities range from coral formations just offshore to the isolated, hard-to-access, coral-ringed islands of the Jardines de la Reina, protected within a vast underwater park teeming with marine life.

The Cuban People. The increasing popularity of the *casa particular* (individual homestay) and the *paladar* (private eatery) provides new opportunities to get to know individual Cubans, witness their everyday lives, and forge friendships.

Great Resorts. Some of the newest Cuban resorts are now found on the cayos of the Jardines del Rey Peninsula. From these island-paradise homebases you can head out to some of the traditional colonial cities.

Ciego de Ávila and Camagüey Provinces. Ciego de Ávila and Camagüey provinces are historically agricultural areas that are due south of the Jardines del Rey, some of the most beautiful cayos of Cuba.

PLANNING

WHEN TO GO

Hurricane season runs from May to November, with September through November presenting a greater risk of your vacation being washed out. The drier December–April season is less susceptible to storms. The fact that most visitors head here in January and February has more to do with northern winters than Santa Lucía sunshine. The rainy season is actually a great time to visit because all is green and crowds are thinner. The busiest months are July through August and January through March, with the last week of December and Easter week being peak. Rates during these times rise and yet rooms book up, making reservations essential.

PLANNING YOUR TIME

The 250-mile slice of the island that makes up Central Cuba has at least a week's worth of things to do. You'll find a good transportation network here in this densely populated part of the country. The region doesn't lie so far from Havana that you can't make a detour from the capital. Santa Clara, Sancti Spíritus, and Camagüey lie along the the Autopista/Carretera Nacional. Other destinations here are no more than 60 to 90 minutes off the main highway. History lives on in well-preserved Cienfuegos, Camagüey, and, especially, Trinidad. Any of the three warrants a couple of days. Remedios, Santa Clara, and Sancti Spíritus make worthwhile stops, too, particularly if you're interested in Cuban history. The spectacular cayos (Coco, Guillermo, Santa María, Las Brujas) off the northern coast give long-established Varadero a run for its money as a beach destination. If you're staying on any of the islands or on mainland Playa Santa Lucía, you're likely here on a resort package, which keeps you there for your stay. All resorts and tour operators offer day trips to give you a taste of non-resort Cuba.

GETTING HERE AND AROUND
AIR TRAVEL
Havana may be Cuba's main international hub, but in winter Canadian charter flights arrive almost daily in Cayo Coco, Cienfuegos, Ciego de Ávila, and Camagüey. Those charters can be much cheaper than scheduled flights to Havana, especially if you wait for a last-minute deal. Domestic flights also wing their way from Havana to Cienfuegos, Ciego de Ávila, Camagüey, and Cayo Coco. ⇨ *See Air Travel in Travel Smart.*

BOAT AND FERRY TRAVEL
Thousands of people visit Cuba on private boats every year, and there are a number of marinas in the central provinces with mooring space, electricity, water, diesel, and other services. The largest operation is Puertosol, with marinas in Cienfuegos, Trinidad, and Cayo Guillermo. Marlin is number two, with marinas in Cayo Coco and Playa Santa Lucía.

Boat and Ferry Information Marina Marlin. ☎ *3330–1323 in Cayo Coco, 3236–5294 in Playa Santa Lucía.* **Marina Puerto Sol.** ☎ *4352–1241 in Cienfuegos, 4199–6205 in Playa Ancón, 3330–1738 in Cayo Guillermo.*

BUS TRAVEL
Well-air-conditioned Víazul buses, the workhorse of comfortable coach transportation, will get you to most larger destinations in this region. Buses depart from Havana for Trinidad, Cienfuegos, Santa Clara, Sancti Spíritus, and Camagüey. There's also service from Varadero to Trinidad. Tickets must be purchased ahead of time.

Less comfortable (no a/c) Astro buses, which have offices in most major terminals, serve the same routes for less money, but they often run late.

Bus Information Cienfuegos. ✉ *Calle 49 y Av. 56, Cienfuegos* ☎ *4352–5720.* **Sancti Spíritus Terminal.** ✉ *Calle Masso [3 km (2 miles) south of town], Sancti Spíritus* ☎ *4132–4142.* **Santa Clara Terminal Inter-Municipal.** ✉ *Carretera Central at Amparo, Santa Clara* ☎ *4220–3470.* **Santa Clara Terminal Inter-Provincial.** ✉ *Carretera Central, Santa Clara* ☎ *4229–2114.* **Trinidad Terminal.** ✉ *Calle Piro Guinart, e/Calle Izquierdo y Calle Maceo/Gutiérrez, Trinidad* ☎ *4199–4448.*

CAR TRAVEL
Central Cuba's roads are generally in good repair. The four-lane Autopista Nacional connects Havana to Sancti Spíritus and the two-lane road continues east from there as an east–west route through which little traffic flows. Peripheral arteries head south to Cienfuegos and north from Ciego de Ávila to Cayos Coco and Guillermo, and from Camagüey to Santa Lucía. The old road loops south from the highway

to Sancti Spíritus at Cabaiguan, continuing east toward Ciego de Ávila; another good road heads southwest from Sancti Spíritus to Trinidad. Cienfuegos and Trinidad are connected via Topes de Collantes by a rough mountain road and a smoother, more direct coastal route.

Driving within Central Cuba's towns can be confusing. There are many one-way streets, and intersections aren't always well marked. If you have any doubts about where you're going, just ask someone; people are happy to help strangers. Traffic is invariably light—mostly bicycles and horse-drawn taxis—and parking spaces are abundant and free.

Local Agencies Transtur. 3227–1015 *in Camagüey, 3330–1175 in Cayo Coco, 4355–1600 in Cienfuegos, 4132–8533 in Sancti Spíritus, 4220–4100 in Santa Clara, 4199–6454 in Trinidad* ⊕ *www.transtur.cu.*

4

TAXI TRAVEL

Cubataxi and Transtur taxis are usually parked outside every major hotel. They have convertible-peso meters only and are relatively expensive. Cheaper Cuban taxis that ply the main routes aren't supposed to pick up tourists but usually will if away from the hotels and traffic police. Unfortunately, Cienfuegos's charming horse-drawn taxis risk a hefty fine if they pick up tourists, so they don't.

Local Companies Transtur. 3227–1015 *in Camagüey, 3330–1175 in Cayo Coco, 4355–1600 in Cienfuegos, 4132–8533 in Sancti Spíritus, 4220–4100 in Santa Clara, 4199–6454 in Trinidad.*

TRAIN TRAVEL

Train service in Central Cuba is a shadow of its former self, but it can get you a few places in this region. Trains depart Havana daily and ply the basic spine of the island with service to Santa Clara and Camagüey, before continuing east to Santiago de Cuba.

Train Information Camagüey Terminal. ⊠ *Calle Quioñes y Calle Padre Olalla, Camagüey* 3228–3214. **Santa Clara Terminal.** ⊠ *Calle Pedro Estévez, north of town, Santa Clara* 4220–2895.

RESTAURANTS

As is true all over Cuba, *puerco* (pork)—prepared the usual variety of ways—figures largely on the region's menus. *Carne de res* (beef) is also common, as are *pollo* (chicken) and *cordero* (lamb). Entrées often come with the traditional *arroz congrí* (fried white rice with beans and pork), which is sometimes called *moros y cristianos* (Moors and Christians). Restaurants in coastal cities and resorts have plenty of seafood on their menus, especially *langosta* (lobster), which abound in the reefs. Because commercial fishing is controlled by the government, however, seafood isn't always as fresh as you might think, even on the coast.

Restaurants are scarce outside Trinidad and Cienfuegos, though every town has a few *paladares* (private eateries), and many *casas particulares* (Cuban homes whose owners have been allowed to rent out rooms) have permits to serve food. Most large beach resorts are all-inclusive, but food quality varies, especially at their buffet restaurants. Because all-inclusiveness confines most beach visitors to eating in their resorts, destinations such as Cayo Coco and Cayo Guillermo have not developed much of a dining scene.

Payment, tipping and reservations. Reservations are rarely necessary, and though there's no tipping policy per se, most travelers feel better if they tip as many people as possible—in and out of restaurants—as Cubans earn paltry wages. You'll be expected to pay in convertible pesos, but credit cards are accepted in all government restaurants and hotels, though never in paladares.

HOTELS

You'll find massive, modern beach resorts here whose guests virtually all arrive on resort packages. (The region is home to Cuba's largest hotel, with 1,100-plus rooms.) Also on the spectrum are historic city-center hotels, with doubles in a budget-pleasing CUC$50 range. The downside is that sheer numbers of city hotels are small. Towns such as Trinidad, Camagüey, and Cienfuegos have only a few quality places to stay. Lodging in *casas particulares* runs CUC$15 to CUC$25, depending on the season. The facilities vary accordingly, but even the *casas particulares* have private baths, air-conditioning, hot water, and in-room phones.

Credit cards are accepted in all government restaurants and hotels, but you pay cash in private accommodations.

Hotel reviews have been shortened. For full information, visit Fodors. com.

WHAT IT COSTS IN CUBAN CONVERTIBLE PESOS			
$	**$$**	**$$$**	**$$$$**
Restaurants under CUC$12	CUC$12–CUC$20	CUC$21–CUC$30	over CUC$30
Hotels under CUC$75	CUC$75–CUC$150	CUC$151–CUC$200	over CUC$200

Restaurant prices are the average cost of a main course at dinner or, if dinner is not served, at lunch. Hotel prices are the lowest cost of a standard double room in high season.

TOURS

The tour operators Cubanacán, Gaviota, and Rumbos provide a variety of local tours. They have representatives in all the large hotels as well as in regional offices.

Tour Companies Rumbos. ✉ *Calle López Recio 108, Camagüey* ☎ *3229-7229.*

VISITOR INFORMATION

Trinidad is the only town that has an Infotur office, but tour-agency desks in the lobbies of most hotels can provide basic information. Maps and other printed material are in scarce supply.

Tourist Information Infotur. ✉ *Calle Simón Bolívar/Desengaño y Calle Maceo/ Gutiérrez, Trinidad* ☎ *4199-2149.*

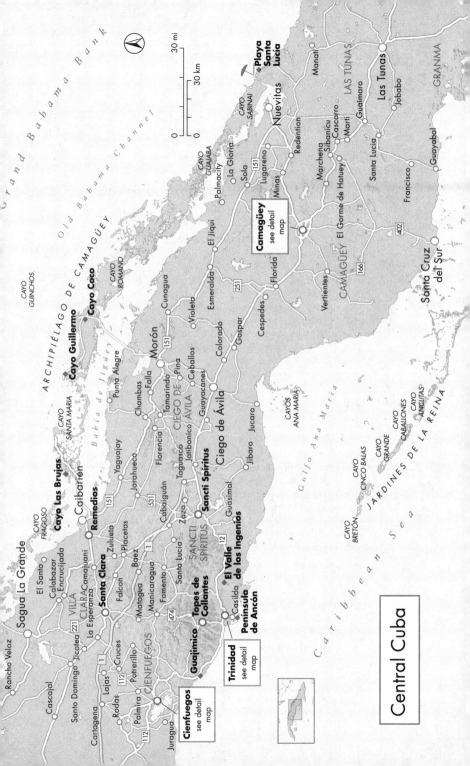

Central Cuba

VILLA CLARA, CIENFUEGOS, AND SANCTI SPÍRITUS PROVINCES

These three provinces contain several historic cities, half a dozen beaches, and natural attractions that range from highland forests to coral reefs. The wonderfully preserved, 18th-century city of Trinidad may be the most spectacular of the colonial towns, but Cienfuegos, Sancti Spíritus, and Remedios all have enough ancient architecture to transport you back in time—and they have fewer visitors. Beaches line the shores just to the south of Trinidad and Cienfuegos, where the ocean holds dozens of dive spots and good angling. In the exuberant valleys of the Sierra de Escambray, the crashing of crystalline waterfalls mixes with the songs of brightly colored birds.

GETTING HERE AND AROUND

The western reaches of Central Cuba are easily and quickly reached from Havana. The six-lane Autopista Nacional extends as far as Sancti Spíritus before narrowing to two lanes, but still a decent highway. Most large cities in this region lie on the highway, or not too far off. Víazul buses serve most destinations here with frequent service. Nightly trains run between Santa Clara and Havana. Santa Clara's Aeropuerto Internacional Abel Santamaría and Cienfuegos's Aeropuerto Internacional Jaime González receive domestic flights from Havana. Both cities lie close enough to Havana that flying, with its added advance check-in times, is probably not much of a timesaver.

SANTA CLARA

258 km (160 miles) southeast of Havana; 61 km (38 miles) northeast of Cienfuegos; 88 km (26 miles) north of Trinidad.

The capital of Villa Clara Province is a pleasant city of 200,000, with a busy center where cobbled streets are lined with historic buildings and a periphery of factories and modern apartment buildings. Santa Clara was the site of a decisive battle during the last days of 1958, and the remains of the quintessential revolutionary, Ernesto "Che" Guevara, rest in a monument at the edge of town. But you need merely visit the central plaza of this provincial capital to discover that its history stretches back centuries and that it has a good bit going on today.

Settled in 1689 by a group of landowners from nearby Remedios, Santa Clara's rich agricultural land and fortuitous location between Havana and Eastern Cuba have made it a relatively affluent provincial center. It's home to Cuba's third-largest university, the Universidad Central de Las Villas, whose students give the city its liberal reputation and youthful vibe. It's one of the few Cuban towns with a visible gay presence.

GETTING HERE AND AROUND

Santa Clara sits just off the six-lane Autopista Nacional, just under a four-hour drive southeast of Havana. Roomy Víazul buses connect the city with Havana, Varadero, Trinidad, Holguín, and Santiago de Cuba. Santa Clara is a stop on the Havana–Santiago train route. The city's

Aeropuerto Abel Santamaría serves flights from Havana and several international charters.

EXPLORING

TOP ATTRACTIONS

Fodor'sChoice **Mausoleo y Museo Ernesto "Che" Guevara.** No matter what your politics,
★ a visit to Santa Clara's most famous attraction is a must if you wish to understand modern Cuba's complex history. A massive bronze sculpture of iconic revolutionary Ernesto "Che" Guevara looms over a site containing his tomb and a museum dedicated to his life. Exhibits under the statue—the entrance is around the back—chronicle Che's eventful life, from his happy childhood in Argentina, to his life-changing 1950's journey through South America chronicled in his own journals and the 2004 film *The Motorcycle Diaries*, to his 1967 assassination in Bolivia. Exhibits here primarily concentrate on his involvement in the Cuban Revolution. The cave-like mausoleum next door holds the remains of Che and 16 others who fought and died with him in the mountains of Bolivia—they weren't discovered and identified by forensic anthropologists until 1997, and the remains didn't arrive in Cuba until 1998. ▪TIP➜ **This is hallowed ground to the lines of Cubans who file through, and proper hushed decorum is required.** Photography is permitted outside the complex but not inside. ✉ *Plaza de la Revolución, southwestern end of Calle Rafael Trista* ☎ *4220–5878* ✆ *Free* ۞ *Tues.–Sun. 9:30–5:30.*

WORTH NOTING

Museo de Artes Decorativas. The oldest building on Parque Vidal is a former home built in 1810 that's now open to the public as a museum. The house itself is half the attraction, with its marble floors, fluted columns, and hand-painted tiles. Its rooms hold an array of antiques—including crystal, china, statues, and furniture—that date from several centuries. ✉ *Northwest corner of Parque Vidal* ☎ *4220–8161* ✆ *CUC$2* ۞ *Mon., Wed., and Thurs. 9–noon and 1–6, Fri. and Sat. 1–10, Sun. 6–10.*

Parque Vidal. Most of the museums and monuments surround Santa Clara's central plaza. The streets that border it are closed to traffic, and locals gather here evenings and weekends, when concerts are often held in the kiosk or on the street in front of the Casa de la Cultura. On the park's northeast end stands the stately **Palacio Provincial,** built in 1912 to house the provincial government but now the city's library. Across the park from the library is the **Palacio Municipal,** or town hall, a structure dating from 1922. The Neoclassical building next to the Palacio Municipal was originally an elite social club but is now a government cultural center, the **Casa de la Cultura;** climb its marble staircase to the old ballroom, which is still lovely despite decades of neglect. ✉ *Santa Clara.*

Teatro La Caridad. On the northwest corner of Parque Vidal stands Santa Clara's principal theater, simple and linear on the outside, ornate and frescoed on the inside. The structure dates from 1885—tenor Enrico Caruso was among the early luminaries who performed here—and underwent a thorough restoration in 2009. *Caridad* means "charity" in Spanish, and proceeds in those early days went to fund projects for the poor. On the opposite side of the park is a statue of Marta Abreu,

The Taíno People

Central Cuba's earliest inhabitants were the Taíno, who island-hopped their way through the Caribbean from South America, arriving on Cuba about 200 years before the Spanish and overrunning the earlier Ciboney, who had settled farther west. The name "Cuba" itself is a Taíno word thought to mean "fertile land" or "great place."

The Taíno developed rather sophisticated agricultural techniques, introducing such mainstays as *yuca* (manioc or cassava), potatoes, corn, tobacco, and cotton. Archaeological evidence suggests that they were also potters, weavers, hunters, and fishermen who plied the waters in powerful canoes.

By the time Columbus arrived on the island in 1492, however, the Taíno were being challenged by the Caribs, a warlike people who also originated in South America. The Caribs never actually settled in Cuba, and although they began the conquest of the Taíno, they left its eventual completion—and the island's settlement—to the Spanish.

a 19th-century philanthropist who financed the theater's construction. ⊠ *Northwest corner of Parque Vidal* ☎ *4220–5548.*

FAMILY **Tren Blindado.** On the north side of Santa Clara, just across the Río Cubanicay, is the armored military train that was carrying soldiers and weapons that was derailed by Che Guevara and a group of rebels on the morning of December 28, 1958—a decisive moment in the Cuban Revolution. Guevara's troops went on to take the city, cutting Havana off from the eastern half of the country, which prompted dictator Fulgencio Batista's flight from Cuba and Castro's victory—all in a matter of days. Several train cars, some containing displays, lie in the grass next to the tracks in memory of that battle; the bulldozer used to destroy the tracks stands on a nearby cement slab. ⊠ *Northern end of Calle Independencia* ☎ *4220–2758* 🖃 *CUC$1* ⊘ *Mon.–Sat. 9–5.*

WHERE TO EAT

$ ✕ **La Concha.** Its only decoration may be a pastoral mural covering
CUBAN one wall, but locals are drawn to this popular restaurant on the western edge of town by the food, the prices, and (we suspect) the air-conditioning—rather than the decor. The menu is a mix of Cuban and international dishes, with such local standards as *escalope de puerco* (breaded pork) as well as a selection of pastas and pizzas. 🖇 *Average main: CUC$10* ⊠ *Carretera Central, esq. de Calle Danielito* ☎ *4221–8124* 🖃 *No credit cards.*

WHERE TO STAY

The best hotels are well outside Santa Clara, near the peripheral highway called the Circunvalación, but budget travelers can choose from several casas particulares near Parque Vidal. The town's one city-center hotel has its flaws but the location can't be beat.

$ ⛬ **Santa Clara Libre.** A plain, bargain option on Parque Vidal has two
HOTEL room sizes: small and not quite so small. **Pros:** the hotel is centrally located; rates are a bargain. **Cons:** the lobby is small and not terribly

pretty. $ *Rooms from: CUC$40* ⊠ *Parque Vidal 6* ☎ *4220–7548* ⊕ *www.islazul.cu* ⤳ *165 rooms* |◉| *Breakfast.*

$

B&B/INN

FAMILY

□ **Villa La Granjita.** On a 5-hectare (12-acre) farm—the name means "little farm"—near Santa Clara's airport, this tranquil resort has plenty of fresh air and birdsong. **Pros:** the rural setting is bliss; the trails make a pleasant diversion for hiking. **Cons:** rooms are small; the hotel is removed from the sights. $ *Rooms from: CUC$58* ⊠ *Carretera la Maleza* ⊹ *3 km (2 miles) northwest of Santa Clara* ☎ *4221–8190* ⊕ *www.hotelescubanacan.com* ⤳ *73 rooms* |◉| *Breakfast.*

NIGHTLIFE AND PERFORMING ARTS

El Boulevard, the pedestrian mall on Calle Independencia, just north of Parque Vidal, has several bars and sidewalk cafés that are popular weekend spots.

NIGHTLIFE

Bar Club Boulevard. At the eastern end of El Boulevard sits Santa Clara's most popular live-music venue; shows start nightly at 10 pm. ⊠ *Calle Independencia 225* ☎ *4221–6236.*

PERFORMING ARTS

Casa de la Cultura. The "House of Culture" hosts several concerts a week at 9 pm and a street concert every Sunday at 4 pm. ⊠ *Parque Vidal 5* ☎ *4221–7181.*

Club Mejunje. It's impossible to pin down what one of Cuba's most famous nightspots exactly is. Sometimes gay and always Bohemian, the Mejunje offers a mix of poetry readings, drag shows, interpretive dance, live theater, and karaoke on rainless nights. ■TIP→**The place has no roof, so plan accordingly.** ⊠ *Calle Marta Abreu 12* ☎ *4228–2572* 🎟 *CUC$2* ⊗ *Closed Mon.*

SHOPPING

CRAFTS

Fondo de Bienes Culturales. This cooperative sells a variety of local handicrafts including straw hats, leather bags, and knickknacks. ⊠ *Calle Estévez 9, just north of Parque Vidal* ☎ *4220–4195.*

SOUVENIRS

ARTEX. Stop by this artisan's cooperative for Cuban music, T-shirts, and other souvenirs. ⊠ *Calle Colón e/Parque Vidal y San Cristóbal* ☎ *4221–4397.*

REMEDIOS

45 km (27 miles) northeast of Santa Clara.

San Juan de Remedios is one of Cuba's oldest towns. Founded in 1515 on the northern coast, it was moved inland to its current location in 1524, after the residents were harassed by pirates. Toward the end of the 17th century, a group of wealthy citizens tried to move Remedios still farther inland, but most of the townspeople resisted; those who wanted to move went on to found Santa Clara, which became the province's principal city. Remedios slipped into its shadow and has retained a sleepy, unspoiled atmosphere.

Though small (20,000-some inhabitants), Remedios is culturally rich and remarkably well preserved. The city is most famous for its Christmastime festival called *las Parrandas*. Legend holds that the festival began in the 1820s when a parish priest, who worried that not enough people where attending Christmas Mass, sent a group of boys through the streets banging drums and making noise to wake people up and get them into the pews. The tradition has developed into an all-night festival lit by homemade lanterns and fireworks and animated by brass bands; its participants are cheered still more by copious food and drink. These days, the partying gets under way in early December.

EXPLORING

TOP ATTRACTIONS

FAMILY **Museo de las Parrandas.** If you can't be here during December for the annual holiday Parrandas celebrations, a visit to this interesting museum makes a nice consolation prize. The carnival-like parades punctuate Christmastime in Central Cuba, and Remedios does them up bigger and better than any city in the region. The city is divided into two neighborhoods—El Carmen and El Salvador—each of which creates its own floats, costumes, lanterns, and fireworks as part of an informal competition during the month-long festival that culminates on Christmas Eve. Though no winner is ever declared, most townspeople will tell you that not only does their neighborhood win every year, but the rest of Remedios isn't even good competition. The museum has photos, costumes, and floats from past Parrandas. ⊠ *Calle Máximo Gómez 71, 1½ blocks west of Plaza Martí* 🕾 *4239–5400* 🖃 *CUC$1* ⏾ *Tues.–Sat. 9–noon and 1–5, Sun. 9–noon.*

WORTH NOTING

Iglesia de San Juan Bautista. The squat colonial structure with a massive bell tower on the plaza's eastern end is the Church of St. John the Baptist. Its splendidly restored 18th-century interior (head for the back door, as the main doors are usually shut) includes high arches, an elaborate beamed cedar ceiling, and gilt-wood altars. Although its stone floor dates from 1550, most of the chapel was rebuilt in 1752; it underwent extensive renovation in the 1940s, including the construction of a new main altar using parts of the original Baroque altar. The smaller altar to the right is dedicated to the Virgen de la Caridad, Cuba's patron saint. The gilt shrines along the walls are dedicated to various saints; note the pregnant Virgin, brought from Seville in the 1700s, to the left of the main door. ⊠ *Plaza Martí* 🖃 *Donation suggested* ⏾ *Mon.–Sat. 8–noon and 3–6, Sun. 4–6.*

Museo de la Música. On the northern side of Plaza Martí you'll find one of the city's best-preserved colonial buildings. The former home of composer Alejandro García Caturla is now a museum dedicated to his life with many of his musical instruments on display. Built in 1875, the house has a small central patio planted with palms and surrounded by rooms that contain antique furnishings or exhibits on the composer's works. ⊠ *Calle Camilo Cienfuegos 5* 🕾 *4239–6851* 🖃 *CUC$1* ⏾ *Tues.– Sat. 9–noon and 1–5, Sun. 9–noon.*

WHERE TO EAT

$ ✕**El Louvre.** This small café with a hardwood bar, brass lamps, and
CUBAN wooden ceiling has been in business since 1866. The view, overlooking Plaza Martí, probably isn't much different than when it opened, and it still serves *ponche de la parroquia*, a rum-and-milk cocktail that wily young men once gave to chaperones. (Once drunk, the chaperones would be less likely to interfere should the young men try to steal kisses from their girlfriends.) Though the menu has a wide array of beverages, dishes are limited to sandwiches, *pollo frito* (fried chicken) and *bistéc de puerco* (grilled pork). $ *Average main: CUC$10* ⊠ *Calle Máximo Gómez 122* ☎ *4239–5639* ▤ *No credit cards.*

WHERE TO STAY

Remedios is a one-hotel town, but it has several *casas particulares*, most of which are west of Plaza Martí.

$ ▥**Hotel Mascotte.** Although such alterations as gleaming white-tile
HOTEL floors detract from its historic atmosphere, this late-19th-century inn, the only real game in town, is still charming. **Pros:** close to local beaches; good on-site Cuban restaurant. **Cons:** rooms in the back have small windows and feel cramped; rooms don't evoke history quite the way the public areas do. $ *Rooms from: CUC$64* ⊠ *Calle Máximo Gómez 112* ☎ *4239–5144* ⊕ *www.hotelescubanacan.com* ⇰ *10 rooms* ⦿*⊙*⦿ *Breakfast.*

SHOPPING

CRAFTS

Fondo de Bienes Culturales. A small selection of wood sculptures and other local handicrafts is available at the artisans' cooperative across from the Hotel Mascotte. ⊠ *Calle Máximo Gómez* ☎ *4239–5617.*

CAYO LAS BRUJAS

50 km (30 miles) northeast of Remedios.

A *pedraplén* (causeway) traverses the shallow waters of Bahía Buena Vista (Buena Vista Bay) from the mainland to Cayo Las Brujas and beyond to the larger Cayo Santa María—both in the western half of the Jardines del Rey archipelago. Although neighboring Cayo Santa María has been developed on a grand scale, with giant, all-inclusive beach resorts and today houses the newest and most desirable properties, Cayo Las Brujas has been spared mass tourism, and we hope it stays that way.

Brujas (pronounced "brew-haas") means "witches," and local legend tells of the clandestine love affair between a fisherman's daughter and a young man. One day he arrived late to their meeting place only to discover a hoary witch in place of his tender love. A statue of the maiden now stares at sea from atop a coral bluff next to the island's one, small hotel—the Villa Las Brujas.

Cayo Las Brujas remains enchanted, but the current spell is cast by the sun as it shines on this key's beige beach, which is backed by dense foliage and fronted by crystalline waters, coral reefs, and uninhabited islets. There's good snorkeling around the point, and a larger reef lies just across the channel, in front of Cayo Francés. The hotel rents snorkeling equipment, kayaks, and catamarans, and offers trips to dive spots and a pristine beach on Cayo Borracho. You can visit Cayo Las Brujas on a day trip, but you'll have to pay 5 cuc to cross the pedraplén. If you spend the night, bring insect repellent.

WHERE TO STAY

$$
B&B/INN
Fodor's Choice
★

🏨 **Villa Las Brujas.** Wooden buildings scattered along a coral bluff house this intimate resort's spacious rooms. **Pros:** the beachfront location is terrific; spacious, modern rooms. **Cons:** the location is remote and can be difficult to find; you dine here for the views rather than the haute cuisine. ⑤ *Rooms from: CUC$115* ⊠ *Cayo Las Brujas* ☎ *4235–0013* ⊕ *www.gaviota-grupo.com* 🛏 *24 rooms* ⦿ *Breakfast.*

CIENFUEGOS

232 km (144 miles) southeast of Havana; 106 km (66 miles) southwest of Remedios; 80 km (48 miles) northwest of Trinidad.

Cienfuegos is an attractive, laid-back port city of 110,000 that overlooks a deep bay of the same name. Keep your disappointment in check as you come into town and pass through neighborhoods of gray cement-block buildings that ring the city. Once you reach its small historic core with the dark green mass of the Sierra de Escambray in the background, you'll understand why Cubans refer to Cienfuegos as *la Perla del Sur* ("the Pearl of the South").

A relatively young provincial capital, Cienfuegos was founded in 1819 by immigrants from Bordeaux as part of a Spanish scheme to establish a city in a region that had long been the haunt of pirates. Originally dubbed Fernandina de Jagua ("Fernandina" honors Spain's King Ferdinand and "Jagua" was the indigenous name for the region), the city was later named after General José Cienfuegos (a colonial governor of the province). It quickly became an important port; sugar plantations came to cover its hinterlands, and slaves were imported to work on them. Families who made fortunes from cane and human bondage built mansions (known locally as *palacios*, or palaces), many of which still stand.

Cienfuegos's French roots are reflected in some of its architecture, and are celebrated every April with a Francophile festival. Nevertheless, it's a very Cuban city where the breeze often carries the melodies of local hero Benny Moré, one of the giants of the Cuban music *son*.

GETTING HERE AND AROUND

If Cienfuegos is your first Central Cuba destination, leave the Autopista Nacional at the town of Aguada de Pasajeros at Km. 170 on the main highway. Cienfuegos lies about one hour southeast. Víazul buses connect Cienfuegos with Havana, Varadero, Santa Clara, and Trinidad.

EXPLORING
TOP ATTRACTIONS

Fodor's Choice
★

Jardín Botánico Soledad (*Soledad Botanical Garden*). East of town lie Cienfuegos's expansive botanical gardens covering 94 hectares (232 acres) and containing more than 2,000 plant species, most of which are not native to Cuba. Created at the turn of the last century by U.S.

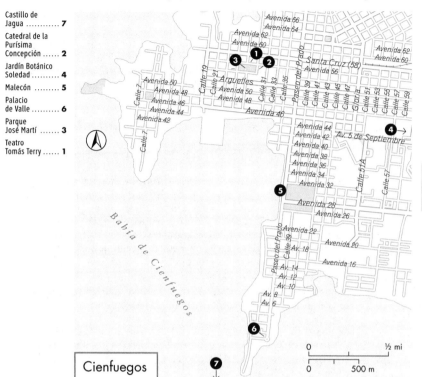

Cienfuegos

sugar farmer Edwin Atkins, the garden was administered by Harvard University until 1961, when it was taken over by the Cuban Academy of Science. It includes palms, bamboos, and other tropical trees as well as medicinal plants and a forest reserve that's home to many native animals. Signage could be better here; a guide can point out what you're seeing, although not all speak English. ■ TIP→ **Tips are greatly appreciated.** ⊠ *Cienfuegos ✚ 17 km (10 miles) east of Cienfuegos* 🕾*4354–5115* 🖭*CUC$3* ☾ *Mon.–Thurs. 8:30–5, Fri.–Sun 8:30–4:30.*

Fodor's Choice **Palacio de Valle.** The most impressive of Punta Gorda's mansions is the ★ Palacio de Valle, which was built in 1917 by the sugar baron Asisclo del Valle. It's a stunning, sumptuous structure full of ornate relief work, crystal chandeliers, hand-painted tiles, Italian-marble columns, French windows, and carved Cuban hardwoods. Though the mansion's design is eclectic, its foremost inspiration was the Alhambra—the Moorish palace in southern Spain. It now houses the city's best restaurant on the ground floor and a rooftop bar that's the perfect spot from which to watch the sun set. ⊠ *Av. 0 y Calle 37* 🕾*4355–1003* 🖭*CUC$1* ☾ *Daily 10–10.*

WORTH NOTING

Casa de Cultura. At Parque José Martí's southwest corner stands the Palacio Ferrer, an elaborate mansion built in 1917 by Spanish businessman José Ferrer and now the Casa de Cultura. The corner room on the second floor was once used by Enrico Caruso, and a spiral staircase leads from here up to a tower that offers a nice view of the plaza. Local musicians and dancers often rehearse here. ⊠ *Av. 54 y Calle 25* ☎ *4351–6584* 💷 *CUC$1* ⊙ *Mon.–Sat. 9–7.*

Castillo de Jagua. Above a fishing village overlooking the narrow entrance to the Bahía de Cienfuegos (35 km [21 miles] south of the historical center) is a Spanish fortress built in 1745 to keep out pirates who had grown accustomed to trading with locals. It's completely refurbished (even the drawbridge works) and has a historical museum with weapons and other antiques. The dungeon houses a bar and restaurant. On your way down, note the small chamber beneath the steps; prisoners were chained and tortured here. ■ **TIP→ If you're a woman, we suggest you not wear blue when you visit. Local legend holds that the site is haunted by the ghost of a mysterious female figure dressed in a blue gown; given the fort's notorious history, who can say for sure?**

You have three ways to get here: take a taxi (or drive) the whole way, looping counterclockwise around the bay; travel overland directly south of Cienfuegos to the Hotel Pasacaballos at the entrance of the bay and take the short ferry that crosses back and forth to the fort all day long; or board the ferry at the south end of Calle 25 in Cienfuegos with departures at 8 am, 1 pm, and 5:30 pm and returns from the fort at 6:30 am, 10 am, and 3 pm. ⊠ *Castillo de Jagua* ☎ *4359–6402* 💷 *CUC$1* ⊙ *Mon.–Sat. 9–5, Sun. 9–1.*

Catedral de la Purísima Concepción. The city's bright yellow Neoclassical cathedral, with its high central bell tower reminiscent of a minaret, was consecrated in 1870. Its interior is less impressive than the renovated exterior, but it does feature a statue of the Virgin of the Immaculate Conception—the city's patron saint—and stained glass windows from France that depict the 12 apostles. ⊠ *Av. 56 y Calle 29, east of Parque Martí* ☎ *4352–5297* 💷 *Free* ⊙ *Weekdays 7–noon, weekends 8–noon.*

Malecón. To the south of the old part of town, Calle 37 runs parallel to the waterfront Malecón, where locals stroll at night. Note the illuminated billboard near the Malecón; it has an image of revered Cuban singer Benny Moré and a line from one of his songs: *"Cienfuegos es la ciudad que más me gusta a mi"* ("Cienfuegos is the city I like most"). The palm-lined promenade stretches south to Punta Gorda, a point dominated by the mansions once owned by sugar barons and ending in a small park surrounded by water where people gather on weekends to swim and relax. ⊠ *Calle 37.*

Parque José Martí. Most of the important buildings of Cienfuegos surround the central Parque José Martí which contains an impressive marble statue, carved in 1902, of the Cuban revolutionary and intellectual for whom it was named. Near the park's western end is a tiny replica of the Arc de Triomphe, a nod to the city's French heritage, and just south of the Martí statue stands a domed kiosk, where the municipal band sometimes gives weekend concerts. East of the park, Avenida 54 is a pedestrian mall—lined with shops and restaurants—called El Boulevard. ⊠ *Cienfuegos*.

Teatro Tomás Terry. The city's principal theater was built in 1889 and named for Venezuelan millionaire Tomás Terry (1808–86) whose fortune funded its construction. If you can't come for a concert or dance performance, you can admire the painted ceilings, statues, and carved hardwoods for a small fee. The small café off the lobby is a perfect place to grab a bite on a hot afternoon. ⊠ *Av. 56, No. 2703, north of Parque Martí* ☎ *4351–3361* 🎫 *CUC$1* ☉ *Daily 9–5.*

BEACHES

Playa Rancho Luna. The coast southeast of Cienfuegos has several nice beaches, the nearest of which is the public Playa Rancho Luna, a pale crescent flanked by rocky points 18 km (11 miles) southeast of town. All go by the name "Rancho Luna." It has various hotels, the largest of which is the Club Amigo Rancho Luna. An extensive coral reef wraps around the point directly to the west—you can rent snorkeling equipment at the Faro Luna Diving Center there. A smaller beach, also called Rancho Luna, lies just around the point to the east. **Amenities:** food and drink; lifeguards; parking; showers; water sports. **Best for:** snorkeling; sunset; swimming; walking. ⊠ *Cienfuegos* ⊹ *16 km (10 miles) southeast of Cienfuegos.*

WHERE TO EAT

$ ✕ **El Palatino.** The low building with the fat pillars south of Parque Martí's bandstand, dates from the 1840s and evokes Cienfuegos's French heyday. Today it's a popular tavern, the perfect place for a quick Cuban coffee, a mojito, or light lunch. ■ TIP➡ **They make a great selection of cheese sandwiches.** You'll occasionally hear live music in the late afternoon and early evening. ⑤ *Average main: CUC$8* ⊠ *Av. 54, esq. de Calle 27* ☎ *4354–1244* ▭ *No credit cards.*

CUBAN

$$ ✕ **La Cueva del Camarón.** One of the smaller mansions in Punta Gorda houses this pleasant seafood restaurant. Its bright interior—full of shiny marble, colorful tiles, and carved hardwoods—makes it an elegant place to dine, and the waterfront terrace in back is a great spot for lunch. The menu is strong on seafood, with dishes ranging from *pescado al camarón* (fish fillets in a white shrimp sauce) to a *grillada mixta* (mixed grill) that contains lobster, fish, and prawns. ⑤ *Average main: CUC$14* ⊠ *Av. 2 y Calle 37* ☎ *4355–1128.*

SEAFOOD

$$$ ✕ **Palacio de Valle.** Elegance abounds on the ground floor of Cienfuegos's most gracious mansion, with its ornate arches, marble columns, and crystal chandeliers. And there's usually someone playing the restaurant's grand piano. The food may play second fiddle to ambience, but it's still some of the best in town. The specialty is *langosta* (lobster), which is prepared five different ways; other choices include *sopa de mariscos* (seafood soup), *camarones al pincho* (shrimp shish kebab), and even filet mignon. ■ TIP➡ **Try to arrive early enough to enjoy a sunset cocktail on the roof deck.** ⑤ *Average main: CUC$21* ⊠ *Av. 0 y Calle 37* ☎ *4355–1003.*

SEAFOOD
Fodor's Choice
★

THE MUSIC OF BENNY MORÉ

No figure better exemplifies the music of Central Cuba than one Bartolomé Maximiliano Moré Gutiérrez, born here in rural Cienfuegos Province in 1919. Benny Moré—his showbiz name sounded a lot snappier—experimented with several genres of music during his short life and left his mark on the guitar-and-percussion *son*, the fast-paced *guaracha*, the methodical bolero, and the brassy mambo. Moré is revered in Cuba to this day for being one of the few prominent musicians who never fled the country. Celia Cruz? Desi Arnaz? Emilio and Gloria Estefan? It's as if they never existed here. Moré did sow his musical oats around Latin America during the 1940s, but returned to Cuba in 1952 and stayed through and after the Revolution, performing up until the time of his death in 1963. You can visit Café Cantante Benny Moré, the place where Moré popularized his version of guitar-and-percussion *son*.

WHERE TO STAY

$
RESORT
FAMILY

Club Amigo Rancho Luna. Most of the rooms at this hotel just west of Playa Rancho Luna have ocean views, especially those in the two-story bungalows. **Pros:** the hotel has its own dive center, which arranges trips to dozens of offshore reefs and wrecks; most of the rooms have ocean views. **Cons:** it's a bit of a walk to the beach; a few of the rooms look a bit shopworn. ⑤ *Rooms from: CUC$58* ✉ *Playa Rancho Luna* ✛ *16 km (10 miles) southeast of Cienfuegos* ☎ *4354–8012* ⊕ *www. hotelescubanacan.com* ⇱ *40 rooms* ⦿ *Breakfast.*

$
HOTEL
Fodor's Choice
★

Hotel E La Unión. This stately hotel in the heart of Ciengfuegos is Cuba's oldest, but the structure has been completely rebuilt and the retooling maintains a faithfulness to the style of its 19th-century heyday. **Pros:** live music enhances the city views in the rooftop bar in the evening; the rates are a bargain for the offerings. **Cons:** ambient noise from the surrounding streets can be annoying. ⑤ *Rooms from: CUC$72* ✉ *Calle 31, esq. de Av. 54* ☎ *4345–1020* ⊕ *www.hotelescubanacan.com* ⇱ *49 rooms* ⦿ *Breakfast.*

$$
HOTEL

Hotel Jagua. This modern six-story structure dates from the 1950s and looks out of place among the palacios of Punta Gorda, but rooms sparkle and service is top-notch here. **Pros:** the rooms gleam here; service is attentive. **Cons:** the hotel is a mammoth concrete megalith, nicer looking on the inside than the outside; nearby oil refinery and other industry can take away from the view. ⑤ *Rooms from: CUC$91* ✉ *Punta Gorda* ☎ *4355–1003* ⊕ *www.gran-caribe.com* ⇱ *139 rooms* ⦿ *Breakfast.*

NIGHTLIFE AND PERFORMING ARTS

After the sun has set, several spots along El Boulevard (Avenida 54) get busy.

NIGHTLIFE

Café Cantante Benny Moré. Local musicians perform nightly at this friendly music club, where you'll hear a few hits that the region's best-known musician made famous. Do not confuse this place with the Disco

Club Benny Moré, which, as its name suggests, is essentially a disco. ⊠ *Av. 54 y El Prado* ☏ *4352–2320* ✆ *CUC$1.*

Disco Club Benny Moré. Despite bearing Benny Moré's name, you're unlikely to hear any of his music here. (For that, you need to visit the Café Cantante Benny Moré.) This spot is a disco, and really little more, but a good place to dance to the hottest Latin tunes. ⊠ *Av. 54, e/Calle 29 y Calle 31* ☏ *4352–1105* ✆ *CUC$5* ⊙ *Closed Mon.*

El Palatino. The historic bar overlooking Parque Martí usually has live music in the afternoon and evening, with killer mojitos to boot. ⊠ *Av. 54 e/Calle 25 y Calle 27* ☏ *4354–1244.*

Hotel E Unión. The bar on the roof of the venerable Hotel Unión has live jazz on Tuesday and Thursday and traditional Cuban music Wednesday, Friday, and Saturday; shows start at 9:30 pm. ⊠ *Calle 31, esq. de Av. 54* ☏ *4345–1020.*

Palacio de Valle. The rooftop bar at the architecturally amazing Palacio de Valle is a great spot for a sunset drink and often has live music. ⊠ *Av. 0 y Calle 37* ☏ *4355–1003.*

PERFORMING ARTS
Teatro Tomás Terry. The city's stately theater hosts frequent concerts and dance performances. Ticket prices are a bargain compared to what you'd pay back home to see a similar production. If you're in town when the Cantores de Cienfuegos, the city's famed a cappella group is performing, grab tickets. ⊠ *Av. 56, No. 2703* ☏ *4351–3361.*

SHOPPING
ART GALLERIES
Galería Moroya. This gallery south of Parque Martí is packed with paintings, sculptures, clothes, and handicrafts. ⊠ *Av. 54, No. 2506* ☏ *4354–1208.*

CIGARS AND TOBACCO
Casa del Fundador. This colonial house overlooking Parque Martí has an excellent selection of cigars, but also sells rum, coffee, T-shirts, CDs, and other souvenirs. ⊠ *Calle 29, esq. de Av. 54* ☏ *4354–2134.*

El Embajador. "The Ambassador" specializes in rum, coffee, and cigars. ⊠ *Av. 54 y Calle 33* ☏ *4345–1343.*

SOUVENIRS
Casa Arco. This small shop offers a decent selection of music, as well as a few T-shirts and other souvenirs. ⊠ *Av. 54, No. 3301* ☏ *4351–1879.*

SPORTS AND THE OUTDOORS
FISHING
The fishing in the waters off Cienfuegos is good, with abundant mahimahi, wahoo, jacks, and other fighters.

Marina Puertosol Cienfuegos. The marina has small charter boats equipped with basic gear for amazingly low rates. ⊠ *Punta Gorda* ☏ *4355–1241.*

SCUBA DIVING
The ocean around Cienfuegos has dozens of dive sites, from shallow reefs to deep shipwrecks. Because the edge of the platform is relatively close to shore, the waters are frequented by big fish. The coral is healthy

and well developed—one column stands 7 meters (23 feet) high—and visibility varies from 15 to 40 meters (45 to 120 feet).

Centro de Buceo Faro Luna (*Faro Luna Diving Center*). The center is next to the hotel of the same name on Playa Rancho Luna, 16 km (10 miles) southeast of Cienfuegos. It costs about CUC$6 a day to rent snorkeling gear and CUC$25 a day for scuba equipment. The center runs one-tank boat dives (CUC$25 per person) to roughly 30 sites; it also offers certification courses for CUC$200. ⊠ *Cienfuegos* ☎ *4354–8040.*

GUAJIMICO

42 km (25 miles) southeast of Cienfuegos; 43 km (26 miles) northwest of Trinidad.

The tiny agricultural community of Guajimico has little to offer in and of itself, but it sits in a wild area halfway between Cienfuegos and Trinidad where the natural attractions range from patches of tropical forest to offshore coral reefs. Tour operators in Cienfuegos or Trinidad can set you up with a day trip.

BEACHES

Playa Inglés. The so-called "Englishman's Beach" has pale sand and is lined with sea-grape trees; it's the essence of tranquillity. The beach is visited almost exclusively by Cubans, who come on weekends and stay in rustic bungalows or camp; during the week, it's deserted. **Amenities:** food and drink; lifeguards; parking; toilets. **Best for:** solitude; sunset; swimming; walking ✛ *10 km (6 miles) south of Villa Guajimico*

SPORTS AND THE OUTDOORS

HORSEBACK RIDING

Hacienda La Vega. A working cattle ranch southeast of the city operates a three-hour horseback tour through pastures and a forest; it includes a swim on a secluded beach and a dairy tour. You can hire horses and a guide at the ranch, or you can go on a half-day tour offered by Rumbos. Costs average around CUC$30 per person. ⊠ *Guajimico* ✛ *50 km (30 miles) southeast of Cienfuegos on road to Trinidad.*

TRINIDAD

85 km (51 miles) southeast of Cienfuegos; 407 km (244 miles) southeast of Havana; 70 km (42 miles) southwest of Sancti Spíritus.

Fodor's Choice Trinidad has weathered five centuries with barely a wrinkle. Its enchant-
★ ing cobblestone streets are lined with houses that have brightly painted adobe walls and wooden shutters. Its historic center, which covers more than 50 blocks, is like a vast, meticulously maintained museum full of restored mansions and manicured plazas. Yet it's also a lively town of 75,000, where the *Trinitarios* are not content merely to reside in a museum exhibit. They live here; they work here; they shop here. Come evening, they pull their chairs out onto the street to gossip, and the air rings with the songs of birds perched in wicker cages and of bands performing in bars or restaurants. Trinidad is one of Cuba's magical places, and it's much more manageable than Havana, to boot.

The city was founded in 1514 by the conquistador Diego Velázquez, who named the settlement for the Holy Trinity. It grew little until the 17th century, when its inhabitants began trading with pirates. Between 1750 and 1825, the population rose from 6,000 to 12,000, as thousands of slaves were brought in to work on sugar plantations in the nearby Valle de los Ingenios. Wealthy families built mansions, filled them with imported treasures, and sent their children to European schools. By the second half of the 19th century, however, Trinidad's star began to fade as sugar prices fell, the struggles for independence began, and slavery ended. By the early 1900s, Trinidad was impoverished and isolated. But the neglect that prevailed during the first half of the 20th century froze the city in a time warp that allowed it to retain its colonial ambience. In 1988, UNESCO declared the historic center a World Heritage Site, and during the past decade the government has worked hard to restore the colonial architecture.

Some people who visit Trinidad stay on the nearby Península de Ancón, but the advantages of staying in the city include many cultural sights and vibrant nightlife. Day-trip options—through such tour operators as Cubánacan—include treks to the beaches of Ancón, hikes in the Sierra de Escambray, train rides through sugar plantations, and sailing or diving excursions to Cayo Blanco. (Note that like many Cuban cities, Trinidad's streets go by pre- and postrevolutionary names. *Both are cited in addresses below.*) Since few Cuban cities wear their history on their sleeves the way Trinidad does, folks here are likely to use the traditional names.

GETTING HERE AND AROUND

Trinidad lies due south of Santa Clara on a narrow, but decent road. Driving time is about one hour. Víazul buses connect Trinidad with Havana, Varadero, Santa Clara, Santiago de Cuba, and several places in between.

EXPLORING

TOP ATTRACTIONS

Fodor's Choice ★ **Museo de la Lucha Contra Bandidos.** This mouthful of a name translates as the "Museum of the Fight Against Bandits." Those so-called bandits were fighters who waged guerrilla warfare—with a little help from their friends at the CIA—from the Sierra de Escambray for the first six years of Castro's Revolutionary government. The museum documents that struggle and their defeat. Doctrinaire exhibits aside, this is Trinidad's most famous landmark, and it adorns postcards, brochures, and T-shirts. The tall, yellow bell tower is all that remains of the original 18th-century Convento de San Francisco, a Franciscan monastery. You can climb the tower for a sweeping view of the city. ⊠ *Calle Fernando Hernández (Cristo) y Calle Piro Guinart (Boca)* ☎ *4199–4121* ☜ *CUC$2* ☼ *Tues.–Sun. 9–5.*

Plaza Mayor. The heart of Trinidad's historic center gets our vote for Cuba's loveliest central plaza. This charming little park is dominated by royal palms and has cast-iron benches, ceramic urns, marble statues, and two brass greyhounds that were probably once cannons. It's surrounded by houses that once belonged to sugar barons and merchants, a few of which now contain museums. The square fills with life each evening as townspeople gather to chat with friends. ⊠ *Calle Simón Bolívar (Desengaño), e/Calle Fernando Hernández (Cristo) y Calle Ruben Martínez Villena (Real de Jigüe).*

WORTH NOTING

La Santísima Trinidad. Although the city's cathedral was consecrated in 1892, the building took the better part of the 19th century to complete (it was built to replace the 17th-century church that was destroyed by a hurricane). Don't let the rather bleak exterior (or limited hours) deter you from stepping inside; its interesting interior is replete with a dozen hardwood altars that date from the early 20th century and various colonial icons. ■ TIP➔ **Local people usually refer to the cathedral as the Parroquial Mayor (major parish).** ⊠ *Calle Fernando Hernández (Cristo)* ⊙ *Mon.–Sat. 10:30–1.*

Museo de Arquitectura. If you really wish to delve into Trinidad's amazing architecture, this museum documents the city's development. (Of course, nothing replaces actually wandering around the city's fabulous streets themselves and soaking it all in.) Exhibits on its most important 18th- and 19th-century buildings fill the rooms of a sky-blue 18th-century house, once the home of the Sánchez Iznaga family. Don't miss the lovely garden patio. ⊠ *Calle Fernando Hernández (Cristo)* ☎ *4199–3208* ⊡ *CUC$1* ⊙ *Mon., Thurs., and weekends 9–5.*

Museo Histórico Municipal. Set in the impressive Palacio Cantero, which was built by a sugar baron in 1830, the History Museum's displays trace the development of Trinidad from its founding by Diego Velázquez to the early years of the Revolutionary government. Two rooms are furnished with antiques, and elaborate murals cover some of the walls. A lookout platform atop the building's large tower affords a wonderful view. (The stairs look rickety, but are safe, although you probably won't want to negotiate their narrowness if you are claustrophobic.) ⊠ *Calle Simón Bolívar (Desengaño) y Calle Peña* ☎ *4199–4460* ⊡ *CUC$2 for entrance; CUC$1 fee for photos* ⊙ *Sat.–Thurs. 9–5.*

Museo Romántico. Rather than the stuff of Cupid's arrows, the romance in this museum's name refers to the one that Trinidad's prominent families had with their precious things. A great variety of antiques—most imported from Europe—fill the 14 rooms of this imposing mansion. Built in 1704, the house belonged to Count Burnet, though nearly all the antiques in it came from the homes of other families. Don't miss the view from the second-floor balcony. ⊠ *Calle Fernando Hernández (Cristo) y Calle Simón Bolívar (Desengaño)* ☎ *4199–4363* ⊡ *CUC$2* ⊙ *Tues.–Sun. 9–5.*

WHERE TO EAT

There's a restaurant on practically every block of the historic center, but the food tends to lag behind the ambience.

$ ✕ **Café Don Pepe.** A rule of thumb: You stand a better chance of finding
CAFÉ good Cuban fare in the diaspora than here on the island. This small café, across from the Museo de la Lucha Contra Bandidos, proves an exception to that rule. The Cuban coffee here just might make you think you're on Calle Ocho in Miami. There's a wide selection of other

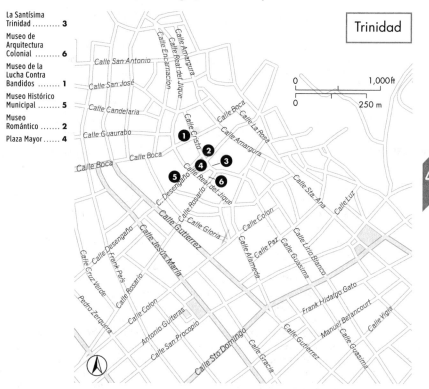

beverages (and snacks, as well) here, too, if you like your coffee drinks a little tamer. $ *Average main: CUC$5* ⊠ *Calle Pedro Guinart (Boca)* ☎ *4199–3573* ⊙ *No dinner* ⊟ *No credit cards.*

$ ✕ **Restaurante El Jigüe.** Set in the Plazuela de Jigüe, a tiny plaza shaded by
CUBAN one tree, this colorful and historic restaurant (dating from 1720) seems to say "come on in." Its bright interior has high ceilings, chandeliers, and landscapes hung on white walls. The menu ranges from *bistec de cerdo grillé* to *enchilado de langosta* (in a red sauce). The specialty, *pollo al jigüe,* is a Cuban version of chicken cacciatore. $ *Average main: CUC$11* ⊠ *Calle Ruben Martínez Villena (Real de Jigüe) 69* ☎ *4199–6476.*

$ ✕ **Restaurante El Mesón del Regidor.** Down the hill from the Plaza Mayor,
CUBAN across from the Museo Histórico, this building is as historic as any in Trinidad: wooden ceilings, brass lamps, terra-cotta floors. The menu is traditional to match the address—*bistec de cerdo grillé* (grilled pork steak), *bistec de res en cazuela* (stewed beef), *filet de pescado grille* (sauteed fish fillet). Sometimes there's live music at lunchtime. $ *Average main: CUC$10* ⊠ *Calle Simón Bolívar (Desengaño) 424* ☎ *4199–6456.*

$ ✕ **Sol y Son.** Trinidad's best paladar is a few blocks south of the Plaza
CUBAN Mayor in an elegant 19th-century home. Upon entering, you may feel as if you've stepped into an antiques shop, but at the back is a garden courtyard complete with candlelight and taped music. The

menu is surprisingly varied, with several vegetarian dishes and such rare ingredients as olives. The service and ambience are first rate, but it's the food that keeps this tiny restaurant packed. $\boxed{\$}$ *Average main: CUC$11* ⊠ *Calle Simón Bolívar (Desengaño) 283* ☏ *4199–2926* ⊟ *No credit cards.*

WHERE TO STAY

$

HOTEL

⚏ **Hotel E La Ronda.** Though it caters mostly to Cubans, some of the rooms in this older hotel several blocks east of the historic center have been fixed up for visitors from abroad, which means there are now such modern amenities as satellite TV and mini-refrigerators. **Pros:** the rooftop bar is a pleasant place for a drink; rates are a bargain for what is offered. **Cons:** rooms are dark, although are undergoing a sprucing-up at this writing; you're several blocks from most of the sights. $\boxed{\$}$ *Rooms from: CUC$60* ⊠ *Calle José Martí (Jesús María) 238* ☏ *4199–2248* ⊕ *www.hotelescubanacan.com* ⤶ *14 rooms* ⏀*Breakfast.*

$$

HOTEL

FAMILY

⚏ **Hotel Las Cuevas.** On a grassy hill at the northern edge of town, this collection of cement duplexes enjoys a sweeping panorama of Trinidad's red-tile roofs, the Península de Ancón, and the blue Caribbean beyond. **Pros:** rooms have porches, some even enjoy nice views. **Cons:** rooms are rather small; the hotel is located on top of a steep hill and is not a place to stay if you have any mobility concerns. $\boxed{\$}$ *Rooms from: CUC$82* ⊠ *Calle Lino Pérez (San Procopio)* ☏ *4199–6133* ⊕ *www. hotelescubanacan.com* ⤶ *114 rooms* ⏀*Breakfast.*

$$$

HOTEL

Fodor'sChoice

★

⚏ **Iberostar Grand Hotel Trinidad.** This centrally located hotel was (believe it or not) newly constructed in 2006, and was built in colonial style directly on Plaza Carrillo at the end of Parque Cespedes—a popular spot in this truly colonial city. **Pros:** free Internet access (rare in Cuba) is in the video game room; hotel offers modern amenities with old-world style. **Cons:** the hotel's restaurant, the Gourmet, is pricey, and the food is okay, at best. $\boxed{\$}$ *Rooms from: CUC$155* ⊠ *Calle José Martí 262, adjacent to Lino Pérez* ☏ *4199–6070* ⊕ *www.thegrandcollection.com* ⤶ *36 rooms, 4 suites* ⏀*Breakfast.*

NIGHTLIFE AND PERFORMING ARTS

NIGHTLIFE

Canchánchara. Pop into Canchánchara, a lively bar in an 18th-century building. There's frequently a live band playing in the shady patio, and there are always plenty of soft drinks, cold beer, and such Cuban cocktails as the mojito and the local specialty *canchánchara* (rum, lime juice, and honey) ⊠ *90 Calle Real del Jigue* ☏ *4199–4345.*

Casa de la Trova. The two blocks east of the Plaza Mayor, Trinidad's Casa de la Trova has live music in the afternoon and after 10 pm. ⊠ *Calle Guasima (Cristo)* ☏ *4199–6445* ▱ *CUC$1.*

Disco Ayala. Dance the night away deep inside a cave at what must be Cuba's most unusual nightspot. Locals call the place La Cueva ("the cave"). Although it is cool (as in "trendy"), it gets very warm and humid here with the throngs of people. About an hour is all most visitors can take. ⊠ *Calle Lino Pérez/San Procopio* ☏ *4199–6133* ▱ *CUC$3* ☾ *Closed Mon.*

PERFORMING ARTS

ARTEX. The open-air theater just north of Parque Martí, has live music and varied shows nightly at 10. ⊠ *Calle Lino Pérez/San Procopio 306* ☎ *4199–6483* 🎫 *CUC$1.*

Ruinas del Teatro Brunet. The open-air ruins of this theater have a nightly folk-dancing and music show at 10. Daily percussion and dance lessons are also on the menu here. ⊠ *Calle Antonio Maceo/Gutiérrez, e/Calle Simón Bolívar/Desengaño y Calle Francisco Javier/Rosario* ☎ *4199–3994.*

SHOPPING

Local artisans sell their wares from stalls on side streets near the Canchánchara, the Museo Histórico, and the Casa de la Trova. They not only offer the best deals, but all the money goes to the artist, rather than a fraction, as is the case with the government stores.

CRAFTS

Fondo de Bienes Culturales. This cooperative in a colonial house across from the Museo Histórico sells paintings and handicrafts by local artists. ⊠ *Calle Simón Bolívar/Desengaño 418* ☎ *4199–4199.*

CIGARS AND TOBACCO

Casa del Tabaco. This is Trinidad's address for cigars, rum, and coffee. ⊠ *Calle Antonio Maceo/Gutiérrez y Calle Francisco Javier/Rosario* ☎ *4199–6149.*

SPORTS AND THE OUTDOORS

Centro de Buceo Puertosol (*Puertosol Dive Center*). To explore a few of the area's 30 dive spots; contact the Centro de Buceo Puertosol, on the Península de Ancón. Equipment rentals run about CUC$60 a day; boat dives and certification courses are also available. ⊠ *Trinidad* ☎ *4199–6120.*

EL VALLE DE LOS INGENIOS

3 km (2 miles) to 12 km (7 miles) east of Trinidad.

Just east of Trinidad, the road winds its way through the verdant Valley of the Sugar Mills, where Trinidad's colonial fortunes were made.

EXPLORING

Manaca Iznaga. This site of an 18th-century farmhouse once belonged to one of the region's wealthiest families. It stands next to the Torre de Iznaga, a 43-meter (141-foot) tower built in the early 1800s. Legend has it that the two Iznaga sons were in love with a beautiful young woman, and their father told one to build a tower and the other to dig a well, with the promise that whoever built higher or dug deeper could have her. But when they were done, both the tower and well were 43 meters, so the old man married the woman himself. The tower actually had a much more practical purpose: it was a place from which to keep an eye on the thousands of slaves who worked the surrounding plantations. The large bell that was rung when slaves tried to escape lies on the ground near the farmhouse. ⊠ *12 km (7 miles) beyond lookout just outside Trinidad.*

COLLOQUIAL CUBAN

Cuban slang is earthy and colorful, and we dare not print some of it in a family publication such as a Fodor's guidebook. Exercise caution, even when choosing from our tamer list below. Cubans sometimes use *monado* with a bit of disdain to refer to the police. You should never do that. Stick with the standard *policía*. Of course, our mention of the *bolsa negra* (black market) is not an endorsement to use the system.

- *asere*: friend
- *bici*: bicycle
- *bici-taxi*: bicycle taxi
- *bodega state*: grocery store
- *bolsa negra*: black market
- *camello*: camello bus
- *chao*: goodbye
- *chebi*: official taxi
- *chopin*: "shopping," a store that takes convertible pesos

- *cola*: queue
- *dale*: okay
- *filtro*: smart person
- *guagua*: bus
- *guajiro*: farmer
- *jama*: food
- *jinetero*: hustler, con artist
- *kiosko*: small shop
- *máquina*: car
- *monado*: police
- *moni*: money
- *pipo*: chap, waiter
- *¿Qué bola?*: What's up? How are you?
- *yuma*: foreigner, more commonly used than "gringo"
- *zafra*: sugarcane harvest

WHERE TO EAT

$$
CUBAN

✕ **Restaurante Manaca.** The Manaca Iznaga family's former manor house is now occupied by a restaurant. The building's ochre walls, square columns, wood-beam ceiling, and terra-cotta floors lend considerable colonial ambience. There's an old sugar mill out back, and scattered on the lawn in front are the cauldrons used to boil down molasses. Lunches are usually accompanied by the music of an excellent little band. The specialty is *puntas de cerdo a la Iznaga* (strips of pork loin in a tomato-vegetable sauce), but the menu includes everything from fresh seafood to grilled chicken. ⑤ *Average main: CUC$14* ✉ *Manaca Iznaga* ☎ *4199–7241* ⊟ *No credit cards* ☉ *No dinner.*

PENÍNSULA DE ANCÓN

12 km (7 miles) south of Trinidad.

The beaches that line the southern edge of this narrow peninsula, which curves eastward into the Caribbean, are two of the best in the province. Many people who visit Trinidad actually stay here; it lies conveniently close to the historic city, and the area's largest hotels overlook its pale sands.

EXPLORING

Cayo Blanco. A 45-minute boat ride southeast of the peninsula takes you to Cayo Blanco, with its white-sand beach and vast coral reef offshore. A tour is the easiest way to get here. Several boats visit the island on day trips offered by local hotels and tour operators. ⊠ *Cayo Blanco.*

BEACHES

Playa Ancón. Sandwiched between the Bahía de Casilda and the sea is the peninsula's most appealing beach, with more than a mile of beige sand sloping into aquamarine water. The large Club Amigo Ancón and Brisas Trinidad del Mar hotels front this strand. **Amenities:** food and drink; lifeguards; parking; showers; toilets. **Best for:** sunset; swimming; walking. ⊠ *Trinidad* ⊹ *10 km (6 miles) south of Trinidad.*

Playa María Aguilar. The first beach on the peninsula is a short strand shaded by a few palm trees and cropped by rocky points. The ocean is littered with coral boulders, part of a colorful reef that wraps around the point to the east, making this the peninsula's best snorkeling beach. **Amenities:** food and drink; parking; water sports. **Best for:** solitude; snorkeling; sunset; swimming; walking. ⊠ *Trinidad* ⊹ *8 km (4 miles) south of Trinidad.*

WHERE TO STAY

$$
RESORT
Brisas Trinidad del Mar. Its many colonial-style arches, columns, Spanish tiles, and pastel colors give this all-inclusive resort a Disneyesque look. **Pros:** the colonial style of the complex here is tasteful and well done; the evening seafood beach grill is a good dinner option. **Cons:** the buffets are nothing to write home about; the place is very popular, and should be reserved well in advance. ⑤ *Rooms from: CUC$90* ⊠ *Playa Ancón, Trinidad* ☎ *4199–6500* ⊕ *www.hotelescubanacan.com* ⇲ *241 rooms* ❍❘ *All-inclusive.*

$$
RESORT
Club Amigo Ancón. This massive beachfront complex has the appearance of two hotels, and you want to choose the right section. **Pros:** the setting here at the end of the peninsula is gorgeous; rooms in Módulo Nuevo are modern and spacious; large pool and tennis courts. **Cons:** about half the rooms here are not so gorgeous, so pick carefully; this is not a place to come for peace and quiet. ⑤ *Rooms from: CUC$98* ⊠ *Playa Ancón, Trinidad* ☎ *4199–6123* ⊕ *www.hotelescubanacan.com* ⇲ *279 rooms* ❍❘ *All-inclusive.*

SPORTS AND THE OUTDOORS

The ocean around the Península de Ancón holds plenty of coral, the most accessible of which lies a mere 300 meters (985 feet) offshore from the Hotel Costasur.

DIVING

Centro de Buceo Puertosol. Located in the marina across from the Hotel Ancón, this center takes people to more than 20 dive spots (CUC$60 for equipment rental), including a shipwreck and several large coral reefs; it also offers certification courses (CUC$200). The marina offers deep-sea fishing. ⊠ *Playa Ancón, Trinidad* ☎ *4199–6205.*

TOPES DE COLLANTES

21 km (12 miles) north of Trinidad.

High in the Sierra de Escambray, at the end of a road that winds its way north from Trinidad, this sylvan enclave has long been a health retreat and a perfect destination for a hike. At an altitude of 800 meters (2,600 feet) above sea level, the climate is a refreshing change from the sultry lowlands (the average temperature is 21°C/70°F), and regular precipitation keeps everything green. Because the area receives mostly Cuban tourism, accommodations aren't as good as those in Trinidad and Ancón. The tour operator Rumbos offers day trips from Trinidad.

GETTING HERE AND AROUND

With no acceptable places to spend the night in the park itself, an organized tour from Trinidad is the easiest way to get up here and spend the day.

EXPLORING

Parque Natural Escambray. The mountains around Topes de Collantes are covered with a mosaic of coffee farms and patches of forest that are protected within the **Parque Natural Escambray**. This nature preserve has several deep, lush valleys that are home to such birds as the Cuban parrot, the emerald hummingbird, and the trogon. Several trails lead to waterfalls; the most accessible is the **Salto de Caburní,** just a 2-km (1-mile) hike along a trail that starts at the Villa Caburní hotel, 2 km (1 mile) north of Topes de Collantes. The spectacular **Salto de Rocío** cascades down a rock face about 17 km (10 miles) north of Topes. Tours (the only way to visit) truck you to a point just 2 km (1 mile) from the falls. The grotto of **La Batata,** several kilometers west of Topes, has a river running out of it with a swimming hole; you can visit on a 7-km (4-mile) guided hike that passes a lookout point. ⊠ *Topes de Collantes.*

SPORTS AND THE OUTDOORS

Enjoying the great outdoors is about the only thing to do in Topes de Collantes, and hiking is the way to do it.

HIKING

Gaviota Tours. This tour company offers inexpensive excursions to the waterfalls, La Batata, and Hacienda Codina, a nearby farm. ☎ *4254–0117.*

SANCTI SPÍRITUS

70 km (42 miles) northeast of Trinidad; 360 km (224 miles) southeast of Havana; 92 km (55 miles) southeast of Santa Clara.

The provincial capital of Sancti Spíritus is a lesser Trinidad—its historic center is much smaller, and it also receives a mere fraction of the visitors that flock to its more famous neighbor. (Sancti Spíritus does have twice the population of Trinidad, though.) City fathers have looked with envy at the tourism boom in nearby Trinidad and have begun to spruce up Sancti Spíritus's own offerings in recent years. It's a tranquil, traditional city, where bicycles and horse-drawn taxis make up much of the traffic and where the locals hang out in the central plaza at night.

The city also has some splendid colonial architecture, much of which the government has restored and painted, including two small museums in colonial homes. It's worth a stop if you have the time.

GETTING HERE AND AROUND

The multilane sector of the Autopista Nacional ends at Sancti Spíritus, making the city an easy five-hour drive from Havana. Víazul buses connect Sancti Spíritus with Havana and Santiago de Cuba and most points between.

EXPLORING

TOP ATTRACTIONS

Iglesia Parroquial Mayor del Espíritu Santo. Built in 1680, the starkly beautiful Iglesia Parroquial Mayor del Espíritu Santo is one of Cuba's oldest and best-preserved churches. Its massive bell tower is visible from much of Sancti Spíritus, and though its interior is sparsely decorated—a carved wooden ceiling and a blue-and-gold wooden arch framing a simple altar—it's extremely well preserved. ⊠ *Calle Jesús Méndez y Calle Rodríguez* ☏ *4132–4855.*

Museo de Arte Colonial (*Museum of Colonial Art*). The meticulously restored mansion that now houses the Museum of Colonial Art was long the property of the Valle Iznaga family, who owned sugar plantations, processing plants, a railroad, and a port, among other things. Dating from 1744, it's furnished with antiques from several centuries, most of which belonged to the Valle Iznagas, so the house appears much as it might have for a party a century ago—the music room is full of instruments, the dining room is set for a banquet, and the kitchen is ready for the cooking to begin. ⊠ *Calle Plácido 74* ☏ *4132–5455* 💲 *CUC$2; CUC$1 fee for photos* ☉ *Tues.–Sat. 9–5, Sun. 8–noon.*

WORTH NOTING

Biblioteca. The Neoclassical Biblioteca, on Plaza Serafín Sánchez's southwest corner, is the most conspicuous edifice. Built in 1929 by the city's wealthiest citizens as an exclusive club, it became a public library following the Revolution, and was meticulously restored in 1998. On the second floor in the former ballroom, students now read beneath painted columns and crystal chandeliers. Be sure to check out the view from the balcony. ⊠ *Calle Máximo Gómez 1 Norte* ☏ *4132–3313* 💲 *Free* ☉ *Weekdays 8 am–9 pm, Sat. 8–4.*

Calle El Llano. Down the hill behind the church is Calle El Llano, a steep, cobbled street lined with some of the city's oldest houses, most of which are private homes. At the bottom of the hill stands the Quinta Santa Elena, a former farmhouse that dates from 1719. It's now a restaurant, and its shaded front terrace has the best view of the 19th-century stone bridge that spans the Río Yayabo. ⊠ *Calle El Llano.*

Calle Independencia. For several blocks south of the Plaza Serafín Sánchez, Calle Independencia is a pedestrian mall lined with an array of shops, a couple of banks, and the main post office. The mall ends in front of the 19th-century Colonia Español building, to the west of which is Sancti Spíritus's ancient church, the Iglesia Parroquial Mayor del Espíritu Santo. ⊠ *Sancti Spíritus.*

Plaza Serafín Sánchez. The heart of Sancti Spíritus is the Plaza Serafín Sánchez, a shady central park, roughly triangular in shape, and surrounded by an eclectic mix of 18th- and 19th-century architecture, including the town library and a museum with displays on the province's history. The park comes into its own as the sun goes down on the torrid afternoon and locals come out to chat and mingle. ⊠ *Sancti Spíritus.*

WHERE TO EAT

$$
CUBAN

✕ **Restaurante Mesón de la Plaza.** This refurbished 19th-century building overlooks Plaza Serafín Sánchez and the porticos of the colonial buildings that surround it. It's an impressive edifice, with large, arched doorways. Seating is at sturdy wooden tables, a couple of which have views of the Iglesia Parroquial Mayor. The menu is traditional Cuban with a few twists, such as *garbanzo mesonero* (garbanzo and pork soup) and *ternero a la villa* (veal stewed in a clay pot). $ *Average main: CUC$12* ⊠ *Calle Máximo Gómez 34* ☎ *4132–8546.*

$
CUBAN

✕ **Restaurante Quinta Santa Elena.** Between the muddy Río Yayabo and the Calle el Llano, this ancient yellow manor house with a large, tree-shaded terrace is an appealing spot. Seating is available on the terrace, which has a river view, or inside, where the terra-cotta floors, thick columns, and wide arches attest to the building's lifespan of almost three centuries. Specialties are *pollo a la quinta* (chicken in a vegetable tomato sauce) and *vaca frita* (strips of beef sautéed with onions), and an array of *criolla* dishes. $ *Average main: CUC$6* ⊠ *End of Calle el Llano* ☎ *4132–8167* ▭ *No credit cards.*

WHERE TO STAY

$
HOTEL

🏨 **Hotel E Plaza.** The historic Hotel Plaza, which overlooks the Plaza Serafín Sánchez, has airy, charming public spaces with arches, wicker furniture, and potted plants. **Pros:** rooms that face the street evoke the history of the place; public spaces so inviting you may forget to go back to your room. **Cons:** the restaurant is ho-hum; newer rooms are dark and unimaginative. $ *Rooms from: CUC$70* ⊠ *Calle Independencia 1 Norte* ☎ *4132–7102* ⊕ *www.islazul.cu* ⤴ *28 rooms* ¶○¶ *Breakfast.*

$
B&B/INN
FAMILY

🏨 **Villa Rancho Hatuey.** Here dozens of two-story, cement bungalows spread around verdant grounds have spacious rooms with white-tile floors, queen-size beds, and lots of windows. **Pros:** there's lots of lush greenery and fresh air here. **Cons:** on weekends, music from the disco might keep you awake. $ *Rooms from: CUC$59* ⊠ *Carretera Central* ✛ *5 km (3 miles) north of Sancti Spíritus* ☎ *4132–8315* ⊕ *www.islazul. cu* ⤴ *76 rooms* ¶○¶ *Breakfast.*

NIGHTLIFE AND PERFORMING ARTS

Casa de la Trova. This spot hosts live-music shows starting at 10 pm Wednesday through Saturday and on Sunday afternoons. ⊠ *Calle Máximo Gómez 26 Sur* ☎ *4132–6802* ▨ *CUC$1.*

SHOPPING

ART GALLERIES

Galería Arcada. This colonial house on the pedestrian mall has been converted into a gallery and sells a wide array of local handicrafts, from paintings to wood sculptures and leather goods. ☒ *Calle Independencia 55 Sur* ☎ *4132–7106.*

SPORTS AND THE OUTDOORS

BIRD-WATCHING

Reserva Ecológica El Naranjal. The best place for bird-watching is the Reserva Ecológica El Naranjal, a protected, mountainous area near the town of Banao. ☒ *20 km (12 miles) south of Sancti Spíritus.*

FISHING

Zaza Reservoir. The reservoir has world-class bass fishing. The Hotel Horizontes Zaza, on the reservoir, can arrange excursions. ☒ *Topes de Collantes* ✛ *10 km (6 miles) southeast of Sancti Spíritus* ☎ *4132–5490 Hotel Horizontes Zaza.*

CIEGO DE ÁVILA AND CAMAGÜEY PROVINCES

These two provinces are known for their white-sand beaches, which are lapped by clear waters rich in marine life. But there's more to the region than sun, sand, and deep-blue sea. Off the northern shore of Ciego de Ávila Province you'll see the mangrove shallows of Cayo Coco and Cayo Guillermo, which are often filled with flamingos. In Camagüey Province, between the northern keys and the coastal resort of Santa Lucía, there are enough coral reefs and wrecks to keep a scuba diver submerged for weeks.

GETTING HERE AND AROUND

The best way to reach this region is by regularly scheduled bus routes on the carrier Víazul. Daily routes travel from Havana to Trinidad and Santiago de Cuba. If you are heading to the cayos by land, you will have little choice but to pay a premium and take an official taxi—which are the only ones allowed onto the small islands. Camagüey's Aeropuerto Internacional Ignacio Agramonte receives regular domestic flights from Havana on Cubana and Aero Caribbean. The superbusy Aeropuerto Internacional Jardines del Rey on Cayo Coco sees domestic traffic as well, but most of the planes that land here are nonstop charter flights from Canada and Europe ferrying sunseekers to nearby resorts.

CAYO COCO AND CAYO GUILLERMO

164 km (98 miles) northeast of Sancti Spíritus.

These two green islands, set in the turquoise sea some 27 km (16 miles) north of the mainland, have more than a dozen white-sand beaches, twice that many coral reefs, and mangrove shallows that attract great flocks of flamingos. The more secluded Cayo Santa María usually gets grouped in with Coco and Guillermo, too; development has been slower to come to Santa María than to its bigger neighbors, but that situation is not expected to last. Ernest Hemingway made frequent fishing trips to these keys and described them in *Islands in the Stream*. Long uninhabited and visited only by local fishermen and the occasional millionaire, the islands now have several modern beach resorts, with even more under construction. They have become Cuba's third most popular tourist destination, following Havana and Varadero.

A causeway traverses the shallow Bahía de Perros (Bay of Dogs) south of Cayo Coco; from this key, shorter causeways stretch west to Cayo Guillermo and east to the undeveloped Cayo Romano. All three islands are covered with a thick scrub vegetation; mangrove swamps line their southern shores; and bleached-sand beaches scallop their northern edges. The fishing is good; in addition to the marlin that so fascinated Papa, there are wahoo, tuna, mahimahi, and sailfish. Sportfishing charters are available out of the marinas on both keys; you can arrange them at any hotel. The diving (particularly off Cayo Guillermo) is even better than the angling, with dozens of healthy coral reefs inhabited by hundreds of fish species—from the delicate butterfly fish to the menacing barracuda—as well as a dizzying array of invertebrates. Visibility averages 20 to 35 meters (66 to 115 feet).

GETTING HERE AND AROUND

If you're here on a resort package, the Aeropuerto Jardines del Rey is your arrival and departure point. A 35-km (21 miles) causeway (*pedraplén*) connects the cayos with the mainland at Morón, northeast of the city of Ciego de Ávila. Only official taxis have permission to use the causeway. Bus transportation is nonexistent.

EXPLORING

Cayo Coco. The island was named for the white ibis, a pale wader called the *coco* in Cuba, but its mangroves and sandy shallows attract dozens of species, including flamingo (which gather by the hundreds in the shallow bay to the south), roseate spoonbill, tricolor heron, and reddish egret. The island's roughly 90 indigenous bird species are joined by another 120 migrants between November and April, and its forests are also home to everything from wild pig to anole lizard.

Despite its varied wildlife, most people visit Cayo Coco for its swaths of sugary sand shaded by coconut palms and washed by cerulean sea—the stuff of travel posters in Toronto storefronts or the daydreams of snowbound accountants. Nine beaches run for a total of 21 km (12 miles) along the northern coast, and only two of them have hotels. The most spectacular beaches are Playa Flamingo, with its extensive sandbars, and nearby Playa Prohibida (Forbidden Beach)—a protected area backed by dunes covered with scrubby native palms. ⊠ *Cayo Coco.*

Cayo Guillermo. The island's beaches are narrow but still captivating. The ocean in front of them is so shallow that you can wade out more than 90 meters (290 feet). Its nicest beach is Playa Pilar, which was named after Hemingway's old fishing boat. Stretching along the key's northwest end, this beach is backed by 20-meter (66-foot) dunes and overlooks Cayo Media Luna, an islet where dictator Fulgencio Batista once had a vacation home. Cayo Guillermo has excellent skin diving, with 37 dive spots nearby. ⊠ *Cayo Guillermo.*

BEACHES

Playa Flamenco. You'll find the mammoth new Meliá Jardines del Rey along with a few other hotels here, but their presence doesn't overpower this scenic white-sand beach. (Remember that all beaches are public in Cuba, resorts or no resorts.) A couple of informal *ranchones* serve lunch here—expect to fork out CUC$15—and offer you a nice break from the confinement of your all-inclusive's dining options. Tourists often call this stretch of sand "Playa Flamingo." **Amenities:** food and drink; parking; toilets; water sports. **Best for:** snorkeling; sunset; swimming; walking. ⊠ *Cayo Coco, east and west of Meliá Jardines del Rey.*

Playa Prohibida (*Forbidden Beach*). Dunes, native palms, and seaweed provide the backdrop at this pretty white-sand, so-called "Forbidden Beach." The name evokes isolation, and that you'll have here, save for the informal thatch-roof ranchón that serves the catch of the day for lunch and has occasional live music. **Amenities:** food and drink; toilets. **Best for:** solitude; swimming; walking. ⊠ *Cayo Coco, 11 km (6½ miles) west of Iberostar Cayo Coco, Ciego de Ávila.*

Fodor's Choice **Playa Pilar.** Cayo Guillermo's nicest beach—and many visitors rank it as
★ their favorite in Cuba—was named after Hemingway's old fishing boat. Stretching along the key's northwest end, the pink-sand beach is backed by dunes and is fairly isolated, although you should expect to see a lot of day visitors from hotels around both Cayos Guillermo and Coco. A couple of ranchónes—informal, thatch-roof eating places—serve lunch, and a few entrepreneurial types rent beach chairs for CUC$2. **Amenities:** food and drink; toilets. **Best for:** solitude; swimming; walking. ⊠ *Cayo Guillermo, 3 km (5 miles) northwest of Meliá Cayo Guillermo.*

WHERE TO STAY

The hotels on Cayo Coco and Cayo Guillermo are megaresorts of the type found throughout the Caribbean. A stay here will put you in full vacation mode, with meals, snacks, drinks, and everything from beach chairs to sea kayaks included in the rates. ■**TIP→ Check the fine print carefully for incidentals that may not be included in the price of your resort package.**) In addition, several resorts have amphitheaters—where the nightly entertainment ranges from Cuban folk dancing to fashion shows—and dance clubs. Most are quite kid-friendly, with children's programs.

An all-inclusive resort will be your home for the duration of your stay, and your dining options will essentially be those in your hotel. Most of the multirestaurant resorts include dining in your rate (usually the buffets), but there are à la carte options as well. Check carefully which is which. A few informal thatch-roof *ranchones* dot the beaches and serve seafood for lunch. The atmosphere is pretty basic, and all seem to fix their meal prices at a standard CUC$15.

$$$ ⬚ **Hotel Colonial Cayo Coco.** The colonial era is also ever-present at this
RESORT resort, with pastel-color colonial-style buildings and walkways. **Pros:** the setting and village-like atmosphere are attractive; sports galore. **Cons:** service can be slow; not a place to go if you crave peace and quiet. ⑤ *Rooms from: CUC$154* ⊠ *Cayo Coco* ☎ *3330–1311* ⊕ *www. hotelescubanacan.com* ⤴ *458 rooms* ⑩*All-inclusive.*

$$$ | **Iberostar Cayo Coco.** Set in an ecological park, this scenic resort—host
RESORT to fauna and flora and adjacent to a pristine coral reef—has numer-
FAMILY ous one-story villas, standard rooms in three-story blocks, as well as
nice rooms that overlook the lagoon itself. **Pros:** lots of kids' activities
make this a great family option; has one of the most scenic settings of
the Cayo Coco resorts. **Cons:** this is not a place where the action is.
⑤ *Rooms from: CUC$190* ☎ *3330–1070* ⊕ *www.iberostar.com* ⇱ *262
rooms, 76 suites* ❙◯❙ *All-inclusive.*

$$$ | **Iberostar Daiquirí.** Second only to its white beach, which extends into
RESORT blue-green shallows, is this hotel's airy lobby, which stretches beneath a
soaring wooden roof and is adorned with shiny marble floors, painted
columns, tinted glass, and a small bar surrounded by tropical greenery.
Pros: active poolside activities; good sports facilities. **Cons:** rooms themselves are rather plain. ⑤ *Rooms from: CUC$178* ✉ *Cayo Guillermo*
☎ *3330–1650* ⊕ *www.iberostar.com* ⇱ *312 rooms* ❙◯❙ *All-inclusive.*

$$$$ | **Iberostar Ensenachos.** Located on a small island adjacent to Cayo Coco,
RESORT this is the most upscale and private of the area's resorts. **Pros:** the rooms
Fodor'sChoice here are superb, meeting international standards; more luxurious than
★ competing hotels. **Cons:** subdued atmosphere, which may or may not
be what you want in a resort stay. ⑤ *Rooms from: CUC$350* ✉ *Cayo
Ensenachos* ☎ *4235–0301* ⊕ *www.iberostar.com* ⇱ *460 rooms, 46 villas* ❙◯❙ *All-inclusive.*

$$$ | **Meliá Cayo Guillermo.** This property has a beautiful layout and is dot-
RESORT ted with ponds with lily pads and numerous palm-tree lined colonnades.
FAMILY **Pros:** babysitter service is available in the kid's club; lots of family-ori-
ented activities. **Cons:** seaweed often litters the beach. ⑤ *Rooms from:
CUC$185* ✉ *Cayo Guillermo* ☎ *3330–1680* ⊕ *www.meliacuba.com*
⇱ *301 rooms* ❙◯❙ *All-inclusive.*

$$$ | **Meliá Cayo Santa María.** This resort on Cayo Santa María, set among
RESORT lush vegetation, offers a bit more privacy and exclusivity than other
properties here in the Cayos. **Pros:** the hotel is noted for its aesthetic
appeal and privacy; adults-only resort; all rooms have balconies or
terraces. **Cons:** restaurants here are unspectacular; not family-friendly.
⑤ *Rooms from: CUC$194* ✉ *Cayo Santa Maria* ☎ *4235–1500* ⊕ *www.
meliacuba.com* ⇱ *358 rooms* ❙◯❙ *All-inclusive* ☞ *No kids under 18.*

$$$$ | **Meliá Jardines del Rey.** Cuba's largest hotel clocks in at an astounding
RESORT 1,176 rooms, and, if you like large resorts with lots of activity, it'll work
Fodor'sChoice for you. **Pros:** tons of activity means you'll never be bored here; nine res-
★ taurants to choose from; web-only specials. **Cons:** this is not a place to
go for solitude; the majority of rooms do not have sea views. ⑤ *Rooms
from: CUC$226* ✉ *Cayo Coco* ☎ *3330–4300* ⊕ *www.meliacuba.com*
⇱ *1,152 rooms, 24 suites* ❙◯❙ *All-inclusive.*

$$$ | **Meliá Las Dunas.** One of the most attractive all-inclusive resorts in
RESORT Cuba has a vibrant atmosphere and beautiful environs. **Pros:** the res-
Fodor'sChoice taurants are top-notch, especially Isabel y Fernando; service here is
★ unfailingly impeccable. **Cons:** with 900-plus rooms, not quite as private
and exclusive as next-door Meliá Cayo Santa María. ⑤ *Rooms from:
CUC$204* ✉ *Cayo Santa Maria* ☎ *4235–0100* ⊕ *www.meliacuba.com*
⇱ *925 rooms* ❙◯❙ *All-inclusive.*

$$$ 🏨 **Memories Caribe.** This family-friendly property is set off from the
RESORT   commotion of other Cayo Coco resorts and faces a beautiful oceanfront
FAMILY   and a long lagoon area. **Pros:** the secluded nature of the resort is an
added plus for those looking for a more private, no-nonsense vacation.
Cons: this is not where the action is, so don't expect a vibrant night-
life at this family-oriented hotel. 💲*Rooms from: CUC$190* ✉ *Cayo
Coco* ☎ *3330–2350* ⊕ *www.memoriesresorts.com* 🛏*328 rooms*
🍽*All-inclusive.*

$$$ 🏨 **Tryp Cayo Coco.** Cayo Coco's original resort, the Tryp is a miniature
RESORT   city, with several pools, more than 20 bars and restaurants, and nearly
FAMILY   a thousand rooms spread along a mile of pale beach. **Pros:** the diving-
instruction center and activities are attractive to younger crowds and
sports enthusiasts; lots of family activities will keep everybody busy.
Cons: not a place to go if you crave solitude. 💲*Rooms from: CUC$153*
✉ *Cayo Coco, due north of causeway* ☎ *3330–1300* ⊕ *www.meliacuba.
com* 🛏*508 rooms* 🍽*All-inclusive.*

CAMAGÜEY

*535 km (321 miles) southeast of Havana; 174 km (104 miles) southeast
of Ciego de Ávila; 255 km (153 miles) northwest of Holguín.*

Cuba's third-largest city (population 315,000) and the capital of the
country's biggest province, Camagüey (pronounced cah-mah- *gway*) is
a sprawling but tranquil town of narrow, cobbled streets—lined with
an eclectic mix of architecture—converging on plazas dominated by
colonial churches. The *camagüeyanos,* as its citizens are known, are
proud of their city and its nearly five centuries of history. They welcome
the few foreigners who pass this way, which makes it an exceptionally
pleasant city to visit.

Camagüey was one of the seven villas founded by Diego Velázquez at
the beginning of the 16th century. Originally called Puerto del Principe
(Prince's Port), the settlement was established on the northern coast and
was moved twice, reaching its current location in 1528. It wasn't until
the early 1900s that it took the name Camagüey, after a tree common
to the region. As the vast plain surrounding it was converted to ranch-
land, the city became a prosperous commercial center. During the 17th
and 18th centuries, buccaneers and pirates, led by the likes of Henry
Morgan, marched inland and sacked the city several times. As protection against such invasions, Camagüey was transformed into a maze of
narrow streets that facilitated ambushing attackers in the old days but
today only make it easier for visitors to get lost. That's the traditional
story that everyone tells, but historians today posit that a simple lack
of urban planning was more likely the cause of Camagüey's spaghetti
entanglement of streets. (Pirates always make for a better story.)

As sugar exports came to complement ranching profits, Camagüey
developed a criollo upper class that was supportive of the independence movements that swept the country in the 19th century. Some of its
most fortunate sons took up arms against the Spanish, and many paid
dearly for their treason. The most famous of these rebels was Ignacio
Agramonte (1841–73); after he was killed by the Spanish, his body was

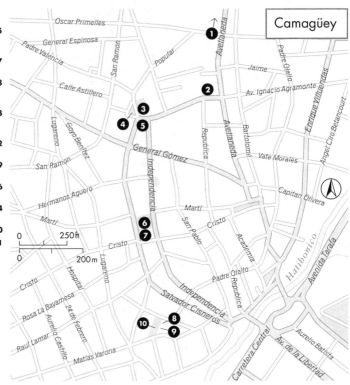

burned in public. Agramonte consequently became the town hero, with the central park and airport named for him.

As the city is set in a fairly dry, flat region, for centuries the camagüeyanos drank rainwater collected in giant ceramic vessels called *tinajones*. In the early 20th century, when a water system was finally built, it's estimated that there were 1,900 such containers, more than enough to give Camagüey its nickname "City of the Tinajones." (You will see tinajones elsewhere in Cuba, but in smaller numbers.) Those giant jugs are now displayed all over town, and the need for them gave birth to a ceramic-making tradition. One popular legend has it that if a local maiden gives a visitor water from a tinajón, he'll fall in love with her and never leave.

GETTING HERE AND AROUND

Camagüey straddles the Carretera Nacional, linking the city with all points east and west. Víazul buses connect Camagüey with Havana, Trinidad, and Santiago de Cuba. Camagüey is a stop on the Havana-Santiago train route. The Aeropuerto Ignacio Agramonte serves flights from Havana, as well as a few international charters.

EXPLORING

If you hoof it, you can explore the city's compact historic center in about half a day. Camagüey will invite you to dally, though, and you can easily stretch the tour into a full day. The city's labyrinthine street pattern means you'll spend a lot of time asking for directions here.

TOP ATTRACTIONS

Fodor's Choice
★

Iglesia de Nuestra Señora de la Merced. Originally erected in 1748, this church was reconstructed in 1848, repaired after a fire in 1906, and renovated yet again in 1998. The clock on its facade was the city's first public timepiece, made in Barcelona in 1773; its current machinery was imported from the United States in 1901. The church's interior has massive square columns and a vaulted ceiling decorated with faded art nouveau frescoes dating from 1915. The painted wooden altar was made in 1909 to replace one destroyed by the 1906 fire, but the paintings on the walls around it date from the 18th and 19th centuries. To the right of the altar is the *Santo Sepulcro* (Holy Sepulchre): a Christ figure in a glass casket that was made in 1762 using the silver from 23,000 Mexican coins donated by parishioners. It's carried out of the cathedral and back every Good Friday in a religious procession that was prohibited for nearly four decades. The crypts beneath the altar have been partially excavated and converted into a tiny museum of tombs, icons, and other antiquities; it's not for the claustrophobic. If the church is closed, enter through the convent next door. ⊠ *Calle Independencia y Av. Ignacio Agramonte* ☎ *3229–2783* 🎫 *Free* ☉ *Daily 8–11 and 4–5:30.*

Iglesia de Nuestra Señora de la Soledad. The restored exterior of this 18th-century Baroque church dedicated to Our Lady of Solitude leads to its well-preserved interior. Thick, square columns rise into high arches decorated with lovely floral frescoes, above which is a *mudejar* wooden ceiling with ornate carved beams. According to legend, a statue of the Virgin fell from a wagon at this spot in the late 1600s; seeing it as a sign from heaven, the locals built a hermitage for it, which was later replaced by this church, completed in 1776. ⊠ *Calle República y Av. Ignacio Agramonte* ☎ *3229–2392* ☉ *Mon.–Sat. 6–11 and 4–6, Sun. 6–noon.*

WORTH NOTING

Casa Natal de Ignacio Agramonte. This yellow colonial building with a high wooden balcony was probably one of the tallest structures in town when Ignacio Agramonte was born to a wealthy ranching family here in 1841. Agramonte grew to become a general in the Ten Years War. When he was killed in battle in 1873, popular acclamation elevated him to the rank of hero. Though only half of the original house remains, it has been restored and converted into a museum. Its courtyard has a tinajón in every corner, and upstairs rooms are furnished with period pieces or filled with displays about the wars for independence. ⊠ *Av. Ignacio Agramonte 59* ☎ *3229–7116* 🎫 *CUC$2* ☉ *Tues.–Sat. 10–5, Sun. 8–noon.*

Catedral de Nuestra Señora de la Candelaria. Camagüey's cathedral, on the southeastern edge of Parque Ignacio Agramonte, was built in fits and starts between 1735 and 1864. The most recent of several renovations took 15 years and included replacing the wood-beam ceiling.

Its refurbished exterior is an attractive beige and yellow. The most impressive aspect of the spacious interior is the large wood-and-marble altar, behind which shine stained glass and a statue of the Virgin Mary. ✉ *Across from southern end of Parque Ignacio Agramonte* ☎ *3229–4965* 💲 *Free* ⊙ *Weekdays 8–11:45 and 2:30–5:30, Sat. 2:30–4, Sun. 8–noon.*

Hospital de San Juan de Dios. On the eastern edge of Plaza de San Juan de Dios, the old hospital now holds the offices of several cultural organizations. In the portico of its large garden, you'll find a simple museum with exhibits on the building's history, some old photos, and surgical instruments from days of yore—thank goodness for modern medicine. It's worth a quick look if you have a curiosity for the history of medicine. More interesting is the view from the roof. ✉ *Plaza de San Juan de Dios* ☎ *3229–1388* 💲 *CUC$1* ⊙ *Mon.–Sat. 7–11 and 2:30–4.*

Iglesia de San Juan de Dios. Camagüey's oldest church was built in 1728 to replace the original (1686) St. John's. It underwent some structural changes in 1847 and an extensive restoration in 1986. Its simple, traditional interior has a terra-cotta floor, white-stucco walls, and a sloped wooden ceiling. Four ancient hardwood altars stand along the walls, each of them dedicated to a different saint—St. John's is the second on the left. The main altar is dedicated to the Holy Trinity, and is unique in that the Holy Spirit is represented as a man instead of as the usual dove. ✉ *Plaza de San Juan de Dios* 💲 *Free* ⊙ *Mon.–Sat. 7–11 and 3–6.*

Parque Ignacio Agramonte. Originally the city's central square, or Plaza de las Armas, this didn't become a proper park until 1912. Note the bronze statue of Agramonte on his steed at its center. In the park's southwestern corner is a 19th-century house that's now the Casa de la Trova, whose courtyard hosts performances by local musicians every day but Monday. The Neoclassical building to the north is the *biblioteca* (library); a few doors farther north is the Palacio Municipal (town hall), which was originally erected in 1730 but almost completely rebuilt in 1906; local artists often exhibit in its foyer. The royal palms that stand at each corner of the park were planted as surreptitious monuments to four freedom fighters executed by Spain during the War of Independence. You'll find the requisite tinajones here too. ✉ *Calle Martí, e/Calle Cisneros y Calle Independencia.*

Plaza de los Trabajadores. Before the Revolution, the Workers Plaza was known as the Plaza de la Merced, after the church and convent that define its eastern edge. (Older people still refer to it by its former moniker.) A large mural of Che Guevara's eternally youthful visage stares past the ancient facade of La Merced in that distinctively Cuban juxtaposition of tradition and revolution. A kapok tree towers over the plaza's center, and in the southwest corner stands the stately La Popular, built in 1928 and the seat of a local cultural society. ✉ *Calle Fernando Hernández y Calle Simón Bolívar.*

Plaza de San Juan de Dios. This splendid cobbled square, surrounded by meticulously restored 18th- and 19th-century buildings (most still private homes), has been declared a national monument. ✉ *Camagüey.*

Tiferet Israel. Cuba's Jewish community numbers under 1,000 and, like all religious groups here, it has struggled since the Revolution. Camagüey's tiny synagogue provides hope for renewal, however. Reestablished in 1998, Tiferet Israel counts about 45 members and is the most active Jewish congregation outside Havana. The Masorti-affiliated community (that's the international counterpart to the Conservative movement in the United States) welcomes visitors to its synagogue, a converted house. Call in advance to make arrangements. ✉ *Calle Andrés Sánchez 365* ☎ *3228–4639* ⏲ *Call for information.*

WHERE TO EAT

Most of Camagüey's casas particulares are near the bus terminal, on the Carretera Central. There are, however, several nice ones in the historic center.

$$ CUBAN ✕ **La Campana de Toledo.** In a restored 18th-century house overlooking the timeless Plaza de San Juan de Dios, this restaurant was named for the *campana* (bell) that hangs in its courtyard, which was brought to Camagüey from Toledo, Spain, by a merchant who lived here. Seating is either in the courtyard, which is shaded by trees and decorated with the tinajones symbolic of Camagüey, or in the front of the house, with a view of the plaza. The Cuban dishes include *boliche mechado* (roast tenderloin stuffed with bacon and served in a light sauce), a specialty here; all come with *arroz congrí* (rice and black beans). $ *Average main: CUC$13* ✉ *Plaza San Juan de Dios 18* ☎ *3229–6812* ▭ *No credit cards.*

$ CUBAN ✕ **Restaurante Don Ronquilo.** A few steps from the Iglesia de la Soledad, this open-air restaurant has several tables overlooking a courtyard and a dozen more in back, surrounded by potted plants and colored glass. The menu is Cuban, but includes variations on common themes. Try the *bistec mayoral* (steak in a wine sauce on toast) and *pollo grillé al huerto* (half a grilled chicken with vegetables). $ *Average main: CUC$11* ✉ *Av. Ignacio Agramonte 406* ☎ *3228–5239.*

WHERE TO STAY

$$ HOTEL **Gran Hotel.** This stately, five-story lodging in Camagüey's historic center has served guests in style since 1939. **Pros:** the rooftop bar is a great place to grab a drink; the hotel still conjures up its pre-Revolution heyday. **Cons:** the public areas here evoke more history than the small rooms do; front-facing rooms pick up street noise. $ *Rooms from: CUC$81* ✉ *Calle Maceo 67* ☎ *3229–2093* 🌐 *www.islazul.cu* *72 rooms* 🍴 *Breakfast.*

$ HOTEL Fodor's Choice ★ **Hotel Colón.** The lobby of this 1927 hotel is a jewel, with ornate columns, a marble staircase, and a dark wooden bar and front desk. **Pros:** this is one of Cuba's nicest city hotels; the hotel evokes a lot of prerevolutionary history and style. **Cons:** the rooms, although nice, are quite small. $ *Rooms from: CUC$69* ✉ *Calle República 472* ☎ *3228–3368* 🌐 *www.islazul.cu* *48 rooms* 🍴 *Breakfast.*

NIGHTLIFE AND PERFORMING ARTS

NIGHTLIFE

El Cambio. This historic bar, across from the Parque Agramonte's northeast corner, is a convenient stop for a little liquid refreshment. Dating from 1909, this proletarian watering hole has a wild interior paint job, ceramic work by local artists, stone floors, and a simple wooden bar. ⊠ *Calle Martí y Calle Independencia* ☏ *3228–6240.*

PERFORMING ARTS

Casa de la Trova. At the Casa de la Trova on the west side Parque Ignacio Agramonte, local musicians perform Cuban *son* in an 18th-century courtyard every day but Monday from 2 to 5 and 9 to midnight. ⊠ *Calle Cisneros 171* ☏ *3229–1357* ▨ *CUC$1* ☉ *Closed Mon.*

Teatro Principal. The impressive Teatro Principal two blocks northwest of the Plaza de los Trabajadores hosts monthly performances by the city's renowned Ballet de Camagüey—consider yourself blessed and grab tickets if you're lucky enough to be in town when they're here— and regular concerts by the city's fine symphony orchestra. ⊠ *Calle Padre Valencia 64* ☏ *3229–3048.*

SHOPPING

Galería ACAA. The large store run by the artists' association ACAA, on the northern end of the Plaza de los Trabajadores, has an extensive selection of ceramics and other handicrafts. ⊠ *Calle Padre Valencia 2* ☏ *3228–8923.*

Fondo de Bienes Culturales. The Fondo de Bienes Culturales sells ceramics, straw work, and other handicrafts. ⊠ *Av. de la Libertad y Calle Vega* ☏ *3229–2877.*

Galéria Colonial. The gallery here in front of the Iglesia de la Soledad is really two shops in one: one sells T-shirts and other souvenirs, and the other sells cigars, rum, and coffee. ⊠ *Av. Ignacio Agramonte 406* ☏ *3228–5454.*

SPORTS AND THE OUTDOORS

HIKING

Rumbos. This tour operator arranges hikes into the forests and caves (including the Cueva del Indio, with its pre-Columbian drawings) of the Sierra de Cubitas, a protected area 45 km (27 miles) northwest of Camagüey. ⊠ *Calle Lopez Recio 108* ☏ *3229–7229.*

PLAYA SANTA LUCÍA

128 km (77 miles) northeast of Camagüey.

Originally a simple fishing and salt-collecting village east of the Bahía de Nuevitas, Santa Lucía has been attracting tourists—mostly Germans and Italians—for decades, and all you need is a glimpse of the beach to understand why. Its 20-km (12-mile) swath of white sand, shaded by coconut palms and lapped by blue-green waters, is as impressive as any beach on the island. About a mile offshore is a barrier reef that beckons both divers and snorkelers, and in the Bahía de Nuevitas are the ruins of a Spanish fort and other reminders of the days when pirates threatened the region. The tourist area consists of five hotels and other facilities scattered along a 2-km (1-mile) stretch of beach just west of town.

GETTING HERE AND AROUND

Your own vehicle is the best way to get here. Plan on a 90-minute drive east of Camagüey. Resorts here provide transportation from the airport in Camagüey.

EXPLORING

Cayo Sabinal. Just west of the Bahía de Nuevitas, the island has deserted beaches, a working lighthouse, and the ruins of a Spanish fortress. A bumpy road and short causeway take you here; hiring a taxi is best, even if you have your own rental vehicle. ⊠ *Cayo Sabinal.*

BEACHES

Playa los Cocos. If you desire a wider—and perhaps even whiter—beach than Playa Santa Lucía, you can drive or take a taxi 4 km (2 mile) west to Playa los Cocos, next to the fishing village of La Boca. This idyllic swath of sun-bleached silica slopes into aquamarine waters at the mouth of the Bahía de Nuevitas, and is shaded by abundant *cocos* (coconut palms), hence its name. The lagoon behind La Boca is a feeding area for flamingos, which you may be able to spot on your way there. **Amenities:** none. **Best for:** solitude; sunrise. ⊠ *Playa los Cocos.*

Fodor's Choice ★ **Playa Santa Lucía.** One of Cuba's postcard-perfect beaches (think palm trees, white sand, and perfect blue water) strings along 20 km (12 miles) of coast. The Brisas Santa Lucía and Club Santa Lucía hotels hold court here. The liveliest activity concentrates in a stretch of sand in front of those hotels, one-tenth the beach's total length. Outside the standard tourist area, seclusion is yours. If you plan to swim, stick to populated areas. **Amenities:** food and drink; parking; toilets; water sports. **Best for:** solitude; snorkeling; sunrise; swimming. ⊠ *Playa Santa Lucía ✛ West of Playa Santa Lucía town.*

WHERE TO EAT

$$
SEAFOOD ✕ **Restaurante La Alfonsina.** At the end of a long dock, this simple restaurant under a thatched roof has the best views in town, not to mention the best ventilation. Though it belongs to the Club Santa Lucía hotel, it's open to guests from other hotels, and it is one of the few places in Cuba that has live lobster. The menu includes an array of seafood dishes, but the langosta, which is prepared a number of ways, is your best bet. $ *Average main: CUC$16* ⊠ *Club Santa Lucía, Playa Santa Lucía* ☎ *3236–5284* ⌾ *Reservations essential.*

WHERE TO STAY

$$
RESORT 🏨 **Brisas Santa Lucía.** The architecture here is a mix of Cuban and Spanish, with arches, marble floors, barrel-tile and thatched roofs, and murals by Camagüey artists. **Pros:** hotel is on a great beachfront; the place is well decorated with interesting local art. **Cons:** a few rooms need refurbishing, but that project is ongoing; buffet meals are filling but ho-hum. $ *Rooms from: CUC$139* ⊠ *Playa Santa Lucía* ☎ *3233–6317* ⊕ *www.hotelescubanacan.com* ⇆ *412 rooms* ⍥ *All-inclusive.*

$$
RESORT 🏨 **Club Santa Lucía.** Although this resort lines a wide swath of sugary sand shaded by palms and thatched parasols, few of its rooms have ocean views. **Pros:** dance club is popular among both guests and locals; rates are a bargain for what is offered. **Cons:** few rooms have ocean views; surcharges for some restaurants and the disco; a few rooms get

noise from the road. $ Rooms from: CUC$128 ⊠ Playa Santa Lucía ☎ 3236–5284 ⊕ www.hotelescubanacan.com ⇌ 232 rooms, 20 suites ⵏ◎ⵏ All-inclusive.

NIGHTLIFE AND PERFORMING ARTS

PERFORMING ARTS

Centro Cultural Mar Verde. The cultural center here has high-season court-yard concerts by musicians from Camagüey. It functions as a dance club other nights. ⊠ Playa Santa Lucía ⊹ By entrance to Villa Caracol, on main road west of Club Santa Lucía ☎ 3233–6205.

NIGHTLIFE

La Jungla. The discotheque at the Club Santa Lucía is the town's most popular dance club. ⊠ Club Santa Lucía ☎ 3236–5284.

SHOPPING

AREAS AND MALLS

Centro Comercial Santa Lucía. The small shopping center on the beach next to the Club Santa Lucía has a number of tiny shops that sell souvenirs, tobacco, rum, coffee, and film, as well as other sundry items. ⊠ Playa Santa Lucía ☎ 3233–6204.

Centro Cultural Mar Verde. Santa Lucía's cultural center has two excellent shops: one sells a good selection of Cuban music, books, and musical instruments; the other sells paintings, sculptures, and ceramics by Camagüey artists. ⊠ Playa Santa Lucía ☎ 3233–6205.

SPORTS AND THE OUTDOORS

FISHING

The ocean off Playa Santa Lucía has good fishing, with everything from sailfish to snapper.

Marlin Marina. The marina offers both trolling and bottom-fishing charters. Basic gear is provided; charters cost around CUC$200 a day, depending on the type of boat. ⊠ Playa Santa Lucía ☎ 3236–5294.

SCUBA DIVING

With a barrier reef 2 km (1 mile) offshore, many shipwrecks nearby, and average visibility of about 25 meters (66 feet), Playa Santa Lucía is a world-class dive destination.

Sharks' Friends Dive Center. Just west of the hotels, the dive center runs trips to 35 different spots, including 24 shipwrecks, the oldest of which dates from the 1800s. It also offers a day trip to Cayo Caguamas, in the Jardines de la Reina. One-tank boat dives cost CUC$50, equipment rental included. Basic certification courses run about CUC$200. ⊠ Playa Santa Lucía ☎ 3236–5182.

EASTERN CUBA

Updated by
Jeffrey Van
Fleet

The region known as El Oriente has a variety of sublimely beautiful settings—from palm-lined beaches to the city of Santiago—the metaphorical seat of the Cuban soul—to the majestic Sierra Maestra. The sagas that unfolded here lent great drama to the island's history, and Cubans speak of the area with awe.

Eastern Cuba brims with tales of rebellion and revolution. The stories go back all the way to the 16th century, when Hatuey, a Taíno leader, rose up against the Spaniards and was captured and burned at the stake near Baracoa in 1523. On October 10, 1868, Carlos Manuel de Céspedes freed the slaves on his plantation near Bayamo and proclaimed Cuba's independence from Spain, launching the Ten Years' War. And what can you say about the resolve of citizens of Bayamo, who, a year later, burned their lovely city to the ground rather than let it fall into Spanish hands? In 1895, patriot and poet José Martí landed on the south coast of the Bahía de Guantánamo; he was killed shortly thereafter in a battle against the Spanish at Dos Ríos in Granma Province. The region is the birthplace of Fidel Castro (who was born in Holguín Province) and his Revolution. (Castro's arch-nemesis, Fulgencio Batista, was born nearby, so the pendulum has swung both ways in this region.) Granma Province itself takes its name from the boat that carried Castro and 81 revolutionaries back to Cuba from exile in Mexico in 1956. Although their landing—at Playa las Coloradas in the province's southwestern corner—was disastrous, the survivors fled to the Sierra Maestra, the eastern mountain range, and continued their fight.

In this region you'll find Cuba's second largest city, Santiago de Cuba, whose proud citizens are second to none and which has always been as open to French, African, and Caribbean Creole influences as it has to those of far-off Havana. It explodes during the July carnival, a week-long festival of music, dancing, and merrymaking. One of the country's great pleasures may be enjoying a *mojito* (light rum, sugar, mint, and soda) on the balcony of Santiago's Hotel Casa Granda. From here, you can watch the goings-on in the Parque Céspedes, the city's historic heart and the hub for *Santiagueros* (as locals are called). The city also sizzles at night, when musicians share a microphone at the Casa de la Trova.

Resorts rise in many a cove on Holguín's northern coast, especially around Guardalavaca. The white-sand beaches here, and their dark-sand counterparts on Granma's southern coast, draw Canadians and Europeans seeking isolated vacations. Along both shores, water-sports outfitters stand ready to help sailors, fishermen, scuba divers, and snorkelers.

From the Caribbean Sea 32 km (20 miles) north to the Atlantic, a legendary highway known as La Farola cuts a sinuous path through jungle. At its northern end, El Yunque, an anvil-shape mountain, rises into the clouds. Beyond, in the far reaches of Guantánamo Province,

TOP REASONS TO GO

Arts and Culture. Santiago, arguably Cuba's cultural capital, is the birthplace of *son,* a forerunner of salsa. You can catch live-music performances at hotels, theaters, clubs, and the Casa de la Trova. The city's musical energy is highlighted in the late-July carnival celebration.

Scuba Diving and Snorkeling. The diving and snorkeling are best on the northern coast, near Guardalavaca. The waters here are perfect for snorkeling, and you'll find an abundance of coral formations and colorful fish just off the shore.

The Revolutionary Trail. Visitors to Cuba increasingly follow the path of Fidel Castro and his Revolution. This takes you from Santiago, where it all

began, to the Sierra Maestra, which was the base for Castro's rebel army.

Stunning Landscapes. Granma province is the home to some of the most varied landscapes, from the forbidding peaks of the Sierra Maestra to the dry south coast. There are nature reserves of the Playa las Coloradas and the Bayamo-Manzanillo roadway, where the jungle and sea coast meet.

Hidden Spaces. Eastern Cuba has historically been the most remote part of the island. It is the home of Baracoa, Cuba's first Spanish settlement, which was founded in 1512 by Diego Velázquez. Eastern Cuba is also home to the now infamous, off-limits American military base at Guantánamo Bay.

are more coastal enclaves, including quirky Baracoa, site of the first Spanish settlement. Throughout the region, hiking trails lead through history to colorful hamlets and old rebel outposts that appear lost in verdant jungle or rugged mountains.

El Oriente remains Cuba's least-visited, least-known, least-developed region. You're a long way from Havana, and traveling here requires a bit more planning than it does elsewhere in the country. Take a hint from Christopher Columbus, who became Cuba's first tourist when he landed near Baracoa in 1492 during his first visit to the New World. He wrote of the southeast coast: it is "the most beautiful land human eyes have ever seen." Make the effort to get here, and you just might agree.

ORIENTATION AND PLANNING

GETTING ORIENTED

The spirit of Eastern Cuba, the birthplace of rum and revolution, is intoxicating. The region includes the provinces of Granma, Holguín, Santiago, and Guantánamo. Together with Las Tunas, they once composed the single province of Oriente, the moniker still used for the whole area today.

The provincial capital of Holguín is a good regional hub—one that's quite close to the beautiful beaches of Guardalavaca. South of it lies Bayamo, the capital of Granma Province and the gateway to the Sierra

Maestra. Directly west is the colorful port town of Manzanillo, with a wide *malecón* (bay-side boulevard) and a beautiful historic center. About 40 minutes east of here is Marea del Portillo, after which the road hugs the southern coast while snaking along in the shadow of the Sierra Maestra to Santiago de Cuba.

Santiago is the gateway to Guantánamo Province. Although famous for its U.S. military base, the province's most outstanding attraction is the colonial town of Baracoa, near Cuba's easternmost point. The town is a 260-km (161-mile) drive from Santiago along the awesome La Farola highway, which brought Baracoa in contact with the rest of Cuba when it was constructed during the 1970s. Pine-covered highlands, jungle-covered foothills, miles of beaches, and surging rivers fill the area around Baracoa. El Yunque looms over the city. The mountain was a sacred place for the indigenous Taíno, and their imprint is still strongly felt in Baracoa. Locals still boast of their Taíno blood, evident in their features.

Holguín and Granma Provinces. An area historically known for its acres of sugar and banana plantations, the area lining Guardalavaca is now an enclave of beaches and resorts. Granma is the province most associated with Fidel Castro's Revolution in the last century, but also of Cuba's original struggle for independence.

Santiago de Cuba and Guantánamo Provinces. Sparsely populated, the province of Santiago de Cuba is home to the Sierra Maestra and Cuba's first capital, the simply amazing city of the same name, Santiago de Cuba. Guantánamo province is best known for the U.S. naval base. (Banish any thoughts of visiting the military installations; they're impossible to access from Cuban soil.) The nearby city of Baracoa is the province's real gem, as attractive as it is isolated.

PLANNING

WHEN TO GO

Although peak season is technically December through April, July is a hectic month owing to Santiago's carnival and the Festival del Caribe. Make reservations well in advance during these peak times. The spring and fall off-seasons see prices drop by as much as 25% in places, though hotels may offer fewer amenities (some may even close entirely). Discounts during these times may not be as great in Guardalavaca—one of the driest spots in the off-season—and Santiago, which tends to draw visitors year-round.

PLANNING YOUR TIME

Few visitors to Havana make it this far east, and that's a shame. Most who get to the Oriente find they have a new favorite region of Cuba. A domestic flight or two can shave off long hours on the road from points west. If you can finagle it, a week makes an ideal length of time to explore the region. You'll likely have fewer days; do some picking and choosing. Two days gives you a slightly rushed opportunity to take in the sights of Santiago de Cuba's historic center and a couple of area attractions. (Three days would be less rushed.) Historic Baracoa is one of Cuba's most charming towns, but it's set off on its own, not near much else, a good four to five hours from Santiago. Bayamo and Manzanillo warrant a day each; either makes a good launching point for the wild and woolly Parque Nacional Turquino. If you stay in Guardalavaca, you likely arrived on an all-inclusive package, meaning a certain amount of confinement to your beach resort. Most do offer a good selection of area tours, so take advantage.

GETTING HERE AND AROUND
AIR TRAVEL
Holguín and Santiago have international airports, and there are smaller airports in Bayamo, Guantánamo, and Baracoa. Cubana Air has several daily flights between Havana and Santiago, a daily flight between Havana and Holguín and Santiago, and weekly flights from Santiago to Baracoa.

Holguín's Aeropuerto Internacional Frank País is just south of the city. A taxi into town costs CUC$10, and transfers are available to both Holguín and Guardalavaca. The airport also sees a good deal of international charter-flight service for passengers headed for the Guardalavaca resorts.

Santiago's Aeropuerto Internacional Antonio Maceo is 8 km (5 miles) south of the city center; a taxi ride into town will cost about $10. Havanatur operates an airport shuttle service, but you must make arrangements in advance; the costs are CUC$15 round-trip, CUC$10 one-way.

BUS TRAVEL
In general city buses aren't recommended. They're crowded, poorly maintained, and slow—all this and tickets are still in great demand. Tourist buses, however, can take you on tours of all lengths. Most can be booked through your hotel or at local offices of Havanatur and other state travel agencies. Víazul has modern, air-conditioned buses that run from Santiago to Havana; trips cost CUC$40 per person each way. You can make arrangements through Rumbos and other tour operators. Payment is accepted in cash and with major credit cards.

Bus Information Rumbos. ⊠ *Parque Céspedes, Santiago* ☎ *2262–5969.*

CAR TRAVEL
The main routes into and out of Eastern Cuba are well maintained, and once you're out of the cities, traffic is light (your biggest concern will be the occasional stray sheep or cow). Renting a car is the best way to cover vast distances, but you're better off hiring a car and driver for short journeys. Note that signage is poor, and it's easy to get mixed up when passing through a city. Ask directions: Cubans will gladly help you out of a mess.

The Autopista Nacional runs from Havana to Santiago (860 km [534 miles]), mostly two lanes through this part of Cuba, but expanding to four between Guántanamo and Santiago de Cuba. You're much more likely to take the northern highway to Bayamo (127 km [79 miles]) and then onward to Holguín (140 km [87 miles]), the gateway to the north coast region. The stunning 200-km (124-mile) road that runs west from Santiago along the coast is squeezed between the Sierra Maestra and the

Caribbean Sea. Equally impressive is the road east to Baracoa (250 km [155 miles]), which runs along the arid coastline before turning north and becoming La Farola highway, which winds through mountains.

State-run Servi-Cupet gas stations line major routes. Many are open 24 hours and sell food and beverages; only convertible pesos are accepted. Stations are also abundant in cities.

TAXI TRAVEL

Modern, well-maintained tourist taxis, which charge convertible pesos, congregate in front of hotels, transportation hubs, and major sights. Private cabs with yellow plates are much cheaper, and you can hire them for a day of driving around town for about CUC$25. The famous *bici-taxis,* or bicycle taxis, are a relaxing way to see the sights. Regardless of which type of taxi you choose, settle on a price before you board.

TRAIN TRAVEL

Rail service in Cuba has seen major cutbacks in recent years. An over-night *especial* train runs between Havana and Santiago (once daily in both directions), with stops at Camagüey, Ciego de Ávila, and Santa Clara in Central Cuba. Santiago is the only stop the train makes in Eastern Cuba. Santiago's modern train station, the Estación de Fer-rocarriles, is on the harbor, six blocks west of Parque Céspedes. The trip from Havana takes about 15 hours and costs CUC$60; payment is accepted only in cash. It's best to buy your ticket as far as possible in advance. The older European-style coaches have air-conditioning and reclining seats. Although a food cart trundles by twice on the trip, you'll definitely need to bring food and bottled water.

RESTAURANTS

Eastern Cuba is the most laid-back part of Cuba, but it's also the least accessible to tourists. If you do get here, though, you will find small family-run restaurants and paladares, usually around the center of town, though they are harder to come by than in the more popular destinations. It's good to plan ahead and check with your hotel concierge when reserving at paladares, although most people eat at their hotel restaurants.

HOTELS

Santiago de Cuba has a few extraordinary lodgings, from the historic, well-situated Hotel Casa Granda to the postmodern Hotel Meliá Santiago de Cuba. Hidden in the decaying elegance of Vista Alegre are some fine *casas particulares,* as well as more conventional lodgings. Other cities in the region have only one or two acceptable hotels each.

Top-notch resorts line this sector of the coast. Most of them charge flat, all-inclusive rates. The prices are economical, and the quality of the service and the food is better than average. To the north, Guardalavaca is becoming a haven for Europeans and Canadians. It has a handful of mostly all-inclusive resorts and a few free-standing restaurants and discos. This area offers the perfect beach vacation, *and* it's a convenient place from which to explore Santiago and Baracoa.

Hotel reviews have been shortened. For full information, visit Fodors.com.

WHAT IT COSTS IN CUBAN CONVERTIBLE PESOS			
$	**$$**	**$$$**	**$$$$**
Restaurants under CUC$12	CUC$12–CUC$20	CUC$21–CUC$30	over CUC$30
Hotels under CUC$75	CUC$75–CUC$150	CUC$151–CUC$200	over CUC$200

Prices in the dining reviews are the average cost of a main course at dinner, or, if dinner is not served, at lunch. Prices in the hotel reviews are the lowest cost of a standard double room in high season.

TOURS

Major hotels throughout the region have tour desks where you can book everything from flights to rental cars to tours. Santiago operators serve all the town's sights as well as such surrounding areas as El Cobre. You can also arrange tours to Baracoa, Marea del Portillo, and Guardalavaca. Companies include Havanatur, Rumbos, and Gaviota.

VISITOR INFORMATION

The tour desks at major hotels throughout the region can provide you with travel information and assistance. Major state-run agencies include Rumbos and Cubanacán. Both of these arrange rental cars and other modes of transportation, tours, hotel stays, and, literally, any tourist service provided on the island.

HOLGUÍN AND GRANMA PROVINCES

These two provinces northeast of Santiago de Cuba are Cuba's center of production for sugar, bananas, rice, and cattle. The eponymous provincial capital of Holguín Province affords a look at a typical Cuban city. But the province is best known for Guardalavaca, a north coast town on a white-sand beach. Although small, it has top-notch resorts, water-sports outfitters, and tour operators; nearby, you'll find several other beaches and attractions.

Granma Province has the most varied landscapes—from the forbidding peaks of the Sierra Maestra to the dry south coast—and was also the sight of events that were important not only to the Revolution but also to Cuba's earlier struggles for independence. Both its capital, Bayamo, and the port town of Manzanillo are interesting stops filled with historic structures. The province is also a gateway to the Sierra Maestra via the Bayamo–Manzanillo roadway. These mountains crash down along the south coast and rise from a jungle interior. The road winds along an awesome turquoise shore in the shadow of steep, muscular rock.

HOLGUÍN

734 km (456 miles) southeast of Havana; 134 km (83 miles) northwest of Santiago de Cuba.

If you've made it as far as Holguín (pronounced *ohl-GHEEN*), Cuba's fourth-largest city, you're probably headed for the beach resorts at Guardalavaca 50 km (31 miles) north. Most foreign visitors take in the

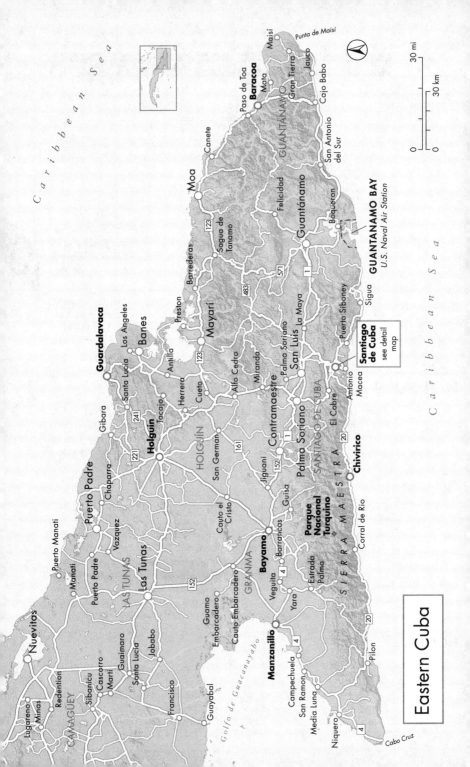

Caribbean Sea

Caribbean Sea

Punta de Maisí

Maisí

Baracoa

Mata

Paso de Toa

Gran Tierra

Jauco

Cajo Babo

GUANTÁNAMO

Cañete

San Antonio
del Sur

Moa

Sagua de
Tanamo

123

Felicidad

Guantánamo

Barrederas

Mayari

483

GUANTÁNAMO BAY
U.S. Naval Air Station

Boqueron

Los Angeles

Preston

57

1

Guardalavaca

Banes

Antilla

Alfo Cedro

Puerto Siboney

Sigua

Santa Lucia

123

Palma Soriano

San Luis

La Maya

Puerto Siboney

Gibara

Herrera

Cueto

Miranda

Santiago
de Cuba
see detail
map

241

Tacajo

San German

161

Contramaestre

1

SANTIAGO DE CUBA

Antonio

Macea

Holguín

221

HOLGUÍN

Palma Soriano

El Cobre

20

Chaparra

Couto el
Cristo

Jiguani

152

Guisa

Chivirico

Puerto Padre

San Ramon

Vazquez

Bayamo

Barrancas

Parque
Nacional
Turquino

Corral de Rio

Puerto Manati

Manati

Puerto Padre

Las Tunas

Guamo
Embarcadero

4

Estrada
Palma

SIERRA MAESTRA

LAS TUNAS

152

Couto Embarcadero

Veguita

Yara

20

Redention

Minas

Guaimaro

Jobabo

Guayabal

Manzanillo

4

Nuevitas

Lugareno

Sibanicu

Santa Lucia

GRANMA

Campechuela

Pilon

Cascorro

Marti

Francisco

San Ramon

Media Luna

CAMAGÜEY

Golfo de Guacanayabo

Niquero

4

Cabo Cruz

Eastern Cuba

30 mi

30 km

Una Cerveza, Por Favor *

(* A beer, please!)

Cuba may mean rum, but Holguín proudly produces the island's beer, with all four nationwide brands brewed at the city's Cervecería Bucanero. Regular travelers to Cuba passionately debate which of the four is best. Sample them—remember that Cubans serve beer very cold—and join the discussion.

Cristal is your standard pale lager and is Cuba's top-selling beer. The brewery's two namesake beers taste stronger and have a higher alcohol content: **Bucanero Fuerte** and the darker premium **Bucanero Max** weigh in respectively at 5.4% and 6.5%. The latter, especially, often generates "Wow! That really packs a punch!" comments. Visitors liken the mass-market **Mayabe** to an American-style light beer. It is always priced more cheaply than Cristal or the two Bucaneros.

As with all products here, ease of access to beer depends on which currency you use. Since you, dear visitor, must navigate in convertible pesos, you'll less notice the beer shortage that has plagued Cuba since early 2014. Cynics suggest that the brewery diverts product to more profitable hard-currency tourist establishments, leaving regular-peso stores, bars, and eateries in short supply. You *will* have trouble finding beer in aluminum cans. Returnable glass bottles are the norm here. Consider that a blessing; beer in glass tastes fresher than it does out of a can.

city as a day tour from those resorts—Holguín does contain a handful of interesting sights. You'll encounter a couple of acceptable lodging options here if you need to spend the night.

GETTING HERE AND AROUND

The Carretera Nacional loops around Holguín when coming from the west, making the city easily accessible from all points in Cuba. Víazul offers easy bus service to Holguín along its Havana–Santiago de Cuba or Trinidad–Santiago de Cuba routes. Cubana Air has flights to Holguín's Aeropuerto Frank País from Havana and Santiago, and many international charters arrive here as well.

EXPLORING

TOP ATTRACTIONS

Fodor's Choice ★ **Loma de la Cruz.** If you're up to the ascent, exactly 456 steps lead up to the Loma de la Cruz, a hill named for the large white cross that has graced it since 1790. ■TIP➡ **Pace yourself—you'll find landings every 50 steps or so—and bring water. The climb up can get hot.** From here you have a lovely view of Holguín and the surrounding limestone hills. There are also artisan shops and a snack bar. ⊠ *Holguín* ✢ *Staircase begins on Calle Maceo, 10 blocks north of Plaza San José.*

WORTH NOTING

Casa Natal Calixto García. The Casa Natal Calixto García contains some of the belongings of General Calixto García, a local patriot. It's worth a visit if you're an aficionado of Cuban history, and you can learn more about the Ten Years' War here. ⊠ *147 Calle Miro, just off Plaza Calixto García* ⊠ *CUC$1* ⊙ *Tues.–Sun. 9–4.*

Museo de la Historia Natural Carlos de la Torre. This museum, a Moorish-style structure with beautiful ceramic tile work, contains a decent natural-history collection with preserved specimens of 11 Cuban ecosystems. Be sure to check out the *Polymita* snail-shell collection from Baracoa. ⊠ *Calle Maceo 129, ½ block south of Plaza Calixto García* ☎ *2442–3935* ⊠ *CUC$1* ⊙ *Tues.–Sat. 9–noon and 1–5, Sun. 9–noon.*

Museo Historia Provincial. The museum, in the former Casino Español at the plaza's northern end, contains an exhibit of pre-Columbian artifacts as well as displays on the Revolution and the province's role in it. Locally, the redbrick building is known as La Periquera ("the Parrot Cage"), because brightly dressed Spanish officers peered through its barred windows while the city was under siege by General García's troops in 1868. ⊠ *Calle Frexes 198* ☎ *2446–3395* ⊠ *CUC$1* ⊙ *Tues.–Sat. 9–4:30, Sun. 9–noon.*

Plaza Calixto García. Holguín's small historic district hugs this square, which is graced by large trees and a marble bust of Calixto García, a local general in the Ten Years' War (1868–78) for independence from Spain. It's lined with colonial buildings containing residences, small shops, the requisite Casa de la Trova (with frequent music performances), the Teatro Comandante Eddy Sunoi, and the Centro de Arte Salón Moncada, with its occasional painting and photography exhibits. ⊠ *Holguín* ✛ *Bounded by Calles Maceo, Marti, Libertad, and Fuentes.*

Plaza de la Revolución. The square has a marble bust of local hero General Calixto García and his marble mausoleum. This broad socialist expanse is used for political rallies and other events. Look for the white colonial building containing the provincial Communist Party headquarters. ⊠ *Holguín* ✛ *3 km (2 miles) northeast of central Holguín.*

WHERE TO STAY

$
HOTEL

🏨 **Hotel Pernik.** Partially paid for by the Bulgarian government (it's named for a town in Bulgaria), this Soviet-inspired hotel has more than 200 rooms and plenty of amenities, and, quite frankly, looks better from the inside than outside. **Pros:** the pool has lively activities; rates are a bargain. **Cons:** typical Soviet-era architecture; not much action going on here. [$] *Rooms from: CUC$52* ⊠ *Av. Dimitrov y Av. XX Aniversario* ☎ *2448–1011* ⊕ *www.islazul.cu* ⤴ *202 rooms* ⦿️ *Breakfast.*

$
B&B/INN

🏨 **Villa Mirador de Mayabe.** At this countryside inn on the outskirts of the city, you can stay in one of the hillside cabins or in the gracious Casa del Pancho, whose rooms have balconies. **Pros:** country location is quiet and refreshing; rates are a bargain for what is offered. **Cons:** in the rainy season, mosquitoes are a problem here, so bring bug repellent; you're a bit removed from the action, such as it is in Holguín. [$] *Rooms from: CUC$52* ⊠ *Loma del Mayabe, La Cuaba* ✛ *10 km (6 miles) southeast of Holguín* ☎ *2442–2160* ⊕ *www.islazul.cu* ⤴ *4 rooms, 20 cabins* ⦿️ *Breakfast.*

CLOSE UP

Honey, Guard the Cow!

Guardalavaca's unusual name translates as a call to "guard the cow." A variety of theories exists about its origins. Pirates plagued this sector of the coast during colonial times, pillaging and looting anything they could. That much is known. Were they after local cattle herds, too? Perhaps, goes one hypothesis. Other historians suggest the name was a mishearing of " *¡Guarda la barca!* " (guard the boat). That warning might be more likely in the face of a pirate onslaught, and Spanish speakers do pronounce *B* and *V* remarkably similarly. Another

modern theory has nothing to do with piracy at all. It posits that the name relates to the region's large population of cattle egrets (*Bubulcus ibis*), the birds, who, in their own peculiar way, "guard" cattle by removing ticks from them. Whatever the origins, the Cuban government is on record as disliking the town's "undignified" name and has tried to change it a few times through the years. Townspeople will have nothing of it. The whimsical moniker sticks, and we hope it always does.

5

GUARDALAVACA

72 km (43 miles) northeast of Holguín.

The northern coast of Holguín Province has some of Eastern Cuba's finest beaches, with Guardalavaca the most famous of these. Its biggest draws are its opportunities for sunning, swimming, sailing, and scuba diving. You'll find a handful of hotels, restaurants, and discos along a single road, behind which is a beautiful white-sand beach. You can make arrangements to participate in water sports, go horseback riding, or visit the Bahía de Naranjo aquarium through your hotel. Tour operators with desks at the various resorts can also set you up for area tours if you want something else to do in addition to lazing on the beach. ■ TIP→ **Most tour operators identify the Guardalavaca resorts in their brochures under the heading of nearby Holguín.**

GETTING HERE AND AROUND

If you're on a tour package, your resort will provide transport from Holguín's airport. If you're on your own, the drive northeast from Holguín is an easy one and takes about an hour. A few local buses ply the route, too.

EXPLORING

Banes. Guardalavaca is part of the county of Banes (pronounced *BAH-nays*). Castro married his first wife at the Iglesia de Nuestra Señora de la Caridad on the town's Plaza Martí. Fulgencio Batista, the dictator Castro eventually toppled, was born here in 1901. But Banes is best known for its archaeological treasures, many of which are exhibited in its Museo Indocubano. ⊠ *Guardalavaca ✛ 30 km (18 miles) southeast of Guardalavaca.*

Museo Indocubano. The museum has one of Cuba's largest collections of such indigenous artifacts (20,000 of them) as pottery, jewelry, and tools. There are also murals depicting indigenous life. ⊠ *Calle General*

Maceo 305, esq. de Av. José Martí ☎ *2448–2487* 📧 *CUC$2* 🕐 *Tues.–Sat. 9–5, Sun. 8–noon.*

BEACHES

Playa Esmeralda. West of Playa Guardalavaca, heading back toward Holguín along the main road, is Playa Esmeralda, a beach that the Spanish chain Meliá has claimed as its own with two all-inclusive hotels: the Paradisus Río de Oro Resort & Spa and the Sol Río de Luna y Mares. (All beaches in Cuba are public, of course, so no one can technically do that.) **Amenities:** food and drink; water sports. **Best for:** sunrise; swimming; walking. ✉ *Guardalavaca* ✛ *5 km (3 miles) west of Guardalavaca.*

Playa Pesquero. West of Playa Esmeralda, along the Carretera Holguín–Guardalavaca (Holguín–Guardalavaca Highway) and enough to be outside the Guardalavaca orbit, is Playa Pesquero. This cove, whose shallow, clear waters and white sands are surrounded by greenery, is often referred to as the Costa Verde (Green Coast). If you stay in one of the resorts here, such as the Hotel Brisas Guardalavaca, consider renting a car for a day trip into the interior. **Amenities:** food and drink; parking; water sports. **Best for:** snorkeling; sunrise; swimming; walking. ✉ *Guardalavaca* ✛ *13 km (8 miles) west of Guardalavaca.*

WHERE TO EAT

The all-inclusive resorts here can take care of all your dining needs, so there's not much of a restaurant scene here. Your resort will likely contain a buffet restaurant, whose offerings are included in your rate, and à la carte options, whose bills are extra.

$ ✕ **Pizza Nova.** This Canadian chain restaurant serves quality pasta
ITALIAN   dishes, salads, and pizza in a low-key, outdoor setting. Look for the yellow sign. 💲 *Average main: CUC$10* ✉ *Guardalavaca* ✛ *Next to Centro Comercial* ☎ *2443–0137.*

WHERE TO STAY

$$ 🏨 **Blau Costa Verde Beach Resort.** If you seek a fun-loving, contemporary
RESORT   beach vacation, don't pass up this resort operated by the Canadian Blau chain. **Pros:** the hotel is on a great beach; lots of activity here. **Cons:** the rooms are tired and could do with a renovation; not all rooms have sea views. 💲 *Rooms from: CUC$128* ✉ *Off Carretera Holguín–Guardalavaca* ☎ *2443–3510* ⊕ *www.blau-hotels-cuba.com* ⇆ *464 rooms, 16 suites* 🍴 *All-inclusive.*

$$ 🏨 **Hotel Brisas Guardalavaca.** Easy access to a white-sand beach, wide-
RESORT   open public spaces, and elegant swimming pools make this resort a solid choice for a relaxing vacation. **Pros:** the villa-type accommodations have modern amenities; nonguests can use the facilities (for a fee). **Cons:** not all rooms have been renovated, so try to snag one of the finished ones; during high season, can feel overrun with day guests. 💲 *Rooms from: CUC$87* ✉ *Playa Pesquero* ☎ *2443–0218* ⊕ *www.hotelescubanacan.com* ⇆ *437 rooms* 🍴 *All-inclusive.*

$$$$ 🏨 **Paradisus Río de Oro Resort & Spa.** Located on the Bahía de Naranjo
RESORT   inlet 3 km (2 miles) west of Guardalavaca, this adults-only resort ben-
Fodor'sChoice   efits from the luxurious sands of Playa Esmeralda. **Pros:** this hotel is
★   among the best in Cuba; excellent spa services are a rarity in Cuba.

Cons: travelers have reported it being hard to find lounge chairs here, so beware of lounge-chair hogs; no-kids policy means this is not a place for families. ⑤ *Rooms from: CUC$239* ✉ *Carretera Holguín–Guardalavaca* ☎ *2443–0090* ⊕ *www.meliacuba.com* ↩ *354 rooms* ▯⦿l *All-inclusive* ☞ *No kids under 18.*

$$ ⛱ **Sol Río de Luna y Mares.** This family-friendly resort has raised the bar
RESORT for luxury along Guardalavaca's coast; Playa Esmeralda is just out your
FAMILY front door, and you have access to two small private beaches on protected coves. **Pros:** lots of family activities to keep everyone busy; this is a particularly scenic sector of the coast. **Cons:** not a place to come if you crave peace and quiet. ⑤ *Rooms from: CUC$142* ✉ *Playa Esmeralda* ☎ *2443–0060* ⊕ *www.meliacuba.com* ↩ *464 rooms* ▯⦿l *All-inclusive.*

NIGHTLIFE

La Roca Disco. This disco has a dance floor that's open to the breezes and an outdoor terrace with ocean views; after the disco's flashing lights, the twinkling stars are soothing. ✉ *Guardalavaca* ⚓ *At west end of Playa Guardalavaca* ☎ *2443–0167.*

SHOPPING

AREAS AND MALLS

Centro Commercial. Fronting the beach near Guardalavaca's western end, Centro Commercial may be in an nondescript building, but it's your place to stock up on sundries (with payment in convertible pesos only). ✉ *Guardalavaca.*

MARKETS

Flea Market. It has no official name, but Anglophone visitors refer to the complex of stalls next to the Club Amigo Atlántico Guardalavaca hotel as "the flea market." (Try *mercado* if you're asking for directions in Spanish.) Around 20 vendors gather here each day, and you'll find a surprisingly nice selection of souvenirs. ✉ *Guardalavaca* ⚓ *Next to Club Amigo Atlántico Guardalavaca hotel.*

SPORTS AND THE OUTDOORS

BOATING

Marina Bahía de Naranjo. This marina has boat rentals and services for boaters, such as mooring space, electricity, water, and diesel. ✉ *Carretera Guardalavaca–Holguín* ☎ *2443–0132.*

WATER SPORTS

Base Nautica Marlin Guardalavaca. This tour operator offers boat rides, waterskiing, snorkeling, scuba diving, and deep-sea fishing. They also rent catamarans and windsurfers. ✉ *Carretera Guardalavaca–Holguín, Rafael Freyre* ☎ *2443–0185.*

BAYAMO

71 km (44 miles) south of Holguín; 127 km (79 miles) northwest of Santiago.

Bayamo, the capital of Granma Province, descends from one of Spain's first seven villas: the 1513 settlement of Villa de San Salvador de Bayamo, which was near present-day Yara before being moved to its current location. The few photos of the city that remain from the mid-19th century suggest a town that looked remarkably like Central Cuba's colonial gem, Trinidad. Alas, little evidence persists of Bayamo's colonial beginnings. In 1869, the townspeople burned their beloved city to the ground rather than let it fall into Spanish hands during the Ten Years' War in the ultimate in scorched-earth war tactics. What exists today is a pleasant, small city with many structures that date from the early 20th century.

GETTING HERE AND AROUND

Bayamo sits astride the Carretera Nacional and is easily reached from all points east and west. The highway doglegs south from Holguín and then veers east toward Santiago. Víazul buses connect the city with Havana, Trinidad, and Santiago de Cuba.

EXPLORING

TOP ATTRACTIONS

Plaza del Himno. One of Bayamo's most peaceful spots is the Plaza del Himno, northwest of Parque Céspedes. The so-called anthem square is dominated by the **Iglesia de San Salvador.** First built in 1613 and rebuilt several times starting in 1740, the church is famous as the first place "La Bayamesa," Cuba's eventual national anthem, was sung in 1868. Its stone-and-wood interior has been restored, and it's open to visitors late in the afternoon, before the 5 pm mass.

The plaza is also the home of **Casa de la Nacionalidad Cubana,** the town's archives. It's not officially open to the public, but you can ask questions of the staff and maybe have a peek at the antique furniture and interior courtyard. A list of cultural events happening around town is usually posted here.

Southeast of the plaza is the **Iglesia de San Juan Evangelista,** a church that was partially destroyed in the 1869 fire but whose tower remains intact. The Retablo de los Héroes is a monument to Cuban independence fighters, from Céspedes to Celia Sánchez (who, in addition to being a revolutionary, was also Castro's lover and confidante). ✉ *Bayamo.*

WORTH NOTING

Casa Natal de Carlos Manuel de Céspedes. This two-story house on the north side of **Parque Céspedes** is the birthplace of Céspedes himself. It has been a museum since 1968, the centennial anniversary of the signing of the Cuban Declaration of Independence, and is filled with period furniture and the belongings of the Cuban patriot. Also on display is the printing press on which Céspedes published Cuba's first independent newspaper. ✉ *Calle Maceo 57* ☎ *2342–3864* ⌨ *CUC$1* ☉ *Tues.–Sat. 9–5, Sun. 9–2, Sun. 10–2.*

Museo Provincial. This eclectic museum is housed in the birthplace of composer and violinist Manuel Muñoz Cedeño (1813–95). There are exhibits on the region's colonial history and its geography. ✉ *Calle Maceo 55, on north side of Parque Céspedes* ☎ *2442–4125* ⌨ *CUC$1* ☉ *Weekdays 9–5, weekends 10–1, and Sat. 7–9 pm.*

Parque Céspedes. Bayamo's central park is a charming square with large trees and long marble benches. It's still the center of local life, and a good place to drink in the rhythms of a quiet Cuban town. Horse-drawn carriage rides are available from here.

At the square's center is the granite-and-bronze **statue of Carlos Manuel de Céspedes,** the hero of the Ten Years' War. He wrote the famous "Grito de Yara" ("Shout of Yara")—the declaration of independence from Spain—which he read aloud on October 10, 1868, after freeing his slaves. Look also for the **statue of Perucho Figueredo,** who wrote Cuba's national anthem; its words describe the valor of the local townspeople: *Run to the battle, Bayamenses / Let the motherland proudly watch you / Don't fear death / To die for the motherland is to live.* On the east side of the square is the **Ayuntamiento,** the old town hall where Céspedes abolished slavery after founding an independent republic briefly in 1868. ⊠ *Maceo at General García.*

WHERE TO STAY

$ ⊞ **Hotel Royalton.** Bayamo's nicest lodging overlooks Parque Céspedes
HOTEL with a terrace bar and restaurant ($) that are great places for whiling away a warm afternoon. **Pros:** this is lovely old style at bargain rates; the central location can't be beat. **Cons:** rooms facing the park do get some street noise. ⑤ *Rooms from: CUC$62* ⊠ *Antonio Maceo No. 53, e/ José Joaquín Palma y Donato Mármol* ☎ *2342–2290* ⊕ *www.islazul. cu* ⟲ *33 rooms* ⦿ *Breakfast.*

$ ⊞ **Hotel Sierra Maestra.** Although it looks unkempt and institutional from
HOTEL the outside, this hotel is well maintained inside. **Pros:** the attraction of this hotel is its central location, adjacent to Plaza del Himno, and other noteworthy spots; rates are a bargain. **Cons:** the noisy lobby takes away from much of the charm of this budget hotel; restaurant meals are ho-hum at best. ⑤ *Rooms from: CUC$54* ⊠ *Carretera Central, Km 1.5* ☎ *2342–7970* ⊕ *www.islazul.cu* ⟲ *132 rooms* ⦿ *Breakfast.*

$ ⊞ **Villa Bayamo.** This attractive complex gives you some peace and
B&B/INN quiet outside the city on the road to Manzanillo. **Pros:** the landscape surrounding the property is beautiful; great on-site Cuban restaurant. **Cons:** the hotel is outside the city itself; Spartan decor in rooms. ⑤ *Rooms from: CUC$29* ⊠ *Carretera via Manzanillo, Calle Mabay* ☎ *2342–3102* ⊕ *www.islazul.cu* ⟲ *12 rooms, 12 cabins* ⦿ *Breakfast.*

NIGHTLIFE

Cabaret Bayamo. Adjacent to the Hotel Sierra Maestra is the Cabaret Bayamo, where high-stepping, costumed dancers perform at dinner shows several evenings a week. Another cabaret is inside the hotel, but it isn't as highly charged as the Bayamo. ⊠ *Carretera Central* ☎ *2342–1698.*

SHOPPING

CRAFTS

Casa de Fondo de Bienes Culturales. Stop by the Casa de Fondo de Bienes Culturales for beautiful ceramics, paintings, and leatherwork. ⊠ *Plaza de Himno* ☎ *2342–5389.*

PARQUE NACIONAL TURQUINO

Entrance at Santo Domingo, roughly 30 km (19 miles) south of Yara.

The Sierra Maestra was the base of Fidel Castro's rebel army, and a tour through its dramatic terrain makes it clear why the revolutionaries chose it as a place to hide from—and launch clandestine strikes against—Batista's forces. Its massive spine, averaging 1,372 meters (4,500 feet) in height, cuts 130 km (81 miles) across El Oriente, throwing a shadow over the southern coast from southwest Granma Province to Santiago de Cuba. The range is covered by moist, tropical forests with huge ferns and towering bamboo. It's cut by steep ravines, rocky valleys, and rushing rivers, and its peaks are often covered with clouds.

GETTING HERE AND AROUND
The village of Santo Domingo sits at the park's entrance and lies on decent roads southeast of Manzanillo or southwest of Bayamo. A taxi can get you here from either city and the lodgings we list will send someone to meet you at Santo Domingo. Access to the park is strenuous from Santiago de Cuba and best avoided.

EXPLORING
Parque Nacional Turquino. It's a steep 5-km (3-mile) ascent from Santo Domingo village to the Alto del Naranjo—a parking lot with beautiful views—which marks the entrance to the park. If you haven't hired a guide in Santo Domingo, you can do so at the visitor center here.

The **Comandancia de la Plata**, the headquarters of the Revolution, is just 3 km (2 miles) west of the entrance to the park. A relaxing, one-hour walk on a clearly marked trail along a ridge brings you to a remote forest clearing. Here you'll find Castro's command post, hospital, and residence—built with an escape route into an adjacent creek. This is the perfect trek if you have limited time: you can get a taste of the region in the morning and return to the lowlands by early afternoon.

If you're feeling truly intrepid, the summit of **Pico Turquino**, Cuba's highest peak at 1,974 meters (6,476 feet), beckons, some 13 km (8 miles) from the Comandancia de la Plata. A journey here involves a night of camping, typically at a tent camp at the mountain's base. Cooks are sometimes available, but you have to bring your own food. Showers and fog alternate with sun and daytime heat, and humidity alternates with chilly windy nights, so in addition to good hiking boots, you need clothing that you can layer and a lightweight rain jacket. ⊠ *Municipio Bartolomé Masó* 🗺 *CUC$10* ⊗ *Daily 7–4.*

WHERE TO STAY
$

B&B/INN

📺 **Villa Balcón de la Sierra.** This 1950s-style complex in the town of Providencia rents rooms in 10 brightly colored cabins. **Pros:** the cabins offer wonderful views; reasonable rates; bar, restaurant, and pool. **Cons:** the restaurant serves only basic fare; this is a remote area and not a place to go if you need actions. ⑤ *Rooms from: CUC$55* ⊠ *Municipio Bartolomé Masó* 🕾 *2359–5180* ⊕ *www.islazul.cu* 🛏 *21 rooms* 🍽 *Breakfast.*

$

B&B/INN

📺 **Villa Santo Domingo.** Its rooms may be on the musty side with furnishings that have seen better days, but this is *the* starting point for trips into the Sierra Maestra. **Pros:** location is everything, and this hotel is literally in the heart of the Sierra Maestra; location offers a nice break from sweltering lowlands. **Cons:** decor is dated; restaurant fare here is filling but selection is limited. ⑤ *Rooms from: CUC$49* ⊠ *Municipio*

Bartolomé Masó, Santo Domingo ☎ *2356–5568* ⊕ *www.islazul.cu* 🥢 *20 cabins* 🍽 *Breakfast.*

MANZANILLO

70 km (43 miles) west of Bayamo.

The charming, cheerful port of Manzanillo stretches 3 km (2 miles) along the Bahía de Guacanayabo. It has a beautiful historic district whose pastel-painted structures have elements of Moorish architecture.

GETTING HERE AND AROUND

Public buses from Bayamo to Manzanillo take about an hour. If you drive, you cut that time in half. Looping around the "foot" of the island to the south makes for a much more difficult journey.

EXPLORING

TOP ATTRACTIONS

Monumento Celia. To reach the Monumento Celia, a monument to revolutionary hero Celia Sánchez, a longtime confidante of Fidel Castro, you climb a beautiful staircase lined with Moorish-style residences. ⊠ *Calle Caridad y Calle Martí.*

WORTH NOTING

Museo Histórico Municipal. The museum has displays on local history and popular culture. One exhibit is dedicated to Taty Labernia, who was so famous for her renditions of *boleros* (traditional Cuban songs descended from troubadour ballads) that she was known as "La Reina del Bolero" (The Queen of the Bolero). ⊠ *Calle Bartolomé Masó* ☎ *2355–2053* 🎫 *CUC$1* 🕐 *Tues.–Sat. 9–5.*

Parque Céspedes. The main plaza, Parque Céspedes, is the best place to experience Manzanillo's unique sense of style. It's dominated by a central bandstand, with colorful, intricately painted tiles and a domed top. Many of the fine buildings surrounding the plaza are Moorish-inspired. You'll also find a café, an art gallery, shops, and the Casa de la Cultura, which has art exhibits, live-music shows, and other cultural events. ⊠ *Manzanillo.*

FAMILY **Parque de Recreación Bartolomé Masó.** Wandering the bay-side malecón and exploring its adjacent Parque de Recreación Bartolomé Masó is a great way to spend an afternoon. This small park features rides and snack vendors in a shady clearing on the shore. It's lit up at night and is particularly lively on weekends. ⊠ *Manzanillo.*

OFF THE BEATEN PATH **La Demajagua.** In the sugar country outside Manzanillo this farm is where poet, patriot, and cane farmer Carlos Manuel de Céspedes freed his slaves and called for rebellion against Spain. There's a large monument at the entrance to the estate, and you can see the bell used by Céspedes to summon his slaves to freedom. The **Museo Histórico La Demajagua,** in Céspedes's former home, displays documents, photos, and other artifacts. ⊠ *Manzanillo* ✛ *3 km (8 miles) south of Manzanillo* 🎫 *CUC$1* 🕐 *Daily 9–5.*

5

WHERE TO STAY

$ **HOTEL** ⚏ **Hotel Guacanaybo.** On a bluff overlooking the bay, this modest, Soviet-era hotel offers the best accommodations, amenities (including satellite TV), and food you're likely to find in the area. **Pros:** visitors can trek in the surrounding forests. **Cons:** while the best hotel in the area, it is far from the Cuban all-inclusive resorts where most people choose to stay. $ *Rooms from: CUC$34* ✉ *Av. Camilio Cienfuegos* ☎ *2357–4012* ⊕ *www.islazul.cu* ➟ *105 rooms, 4 suites* ❒ *Breakfast.*

CHIVIRICO

60 km (37 miles) west of Santiago de Cuba.

West of Santiago lies Chivirico, a little beach town with a decent all-inclusive resort that operates as two adjoining hotels. The beaches here offer all kinds of water-sports activities; the diving is particularly noteworthy owing to several area wrecks and the deep Cayman Trench nearby.

GETTING HERE AND AROUND

Chivirico is most easily accessed by car or public bus—a few run each day—from Santiago de Cuba. The road running west from Santiago is smooth, but winds in sectors along the coast. The lodgings we list are east of town.

WHERE TO STAY

$$ **RESORT**   **Fodor's**Choice   ★   ⚏ **Brisas Los Galeones.** How many lodgings proudly proclaim that they are "only" a three-star resort and their devoted return customers revel in that claim? A mostly Canadian retiree clientele makes up the guest list here, but all are welcome, of course. **Pros:** the place is wonderfully low-key and friendly; rooms have great views. **Cons:** it's a steep walk (296 steps) down to the beach; this is not where the action is. $ *Rooms from: CUC$89* ✉ *Playa Sevilla* ☎ *2232–9110 through Brisas Sierra Mar* ⊕ *www.hotelescubanacan.com* ➟ *32 rooms* ❒ *All-inclusive.*

$$ **RESORT** ⚏ **Brisas Sierra Mar.** High-quality food and service are among this resort's hallmarks. **Pros:** rooms have great views; friendly staff at resort. **Cons:** this is an older resort with a few shopworn rooms. $ *Rooms from: CUC$89* ✉ *Playa Sevilla* ☎ *2232–9110* ⊕ *www.hotelescubanacan.com* ➟ *200 rooms* ❒ *All-inclusive.*

SANTIAGO DE CUBA AND GUANTÁNAMO PROVINCES

Santiago Province is home to the Sierra Maestra to the west, the Cordillera de la Gran Piedra to the east, and the Sierra de Cristal to the north. Although rugged and sparsely populated, the province is El Oriente's geographic and cultural center. The region's most important city, Santiago de Cuba, sits on a wide, south-coast bay, smack in the middle of the province. Founded in 1515, it was Cuba's first capital and still rivals Havana in art, culture, music, and historical sights.

Most famous for being the site of the U.S. naval base—one of the few remaining outposts of the Cold War—Guantánamo Province embodies

El Oriente's untamed spirit. Much of the region is within the protected biosphere reserve known as the Cuchilla del Toa, and its topography varies from a flat arid coastal zone to rain forest to pine-covered mountains. The main destination, Baracoa, was reachable only by water until the 1970s, when Castro had the Farola highway built over a formidable mountain range. Much of the east coast is still remote, served only by a string of country roads.

GETTING HERE AND AROUND

Although Cubans think of this region as isolated, and most have never traveled this far east, Santiago serves as El Oriente's highway, bus, air, and rail hub. The Autopista Nacional reaches here, 860 km (534 miles southeast of Havana) and expands to four lanes again between Santiago and Guantánamo. (Off the main highways, though, be prepared for some of Cuba's most potholed roads.) Víazul buses ply the spine of the island with long-distance coach service from Havana and Trinidad and cities in between. Cuba's dwindling rail service still makes an overnight run every night between the capital and Santiago. The fastest way here is to fly. The Aeropuerto Internacional Antonio Maceo, just south of Santiago, receives domestic flights from Havana on Cubana and Aero Caribbean.

SANTIAGO DE CUBA

860 km (534 miles) southeast of Havana; 86 km (53 miles) southwest of Guantánamo.

Fodor's Choice ★ Santiago de Cuba celebrated 500 years of history in 2015 with its own unique panache. The city has played an important role in Cuban development, from the beginnings of the wars for independence to the launching of the Revolution. No wonder it has earned the title *Ciudad Héroe* ("hero city"). It has fostered an independent spirit, bred through its isolation from Havana and its tradition of trading with and welcoming settlers from neighboring Caribbean islands.

As Cuba becomes a hot tourist destination, sultry, seductive Santiago is positioning itself to become a well-deserved mecca for tourism. The city's unique architecture blends Caribbean, Spanish, and other European influences. The African roots of Cuba's people are the most pronounced in Santiago, and this adds considerable flavor to the food as well as a lyrical lilt to the Spanish that's spoken here. You'll hear music in the air, from hypnotizing Cuban salsa to the folksy *nueva trova* to the latest Latin hits. Sightseeing here can keep you busy for days, if you like. Nightlife here can keep you busy for just as many corresponding evenings, too. To top it off, unlike most non-Havana urban areas on the island, this city actually has a good, decent variety of lodgings. None of them—not even the venerable, historic Casa Granda or the hip, trendy Meliá Santiago de Cuba—will break your budget. After 10 minutes here, you'll shorthand the city's official name to "Santiago," like the half-million people who live here do. After a couple of days here, soaking up the uniquely santiaguero vibe, you may say, "Havana? Where's that?" There's good reason why many visitors who make it this far east count Santiago as their favorite Cuban city.

GETTING HERE AND AROUND

Eastern Cuba's transportation hub is easily accessible from all points. The two-lane Carretera Nacional becomes the four-lane Autopista Nacional between Bayamo and Santiago, allowing you to zip along in your own vehicle for the final sector of the island journey. Víazul buses ply the route from Havana and Trinidad and points in between. Cutbacks have made rail service a shadow of its former self; overnight trains still connect Santiago with Havana. The Aeropuerto Antonio Maceo receives domestic flights from Havana, Holguín, and Varadero, as well as many international charters.

Contacts **Estación de Ferrocarriles.** ⊠ *Av. Jesús Menéndez, Centro Histórico, Santiago* ☎ *2262–2836.*

GUIDED TOURS

Contacts **Havanatur.** ⊠ *Calle 8, No. 54, Reparto Vista Alegre, Santiago* ☎ *2264–3603.* **Rumbos.** ⊠ *Parque Céspedes, Centro Histórico, Santiago* ☎ *2262–5969.* **Transtur.** ⊠ *Hotel Casa Granda, Calle Heredia 201, Parque Céspedes, Centro Histórico, Santiago* ☎ *2264–1121.*

EXPLORING CENTRO HISTÓRICO

At the center of the city's historic district you'll find Parque Céspedes. The plaza and the streets just off it form the city's cultural heart. They're filled with museums, art galleries, bookstores, and spots where the music never seems to stop. Note that, as in many Cuban cities, Santiago's streets often go by pre- and postrevolutionary names. *Both are provided in the addresses below.*

If you wear your most comfortable shoes, get an early start, and are selective about which museums you explore (or visit each only briefly), you could probably hit the highlights of the Centro Histórico in a seven-hour day. But Santiago really deserves at least two days—seeing the sights just west of Parque Céspedes and visiting the Castillo San Juan on one day and then visiting the many museums east of Parque Céspedes on another. Be sure to paint the Historic Center red at least one night during your visit—perhaps taking in a show at the Casa de la Trova or the Casa del Estudiante.

Santiago suffered significant damage during 2012's Hurricane Sandy, the same storm that later wreaked havoc on New York and New Jersey. Structural repairs are ongoing at this writing. The condition of most public buildings is back to normal, but some residential neighborhoods have yet to recover. Vegetation in some parks has required replanting.

TOP ATTRACTIONS

Casa de Diego Velázquez. Constructed in 1516, this structure is reputed to be Cuba's oldest house, although many historians now doubt that claim. First or not, it is one of Santiago's top attractions. Diego Velázquez, the Spanish conquistador who founded the city and was the island's first governor, lived upstairs. Inside you'll find period beds, desks, chests, and other furniture. On the first floor is a gold foundry. Memorable are the star-shape Moorish carvings on the wooden windows and balconies, and the original interior patio with its well and rain-collecting *tinajón* vessel. An adjacent house is filled with antiques intended to convey the

French and English decorative and architectural influences—such as the radial stained glass above the courtyard doors—in the late 19th-century. ✉ *Calle Félix Peña (Santo Tomás) 612* ☎ *2265–2652* 🎟 *CUC$2* 🕐 *Sat.– Wed. 9–5, Fri. 1–5.*

Museo Provincial Bacardí Moreau. Cuba's oldest museum was founded in 1899 by Emilio Bacardí Moreau, the former Santiago mayor whose rum-making family fled to Puerto Rico after the Revolution. Although the Neoclassical structure's interior was horrendously remodeled in 1968—destroying many elegant details and cutting off air circulation—the collection it contains is fantastic. The basement, which you enter from the side of the building, has artifacts—including mummies and a shrunken head—from indigenous cultures throughout the Americas. In the first-floor displays of colonial objects, the antique weapons and brutal relics of the slave trade are especially thought-provoking. Step outside a door to a cobblestone alley, along which are houses from the 16th to the 19th centuries. Around the corner is a traditional colonial patio. The second-floor art gallery has works from the 19th and early 20th centuries. ■TIP➔ **Although the museum bears the Bacardí name, this is not Santiago's rum museum. That's the Museo del Ron, two blocks away.** ✉ *Calle Pío Rosado (Carnicería) y Calle Aguilera* ☎ *2262–8402* 🎟 *CUC$2* 🕐 *Mon. 1–4:30, Tues.–Sat. 9–4:30, Sun. 9–12:30.*

Parque Céspedes. At times it seems that Santiago's main activity is the curious stare-down that takes place in Parque Céspedes between mojito-sipping tourists at the Hotel Casa Granda's café and white-hatted locals, who sit across the way. Long the central meeting place for santiagueros, this large plaza buzzes with sound and movement day and night. Musicians wander past and around its shady benches, which are occupied from early in the morning to late in the evening. At the park's center is a large bronze statue of Carlos Manuel de Céspedes, whose Grito de Yara declared Cuba's independence from Spain in 1868 and began the Ten Years' War. Hurricane Sandy uprooted most of the park's trees in 2012; residents here patiently wait for the vegetation to grow back. ✉ *Santiago de Cuba.*

WORTH NOTING

Balcón de Velázquez. This ceramic-tiled terrace is all that remains of a fort once used by authorities to monitor boat traffic. It's a great place to linger while taking in views of both the city and the bay. Music shows and other events are often held here, particularly on weekend evenings. ✉ *Calle Bartolomé Masó (San Basilio) y Calle Corona* 🎟 *Free; CUC$1 photo permit; CUC$5 video permit.*

Calle Padre Pico. The climb up the stone steps to this street will reward you with more than just dramatic views. It's part of the Tivoli neighborhood, where 18th-century French-colonial mansions sit side by side with 16th-century structures. Locals gather on its shady edges to gossip, play dominoes, or watch visitors like you make their ascent. ✉ *Santa Rita at Hospital.*

Casa Natal de José María Heredia. This Spanish-colonial mansion was the birthplace of poet José María Heredia, who, because of his pro-independence writings, is considered Cuba's first national poet. Heredia died in

Santiago de Cuba

1839 at age 36 while exiled in Mexico. The house, now just a fraction of its original size, displays period furniture and some of the poet's works and belongings. The home's traditional interior patio is planted with trees and plants—including orange, myrtle, palm, and jasmine—associated with Heredia's verse. A marble plaque on the house's Calle Heredia facade excerpts one of the poet's most famous works, "Niágara" ("Ode to Niagara Falls"). ⊠ *Calle Heredia 260* ☎ *2262–5350* 🖃 *CUC$1* ☉ *Tues.–Sat. 9–5, Sun. 9–1.*

Catedral de Nuestra Señora de la Asunción. The twin towers and central dome of Santiago's Neoclassical cathedral loom over the southern edge of **Parque Céspedes**. Because this area is atop a hill, the cathedral's profile is visible from afar and creates a recognizable silhouette. Although it was first built on this site in 1523, the current building dates primarily from 1922. Inside, the painted ceiling has been beautifully restored, and there are several noteworthy works of religious art, including a sculpture of Cuba's patron saint, La Virgen de la Caridad. A two-room museum near the east entrance displays objects relating to the history of the Catholic Church in Cuba. ⊠ *Calle Heredia* 🖃 *Donation suggested for church; CUC$1 for museum* ☉ *Church daily 8–10 am and 5–7:30 pm. Mass Mon. and Wed. 6:30 pm, Sat. 5 pm, Sun. 9 am, and 6:30 pm. Museum Mon.–Sat. 9:30–5:30.*

FAMILY **Museo del Carnaval.** The spirit of one of the Caribbean's most vibrant street parties, Santiago's annual July carnival, is recalled in photos and newspaper clippings, floats, costumes, and musical instruments. To be honest, the artifacts here are rather ho-hum and do not justify the added camera fee on top of the admission price. ■ **TIP→ Late afternoons here give a better sense of what carnival is like; stop by at 4 pm Tuesday through Saturday for a performance by music and dance troupes.** The short spectacle of colorful costume, Afro-Cuban rhythms, and stirring song might justify the photo fee and might have you planning your next trip to coincide with the main event. The performers are always grateful for tips. ⊠ *Calle Heredia 303* ☎ *2262–6955* 🖃 *CUC$1; CUC$5 for photos* ☉ *Tues.–Sat. 9–5, Sun. 9–1.*

Museo de la Lucha Clandestina. Every Cuban city of any size has a museum dedicated to the Revolution. To be frank, most begin to blur together after awhile. This so-called Museum of the Clandestine Struggle is one of the country's better such facilities. It is housed in a 19th-century building that was once the city's police headquarters. It was attacked and burned by Frank País and a band of rebels on November 30, 1958. Displays in this now-restored structure give you a complete overview of the struggle, and the architecture and bay views are as compelling as the exhibits. ⊠ *Calle General Jesús Rabí 1* ☎ *2262–4689* 🖃 *CUC$1* ☉ *Tues.–Sat. 9–5, Sun. 9–noon.*

Museo del Ron. Exhibits here take you through the rum-making process. You'll also find displays of antique rum paraphernalia and bottles, as well as exhibits documenting the history of the former Bacardí factory. The Bacardís, one of Santiago's oldest families, initially supported Castro's revolutionary goals but left Cuba for Puerto Rico when their installations were nationalized. In the same building (but accessible only through an entrance around the corner) is the **Taberna del Ron**, which sells rum products and gifts. ✉ *Calle Bartolomé Masó (San Basilio) 358* ☎ *2662–3737* 💲 *CUC$1* ☉ *Tues.–Sun. 9–6.*

Plaza de Dolores. Four blocks from Parque Céspedes, this long plaza—the city's former marketplace—is ringed with cafés, open-air restaurants, and 18th-century homes with noteworthy wooden balconies. It takes its name from the church overlooking its eastern end, the Iglesia de Nuestra Señora de los Dolores, which was renovated and turned into a concert hall. Several of the trees here were felled by Hurricane Sandy in 2012; it will be several years before the new plantings grow back. ✉ *Calvario at Francisco Vicente Aguilera.*

Plaza de Marte. For a memorable photo, visit this park, Santiago's third largest, at the edge of the Old City. Children ride in colorful carts pulled by goats—a pleasure formerly enjoyed in Parque Céspedes. This relaxed square, filled with families and sweets vendors, captures the rhythm of Santiago life. Most of the trees here were uprooted by 2012's Hurricane Sandy. Replanting has begun, but it will be some time before the park achieves its cool shadiness once again. ✉ *Francisco Vicente Aguilera at Paraíso.*

EXPLORING NEARBY SANTIAGO DE CUBA

If you have an extra day, take in some of the sights around Santiago. There are several places of interest on and near the bay just to the north of the Centro Histórico. Avenida de las Américas edges modern Santiago's northern perimeter before arcing sharply southeast. Along and just off this boulevard are several noteworthy contemporary and historical sights.

Except for the basilica at El Cobre, you can hit most of the city's sights in greater Santiago in a day. You'll save money and your sanity by hiring a car and driver rather than renting a car and driving yourself. A taxi will charge roughly CUC$50 for this tour. In addition, many hotels offer half-day Havanatur excursions that hit many of these sights.

TOP ATTRACTIONS

Antiguo Cuartel Moncada. If you have an interest in all things revolutionary, a visit to the Moncada Barracks is a must, because here's where it all started. On July 26, 1953, Castro and 100 men attempted to storm this former army barracks. It was carnival time in Santiago; the streets were full of revelers, and Castro had hoped that security would be lax. Unfortunately, his hopes were dashed, and the rebels were either killed or captured. Castro, who fled to the mountains, was eventually caught, tried, and imprisoned on the Isla de la Juventud off Western Cuba's southern coast. Although unsuccessful, the attack ignited the sparks of Castro's Revolution. He wrote his famous speech "*La historia me absolverá*" ("History will absolve me"), which was smuggled out of prison, printed, and distributed throughout the island. Although luck had not been on his side in 1953, it certainly was in 1955, when Batista granted many political prisoners their freedom. Castro left for the United States, where he began soliciting support for his 26th of July Movement (named in honor of the ill-fated barracks attack) to rid Cuba of Batista's regime. From there, he took his cause to Mexico. In 1956, just a year after being released from prison, Castro made his historic journey from Mexico to Cuba aboard the *Granma.*

Today the former stronghold of Batista's troops contains a grammar school and the **Museo de 26 de Julio.** The bullet holes surrounding the doorway to the museum are re-creations of those left after the original attack, which were quickly patched over by Batista's men. The exhibits here tell, in Spanish only, the entire story of the attack and the events that followed. They're among the nation's most comprehensive ones on revolutionary history. Take the guided tour (it's customary to tip docents CUC$1). ✉ *Av. General Portuondo (Trinidad) y Av. Moncada, Reparto Sueño* ☎ *2266–1157* ◩ *CUC$2* ۞ *Tues.–Sat. 9:30–5:15, Sun. 9–2:30.*

Fodor's Choice ★ **Basilica del Cobre.** After a drive through the countryside west of Santiago you'll see the red-tile tower of La Basilica de Nuestra Señora de la Caridad del Cobre—dedicated to Cuba's patron saint in 1926—before the turn-off to the copper mining town of El Cobre in which it is located. The story of the Virgin dates from the early 1600s, when three men in a boat first saw her floating on water during a storm; tradition holds that the Virgin saved the men from certain drowning. Records show that the statue was most likely brought from Spain on order of the then-governor of Cuba, but don't play iconoclast with the millions of faithful who take seriously the Virgin's reputed miraculous powers. (Her image has also been blended with that of Ochún, the *orisha*, or goddess, of love in the Santería religion.) Each September, pilgrims journey here—sometimes crawling uphill on their knees—on the Virgin's feast day (September 8) to pay homage to the image housed in a glass case high above the main altar. Her shrine is filled with gifts from the faithful, including Ernest Hemingway's 1954 Nobel Prize, which he won largely for his novel *The Old Man and the Sea.* The Nobel medal was stolen in 1986 but recovered. It is no longer on display, except during special occasions. A staircase at the back of the cathedral leads to the chapel containing the Virgin's wooden image. In front of the cathedral you'll find a plaque commemorating Pope John Paul II's visit here during his 1998 trip to Cuba. A taxi is the quickest way to get out here. Plan to pay CUC$30. Most area tours feature the basilica as a stop, too. ✉ *Carretera Central, El Cobre* ✛ *20 km (12 miles) west of Santiago de Cuba* ☎ *2234–6118* ◩ *CUC$1 suggested donation* ۞ *Daily 6:30 am–6 pm.*

Fodor's Choice ★ **Cementerio Santa Ifigenia.** This well-kept cemetery is home to the majestic mausoleum of the great poet-patriot in the wars of independence, José Martí. The structure is true to Martí's wishes (expressed in one of his poems) that he be buried below the flag of Cuba and surrounded by roses. Marble steps lead to the tomb, above which is a domed tower. An honor guard keeps watch over Martí's tomb 24 hours a day and changes guard every 30 minutes in an eye-catching, goose-stepping ceremony. Other highlights include a memorial to Cuban soldiers who have fallen in battle—many of the partisans who fought in Angola, in southern Africa, are buried here—and the tombs of Carlos Manuel de Céspedes and those who died in the Moncada Barracks attack. While admission is technically free, you may enter only in the accompaniment of a guide, for which you must pay. You'll also be charged a hefty photo fee, whether taking stills or videos. The changing-of-the-guard ceremony is impressive enough that most visitors pony up and pay the photo fee. ⊠ *Av. Crombet, Reparto Santa Ifigenia* ☎ *2263–2723* 🖳 *Free (but only with guide); guide, CUC$1; photo permit, CUC$10* ⊙ *Daily dawn–dusk.*

OFF THE BEATEN PATH **Castillo del Morro.** The Spanish fortress known as El Morro, south of Santiago, was constructed between 1638 and 1700 and was designed by Giovanni Antonelli, the Italian architect and engineer responsible for fortresses bearing the same name in both Havana and San Juan, Puerto Rico. Dominating a bluff at the entrance to the Bahía de Santiago de Cuba, El Morro was built to ward off pirates (and rebuilt after a 1662 attack by the English pirate Henry Morgan). Inside you'll find a museum with exhibits on, appropriately enough, pirates. Signage is in Spanish only, but English-speaking guides can lead you around. (Tip them, of course.) There are wonderful views from interior rooms, which have wooden floors and stone walls, as well as from various terraces. From the lowest terrace, the view of the fortress itself, formed from the sheer face of the bluff, is powerful. The way into the structure takes you down and then back up a 207-step staircase; a drawbridge over a moat leads to the entrance. You'll find little shade here; sunscreen and a brimmed hat are musts. Midday gets unbearably hot. ■ **TIP→ Visit early in the morning or late afternoon if your schedule permits.** An impressive flag-lowering, cannon-firing ceremony winds up the day, and that makes a good case for a late-afternoon visit. ⊠ *Carretera del Morro, Km 7.5* ☎ *2269–1569* 🖳 *CUC$4* ⊙ *Daily 8–sunset.*

WORTH NOTING

Fábrica de Ron Caney. Cuba's oldest rum distillery, the former Bacardí family enterprise, now makes the Caney, Santiago, and Varadero brand rums. The on-site shop—which has a bar, live music, and free samples—is the central attraction. Unfortunately, there are no factory tours. ⊠ *Av. Jesús Menéndez y Calle Gonzalo de Quesada, Centro Histórico* ☎ *2662–5576* 🖳 *Free* ⊙ *Mon.–Sat. 9–6.*

FAMILY **Loma de San Juan.** Made famous by Teddy Roosevelt and his Rough Riders, San Juan Hill marks the sight of the decisive July 1, 1898 battle in the Spanish-American War. (The conflict is known here as the *Guerra hispano-cubano-norteamericana*, or Spanish-Cuban-American War.) Today it's a park, in the Reparto San Juan neighborhood, covered by monuments left by U.S. and Cuban militaries, dedicated to the battle fought here during the Spanish-American War. It's a lovely passive spot, with amusements for small children in the **Parque de Diversiones**—identifiable by its large Ferris wheel—at the base of the hill. ⊠ *Santiago de Cuba* ✛ *Just south of Reparto Vista Alegre.*

Plaza de la Revolución. Just about every city on the island has a Revolution Square, a vast expanse of space and perhaps every community's most prominent marker of Cuban socialism. This one in the Reparto Sueño neighborhood was the site of Pope John Paul II's Mass celebrated here in Santiago. Towering above the plaza is the dramatic **monument to Major General Antonio Maceo**, one of the heroes of the wars of independence. It shows the general on his horse, going down in a battlefield

5

portrayed by 23 steel machetes that rise from the ground around him. ⊠ *Plaza de la Revolución, Reparto Sueño.*

Reparto Vista Alegre. This elegant neighborhood of mansions is a place of historical splendor. French-inspired plantation homes, stately Spanish-colonial mansions, even Art Deco gems are beautifully decaying amid riotous vegetation under the clear Caribbean sun. Chevy Bel Airs and Cadillacs from the late 1950s roll down the wide, quiet streets where time seems to have frozen four decades ago, just before the Revolution. The district, framed in bougainvillea and hibiscus, resembles Havana's Vedado and older residential neighborhoods in Miami. ⊠ *Reparto Vista Alegre.*

WHERE TO EAT

$

ITALIAN

✕ **La Teresina.** The Italian fare—pizza, pastas, and seafood dishes—is good by local standards. The white-tile, European café–style setting overlooking the plaza is pleasant, and the staff is friendly. ⑤ *Average main: CUC$10* ⊠ *Plaza de Dolores, Calle Aguilera, Centro Histórico* ☎ *2268–6484.*

$

CUBAN

✕ **Restaurante Don Antonio.** Although this state-run spot serves much of the same fare as its many like-owned neighbors, its setting in a restored colonial mansion on Plaza de Dolores is terrific. Fans spin slowly overhead from a lofty wooden ceiling, and large windows open to the plaza's northwest corner. ⑤ *Average main: CUC$10* ⊠ *Plaza Dolores, Calle Aguilera y Calle Porfiro Valiente, Centro Histórico* ☎ *2265–2307.*

$

SEAFOOD

✕ **Restaurant Zun Zún.** The well-prepared seafood dishes and extensive wine list befit Zun Zún's elegant Vista Alegre setting. You can dine outdoors on a wraparound porch adorned with potted ferns or inside amid the unique decor of the house's former owner, an Arab merchant. ⑤ *Average main: CUC$8* ⊠ *Av. Manduley 159, Reparto Vista Alegre* ☎ *2264–1528.*

$$

CUBAN

✕ **Santiago 1900.** In the former mansion of the rum-making Bacardí family, this restaurant is an old Santiago standard. Although the dishes lack a sense of adventure, you can't beat the ambience. The formal dining room, with its antique furnishings, is particularly striking; the informal back patio, whose offerings vary only slightly from those inside, is a great spot for a drink. ⑤ *Average main: CUC$14* ⊠ *Calle Bartolomé Masó (San Basilio) 354, e/Calle Pío Rosado/Comisaria y Calle Hartman/San Félix, Centro Histórico* ☎ *2262–3507.*

$$

CUBAN

✕ **Taberna de Dolores.** Conversation and music linger in the air at this authentic Cuban restaurant. Long white flowers known as *campanitas blancas* hang from the trellis of a broad interior courtyard. A marble staircase leads up to a narrow second floor and its long bar. Diners at tables on the balcony survey Plaza Dolores. ⑤ *Average main: CUC$15* ⊠ *Plaza Dolores , Calle Aguilera y Calle Maya Rodriguez/Reloj, Centro Histórico* ☎ *2262–3913* ▭ *No credit cards.*

WHERE TO STAY

Santiago has some fine casas particulares, particularly in the Vista Alegre neighborhood. On a leisurely stroll through this barrio you can pick out a favorite house; if you're lucky, it will have a sticker with a blue triangle on its door, which means it's a licensed, private lodging establishment. Most such homes charge CUC$20 for one person, CUC$35 for two.

Santiago's Specialties

Santiago is known for its roast pig and its marinated *yuca* (cassava or manioc). Other eastern Cuba specialties include *fufu*, a mashed plantain side dish laced with crumbs of crispy pork, and *pru*, a soft drink made from pine needles, sugar, roots, and herbs. Baracoa's cuisine is closer to that found elsewhere in the Caribbean in that it relies heavily on the coconut. Fish and shellfish, for example, are served in a flavorful orange coconut sauce. *Bacán* is mashed plantain and coconut stuffed with pork, wrapped in plantain leaves, and then cooked.

All along the roadsides, children sell *cucurucho*, a desert of shredded coconut, fruits, nuts, and sugar ingeniously wrapped in a palm leaf.

When looking for a place to eat, good bets are the privately operated *paladares*, which serve *comida criolla* (the island's own mixture of Spanish and New World cuisines). Roasted pork or chicken and stewed or spiced beef are common main courses. They're usually served with *arroz* (rice) and red-kidney or black beans or fried sweet bananas or plantains (*plátanos*).

$ **Hotel Balcón del Caribe.** On a coastal cliff a few minutes' walk from
HOTEL Castillo del Morro, this hotel has spectacular views. **Pros:** as close to Castillo del Morro as it gets; friendly service. **Cons:** long way from other city sights; not a place to stay if you're looking for action. $ *Rooms from: CUC$39 ⊠ Carretera del Morro, Km 7, El Morro ⊹ 6 km (4 miles) southwest of Santiago de Cuba ☎ 2269–1506 ⊕ www.islazul.cu ⤳ 72 rooms, 22 cabins ⦿ Breakfast.*

$$ **Hotel Casa Granda.** From the grand old Casa Granda, the best hotel in
HOTEL the Centro Histórico, you can see Parque Céspedes, with its wandering
Fodor's Choice musicians and guayabera-clad men in conversation. **Pros:** the formal
★ dining room offers delectable seafood and steak dishes; few lodgings in Cuba evoke history the way this one does. **Cons:** guest rooms don't have as elegant an aura as architecture of the place; the furniture isn't new and rooms are on the small side, though still among the best in the city. $ *Rooms from: CUC$105 ⊠ Calle Heredia 201, adjacent to San Pedro, Parque Céspedes ⊹ Centro Histórico ☎ 2265–3021 ⊕ www. hotelescubanacan.com ⤳ 55 rooms, 3 suites ⦿ Breakfast.*

$ **Hotel San Juan.** The setting is bucolic: you're at the foot of San Juan
HOTEL Hill and surrounded by trees and fields. **Pros:** a quiet option away from the commotion of central Santiago; rates are a bargain for the offerings. **Cons:** you're a distance from most city sights here. $ *Rooms from: CUC$60 ⊠ Carretera a Siboney, Km 1.5, Reparto San Juan ☎ 2268– 7200 ⊕ www.islazul.cu ⤳ 112 rooms ⦿ Breakfast.*

$$ **Hotel Versalles.** Situated on a hill less than a mile from the airport,
HOTEL you'll get nice views of the city from out here, and it's very quiet at night. **Pros:** peace and quiet are yours at this countryside lodging; the slight elevation on a hill keeps things cooler than in the city itself. **Cons:** you're a long way from Santiago's sights; rooms are very plain. $ *Rooms from: CUC$84 ⊠ Carretera del Morro, Km 1, Alturas del Versalles ⊹ 2 km (1 mile) from airport just south of Santiago on road*

CLOSE UP

Carnival in Santiago

Carnaval in Latin America usually means pre-Lenten festivities, with one final blowout before settling in for the sacrifices of Lent. The rhythms and rituals of Santiago's festival, the country's largest, take place, instead, in July to honor the city's patron, St. James, during the week bracketing his July 25 feast day. Neighborhood associations called *comparsas* compete to build the most colorful floats, create the most inspired costumes, and stage the most spectacular processions. Men dress in colorful outfits and wear papier-mâché masks; women don bikinis and wraps of see-through silk and feathers. The primal rumba beat—accentuated by maracas, Chinese coronets, and wooden flutes—drives the processions, which take place throughout the city. Socialism enters the fray these days, with Cuba's late-July Revolution holidays falling during Carnaval. (The timing is no coincidence: Fidel Castro planned the attacks on Santiago's Moncada Barracks during Carnival, thinking that security would be lax. He was wrong, but the event kicked off the Revolution, which would ultimately be successful six years later.) Think of Santiago's Carnival as mixing conga with a layer of Communism.

to *El Morro* ☎ 2269–1016 ⊕ *www.hotelescubanacan.com* ➣ *46 rooms, 15 cabins* ❍❙ *Breakfast.*

$$
HOTEL
Fodor's Choice
★

🖭 **Meliá Santiago de Cuba.** With the look of a tropical erector set, this red, white, and blue high-rise is either playfully appealing or pompously postmodern, depending on your point of view. **Pros:** the hotel is the most up-to-date facility in town; there is a great night club on the top floor. **Cons:** the hotel is a good walk from downtown, requiring a short taxi ride. ⑤ *Rooms from: CUC$140* ⊠ *Av. de las Américas, e/Av. Manduley y Av. Cuarto, Reparto Sueño* ☎ 2268–7070 ⊕ *www.meliacuba. com* ➣ *270 rooms, 32 junior suites* ❍❙ *Breakfast.*

$
B&B/INN

🖭 **Villa Santiago.** At the edge of the Vista Alegre neighborhood are these accommodations in 12 one-storey houses, all former residences built in the 1940s and 1950s. **Pros:** house accommodations are a nice change from standard hotel fare; neighborhood is a quiet respite from the bustle of Santiago. **Cons:** a few of the houses have a lot of front steps; you're quite a distance from most sights here. ⑤ *Rooms from: CUC$60* ⊠ *Av. Manduley 502, esq. de Calle 19, Reparto Vista Alegre* ☎ 2264–1368 ⊕ *www.gaviota-grupo.com* ➣ *49 rooms* ❍❙ *Breakfast.*

NIGHTLIFE AND PERFORMING ARTS
NIGHTLIFE
Casa de la Trova. The folksy *trova* combines African rhythms with Spanish guitar, and the lyrics explore themes of romance or social protest. The **Casa de la Trova** has daily shows where groups play in one of four shifts: 10 am–2 pm, 3–7, 8:30–10, and 10 pm–2 am. Former Beatle Paul McCartney once visited; his autographed picture hangs on the wall here. ⊠ *Calle Heredia 208, Centro Histórico* ☎ 2265–2689 🎟 *CUC$1–CUC$2* ⊙ *Closed Mon.*

Claqueta Bar. Just off Parque Céspedes, this bar serves cheap drinks on its outdoor terrace; sometimes there's live music here weekend evenings. ⊠ *Calle Félix Peña (Santo Tomás) 654, Centro Histórico.*

Hotel Casa Granda. Early in the evening, a band plays at the bar-café on the porch of the Hotel Casa Granda. Its rooftop bar occasionally has live-music shows and is also a nice spot for a drink. ⊠ *Calle Heredia 201, Parque Céspedes, Centro Histórico* ☎ *2265–3021.*

PERFORMING ARTS

Ballet Folklórico Cutumba. When they're not on tour, the highly regarded Afro-Cuban Ballet Folklórico Cutumba rehearses mornings from 9 to 1 from Tuesday through Friday. They present a show most Saturday evenings. ⊠ *Calle Trocha at Santa Ursula, Centro Histórico* ☎ *2265–5173* ☞ *CUC$2 for rehearsal; CUC$10 for show.*

Teatro Heredia. The Teatro Heredia hosts performances of classical and Cuban music and opera as well as poetry readings. ⊠ *Av. de las Américas y Av. de los Desfiles, Reparto Sueño* ☎ *2264–3134.*

Tropicana Santiago. Sibling of the Havana original, the Tropicana puts on a full cabaret, with dozens of dancers—men in Spandex, women in feathers and jeweled bikinis—floating through the colored lights and tropical decor. It's undeniably touristy and Vegas-like. You'll come away entranced by the spectacle or a tad bored. It depends on your tastes. Most hotels offer cabaret packages for CUC$40 per person (including transport, entrance, and one drink). ⊠ *Circunvalación , Reparto Sueño* ✛ *4 km (2 miles) north of Hotel Meliá Santiago de Cuba* ☎ *2264–2579.*

SHOPPING

Santiago and its environs have some of the best arts and crafts in the region—from surrealist oil paintings to stuffed dolls to wood carvings. The city's painters are particularly good; if you buy an artwork, just remember to purchase a CUC$10-export permit from the artist.

ART GALLERIES

Arte Universal. There are art exhibits and works for sale at Arte Universal. ⊠ *Calle 1, e/Calle M y Calle Terraza, Reparto Vista Alegre* ☎ *2265–7399* ⊙ *Mon.–Sat. 9–7, Sun. 9–5* ☞ *Admission CUC$1.*

BOOKS

Casa del Caribe. This book store offers a good selection of Spanish-language books with Cuban themes. ⊠ *Calle 13, No. 154, esq. de Calle 5, Reparto Vista Alegre* ☎ *2264–2285.*

CRAFTS

Cubartesania. Just off Parque Céspedes, this state-run store sells high-quality paintings, prints, and a wide selection of crafts. ⊠ *Calle Bartolomé Masó/San Basilio y Calle Félix Peña/Santo Tomás, Centro Histórico.*

TOBACCO

Fábrica de Tabacos César Escalante. If cigars are your passion, this small factory uses the traditional way to roll some of the region's best. ⊠ *Av. Jesús Menéndez 703, esq. de Calle Bartolomé Masó (San Basilio)* ☎ *2262–2366* ⊙ *Closed Sun.*

SPORTS AND THE OUTDOORS

There are beaches and plenty of hiking opportunities here. The beach zone west of Santiago, along the coastal road into Granma Province, is also just a day trip away.

BASEBALL

Estadio Guillermón Moncada. Cuba goes crazy for America's pastime of baseball. You can catch the madness at Estadio Guillermón Moncada, the stadium of the hometown team, the Santiago Orientales. The season runs November through March (which brackets the dry season), and games are played Tuesday and Thursday at 7:30 pm, Saturday at 1:30 and 7:30 pm, and Sunday at 1:30. ⊠ *Av. de las Américas, Reparto Sueño* ☎ *2264–1090.*

BARACOA

250 km (155 miles) northeast of Santiago.

Cuba's first Spanish settlement was founded in 1512 by Diego Velázquez, who went on to settle six other cities. Today Baracoa is one of the island's most charming towns. Its historic center is bounded by three fortresses and El Malecón, a wide ocean-side roadway (La Farola runs into it) bordered by sea-grape trees and coral coastline on one side and buildings—some historic, some modern and sterile—on the other.

GETTING HERE AND AROUND

One Víazul bus each day connects Baracoa with Santiago de Cuba in each direction. Tickets sell out quickly, especially on weekends. The ride takes about five hours. (Local buses are agonizingly slower.) You can shave about an hour off that five-hour time if you drive yourself. Either way, the drive is scenic but twisting and winding in sectors.

EXPLORING

TOP ATTRACTIONS

Catedral de Nuestra Señora de la Asunción. The Parque Independencia is home to the Baracoa's cathedral, built in 1833. The church is best known for preserving the Cruz de la Parra that Columbus supposedly used when he came ashore in 1492 to claim Cuba for Spain and Christianity. Indeed, carbon dating has confirmed that the cross was fashioned in the late 1400s and is old enough to have been brought by the explorer. One pesky detail pokes holes in the story, though: the cross is made of hardwoods native to the island and could not have been brought here by Columbus. No matter. It can be stated with certainty that this is one of oldest crosses (perhaps *the* oldest) in the New World. For years, parishioners were permitted to carve slivers of wood from the cross to keep as relics. That practice is no longer permitted. ⊠ *Calle Antonio Maceo 152* ☎ *2164–3352* ☉ *Tues.–Sat. 8–noon and 2–4.*

WORTH NOTING

El Castillo de Seboruco. This fortress, which now houses the Hotel El Castillo, dominates a hill overlooking Baracoa. Although construction on it started in 1739, the fort wasn't finished until nearly 200 years later. Even if you don't stay here, stop by for the views of El Yunque and the city. ⊠ *Calle Calixto García, Loma El Paraíso.*

GUANTANAMERA

One of Cuba's most famous exports, the song "Guantanamera," began life as a ballad about an attempt to court a country woman from Guantánamo Province. (*Guantanamera* is the feminine form for a person from this region.) The version we know today includes lyrics written by poet José Martí. ("I am a sincere man from where the palm trees grow, and, before dying, I want to share the verses of my soul.") Folk singer/activist Pete Seeger first introduced the song to an international audience during a 1963 concert at New York's Carnegie Hall. He always delighted in having concert attendees sing the simple refrain. For Seeger, the song symbolized the peace movement in the aftermath of the Cuban missile crisis. Covers came from all points on the political and apolitical spectrum, most famously by the Sandpipers, but also José Feliciano, Joan Baez, Celia Cruz, Gloria Estefan, Wyclef Jean, Jimmy Buffett, Tito Puente, and Julio Iglesias. A 2014 Jackson Browne-produced arrangement brought together 75 Cuban musicians, both inside the country and in the diaspora in a rare spirit of cooperation between the two, as part of the Playing for Change project.

Finca Duaba. You can get a taste of country life at this replica of a typical Cuban plantation. A tour takes you past mango and coconut trees as well as coffee and cocoa crops. You'll also visit a typical *bohío*, or peasant's hut, where staff members actually live. A rustic restaurant serves a good comida criolla lunch for about CUC$10 per person. ✉ *Ruta Duaba* ⊕ *7 km (4 miles) west of town, take left at Campismo El Yunque and follow dirt road to right* 🔲 *CUC$1* ⊙ *Tues.–Sun. 9–4.*

Fuerte de la Punta. Baracoa's third fortress, Fuerte de la Punta, was built in 1803 on a spit of land over the entrance to the bay. The fortress now contains the Restaurante La Punta. ✉ *Av. Los Mártires y el Malecón.*

Fuerte Matachín. One of Baracoa's three fortresses, Fuerte Matachín, was completed in 1802. Today it houses the **Museo Histórico Matachín**, whose displays discuss the city's history, including its Taíno roots. There are examples of Taíno pottery, sculpture, and other artifacts; exhibits on famous citizens; and displays explaining the community's role in the wars for independence and the Revolution. ✉ *Calle Martí y El Malecón* 🕿 *2164–2122* 🔲 *CUC$1* ⊙ *Daily 8–noon and 2–6.*

Parque Independencia. This park forms Baracoa's historic heart; local people refer to the triangle-shaped park as "Parque Central." Note the large bust of indigenous leader Hatuey—Cuba's first rebel—who fought against the Spanish and was burned at the stake for his audacity in 1512. ✉ *Félix Ruene at Antonio Maceo.*

BEACHES

Playa Baragua. East of town lies Playa Baragua, one of the area's few light-sand beaches. Not far from here, the road passes beneath a natural arch called the Túnel de los Alemanes (Germans' Tunnel) before ending 25 km (16 miles) east of Baracoa, at the Río Yumurí and the adjacent village of the same name. The river tumbles out of a steep canyon. Boats ferry passengers across the river and up into the canyon for nominal fees. **Amenities:** none. **Best for:** solitude; sunrise; walking. ☒ *Baracoa* ✛ *20 km (12 miles) east of Baracoa.*

Playa Maguana. West of town, you'll find the lovely, dark-sand Playa Maguana, site of the Gaviota Villa Maguana hotel. **Amenities:** food and drink; parking; water sports. **Best for:** sunrise; swimming; walking. ☒ *Baracoa* ✛ *20 km (12 miles) west of Baracoa.*

Río Miel. Right outside the east end of town you'll cross the Río Miel. Legend has it that after swimming in these waters you'll fall in love in Baracoa and stay here forever. ☒ *Baracoa.*

WHERE TO EAT

$ ✕ **Restaurante La Punta.** At this restaurant in the Fuerte de la Punta you
CUBAN can dine on traditional food 24 hours a day. Tables are set within the old fort walls. Just outside are wonderful bay views. Live music and dance shows take place nightly. $ *Average main: CUC$10* ☒ *Av. Los Mártires y el Malecón* ☎ *2164–1480* ▭ *No credit cards.*

WHERE TO STAY

$ ⊡ **Hotel El Castillo.** Baracoa's Seboruco Castle was renovated and trans-
HOTEL formed into this charming hotel with views of the town—from its quaint Historic Center to its Malecón—El Yunque, and the sea. **Pros:** the most impressive hotel in town with the best views of the city; here's an opportunity to stay in a converted fort. **Cons:** a few of the rooms are looking a bit shopworn; noise from the city travels up the hill. $ *Rooms from: CUC$65* ☒ *Calle Calixto García, Loma El Paraíso* ☎ *2164–5165* ⊕ *www.gaviota-grupo.com* ⇨ *62 rooms* ⫶❍⫶ *Breakfast.*

$ ⊡ **Villa Maguana.** If you like the idea of sitting in the shade on a rocking
B&B/INN chair steps from a secluded, palm-lined beach, this guest house is perfect. **Pros:** the setting is intimate; on a stunning beachfront. **Cons:** a little hard to find, especially at night. $ *Rooms from: CUC$60* ☒ *Playa Maguana* ☎ *2164–5106* ⊕ *www.gaviota-grupo.com* ⇨ *16 rooms* ⫶❍⫶ *Breakfast.*

NIGHTLIFE AND PERFORMING ARTS

The town band plays in Plaza Independencia every Sunday, and the adjacent Plaza Martí hosts weekend chess tournaments.

Casa de la Trova. This is the best spot to hear live music. It's open nightly until about 2 am. Listen for *el nengen* or *el kiribá,* two styles of music that predate the Cuban son. ☒ *Calle Antonio Maceo 149* ☒ *CUC$1.*

SPORTS AND THE OUTDOORS

HIKING

You can hike the mysterious El Yunque, an anvil-shape mountain covered in green jungle and mist.

RAFTING

Gaviota. Gaviota offers rafting trips along the Río Yumurí, 28 km (18 miles) east of town (seven hours, CUC$12); the Río Toa (five hours, CUC$8); and the Río Duaba (four hours, CUC$8), as well as area treks. ☒ *Hotel El Castillo, Calle Calixto García* ☎ *2164–2147.*

UNDERSTANDING CUBA

Cuban History

Vocabulary

CUBAN HISTORY

Ever since Christopher Columbus called the largest of the Antilles islands "the most beautiful thing human eyes ever beheld," Cuba has amassed a string of passionate admirers: In recent history Graham Greene, Ernest Hemingway, Ava Gardner, and Winston Churchill are just a few luminaries who've been enchanted by the "Pearl of the Antilles." But over the centuries Cuba has also amassed more than its fair share of foreign invaders and undergone a series of revolutions and counter-revolution, struggling through Spanish colonization and slavery, devastating wars for independence, and despotism.

Wars of Independence

For 400 years Spain ruthlessly exploited Cuba through trade monopolies, slavery, and political control. Although Cuba saw many skirmishes for greater freedom, including several slave rebellions, the struggle for independence marked its first major milestone in 1868 when landowner Carlos Manuel de Céspedes freed his slaves and declared his *Grito de Yara* (a Cuban Declaration of Independence), sparking the Ten Years' War—the first Cuban War of Independence, against the Spanish.

Two of Cuba's great military leaders, Dominican-born Máximo Gómez and Cuban mulatto Antonio Macéo, emerged during this conflict. Despite their initial military gains and glimpses of a potential rebel victory, the Spanish managed to maintain a deadlock that cost tens of thousands of lives on both sides. The movement collapsed, and an uneasy peace agreement was reached with the 1878 Pact of El Zanjón. The pact did little other than acknowledge that both sides were exhausted and their resources depleted. Its terms were unsatisfactory to many (including Macéo, who fought for another year and never did surrender). The island seemed far from achieving true local autonomy; and although steps were taken to abolish slavery, its complete abolition—a goal for many revolutionaries—had not been realized.

In 1895 a Second War of Independence was launched. Gómez and Máceo once again served as top generals. José Martí, a beloved poet and patriot, served as the movement's chief ideologue. Martí's battle did not last long—he was one of the first to fall in the fighting. But Cubans still remember Martí as a martyr famous for the motto: "To die for the fatherland is to live." Cuban nationalists continued to fight across the country, and by 1897 they controlled much of Cuba.

The country was becoming increasingly unstable with riots occurring in Havana. In 1898 the United States sent its battleship *Maine* to Havana in a show of military power meant to protect U.S. citizens in Cuba's capital city. However, while docked in Havana Harbor the ship exploded. The Spanish denied destroying the ship, but American public opinion turned sharply against Spain. "Remember the *Maine*, to hell with Spain!" became an American rallying cry, and on April 25, 1898, the United States declared war with Spain. American forces quickly wrested Guam, Puerto Rico, and the Philippines from Spanish control. Later that year the United States won Cuba. To many political strategists, this was no surprise. Starting as early as 1808, the United States had made a number of attempts to purchase Cuba in an effort to acquire "the Key to the New World," a prize of enormous strategic and economic value. The destruction of the *Maine* was considered by many Cuban nationalists to be the perfect pretext for U.S. military action against the Spanish, and an opportunity for imperial advancement. In 1899 the island became an independent republic under U.S. protection, effectively ending Spanish rule, but creating growing concerns among Cubans over U.S. occupation.

The Way to Revolution

The fears that the United States would subsume Cuba played out soon enough. The 1901 Platt Amendment, accepted grudgingly by Cuba, stipulated that the United States could intervene in Cuban affairs should the U.S. protectorate become unstable. The amendment also allowed the United States to buy or lease Cuban land for a military outpost (hence the Guantánamo Naval Base).

Within a few short years American interests owned large majority interests in Cuba's nickel and copper mines, the country's sugar and tobacco plantations, and its public services. The American mafia made Havana its headquarters, making the port a haven for gambling and prostitution. U.S. diplomats supported Cuban leaders, including Fulgencio Batista, who ruled Cuba with an iron grip. By the 1950s, average Cubans were in no better shape economically than many of their forebears had been at the beginning of the Wars of Independence. In 1952, when a charismatic lawyer named Fidel Castro entered the stage to run against Batista (in elections that Batista cancelled by way of a military coup recognized by the United States), Cubans were more than ready for change.

In 1953 Castro was captured after he led 119 rebels in a failed attack on the strategically important Moncada army barracks. Passionate and eloquent, Castro used his very public trial as a platform for his political aspirations and visions for reform. He famously declared "condemn me if you will, but history will absolve me," and his status as a national hero was firmly established. He was sentenced to 15 years' imprisonment but was exiled to Mexico by Batista after only three years.

In 1956, Castro led 81 rebels aboard the yacht *Granma* and landed in Eastern Cuba but was met by an ambush by Batista forces. It was a devastating defeat, but Castro reorganized and led an improbable guerrilla movement in the island's highland jungles. Chief among Fidel's aides was Ernesto "Che" Guevara, an Argentine-born physician, poet, and idealist. Obsessively opposed to capitalism, Che strove to create *El Hombre Nuevo* (the New Man), who would work for the common good rather than personal gain. To this day Che remains something of a Cuban saint among many Cubans (although many also view him unfavorably as a violent Marxist revolutionary), and his likeness is depicted in statues, propagandistic billboards, and on Cuban currency and T-shirts.

Castro's rebels took Havana in January 1959 and deposed the government of Fulgencio Batista. Castro's government was to become one of the world's last totalitarian, Soviet-style regimes. The Cuban people struggled under the yoke of a society significantly short on civil liberties and material wealth, but they took pride in their hard-won national independence as well as their educational, health care, and cultural successes.

American Conflict . . . and Reconciliation?

To protect its interests after Castro's Revolution, the United States compiled a troubled record vis-à-vis Cuba. In 1961 came an incident that Americans termed the Bay of Pigs invasion. (Cubans call the incident the Battle of Girón or *La Victoria*, "The Victory.") Counterrevolutionaries opposed to Castro's repressions banded together under the support of the CIA. But Castro got wind of the U.S.-Cuban plan, shored up his defenses, and stopped the invasion in its tracks.

Just 18 months later, in October 1962, American-Cuban tensions flared again. The Soviet Union, feeling endangered by American missiles in Europe and emboldened in the wake of the failed Bay of Pigs invasion, began to build up a military presence in Cuba. The United States felt threatened not only by the presence of Soviet missiles but by the existence of a Communist regime just 90 miles south of

Florida. A stand-off that became known as the Cuban Missile Crisis caused the very real fear of a proxy American-Soviet war in the Caribbean, and it was only averted at the 11th hour when Soviet leader Khruschev backed down.

Although Soviet and American missile strikes were avoided, a Cold War battle nearly as painful ensued and continued for decades—a clash that has included allegations of assassination attempts on Castro as well as a U.S. trade and tourism embargo enforced by half a dozen statutes.

However, U.S.-Cuba relations have slowly improved. In 2006 Fidel Castro, in flagging health, ceded power to his younger brother Raúl, who has issued modest liberal reforms, including expanded foreign investment and private enterprise opportunities for Cubans. And in December 2014 President Obama announced an historic accord between the two nations, further loosening restrictions on tourism and personal remittances to Cuba. In August 2015 Secretary of State John Kerry officially reopened the U.S. Embassy in Havana, paving the way for full diplomatic relations.

So how soon before you can order your Americano at a Cuban Starbucks? Currently, participation in the coming Cuba boom remains officially off limits to American firms. That, along with totally unfettered travel for U.S. citizens, would require a complete lifting of the embargo by Congress. Bills have been introduced, and the U.S. business sector has lobbied hard to lift economic restrictions. But Cuba is a contentious issue in Washington. During the clamor of the 2016 U.S. presidential election year, few expect much to be accomplished on this front for at least a year.

VOCABULARY

ENGLISH	SPANISH	PRONUNCIATION
BASIC PHRASES		
Yes/no	Sí/no	see/no
OK.	De acuerdo.	de a- **kwer**-doe
Please.	Por favor.	pore fah- **vore**
May I?	¿Me permite?	may pair- **mee**-tay
Thank you (very much).	(Muchas) gracias.	(**moo**-chas) **grah**-see-as
You're welcome.	Con mucho gusto.*	con **moo**-cho **goose**-toe
Excuse me.	Con permiso.	con pair- **mee**-so
Pardon me.	¿Perdón?	pair- **dohn**
Could you tell me?	¿Podría decirme?	po-dree-ah deh- **seer**-meh
I'm sorry.	Disculpe.	dee- **skool**-peh
Good morning!	¡Buenos días!	**bway**-nohs **dee**-ahs
Good afternoon!	¡Buenas tardes!	**bway**-nahs **tar**-dess
Good evening!	¡Buenas noches!	**bway**-nahs **no**-chess
Goodbye!	¡Adiós!/¡Hasta luego!	ah-dee- **ohss** / **ah**-stah-lwe-go
Mr./Mrs.	Señor/Señora	sen- **yor** /sen- **yohr**-ah
Miss	Señorita	sen-yo- **ree**-tah
Pleased to meet you.	Mucho gusto.	**moo**-cho **goose**-toe
How are you?	¿Cómo está usted?	**ko**-mo es- **tah** oo- **sted**
Very well, thank you.	Muy bien, gracias.	**moo**-ee bee- **en**, **grah**-see-as
And you?	¿Y usted?	ee oos- **ted**
DAYS OF THE WEEK		
Sunday	domingo	doe- **meen**-goh
Monday	lunes	**loo**-ness
Tuesday	martes	**mahr**-tess
Wednesday	miércoles	me- **air**-koh-less
Thursday	jueves	hoo- **ev**-ess
Friday	viernes	vee- **air**-ness
Saturday	sábado	**sah**-bah-doh

ENGLISH	SPANISH	PRONUNCIATION

USEFUL PHRASES

ENGLISH	SPANISH	PRONUNCIATION
Do you speak English?	¿Habla usted inglés?	**ah**-blah oos-**ted** in-**glehs**
I don't speak Spanish.	No hablo español.	no **ah**-bloh es-pahn-**yol**
I don't understand (you).	No entiendo.	no en-tee-**en**-doh
I understand (you).	Entiendo.	en-tee-**en**-doh
I don't know.	No sé.	no seh
I am American/ British.	Soy americano (americana) / inglés(a).	soy ah-meh-ree-**kah**-no (ah-meh-ree-**kah**-nah)/in-**glehs (ah)**
What's your name?	¿Cómo se llama usted?	koh-mo seh **yah**-mah **oos**-ted
My name is . . .	Me llamo . . .	may **yah**-moh
What time is it?	¿Qué hora es?	keh **o**-rah es
It is one, two, three . . . o'clock.	Es la una. . . . Son las dos, tres.	es la **oo**-nah/sohn lahs dohs, tress
How?	¿Cómo?	**koh**-mo
When?	¿Cuándo?	**kwahn**-doh
This/Next week	Esta semana / la semana que entra	**es**-teh seh-**mah**-nah/ lah seh-**mah**-nah keh **en**-trah
This/Next month	Este mes/el próximo mes	**es**-teh mehs/el **proke**-see-mo mehs
This/Next year	Este año/el año que viene	**es**-teh **ahn**-yo/el **ahn**-yo keh vee-**yen**-ay
Yesterday/today/ tomorrow	Ayer/hoy/mañana	ah-**yehr** /oy/ mahn-**yah**-nah
This morning/ afternoon	Esta mañana/tarde	**es**-tah mahn-**yah**-nah/ **tar**-deh
Tonight	Esta noche	**es**-tah **no**-cheh
What?	¿Qué?	keh
What is it?	¿Qué es esto?	keh es **es**-toh
Why?	¿Por qué?	pore **keh**
Who?	¿Quién?	kee-**yen**

ENGLISH	SPANISH	PRONUNCIATION
Where is . . . ?	¿Dónde está . . . ?	**dohn**-deh es- **tah**
the bus stop?	la parada del bus?	la pah- **rah**-dah del **boos**
the post office?	la oficina de correos?	la oh-fee- **see**-nah deh koh- **reh**-os
the museum?	el museo?	el moo- **seh**-oh
the hospital?	el hospital?	el ohss-pee- **tal**
the bathroom?	el baño?	el **bahn**-yoh
Here/there	Aquí/allá	ah- **key** /ah- **yah**
Open/closed	Abierto/cerrado	ah-bee- **er**-toh/ ser- **ah**-doh
Left/right	Izquierda/derecha	iss-key- **er**-dah/ dare- **eh**-chah
Straight ahead	Derecho	dare- **eh**-choh
Is it near/far?	¿Está cerca/lejos?	es- **tah sehr**-kah/ **leh**-hoss
I'd like . . .	Quisiera . . .	kee-see-ehr-ah
a room.	un cuarto/una habitación.	oon **kwahr**-toh/ **oo**-nah ah-bee-tah-see- **on**
the key.	la llave.	lah **yah**-veh
a newspaper.	un periódico.	oon pehr-ee- **oh**-dee-koh
a stamp.	una estampilla.	**oo**-nah es-stahm- **pee**-yah
I'd like to buy . . .	Quisiera comprar . . .	kee-see- **ehr**-ah kohm- **prahr**
a dictionary.	un diccionario.	oon deek-see-oh- **nah**-ree-oh
soap.	jabón.	hah- **bohn**
suntan lotion.	loción bronceadora.	loh-see- **ohn** brohn- seh-ah- **do**-rah
a map.	un mapa.	oon **mah**-pah
a magazine.	una revista.	**oon**-ah reh- **veess**-tah
a postcard.	una tarjeta postal.	**oon**-ah tar- **het**-ah post- **ahl**
How much is it?	¿Cuánto cuesta?	**kwahn**-toh **kwes**-tah

ENGLISH	SPANISH	PRONUNCIATION
Telephone	Teléfono	tel- **ef**-oh-no
Help!	¡Auxilio!	owk- **see**-lee-oh
	¡Ayuda!	ah- **yoo**-dah
	¡Socorro!	soh- **kohr**-roh
Fire!	¡Incendio!	en- **sen**-dee-oo
Caution!/Look out!	¡Cuidado!	kwee- **dah**-doh

SALUD (HEALTH)

I am ill.	Estoy enfermo(a).	es- **toy** en- **fehr**- moh(mah)
Please call a doctor.	Por favor llame a un médico.	pohr fah- **vor** ya-meh ah oon **med**-ee-koh
acetaminophen	acetaminofeno	a-say-ta- **mee**-no-fen-oh
ambulance	ambulancia	ahm-boo- **lahn**-see-a
antibiotic	antibiótico	ahn-tee-bee- **oh**-tee-co
aspirin	aspirina	ah-spi- **ree**-na
capsule	cápsula	**cahp**-soo-la
clinic	clínica	**clee**-nee-ca
cold	resfriado	rays-free- **ah**-do
cough	tos	toess
diarrhea	diarrea	dee-ah- **ray**-a
fever	fiebre	fee- **ay**-bray
flu	gripe	**gree**-pay
headache	dolor de cabeza	doh- **lor** day cah- **bay**-sa
hospital	hospital	oh-spee- **tahl**
medication	medicamento	meh-dee-cah- **men**-to
pain	dolor	doh- **lor**
pharmacy	farmacia	fahr- **mah**-see-a
physician	médico	**meh**-dee-co
prescription	receta	ray- **say**-ta
stomachache	dolor de estómago	doh- **lor** day eh- **sto**-mah-go

TRAVEL SMART
CUBA

GETTING HERE AND AROUND

Most travelers fly to Havana, while others arrive on charter flights to a handful of smaller airports near the all-inclusive resorts at Varadero or the provincial cities of Santiago de Cuba, Cayo Coco, Holguín, Santa Clara, Camagüey, Cienfuegos, or Cayo Largo del Sur. Getting around the island by bus for tourists is comfortable, reliable, generally clean, and efficient with Víazul. A car is an appealing option for those seeking more freedom, although the substandard road conditions and unusual obstacles like horse-drawn carriages deter many from this option.

▌AIR TRAVEL

Several international airlines now serve Cuba, although air travel to the island is still dominated by charter flights. Most charters to Cuba originate in Canada, Mexico, and Europe and are part of package deals that include stays in one of Cuba's burgeoning number of all-inclusive resorts.

Although there's still no regular commercial service from the United States to Cuba (Americans flouting the embargo often fly to the island from elsewhere in the Caribbean or from Canada, Mexico, or Central America), direct charter flights operate between the two nations. ⇨ *See box on travel restrictions for U.S. citizens.*

Before you leave Cuba, you'll need to pay an airport departure tax of CUC$2–in cash. Cuba is slowly moving to a system of bundling the tax into the airfare, so confirm with your airline or tour operator if this requirement persists when you visit.

Airlines and Airports Airline and Airport Links.com. ⊕ *www.airlineandairportlinks.com.*

Airline-Security Issues Transportation Security Administration. ⊕ *www.tsa.gov.*

FLIGHTS

Most visitors to Cuba arrive on charter flights, usually in conjunction with a package tour. Flights from the United States are filled with U.S. citizens who are visiting relatives in Cuba and those few other travelers who have authorization to travel there. Charters from Canada and elsewhere are filled with vacationers.

Flight times. Approximate non-stop flight times to Havana are: New York, 3 hours; Miami, 1 hour; Toronto, 3 ½ hours; Mexico City, 2¾ hours; Nassau, Bahamas, 1 hour.

FROM THE UNITED STATES

Several U.S.-based commercial airlines have expressed interest in serving Cuba with regularly scheduled commercial flights. All await the full lifting of the embargo and the eventual negotiation of landing rights with the Cuban government. Neither is expected to be a quick process. For now, booking regularly scheduled flights to Cuba remains in a state of flux for Americans. A few flight search engines are beginning to hack itineraries together via connecting flights in Mexico and Canada. In some cases, results are presented as information only, and you cannot complete the booking without going through the airline itself. Airline websites themselves also run the spectrum on what they permit: Some do allow you to purchase a U.S.–Cuba flight with third-country connections; others still caution you that you cannot, but may allow you to purchase the tickets separately.

Charter flights. The U.S.-based airlines that do fly to Cuba—American, Delta, United, JetBlue, and Sun Country—have been doing so for years, only under the guise of what are called Special Authority Charters. These are open solely to U.S. citizens approved for travel to Cuba, and may not be booked with the airline directly.

CLOSE UP

Travel Restrictions for U.S. Citizens

The August 2015 reopening of the U.S. Embassy in Havana brought hope that Cuba could once again be fully accessible to U.S. visitors and that the half-century trade embargo against the island might be lifted. Indeed, some longtime travel restrictions have been eased , with "some" being the operative term. At this writing, the embargo remains in place for the foreseeable future. Lifting it fully would require an act of Congress, no small feat for a contentious issue in today's politically charged U.S. capital. Until such time Americans still face legal constraints for travel to Cuba.

The U.S. Department of the Treasury's Office of Foreign Assets Control (OFAC) oversees rules for Cuba visits by Americans. Technically, it's not illegal for Americans to travel to Cuba; what *is* restricted is spending money in the country, hence the Treasury Department's involvement in the matter. (Proving you went to Cuba and spent no money would be a nearly insurmountable task.) Presently, OFAC authorizes several categories of travel to Cuba, including family visits, humanitarian missions, journalism, religious activities, educational activities, government business, athletic competitions, artistic performances, and professional research. OFAC no longer issues specific licenses for each category of travel, but rather one general license, so long as the reason for your visit falls within the approved categories. There's a certain degree of being on the honor system when making such trips, but your motives are always subject to scrutiny when you return home.

Note that routine, independent tourism is not among the approved reasons for travel to Cuba—yet.

OFAC does authorize guided people-to-people tours whose focus is cultural exchange. You will not get to sunbathe on the island's famed beaches; you will meet Cubans working in art, education, and agriculture. Such excursions win accolades among visitors for providing a deeper insight into Cuba than a stay at a beach resort could ever offer. ⇨ *See Tour Operators for more information.*

All the above aside, many U.S. citizens do visit Cuba on their own by flying through third countries: Canada, Mexico, and the Bahamas are the most common gateways, with Costa Rica, Panama, El Salvador, and Jamaica next. Third-country tour operators and travel agents arrange such trips. Such travelers enter Cuba on tourist cards, which they purchase from their airline or travel agent. ⚠ **Cuban officials stamp all passports upon entry and exit. There is no concealing any travel to the country.** Although few people have been prosecuted for violating the restrictions, there are stiff penalties (up to $250,000) on the books for unauthorized travel to Cuba.

Information **U.S. Department of the Treasury, Office of Foreign Assets Control** (*OFAC*). ☎ *202/622–2480 in Washington* ⊕ *www.treas.gov/ofac.* **U.S. State Department.** ⊕ *travel.state.gov.*

Marazul Tours—which pioneered charters between the United States and Cuba—offers flights from Miami to Havana, Camagüey, Santa Clara, and Santiago de Cuba. Cuba Travel Services books weekly Tuesday flights from New York (JFK) to Havana.

FROM OUTSIDE THE UNITED STATES

Cubana (officially Cubana de Aviación), Cuba's national carrier, flies international routes on mostly Russian-built planes, with a few European Airbus and ATR aircraft in the mix. Service is adequate but somewhat below North American and European standards. Cubana offers nonstop service between Havana and Toronto and Montréal, Canada; and Cancún and Mexico City, Mexico. Cubana also connects various Canadian cities with nonstop flights to Varadero, Holguín, Cienfuegos, Santiago de Cuba, Camagüey, Santa Clara, Cayo Coco, and Cayo Largo.

Several foreign carriers also serve Cuba. Air Canada flies from Toronto to Havana, as well as connecting various Canadian cities with nonstop flights to Varadero, Holguín, Santa Clara, Cayo Coco, and Cayo Largo. Canadian airline WestJet flies nonstop from several Canadian cities to Varadero, Holguín, Santa Clara, and Cayo Coco. AeroMéxico connects U.S. gateways to Havana via Mexico City or Cancún. Bahamasair connects to Havana via its hub in Nassau; Cayman Airways does the same through its hub in Grand Cayman.

Charter flights. Air Transat offers flights and packages from Montréal and Toronto to Varadero, Cayo Largo, Santa Clara, and Holguín. It also flies from Vancouver, Edmonton, and Calgary to Varadero. Canada-based Sell Off Vacations books charter flights from several Canadian cities to Varadero.

International Airline Contacts AeroMéxico. 🕾 7203-9796 in Cuba, 800/237-6639 in North America ⊕ www.aeromexico.com. **Air Canada.** 🕾 7836-3226 in Cuba, 888/247-2262 in North America ⊕ www.aircanada.com. **Avianca.** 🕾 7833-3114 in Cuba, 800/284-2622 in North America ⊕ www.avianca.com. **Bahamasair.** 🕾 7649-7311 in Cuba, 800/222-4262 in North America ⊕ www.bahamasair.com. **Cayman Airways.** 🕾 7204-2331 in Cuba, 800/422-9626 in North America ⊕ www.caymanairways.com. **Copa.** 🕾 7204-1111 in Cuba, 800/359-2672 in North America ⊕ www.copaair.com. **Cubana.** 🕾 7834-4446, 866/428-2262 in Canada ⊕ www.cubana.cu. **WestJet.** 🕾 888/937-8538 in North America ⊕ www.westjet.com.

Charter Flights Contacts Air Transat. 🕾 866/847-1112 ⊕ www.airtransat.com. **Cuba Travel Services.** ✉ 112 W. 34th St., Suite 17018, New York 🕾 800/963-2822 ⊕ www.cubatravelservices.com. **Marazul Tours.** ✉ 771 N.W. 37th Ave. 🕾 800/993-9667 ⊕ www.marazul.com. **Sell Off Vacations.** 🕾 877/735-5633 ⊕ www.selloffvacations.com.

DOMESTIC FLIGHTS

Flying on regional airlines in Cuba is extremely affordable by North American and European standards and provides the fastest and most comfortable way to get around. Routes connect most major cities in the country. Cubana, the national carrier, offers daily service from Havana to several destinations around Cuba. You can buy tickets at agencies or local airport representatives in major cities. Domestic plane tickets are never refundable, no matter what the reason. If you miss your flight or your plans change, you're out the money and just buy a new ticket. ⚠ Note that it's illegal for U.S. citizens to fly on Cubana, as it constitutes a cash payment to the Cuban government—a trade-embargo no-no.

AIRPORTS

Cuba's major international airport is Havana's Aeropuerto Internacional José Martí, 15 km (9 miles) south of the city. It has four terminals: Terminal 1, for domestic flights; Terminal 2, for U.S. charter flights; Terminal 3, for other international flights; and Terminal 5, for some flights of domestic airline Aero Caribbean. (There is no Terminal 4.) Buses connect the four terminals.

Cuba has eight other international airports—in Varadero, Cayo Largo, Cienfuegos, Cayo Coco, Camagüey, Holguín, Santa Clara, and Santiago de Cuba—and several smaller, regional airstrips. If you book a resort package in Varadero, Guardalavaca, or the Cayos, you'll fly directly to those places and never pass through Havana.

Airport Information **Aeropuerto Internacional Abel Santamaría** (*SNU*). ✉ *Carretera Malezas, Km 11, Santa Clara* ☎ *4222-7525*. **Aeropuerto Internacional Antonio Maceo** (*SCU*). ✉ *Carretera Ciudamar, Km 3½, Santiago de Cuba* ☎ *2269-1053*. **Aeropuerto Internacional Frank País** (*HOG*). ✉ *Carretera Vía Bayamo, Km 12, Holguín* ☎ *2446-2512*. **Aeropuerto Internacional Ignacio Agramonte** (*CMW*). ✉ *Avenida Finlay, Km 7½, Camagüey* ☎ *3226-1010*. **Aeropuerto Internacional Jaime González** (*CFG*). ✉ *Carretera Caonao, Km 7½, Cienfuegos* ☎ *4355-1328*. **Aeropuerto Internacional Jardines del Rey** (*CCC*). ✉ *Carretera Cayo Coco, Cayo Coco* ☎ *3330-9161*. **Aeropuerto Internacional José Martí** (*HAV*). ✉ *Avenida Nguyen Van Troi al final, Havana* ☎ *7275-1200*. **Aeropuerto Internacional Juan Gualberto Gómez** (*VRA*). ✉ *Avenida Mártires de Barbados, Varadero* ☎ *4524-7015*. **Aeropuerto Internacional Juan Vitalio Acuña** (*CYO*). ✉ *Cayo Largo del Sur, Km 5, Cayo Largo* ☎ *4524-8207*.

CUSTOMS AND DUTIES

Expect X-ray machines and a thorough search by customs officials upon your arrival. You may enter Cuba with three bottles of wine or liquor, a carton of cigarettes *or* 50 cigars, gifts totaling no more than $100 in value, and prescription medicines (for personal consumption) either in their original bottles or in other bottles accompanied by a doctor's prescription. A laptop computer, tablet, mobile phone, and camera are also permitted as personal effects. Be sure to declare valuable items (such as a laptop) upon entering Cuba.

Firearms and illicit drugs aren't allowed—pretty standard anywhere—and Cuban authorities may confiscate written or visual material viewed either as "pornographic" or "counter-revolutionary."

Upon departure from Cuba, you are allowed to export up to 50 cigars and five bottles of liquor. Cuban officials require you to show store receipts. U.S. Customs is far less generous, however, allowing authorized travelers to Cuba the import of just a combined $100 of alcohol and/or tobacco products of Cuban origin for personal use only; with quality Cuban cigars selling for $25 each, that $100 does not go far.

Cuban Information **Cuban Customs** (*Aduana de Cuba*). ☎ *7883-8282* ⊕ *www.aduana.co.cu*.

U.S. Information **U.S. Customs and Border Protection** (*CBP*). ⊕ *www.cbp.gov*.

GROUND TRANSPORTATION

Visitors arriving on an all-inclusive package will be picked up at the airport and shuttled to their respective hotel. Independent travelers flying into Havana can take one of the taxis lined up outside each terminal. The 30-minute trip into town costs CUC$25; Vedado and Miramar districts are slightly more expensive. While there is a public bus to Havana from Terminal 1 (the domestic terminal), fares must be paid in local CUP; even if you succeed at boarding, you're in for a slow and crowded trip, especially if you're carrying bags. Some hotels offer airport transfers, so do inquire in advance.

▌ BUS TRAVEL

For overland travel, your best bet is the tourist bus company Víazul, which has comfortable, air-conditioned coaches that depart fairly punctually and connect all major cities. (The biggest visitors' complaint about Víazul is the icy air-conditioning. You'll appreciate a jacket and long trousers.) Víazul offers daily service between Havana and Varadero,

Viñales, Trinidad, Holguín, and Santiago de Cuba, plus daily service between Varadero and Trinidad and between Trinidad and Santiago de Cuba. Fares range from CUC$10 (Havana–Varadero) to CUC$51 (Havana–Santiago). Note that most cities have two types of terminals: the *terminal de omnibus interprovincial* serves long-distance buses; the *terminal de omnibus intermunicipal* serves buses to nearby towns and beaches.

Outside the Víazul orbit, Cubans contend with an unreliable bus system—one with crowded, badly maintained vehicles and slow service. (The 2000 Cuban film *Lista de Espera,* or "The Waiting List," detailed the trials and tribulations of local bus travel and teetered tantalizingly close to commentary on the problems with Cuban socialism.) Even long-distance buses, called *especiales,* are well below North American and European standards.

In most of the country, the only way to reserve seats is to buy your ticket in person at the bus station. In Havana, you can also purchase tickets at Infotur offices and at a Víazul counter in the arrivals area of Terminal 3 at Havana's Aeropuerto Internacional José Martí, though the company does not serve the airport and you'll still need to take a taxi to the bus terminal in town. Tickets should be purchased several days ahead of time in high season; for much of the year, however, tickets are available only on the day you plan to depart or the day before.

Though public buses charge Cubans in CUP pesos, tourists tend to pay much inflated prices in CUC pesos. Víazul accepts credit cards.

Pickpocketing and groping are common on Havana's city buses. Avoid them and take a taxi instead.

Contacts Víazul. ☎ 7883–6092 ⊕ www.viazul. com.

▌ CAR TRAVEL

Road conditions are quite different in Cuba from those in North America. Vehicles regularly share the road with horse-drawn carriages, bicycles, tractors, and pedestrians. Most highways lack proper lighting at night. While your rental vehicle will be modern and spiffy, most of Cuba's colorful 1950s cars lack turn signals, and you can rarely be sure of drivers' intentions. Indeed, the potential for accidents should lead you to balance your options.

GASOLINE

While Cuba's vintage 1950s cars still use leaded gas, your new rental vehicle cannot. Gas prices are high: A liter costs about CUC$1.10 (translating to roughly US$4.15 a gallon). Make sure you fill up with high-octane *especial.* State-run Cupet-Cimex and Oro Negro stations are spread out along major routes; many are open 24 hours a day. Nonetheless, it's best to start a long journey with a full tank. These stations, which accept payment only in CUC, also sell snacks and beverages.

PARKING

Parking is easy in most Cuban cities outside Havana. On-street spaces are plentiful, and many hotels have large lots. Never leave valuables unattended in your car, and don't leave a car on an unguarded street overnight.

RENTAL CARS

Americans have historically not rented cars in Cuba. It's an expensive proposition: rates start at CUC$60 per day for a basic economy car and run up to CUC$225 for a van. Further, if your credit cards is issued by a U.S. bank and is still restricted for use, you'll need to leave a hefty security deposit—in cash. With the credit-card issue slowly being resolved, that situation is expected to change.

The embargo has prevented U.S. firms from setting up shop here—so you won't see an Avis or Hertz. Instead, rentals are handled by Transtur, a state-owned agency. A number of brand names under the Transtur umbrella (Cubacar, Havanautos, Micar, Rex, Transautos, Vía) still appear on signs; these are being phased out. Vehicles are all Japanese or Korean models.

If you're traveling during a holiday period, make sure that a confirmed reservation guarantees you a car. Unfortunately, Transtur's online reservation system doesn't always hold up and you may arrive to find you have no vehicle. Before setting out, check the car carefully for defects, and make sure your car has a jack and spare tire.

You must be 21 years old and have a valid national driver's license or an international driver's license to rent an automobile.

Contacts Transtur. ☎ 7214–0090 ⊕ www. transturcarrental.com.

RENTAL CAR INSURANCE
Insurance adds greatly to cost of renting a vehicle. Transtur's charges begin at CUC$15 per day for an economy vehicle, and deductibles are high, running CUC$200–CUC$1,000. Note that insurance charges must be paid separately and in cash. Check if your own auto insurance policy or credit card will cover you while driving in Cuba. If you are a U.S. citizen, they likely do not— yet.

ROADSIDE EMERGENCIES
Roadside assistance for rental vehicles is handled through Transtur; your rental office will provide you with contact numbers tailored to where you'll be driving.

ROAD CONDITIONS
The good news is that most main roads in Cuba are well-maintained and traffic is very light once you're out of the cities. The bad news is that signage is very poor and it's easy to get lost, so get good road maps. The Havana metro area has the densest concentration of freeways, with six *autopistas* fanning out from the Havana Ring Road (*Primer Anillo*). The country's main artery, the six-lane Autopista Nacional, runs from Havana to just east of Sancti Spíritus before hitting the two-lane Carretera Central, which continues east. The highway expands to four lanes between Santiago and Guantánamo. The Autopista Nacional also runs westward from Havana to Pinar del Río. All Cuban highways are free except for the north coast's tolled Matanzas–Varadero Expressway, which costs CUC$2. In general, road conditions decline the farther east you travel, with rural byways in Eastern Cuba turning downright quaint and potholed. Signage becomes annoyingly sparse once you get off major highways anywhere in Cuba. Wherever you are, remember the major place-name spelling difference between English and Spanish: *LA HABANA* directs you to Havana.

RULES OF THE ROAD
Obey traffic laws religiously. Fines are high, transit police are ubiquitous and efficient, and your car's maroon license plates target it as a rental vehicle. Any fines you incur for traffic violations will be deducted from your rental car deposit. Driving is on the right. Speed limits are posted and range from 100 kph (60 mph) on freeways, to 90 kph (54 mph) on other highways, to 60 kph (30 mph) on rural roads, to 50 kph (30 mph) in urban areas, to 40 kph (25 mph) in school zones. Seatbelt use is mandatory. Children under two must be seated in car seats, and children under 12 may not sit in the front seat. Cell phone use and texting while driving are not allowed. Drivers are prohibited from having any alcoholic beverages before getting behind the wheel. The law is absolute; the maximum permitted blood-alcohol level is 0.0%.

▌ CRUISE-SHIP TRAVEL

Cuba's cruise season runs November through April. At this writing, Carnival (under its new Fathom brand) and Haimark Line have announced plans for Cuba cruises with cultural exchange itineraries, a category of travel permitted by the U.S. government for its citizens.

Cruise Lines **Cuba Cruise.** ☎ *855/364–4999* ⊕ *www.yourcubacruise.com.* **Fathom.** ☎ *855/932-8466* ⊕ *www.fathom.org.* **Haimark Line.** ☎ *855/424-6275* ⊕ *www.haimarkline.com.* **Star Clippers.** ☎ *800/442-0551* ⊕ *www.starclippers.co.uk.* **Voyages of Discovery.** ☎ *800/510-9061* ⊕ *www.voyagesofdiscovery.com.*

▌FERRY TRAVEL

At this writing, passenger ferry service between the United States and Cuba is being reestablished for the first time since the 1950s. One-way travel time between Miami and the island is expected to be around nine hours with an estimated fare of $350 roundtrip. Future departures from other ports in South Florida will be available, too. Passage is limited to those U.S. citizens authorized to travel to Cuba. Vehicular traffic is not yet allowed.

Ferries **Baja Ferries USA.** ⊕ *enbajaferries.com.mx.* **Cuba Ferry International.** ⊕ *www.havanaferrypartners.com.* **United Caribbean Lines.** ⊕ *www.unitedcaribbeanlines.com.*

▌TAXI TRAVEL

Modern, well-maintained tourist taxis with CUC meters congregate in front of hotels, transportation hubs, and major sights. Rates are affordable by North American and European standards. Metered cabs from the companies Havanatur, Cubataxi, and Taxi OK charge about CUC$5 for every 10 km (6 miles) traveled. Smaller yellow cabs that park at public areas in Havana and other large cities charge fares in convertible pesos, about CUC$3 for a 10 km (6 mile) trip. Havana's and Varadero's cute little *cocotaxis*—three-wheeled motorcycles with round, yellow fiberglass shells—charge a bit more than yellow cabs but with an alarmingly high accident rate, we sadvise against using them. Unmetered *taxis particulares* (private cabs) aren't supposed to pick up tourists, but they will, and they tend to be inexpensive—determine the fare before you get in. Photogenic *taxis colectivos,* most of which are vintage American cars, aren't permitted to transport tourists, but they often will. The fare for these trips is officially CUC$0.50.

Contact **Cubataxi.** ☎ *7855-5555.*

▌TRAIN TRAVEL

Ferrocarriles de Cuba operates the Caribbean's only comprehensive passenger-rail system, even if cutbacks have exacted a toll on services in recent years. (An influx of Chinese capital and locomotives is expected to reverse the decline in the near future.) Rail service spans the length of the island, with one line offering frequent service going east Havana–Santa Clara–Ciego de Ávila–Camagüey–Santiago, and another running west Havana–Pinar del Río a few days a week. Because they're the island's cheapest form of transportation, trains are popular with Cubans. Foreigners, however, pay inflated, though still reasonable, fares; the 15-hour, overnight Havana–Santiago train, for example, costs CUC$60 one-way. Tickets are sold by the eLadis travel agency inside most stations; it's in a separate building behind Havana's Estación Central. The railroad operates no website.

Contacts **Ferrocarriles de Cuba.** ✉ *Behind Estación Central, Havana* ☎ *7861-8540.*

ESSENTIALS

▌ACCOMMODATIONS

Accommodations include large, modern hotels; smaller, restored colonial classics; and rooms in *casas particulares* (private homes). All hotels belong to one of five state-owned chains: Cubanacán, Gaviota, Gran Caribe, Habaguanex, or Islazul. To improve its tourist infrastructure, the government has entered into joint ventures with foreign hoteliers such as Spain's Meliá and Canada's Blau; American chains such as Hilton, Marriott, and Sheraton have yet to set up shop here. To get the best deal, book your room in advance.

CASAS PARTICULARES

Since 1996, Cubans have been allowed to rent out rooms to visitors. Homes with a license to rent will have a blue triangle on their front door or window. Havana now has hundreds of these *casas particulares*, and other towns frequented by foreigners have at least a few. The rates are excellent (CUC$25–CUC$50 daily, payable in CUC cash), and the accommodations are often charming. Some *casas particulares* are mansions that may have passed their heyday but still have the power to impress; most offer such amenities as private baths and air-conditioning. A number of them are also licensed to serve meals to guests, and Cuban home cooking often puts the institutional buffets at the big hotels to shame.

Quality varies widely from one casa to the next. Some owners will welcome you as one of the family; others will be strictly businesslike in their dealings with you. It is difficult to book reservations for private homes through a tour operator, but the vacation rental site Airbnb now lists hundreds of properties, with more listings coming on all the time. A good strategy is to book your first two nights at a tourist hotel, and then investigate nearby *casas particulares*. Many atmospheric buildings in Habana Vieja have rooms for rent in them—look for the blue triangles and other signs. Casa owners also tend to offer their rooms at city's bus terminals. Shop around, and don't be shy, ask to see the rooms before booking. Just beware of recommendations from street hustlers; their desire to take you to a casa particular is based only on the commission they get, which will invariably affect the rate you pay.

Contacts Airbnb. ⊕ *www.airbnb.com.*

HOTELS

Construction of new hotels took off with the opening of tourism in the 1990s. It continued in fits and spurts, depending on the state of the world economy, but, these days, expansion is going gangbusters. The island has some 61,000 rooms and counting. All new hotels and resorts are up to North American and European standards, and many of the older ones have undergone renovations. Still others exude what could politely be called "faded elegance"—you may be charmed, or not—and some have simply faded. Most new accommodations are in massive beach resorts whose room count is frequently measured in the mid-three figures; Cuba's first four-figure hotel, a 1,100-room beachside resort in Cayo Coco, opened in 2015. These resorts offer an array of services—from day tours to nightly entertainment and children's programs—and include most if not all food and drink in the room rates. Urban hotels are still lacking in number: Havana, a capital of more than 2 million people, could stand more quality lodging than it has, and smaller cities may have only a couple of decent hotels each. Rooms in all hotels invariably have air-conditioning and cable TV; many also have refrigerators and other modern conveniences.

■ ADDRESSES

Addresses are frequently cited as street names with numbers and/or locations, as in: "Calle Concordia, e/Calle Gervasio y Calle Escobar" or "Calle de los Oficios 53, esquina de Obrapía." It's helpful to know the following terms and abbreviations: "e/" is *entre* (between); *esquina de* (sometimes seen as "esq. de") is "corner of"; and *y* is "and." Some streets have pre- and postrevolutionary names; both are often cited on local maps and on maps and in text throughout this guide.

■ COMMUNICATIONS

INTERNET

Cuba remains largely off the grid, thanks to scarce, sluggish, expensive Internet connectivity. ETECSA, the government telecommunications monopoly, operates a few cybercafés in Cuba's more populated areas. These operate under various names (Telepunto, Minipunto, or Centro Multiservicios) and there are less than 200 in the entire country. (Havana has only a dozen outlets.) You purchase a scratch card with PIN number at a cost of CUC$6 per hour of access—you must show a photo ID to buy the card—and can use the remaining balance at other branches. Waits for a computer can be long. Large hotels offer Internet access to guests, usually in the form of a public terminal or two, never free and always slow. Only a tiny number of hotels in Havana and Varadero offer Wi-Fi, and it's neither free nor speedy. ETECSA has begun setting up a few Wi-Fi hotspots around the country for the standard CUC$6 hourly charge. Many websites are blocked. In theory, social-networking sites such as Facebook and Twitter are permitted, as are foreign news media such as the *New York Times* and *Miami Herald,* but bandwidth is so lethargic the pages will likely never appear. If you can tap in, plan on checking email and little else.

PHONES

Cuban phone service has been improving, due to partial privatization and joint ventures with foreign investors. Cuba has been upgrading its phone system over the last few years to a nationwide system of eight-digit phone numbers that does away with area codes. You'll still see area codes on signs, stationery, and business cards; simply scrunch everything together to get the current number (old area code + old phone number = 8 digits total). Though Cuban homeowners suffer a phone shortage, hotels and other tourist enterprises do have the newest equipment. The blue public phones operated by the government-run ETECSA are cost-effective, abundant, and allow you to dial direct to anywhere in the world. Most hotels offer fax service to guests and, sometimes, non-guests, though you can send faxes for less from the local post office. Thanks to Raúl Castro's attempts at reform, private individuals may now purchase cell phones, a boon for those few who can actually afford them.

CALLING CUBA

Cuba's country code is 53, and there's direct-dial service to the country from North America and Europe. The quality of the connection can leave much to be desired. All eight-digit mobile numbers begin with a 5.

CALLING WITHIN CUBA

To make a call within Cuba, dial the eight-digit number.

CALLING OUTSIDE CUBA

All major hotels offer international phone service at very high rates—the more expensive the hotel, the higher the phone rates—so be sure to check the price beforehand. It's considerably cheaper to dial direct from an ETECSA pay phone. To make an international call, dial 00 plus the country code, area code, and number. The country code for the United States and Canada is 1.

CALLING CARDS

You can buy cards in denominations CUC$5, CUC$10, or CUC$15 at most hotels, or centrally located *telecorreos* and *centros de llamadas internacionales*. Many phone centers are open 24 hours a day. All ETECSA pay phones accept cards.

MOBILE PHONES

ETECSA is also Cuba's wireless provider, alternately referred to as Cubacel. The mobile network extends to all but the most remote areas of the island and allows for the use of AMPS cell phones (American norm).

You may be able to purchase a new SIM card from ETECSA to use your own wireless phone in Cuba (assuming your phone is unlocked and uses GSM-900), or you can rent one of theirs—an expensive proposition. The temporary line can be set up only at the ETECSA/Cubacel office in the arrivals area of Terminal 3 at Havana's Aeropuerto Internacional José Martí. Security deposits run several hundred dollars (depending on the length of usage), and rental fees are about CUC$6 a day for the equipment plus a daily CUC$3 for the line. Expect to pay CUC$0.40–0.60 cents per minute for a call within Cuba and CUC$2.45 per minute to the United States. A hefty per-minute airtime fee is charged, in addition to long-distance or international fees. Several car-rental agencies include cell phones with the rental of standard or luxury vehicles.

Cuba has no roaming agreements yet with wireless carriers in the United States. If you have an account with a non-U.S. company, you may be able to use your own phone while traveling in Cuba. Roaming fees can be steep, however: CUC$1 a minute is average. You normally pay the toll charges for incoming calls. It's almost always cheaper to send a text message than to make a call, because text messages have a very low set fee.

Contacts ETECSA/Cubacel. ⊠ *Calle 28, No. 510, e/Calle 5 y Calle 7, Havana* ☎ *5264-2266*

⊕ *www.etecsa.cu.* **Mobal.** ☎ *888/888–9162* ⊕ *www.mobalrental.com.*

∎ DINING OUT

Decades of socialism, isolation, and hard economic times have taken their toll, often leaving Cuban food (and service in restaurants) uninspired and uninspiring. Many of the country's best chefs and restaurateurs followed their upper- and middle-class clients into exile after the Revolution, and even local *comida criolla* (Creole cuisine) isn't as good as the Cuban food served in the exile communities of Miami, New York, or Puerto Rico.

As the economy has become increasingly reliant on tourism, the government has made efforts to improve the quality of both the service and the food in state-run restaurants. Foreign management of hotels and their restaurants, through joint ventures with the Cuban government, is also helping matters.

Most hotel restaurants serve buffet-style breakfasts from 7 am to 10 am and dinners from 7 pm to 10 pm. Good, interesting meals—sometimes only dinner—are served in *paladares*, tiny eateries in private homes that are allowed a maximum of only 12 seats and must be staffed by family members. (It's the dining equivalent to a *casa particular*.) Although there are restrictions on what can be served (seafood, for example, is officially forbidden at *paladares*), the food is usually fresh and relatively inexpensive; a full meal with generous portions can cost as little as CUC$8. Unfortunately, the government has closed many *paladares* in recent years, so most towns have only two or three; some have none at all. There are also a number of illegal *paladares*, toward which *jineteros* (street hustlers) will likely try to steer you. Although the food in these establishments can be good, in general you're better off avoiding such recommendations.

CUBAN CUISINE

Cuban cuisine is a fusion of African, Spanish, and Caribbean fare, and generally only very lightly spiced. The best criollo fare can actually be found at the many *paladares* that have sprouted up throughout the country. Dining in what is literally somebody's home will give you the most authentic experience. Small private restaurants are also increasingly popular among locals. Typical criollo fare includes rice and beans, pork, beef or fish with potatoes, plantains and a simple lettuce and tomato salad.

PAYING

Convertible pesos (CUC) are almost always required in places frequented by tourists. Local establishments generally take only local pesos. Credit cards are accepted at government establishments but not in *paladares*.

RESERVATIONS AND DRESS

Cuban meals are relaxed affairs, and reservations are rarely required. Note that some restaurants frown on shorts for both men and women; beach attire is usually acceptable only on the beach.

WINES, BEER, AND SPIRITS

Cuba's three signature rum libations—the mojito, the daiquiri, and the Cuba Libre (referred to in North America as a rum and coke)—appear on the drinks menu at every tourist joint. A "rum and coke" is actually a "rum and cola" here, as Coca-Cola is not available anywhere in Cuba, thanks to the embargo. Cristal, Bucanero, and Mayabe are the most widely available beers. Don't count on finding any imported brands at local watering holes. Wines are a hit and miss—maybe a Chilean or Argentine vintage or two—and rare is the restaurant that boasts an extensive wine menu.

▌ ELECTRICITY

Cuba uses both the North American system of 110 volts, 60 cycles, and the 220-volt European system. North American–style plugs are the norm here. If your appliances are dual-voltage (as many laptop computers are), you'll need only an adapter. However, if they're strictly 110 volts, as most appliances sold in North America are, plugging them into a 220-volt outlet will destroy them. Outlets are often marked either 110 or 220, but if they aren't, be sure to ask what the voltage is before plugging in an appliance. Consider buying a universal adapter; Swiss Army's adapters have several types of plugs in one handy unit.

Although conditions are improving, blackouts are still an occasional reality. Most hotels have a backup power system, but these are designed to keep electricity flowing only to lights in lounges and hallways and to emergency lamps in guest rooms.

▌ EMERGENCIES

Dial 106 nationwide for emergencies (police, ambulance, and fire), although you will not necessarily get an English-speaking operator on the other end. The police are generally helpful in emergencies.

The United States reopened its embassy in Havana in 2015, which meand that officials will respond to emergencies involving U.S. citizens, whether or not they have legally traveled to Cuba.

All but the smallest hotels have their own nurses and doctors, who have access to medicines you won't find in most pharmacies or hospitals. Travelers who stay in *casas particulares* (private houses with rooms to rent) can head for 24-hour *clínicas internacionales* (international clinics), which have well-stocked pharmacies, or contact Asistur, which specializes in helping tourists in trouble. Its staff can handle anything from insurance claims and lost luggage to repatriation of the deceased. A visit with a doctor at a clinic costs about CUC$25; house calls can sometimes be made for an extra CUC$25. Traveler's insurance is available through Asistur, which can also help you with sorting out various medical, financial, legal, and other problems.

The Clínica Central Cira García, just across the Río Almendares and in a district near Miramar, is dedicated to medical care for foreigners. Considered the best hospital in Havana, the clinic handles emergencies expertly and pleasantly and expects payment in convertible pesos (CUC). Servimed Internacional, part of the Clínica Cira García, is the pharmacy to use; it's open 24 hours a day.

Contacts Asistur. ⊠ *Paseo Martí/Prado 212* ☎ *7866–4499* ⊕ *www.asistur.cu.* **Clínica Central Cira García.** ⊠ *Calle 20, No. 4101, Playa* ☎ *7204–2811* ⊕ *www.cirag.cu.* **United States Embassy.** ☎ *7839–4100 24 hours* ⊕ *havana.usembassy.gov.*

▌ HEALTH

All visitors are required to demonstrate health-insurance coverage upon arrival in Cuba. Since U.S. policies are not valid here, American visitors cannot meet this requirement and are obliged to buy a temporary policy for their trip's duration. Asistur sells such policies in the airport-arrivals area at a cost of CUC$3 per day. In practice, you may not be asked about health insurance when you arrive.

In Cuba the major health risk is traveler's diarrhea, caused by eating contaminated fruit or vegetables or drinking contaminated water. So watch what you eat. Stay away from ice, uncooked food, and unpasteurized milk and milk products, and drink only bottled water, or water that has been boiled for at least 20 minutes, even when you're brushing your teeth. Make sure that fruit is thoroughly washed and/or peeled before eating it. Although Cuban lobsters are beyond reproach, avoid eating clams and mussels.

Locals call the *almacigo* tree the "tourist tree" owing to its red, peeling bark (and its bulging trunk), a nod to Cuba's greatest health risk: the Caribbean sun. Use plenty of sunscreen with a high SPF.

Despite official claims to the contrary, the risk of contracting HIV in Cuba has grown in recent years, thanks to tourism-related prostitution. Other sexually transmitted diseases are more common. Extreme caution is advised in this area. Local condoms are of poor quality, so bring your own supply from home.

OVER-THE-COUNTER REMEDIES

Since medical supplies in Cuba are short, pack a small first-aid kit/medicine bag with basic bandages and topical ointments as well as sunscreen; insect repellent; and your favorite brands of over-the-counter allergy, cold, headache, and stomach/diarrhea medicine. (No U.S. brands are available in Cuba.) Bring enough prescription medications to last the entire trip. You may want to pick up some cheap vitamins, aspirin, and other common remedies at the discount drug store to give away, since most Cubans have a hard time getting even the most basic medicines.

SHOTS AND MEDICATIONS

No vaccinations are required for travel to Cuba, but make sure you are up-to-date on all routine immunizations. There's some risk of contracting Hepatitis A and typhoid, so it's generally a good practice to be vaccinated against both. Another ongoing problem is the mosquito-carried dengue fever, though it is not preventable by any vaccination. Incidents of all three diseases are rare, and practically nonexistent in tourist zones. Malaria has been eradicated in Cuba. Visitors with allergies take note: the air quality in cities can be horrible, particularly in summer, when the thick, smoky exhaust from aging Eastern European trucks and buses mixes with choking dust and lingers in the humid air.

Health Warnings Centers for Disease Control and Prevention (*CDC*). ☎ *800/232–4636* ⊕ *www.cdc.gov/travel.* **World Health Organization** (*WHO*). ⊕ *www.who.int.*

▌ HOURS OF OPERATION

Banks are open weekdays 9–3, and offices are usually open weekdays 8–noon and 1–5. Museums are generally open weekdays 9–5, with slightly shorter hours on weekends (e.g., 10–4 or simply an afternoon or morning off); some close on Monday. Most shops conduct business Monday–Saturday 9–6, though some may close for an hour at lunchtime. Many gas stations are open 24 hours.

HOLIDAYS

Cuba marks 10 public holidays, including two Christian observances in this officially atheist country.

January 1–2 (Liberation and Victory days)

March or April (Good Friday)

May 1 (International Workers Day)

July 25–27 (Revolution Day)

October 10 (Independence Day)

December 25 (Christmas)

December 31 (New Year's Eve)

▌ MAIL

Mail service is slow but reasonably reliable. A postcard sent to anywhere in the Americas or Europe will cost no more than USD50¢, a letter 75¢. Until Cuba and the United States hammer out a postembargo postal agreement, mail between the two countries travels via Canada or Mexico and takes three or four weeks to reach its destination. Evidence exists that officials read mail; stick to postcards with "Having a wonderful time" pleasantries and you'll be fine.

SHIPPING PACKAGES

DHL Express is the international air courier service with the biggest presence in Cuba. It has desks at some major hotels and offices in Havana, Camagüey, Cienfuegos, Holguín, Pinar del Río, Santiago de Cuba, and Varadero. The company offers package and letter delivery to international points within 24–48 hours, but it will cost you dearly. A less expensive option is Cubanacán Express.

Courier Service Cubanacán Express.
✉ Calle Manglar 578, e/ Infanta y Retiro, Centro Habana ☎ 7873–6660 ⊕ www. cubanacan-express.cu. **DHL.** ✉ Main office, Av. 1 y Calle 26, Centro Habana ☎ 7204–1876 for customer service ⊕ www.dhl.com.

▌ MONEY

The official currency is the peso, often abbreviated *CUP*, and sometimes referred to as *moneda nacional* (national currency).The state has also created a secondary currency, the convertible peso (abbreviated *CUC*). The *peso convertible* is largely on par with the U.S. dollar, with one big caveat. (⟹ *See Currency Exchange below.*) The nonconvertible peso, worth about 25 times less than its CUC counterpart, is used by Cubans to buy basic everyday products, amenities, and food. Cubans with access to CUC can purchase a wider range of quality consumer goods, an endless source of resentment among the majority population who cannot. In 2013, the government announced an eventual end to the dual-currency system. It has yet to publicly specify a timetable. Nearly all travelers' expenses will be charged in CUC. (U.S. dollars are not accepted for payment.)

Both currency series come in bills of 1, 3, 5, 10, 20, 50, and 100 pesos, with the CUP currency also having denominations of 200, 500, and 1,000 pesos. In addition, the convertible currency has coins of 5, 10, 25, and 50 centavos, and 1 peso. (One peso = 100 centavos.) Though not common, the occasional unscrupulous vendor will try to pawn off nonconvertible pesos as change for convertible pesos on unsuspecting visitors. Learn to recognize the difference. CUC pesos are brighter, with a variety of colors, and bear the words *PESOS CONVERTIBLES*; CUP pesos look duller.

ATMS AND BANKS

Most travelers use the Banco Financiero Internacional or the Banco de Crédito y Comercio. Both change hard currencies

Local Customs

LANGUAGE
Spanish is Cuba's official language. Those connected with the tourist industry in places that see a lot of foreign visitors will speak English, thanks to all the Canadians who come here. The person on the street will know very little. Learning even a few words of Spanish helps. The basic niceties such as *por favor* (please) and *gracias* (thank you) should be a minimum along with a friendly *Buenos días* (Good morning), *Buenas tardes* (Good afternoon), or *Buenas noches* (Good evening), and will always be appreciated. For more words and phrases, see the Spanish glossary in the back of this book. Phrase book and language-tape sets can augment that list. We recommend *Fodor's Travel Phrases,* an app for smartphone or tablet, which includes Spanish among its 22 languages, and *Living Language Spanish* courses.

Español cubano (Cuban Spanish or, nicknamed, *"cubañol"*) fascinates and frustrates travelers. Cubans' rapid speech will test the careful textbook Spanish you studied in school. Compound that with the tendency of people here to "swallow" consonants, especially the *S* at the end of words, and to pronounce *L* like *R* and vice versa. Listen closely and make ample, good-hearted use of this request: *"Más despacio, por favor"* (slower, please).

GREETINGS
Cubans embrace each other and often kiss friends and family of the opposite sex. We visitors will never cross that barrier, but shaking hands with someone you meet is the norm here. The formal pronoun *usted* (you) is almost always used; the familiar *tú*

(you) is reserved only for close friends and relatives. After decades of socialism, you'll hear Cubans address each other as *Compañero* or *Compañera,* for males and females respectively and loosely meaning "comrade." Some Cubans we speak to suggest it sounds awkward coming from a foreigner. You'll never go wrong with *Señor* or *Señora.*

SIGHTSEEING
Even in officially atheist Cuba, a church is a place of reverence, and respectful dress and decorum are expected. Men and women should not wear shorts, sleeveless shirts, or sandals inside a church; women should wear pants or skirts below the knee. Bathing suits and other assorted skimpy attire work inside the confines of your beach resort but never in cities or towns. Cuban adults do not wear shorts except at the beach; they regard them as children's wear. It does get hot here. You'll have to make that call.

POLITICS
Despite a half-century of poor government-to-government relations and an economic embargo, most Cubans warmly welcome American visitors. Life here is far more nuanced and complex than many assume; you may be surprised at the frankness with which Cubans across the political spectrum speak. As a visitor, you should be positive. Complaining to local people about things that go wrong serves little purpose. There may be a hitch or two in your travel plans—voice your concerns to your tour representative.

into convertible pesos and give cash advances from credit cards. Automatic teller machines (a *cajero automático* in Spanish) accept international bank cards. ATMs are becoming more common, but are still scarce the farther you get from Havana. Inquire at your hometown financial institution to check on fees for ATM use in Cuba.

CREDIT CARDS

The longtime restrictions on use of U.S. credit cards in Cuba are in the process of being lifted. MasterCard and Visa are accepted, and American Express and Discover are soon to follow. In the case of Visa and MasterCard, we recommend that you contact your issuing financial institution to be sure that their specific cards are supported—not all are. In any case, realize that credit cards are still not widely accepted in Cuba, especially outside Havana. Even places that do accept them might find their systems down and unable to process transactions, so be sure to carry sufficient cash.

If you plan to use your credit card for cash advances, you'll need to apply for a PIN at least two weeks before your trip. Although it's usually cheaper (and safer) to use a credit card abroad for large purchases (so you can cancel payments or be reimbursed if there's a problem), note that some credit-card companies *and* the banks that issue them add substantial percentages to all foreign transactions, whether they're in a foreign currency or not. Check on these fees before leaving home, so there won't be any surprises when you get the bill.

CURRENCY EXCHANGE

U.S. currency can and must be exchanged for convertible pesos to pay for your travel expenses in Cuba, at an approximate rate of US$1 to CUC$1. (If you're on a package tour, most of those expenses will already be paid for in advance, and you'll be concerned only with incidental costs.) The big kicker here? ⚠ **Each and every time you change dollars to convertible pesos you will incur a 10% penalty.** (Thus US$100 fetches you around CUC$90.) Other currencies are not assessed this fee, and if you have euros, Canadian dollars, or pounds sterling, exchange rates will resemble those on the international market without the 10% hit. Some U.S. travelers convert their dollars to other currencies before arrival in Cuba. However, that transaction also costs you a percentage. Gauge if it's worth your time and effort. Plus, outside Havana, few banks can exchange non-U.S. currencies. You can freely exchange CUC back to dollars, and it will be at a 1:1 rate. Nonconvertible pesos may not be changed for dollars. Nothing prohibits you from changing convertible pesos to regular Cuban pesos, but there are few opportunities for travelers to spend this currency—save for ice cream, popcorn, or some street food. The shops, restaurants, hotels, taxis, *paladares*, and *casas particulares* you'll patronize accept only convertible pesos. Import or export of either type of peso is prohibited, although no one will look askance if you take a small bill or two home as a souvenir. The nonconvertible 3-peso bill with the iconic portrait of Che Guevara is a favorite.

Major banks change Western currencies for CUC pesos, as do branches of CADECA, the state exchange bureau. International airports have CADECA branches that offer a slightly less favorable exchange rate than their in-town counterparts. ⚠ **Never exchange money on the street.** Black-market transactions are illegal.

TRAVELER'S CHECKS

Traveler's checks issued by U.S. banks can't yet be cashed in Cuba. Those issued by a foreign company can be cashed at banks and branches of CADECA in Cuba. They cannot be replaced if lost or stolen.

PACKING

For sightseeing, casual lightweight clothing and good walking shoes are appropriate; most restaurants don't require very formal attire. For beach vacations, you'll need lightweight sportswear, a bathing suit, a sun hat, and lots of sunscreen. A sarong or a light cotton blanket makes a handy beach towel, picnic blanket, and cushion for hard seats, among other things.

Travel in forest areas will require long-sleeve shirts, long pants, socks, sneakers and/or hiking boots, a hat, a light waterproof jacket, a bathing suit, and plenty of insect repellent. Other useful items include a screw-top water container that you can fill with bottled water, a money pouch, a travel flashlight and extra batteries, a Swiss Army knife with a bottle opener, a medical kit (with first-aid supplies and basic over-the-counter remedies), and binoculars. If you have the room, try to take any clothes you don't wear as well as extra soap, over-the-counter medicines, and so on, to give away. That bottle of aspirin you bought at a discount drugstore back home could be a godsend for a retired school teacher trying to survive on CUC$10 a month; the blouse that no longer fits might be the perfect gift for the housekeeper at your hotel.

PASSPORTS AND VISAS

All foreigners must have passports to enter Cuba. Beyond that, in most cases Cuba recognizes visitors as tourists, which requires the purchase of a tourist card ($20), rather than a visa. Tourist cards are valid for 30 days. Business travelers, working journalists, and some other visitors require visas. Visas cost $100 and can take up to three weeks to process. Apply at your local Cuban embassy or consulate. Visas start at 30 days and can be extended for stays of up to six months.

Information **Cuban Embassy.** ☎ *202/797–8518* ⊕ *www.cubadiplomatica.cu/eeuu.*

RESTROOMS

All major public areas, from hotels to airports, have facilities, though the more public the area, the less likely they are to be clean. The words for "restroom" are *servicio* and *baño*. "Men" is *caballeros*; "women" is *mujeres* or *damas*.

The most reliable restrooms are in good hotels. No one minds if you choose to use one and you're not a guest of the hotel.

SAFETY

Cuba is among the safest travel destinations. Sentences for committing crimes are heavy and police are quite visible. This said, take the same precautions you would elsewhere in Latin America or the Caribbean; keep a close eye on personal belongings. Avoid adorning yourself with expensive jewelry, and follow local advice about where it's safe to walk, particularly at night.

There are increasing numbers of *jineteros* (hustlers) wanting to serve as your guide or refer you to a *casa particular* or *paladar* and *jineteras* (prostitutes), especially in Havana; it's best to decline their services. Panhandlers looking for anything from cash to clothing to soap are also becoming more prevalent. If you consider the local economic conditions, it shouldn't be hard to remain polite and still keep confrontation to a minimum.

GOVERNMENT ADVISORIES

The same warnings about travel during hurricane season elsewhere in the Caribbean apply to Cuba, which sees its fair share of storms almost every year. The U.S. Department of State also advises visitors to be aware that the Cuban government relies on repressive methods to maintain its governmental control. This includes physical or electronic surveillance of both Cuban and foreign visitors.

General Information and Warnings U.S. Department of State. ⊕ *travel.state.gov.*

▌TAXES

No sales taxes are levied on goods and services. If you buy fine artwork, however, you need to get a CUC$10 export permit. Most galleries and shops can handle this for you. Otherwise, you can wait until your departure. Airport customs will make the assessment.

▌TIME

Cuba shares a time zone (GMT-0500) with Miami and New York. The country switches to daylight saving time from the second Sunday in March to the first Sunday in November, on the same calendar as the United States.

Time Zones **Timeanddate.com.** ⊕ *www.time anddate.com/worldclock.*

▌TIPPING

First, the "what," before the "how much": *Tip in convertible pesos only.* With CUC, you give that person access to purchase otherwise scarce goods. Some visitors "tip" in consumer goods, leaving behind aspirin, vitamins, school supplies, or pens for the hotel maid or a Spanish-English dictionary for a tour guide. That is fine, but always consider such items additional gifts. Cash provides the best help for these struggling, hard-working people.

In hotel restaurants with buffet-style meals, you can tip the waitstaff CUC$2–CUC$3, depending on the extent of service and the number of people in your party. Elsewhere, tip waiters and waitresses 10%–15% of the check. Tip hotel maids CUC$1 a day and porters CUC$1 a bag. Tour guides should get CUC$5 per person. Tips should also be given to museum docents, taxi drivers, and anyone who keeps an eye on your rental car for you. For most of these people, CUC$1 is usually enough; if your cab fare comes to more than CUC$10, tip the driver 10%–15% of the total. Cubans who work in the service industry rely heavily on tips to merely subsist; therefore, you may feel better if you err on the generous side. You should also consider tipping people you wouldn't elsewhere, such as receptionists, rental-car agents, public-relations people, travel agents—all of whom earn CUC$10–CUC$15 a month—and hotel doctors, who earns less than CUC$30.

▌TOUR OPERATORS

⇨ *For more information on Cuban tour operators, see Top Tour Operators in the Experience Cuba chapter.*

The majority of Cuba's 3 million annual visitors arrive on the island on a tour package, with flights, accommodations, and meals included. Independent travel to the island is still a bit on the adventurous side—conditions are improving all the time, though—and an organized tour does make things easier.

The preponderance of these packages feature multiday stays at beach resorts and Havana hotels—5 to 10 days is most common. Most excursions are managed by tour operators in Canada and Europe. The Cuban government works directly with them to book rooms in the many hotels and resorts that have been constructed in the past two decades. Canadian tour operators fly charters from various north-of-the-border cities directly to airports near the resorts. Resort-focused tours offer frequent departures year-round, with better deals to be found in the May–November off season. Until the embargo is fully lifted, this type of leisure tourism is officially prohibited to U.S. citizens, although some Americans do book such tours. ⇨ *See Resort Packages below.*

Newer to the mix are excursions that fall under the broad umbrella of people-to-people or cultural exchange tours, and several such operators are approved by the U.S. government. Group sizes are small (15–20 people max) and the tours are designed to give you an opportunity to meet Cuban people, with activities such as visits to schools and cooperatives, in addition to standard sightseeing. Look carefully at a tour operator's itinerary on its website. Most offer an eclectic look at art, dance, sugarcane, schools, and cigars. You're bound to find something on the schedule to pique your interest, even if that's not the entire focus of the tour. A handful of operators do provide more theme-based itineraries in addition to their general all-Cuba tours. Know also that itineraries occasionally (only rarely) need to be tweaked at the last minute. Your morning at the artisans' cooperative might be substituted with a salsa lesson. You are required to stay with the group and participate in all scheduled activities. (No, you may not break away to laze on the beach.)

The Havana-Trinidad-Cienfuegos circuit is a common itinerary among these tours; beach resorts such as Varadero are never included. These tours usually begin and end in Miami and use special charter flights by U.S. airlines. Arriving in Cuba early or staying on posttour are not allowed. Since activities don't depend on good weather, few seasonal-based price variations exist. A given company's Cuba tour might depart only a limited number of times a year. The biggest complaint about the cultural tours is their price, and they do look expensive at first glance. Accommodations, food, guide services, in-country transport, and flights from Miami are included, but that costly round-trip Miami–Cuba–Miami charter airfare contributes substantially to the tour price. You also need to find your own way to Miami; remember to factor that extra cost into your budget. Sticker shock aside, most participants in people-to-people tours come away with glowing impressions of their visits to Cuba.

PEOPLE-TO-PEOPLE TOURS

Abercrombie & Kent. A 10- or 13-day tour offered by Abercrombie & Kent takes in much of the island and focuses on Cuban art, cuisine, dance, and health care. ✉ *1411 Opus Pl., No. 300, Downers Grove* ☎ *800/554–7016* ⊕ *www. abercrombiekent.com* ✉ *Tours from $5,695 per person.*

Alexander & Roberts. A 9- or 13-day itinerary takes you to Havana, Camagüey, Santiago, and Baracoa with visits to theaters, schools, art studios, and cooperatives. ✉ *53 Summer St.* ☎ *800/221–2216* ⊕ *www.alexanderroberts.com* ✉ *Tours from $4,995 per person.*

Classic Journeys. Autos, architecture, and agriculture are the focus of Classic Journeys' four- or seven-day tours that take you to Havana and Viñales. ✉ *7855 Ivanhoe Ave., Suite 220* ☎ *800/200–3887* ⊕ *www.classicjourneys.com* ✉ *Tours from $3,995 per person.*

Coda International Tours. In keeping with the interests of Coda's predominantly gay-lesbian clientele, its tours include time devoted to issues of LGBT advocacy in Cuba as well as the standard looks at art and education. Eight-day tours take you to Havana, Cienfuegos, and Trinidad. ✉ *12794 Forest Hill Blvd, Suite 1A, West Palm Beach* ☎ *888/677–2632* ⊕ *www. coda-tours.com* ✉ *Tours from $3,754 per person.*

Collette. A mix of music, agriculture, and cigar making is on tap with Collette's nineday tour that takes you to Havana and Cienfuegos. ✉ *162 Middle St., Pawtucket* ☎ *855/355–8687* ⊕ *www.gocollette.com* ✉ *Tours from $3,779 per person.*

Cuba Explorer. The eight- or nine-day excursions of Cuba Explorer include a general trips around the island as well as more focused tours dealing with nature or photography. The operator also customizes tours for educators and students. ✉ *816 Peace Portal Dr., Suite 151* ☎ *888/965–5647* ⊕ *www.cubaexplorer. com* ✉ *Tours from $1,839 per person.*

Cultural Explorations Cuba. Focused solely on Cuba, Cultural Explorations Cuba offers three tours of five, seven, or eight days that take in a mix of painting, ceramics, cigars, Hemingway, and Jewish Cuba. ✉ *352 N.E. 3rd Ave, Delray Beach* ☎ *561/921–2425* ⊕ *www.cultural-explorations.com* ✉ *Tours from $3,325 per person.*

★ Fodor's Choice **Drod Culinary Adventures.** Cuban cuisine is the focus of five- or seven-day tours led by Chef Douglas Rodriguez, award-winning master of Cuban restaurants in Philadelphia and Miami Beach. The entire process is on display, from sea or field to preparation to plating and eating. ✉ *8011 N.E. Bayshore Ct.* ☎ *954/693–6562* ⊕ *www.chefdouglasrodriguez.com* ✉ *Tours from $4,995 per person.*

Gate 1 Travel. Gate 1's nine-day tour takes you to Havana, Cienfuegos, Trinidad, and Santa Clara for a look at education, literacy, theater, art, and revolution. ✉ *455 Maryland Dr.* ☎ *800/682–3333* ⊕ *www.gate1travel.com* ✉ *Tours from $3,399 per person.*

Global Volunteers. The nonsectarian Global Volunteers focuses on interaction with Cuba's different faith groups during its eight-day tour that takes you to Havana, Santa Clara, and Ciego de Ávila. ✉ *75 E. Little Canada Rd., St. Paul* ☎ *800/487–1074* ⊕ *www.globalvolunteers.org* ✉ *Tours from $3,795 per person.*

Globus. The three tours offered by Globus last 9 or 17 days. Shorter tours delve into central or eastern Cuba, with a longer island-wide tour if you have more time. ✉ *5301 S. Federal Circle, Littleton* ☎ *877/797–8791* ⊕ *www.globusjourneys.com* ✉ *Tours from $2,459 per person.*

Havanatur. In Havana they offer one main city tour, which visits most of the major sights in the historic center. They also offer a number of guided day trips in Viñales, Varadero, and Cayo Largo. ✉ *Calle 3, esq. de Calle 74, Miramar* ☎ *7204–6417.*

★ Fodor's Choice **Insight Cuba.** Pioneering Insight Cuba focuses solely on the island and offers an impressive 10 excursions of 4 to 13 days. In addition to island-wide tours, you'll find excursions devoted to jazz or Cuba's vintage cars, as well as the opportunity to do a long weekend or even to participate in the Havana Marathon. ✉ *2 Clinton Pl.* ☎ *800/450–2822* ⊕ *www.insightcuba.com* ✉ *Tours from $2,895 per person.*

International Expeditions. IE's 8 or 10 day tours take you to Havana, Trinidad, Cienfuegos, and Viñales, with close-up looks at art, ecology, and Hemingway. ✉ *One Environs Park, Helena* ☎ *844/684–9462* ⊕ *www.ietravel.com* ✉ *Tours from $3,998 per person.*

Intrepid. An impressive 12 tours of 8 to 22 days make up Intrepid's offerings, including culture-focused excursions devoted to sailing the Cayos and cycling. Not all tours qualify as People-to-People excursions. ✉ *380 Lonsdale St., Level 3* ☎ *800/ 970–7299* ⊕ *www.intrepidtravel.com* ✉ *Tours from $965 per person.*

Mayflower Tours. A nine-day tour by Mayflower mixes sugarcane, cigars, theater, and gardens in Havana, Trinidad, Cienfuegos, and the Cayos. ✉ *1225 Warren Ave., Downers Grove* ☎ *800/323–7604* ⊕ *www.mayflowertours.com* ✉ *Tours from $4,199 per person.*

National Geographic Expeditions. National Geographic's nine-day tour takes you to Havana, Cienfuegos, Trinidad, and the Bay of Pigs at Playa Girón, with looks at art, education, and nature. ✉ *1145 17th St. NW, Washington* ☎ *888/966–8687* ⊕ *www.nationalgeographicexpeditions.com* ✉ *Tours from $5,995 per person.*

Overseas Adventure Travel (*OAT*). OAT's 12-day tour delves into Cuban art, literature, farming, and fishing and takes you to Havana, Cienfuegos, and Trinidad. ✉ *1 Mifflin Pl., Suite 400, Cambridge* ☎ *800/955–1925* ⊕ *www.oattravel.com* ✉ *Tours from $3,995 per person.*

★ Fodor's Choice **Road Scholar.** The 10 Cuba offerings of Road Scholar include island-wide tours with a variety of cultural activities, as well as excursions focusing on photography, homestays, and family outings. Tours are 7 to 22 days. ✉ *11 Ave. de Lafayette, Boston* ☎ *800/454–5768* ⊕ *www.roadscholar.org* ✉ *Tours from $2,995 per person.*

Smithsonian Journeys. History, art, literature, and economics are the focuses of Smithsonian's eight- or nine-day tours that take you to Havana, Trinidad, and Cienfuegos, with a pretrip panel discussion in Miami to get you informed and up to speed. ✉ *Smithsonian Institution, Box 23182, Washington* ☎ *855/330–1542* ⊕ *www.smithsonianjourneys.org* 🖃 *Tours from $4,995 per person.*

Tauck. Looks at art, artisans, clothing, sugarcane, and the revolution are highlights of Tauck's 13-day tour that takes you to Santiago, Remedios, Holguín, and Sancti Spíritus. ✉ *10 Norden Pl., Norwalk* ☎ *800/788–7885* ⊕ *www.tauck.com* 🖃 *Tours from $7,465 per person.*

Travcoa. Two island-wide tours of 7 or 10 days make up Travcoa's offerings and focus on art, entrepreneurs, and education. ✉ *100 N. Sepulveda Blvd., Suite 1700, El Segundo* ☎ *888/979–4280* ⊕ *www. travcoa.com* 🖃 *Tours from $4,995 per person.*

RESORT PACKAGES

Air Canada Vacations. Tour packages of 5 to 16 days to Havana, Varadero, Guardalavaca, and the Cayos are offered by Air Canada Vacations. Airfare from several Canadian cities is included on its namesake airline. ✉ *5925 Airport Rd., Suite 700, Mississauga* ☎ *877/529–2079* ⊕ *vacations.aircanada.com* 🖃 *Packages from $832 per person.*

Nolitours by Transat. Resort stays in Havana, Varadero, Guardalavaca, and the Cayos of five to 16 days are offered by Nolitours with airfare included on its affiliated Transat Airlines. Departures take place from several Canadian cities. ✉ *300 Léo Pariseau, 2nd fl., Montréal* ☎ *866/556–3948* ⊕ *www.nolitours.com* 🖃 *Packages from $949 per person.*

Sunquest. Sunquest offers 4- to 16-day resort packages at beach hotels in Varadero, Guardalavaca, and the Cayos, with airfare included from several Canadian cities. ✉ *2355 Skymark Ave., Suite 200, Mississauga* ☎ *877/485–6060* ⊕ *www. sunquest.ca* 🖃 *Packages from $1,089 per person.*

Sunwing Vacations. Tour packages of 5 to 16 days from several Canadian cities to Havana, Varadero, Guardalavaca, Santiago, and the Cayos are offered by Sunwing Vacations, with airfare included on Sunwing Airlines. The operator offers many last-minute Web-only specials. ✉ *27 Fasken Dr., Toronto* ☎ *877/786–9464* ⊕ *www.sunwing.ca* 🖃 *Packages from $595 per person.*

TMR Holidays. An operator dealing only in Cuba travel, longtime specialist TMR Holidays offers 5- to 16-day packages to Havana, Varadero, Trinidad, Santiago, Guardalavaca, and the Cayos, with charter airfare included on departures from Montréal. ✉ *300 rue Léo-Pariseau, Suite 500, Montréal* ☎ *855/453–3936* ⊕ *www. vacancestmr.com* 🖃 *Packages from $919 per person.*

▌ VISITOR INFORMATION

Cuba's government tourist office is the Oficina Nacional de Información Turística (often shorthanded to Infotur on signs), whose staffers answer questions, distribute maps (often free), and sell tickets for Víazul buses. Abroad, Infotur does business as the Cuba Tourist Board. It has no U.S. office; the closest outlet is in Toronto. The Havana and Toronto offices are not diligent about responding to email inquiries. State-operated tour and travel agencies—Havanatur (a tour operator), Cubanacán (a hotel and tour operator), or Cubana (the national airline)—have desks in the lobbies of large hotels, where representatives can arrange flights, tours, and rental cars.

A few other sites provide general material in addition to standard tourist info. One of the best U.S.-based sources of information is the Center for Cuban Studies, which publishes the bimonthly *Cuba Update*. The free monthly web magazine *What's On, Havana!* focuses primarily on the capital, but also presents articles of interest on culture and tourism around Cuba. It comes in English, Spanish, and

French editions and can be downloaded to ebooks on devices with iOS platforms. *Havana Times* does a lot of good reporting on Cuban affairs, tourism among them. It's not all politics at *Granma*, the official organ of the Cuban Communist Party. You'll find articles on sports, culture, and tourism, too.

Visitor Information Center for Cuban Studies. ⊕ *www.cubaupdate.org.* **Cuba Tourist Board.** ✉ *1200 Bay St., Suite 305, Toronto* ☎ *416/362–0700* ⊕ *www.gocuba.ca.* **Granma.** ⊕ *en.granma.cu.* **Havana Times.** ⊕ *www.havanatimes.org.* **Oficina Nacional de Información Turística** (*Infotur*). ✉ *Calle 28, No. 303 e/3. y 5. Av., Playa* ☎ *7204–0624.* **What's On, Havana!** ⊕ *www.cubaabsolutely. com.*

INDEX

PHOTO CREDITS

NOTES

NOTES

NOTES

NOTES

NOTES

NOTES

NOTES

NOTES

NOTES

NOTES

Fodor's CUBA

Publisher: Amanda D'Acierno, *Senior Vice President*

Editorial: Arabella Bowen, *Editor in Chief*; Linda Cabasin, *Editorial Director*

Design: Tina Malaney, *Associate Art Director*; Chie Ushio, *Senior Designer*

Photography: Jennifer Arnow, *Senior Photo Editor*; Mary Robnett, *Photo Researcher*

Production: Linda Schmidt, *Managing Editor*; Evangelos Vasilakis, *Associate Managing Editor*; Angela L. McLean, *Senior Production Manager*

Maps: Rebecca Baer, *Senior Map Editor*; Mark Stroud (Moon Street Cartography), *Cartographer*

Sales: Jacqueline Lebow, *Sales Director*

Marketing & Publicity: Heather Dalton, *Marketing Director*; Katherine Punia, *Publicity Director*

Business & Operations: Susan Livingston, *Vice President, Strategic Business Planning*; Sue Daulton, *Vice President, Operations*

Fodors.com: Megan Bell, *Executive Director, Revenue & Business Development*; Yasmin Marinaro, *Senior Director, Marketing & Partnerships*

Writers: Amy S. Eckert, Esme Fox, Dorothy MacKinnon, Jeffrey Van Fleet

Editors: Eric B. Wechter (Lead Editor), Alexis Kelly, Mark Sullivan

Production Editor: Elyse Rozelle

3rd edition

ISBN 978-1-101-88023-4

ISSN 1091–4749

All details in this book are based on information supplied to us at press time. Always confirm information when it matters, especially if you're making a detour to visit a specific place. Fodor's expressly disclaims any liability, loss, or risk, personal or otherwise, that is incurred as a consequence of the use of any of the contents of this book.

The information in this book is intended to provide general guidelines on travel to Cuba. It does not provide advice on what is legal, or illegal, with respect to Cuban travel. Inclusion of suggested activities or itineraries in this guide does not necessarily mean that these suggested activities or itineraries comply with current U.S. law. As the application and impact of laws specific to Cuban travel can vary widely from case to case, and current U.S. rules are subject to change, readers are encouraged to consult with professional advisors concerning the legality of their specific travel plans and refer to the current travel rules outlined by the U.S. Department of Treasury at treasury.gov.

SPECIAL SALES

This book is available at special discounts for bulk purchases for sales promotions or premiums. For more information, e-mail specialmarkets@penguinrandomhouse.com.

PRINTED IN THE UNITED STATES OF AMERICA

10 9 8 7 6 5 4 3 2 1

ABOUT OUR WRITERS

Amy S. Eckert has lived her whole life near Detroit but her writing career has taken her around the world. She's contributed to more than a dozen guidebooks covering destinations in North America and Europe and including activities ranging from riding the rails to riding motorcycles. Amy has also written about travel hot-spots on six continents for Alaska Airlines, *Wine Enthusiast*, *Hemispheres*, and numerous AAA magazines.

Esme Fox is a professional travel writer who regularly visits Havana and other Cuban destinations. A Hispanophile, she spends much of her time in Spain and Latin America and speaks fluent Spanish. She has contributed to a number of travel publications including a Time Out guide to Argentina and Uruguay, Rough Guides, *BA High Life*, *b.there magazine*, and *Food and Travel Magazine*.

 Canadian travel writer **Dorothy MacKinnon** first covered the length and breadth of Cuba in 2003 on an intensive bird-watching tour, alighting in the serene Viñales Valley for a long holiday. Based in Costa Rica since 1999, she has helped update Fodor's *Costa Rica* for the past 13 years. Along the way she has learned to speak passable Spanish and become a passionate birder and enthusiastic nature lover, writing about ecotourism and reviewing restaurants for *The Tico Times* in San José. In her past life she was a feature writer and copy editor for *The Financial Post* in Canada, and for the Weekend section of *The Washington Post*. For this new guide, she was delighted to re-visit Cuba and update the Western Cuba chapter.

 Costa Rica-based writer and pharmacist **Jeffrey Van Fleet** has spent the last two decades enjoying Wisconsin's winters and Central America's long rainy seasons. Most people would try to do it the other way around. He has covered nearly every Latin American country for Fodor's and was pleased to add Cuba to the mix. Jeff updated Travel Smart and the Central and Eastern Cuba chapters for this edition.